EViews Illustrated
for Version 7

Richard Startz

University of Washington

EViews Illustrated for Version 7

ISBN: 978-1-880411-44-5

Disclaimer

Trademarks

Quantitative Micro Software, LLC
4521 Campus Drive, #336, Irvine CA, 92612-2699
Telephone: (949) 856-3368
Fax: (949) 856-2044
web: www.eviews.com

First edition: 2007
Second edition: 2009
Editor: Meredith Startz
Index: Palmer Publishing Services

EViews Illustrated is dedicated to my students of many years, especially those who thrive on organized chaos—and even more to those who don't like chaos at all but who nonetheless manage to learn a lot and have fun anyway.

Acknowledgements

First off, I'd like to thank the entire EViews crew at Quantitative Micro Software for their many suggestions—and you'd like to thank them for their careful review of the manuscript of this book.

Next, thank you to David for letting me kibitz over the decades as he's built EViews into the leading econometric software package. Related thanks to Carolyn for letting me absorb much of David's time, and even more for sharing some of her time with me.

Most of all, I'd like to thank my 21-year-old editor/daughter Meredith. She's the world's best editor, and her editing is the least important contribution that she makes to my life.

Table of Contents

Foreword

Sit back, put up your feet, and prepare for the E(Views) ticket of your life.

My goal in writing *EViews Illustrated* is that you, the reader, should have some fun. You might have thought the goal would have been to teach you EViews. Well, it is—but books about software can be awfully dry. I don't learn much when I'm bored and you probably don't either. By keeping a light touch, I hope to make this tour of EViews enjoyable as well as productive.

Most of the book is written as if you were seated in front of an EViews computer session and you and I were having a conversation. Reading the book while running EViews is certainly recommended, but it'll also work just fine to read—pretending EViews is running—while you're actually plunked down in your favorite arm chair.

> Hint: Remember that this is a tutorial, not a reference manual. More is not necessarily better. EViews comes with over 2,500 pages of first class reference material in four volumes. When details are better explained by saying "See the *User's Guide*," that's what we do.
>
> And if 2,500 pages just isn't enough (or is perhaps too much), you can always visit the EViews Forum (http://forums.eviews.com) where you can find answers to commonly asked questions, share information, and mingle with like-minded EViews users.

EViews is a *big* program. You don't need to learn all of it. Do read Chapter 1, "A Quick Walk Through" to get started. After that, feel comfortable to pick and choose the parts you find most valuable.

EViews Illustrated for Version 7 is keyed to release 7 of EViews. Most, but not all of *EViews Illustrated* applies to release 4 as well. EViews workfiles discussed in the book are available for download from www.eviews.com or on a CD bundled with *EViews Illustrated*.

Despite all care, an error or two undoubtedly remain. Corrections, comments, compliments, and caritas all gratefully received at EViewsIllustrated@eviews.com.

Dick Startz
Castor Professor of Economics
University of Washington
Seattle
August 2009

Chapter 1. A Quick Walk Through

You and I are going to start our conversation by taking a quick walk through some of EViews' most used features. To have a concrete example to work through, we're going to take a look at the volume of trade on the New York Stock Exchange. We'll view the data as a set of numbers on a spreadsheet and as a graph over time. We'll look at summary statistics such as mean and median together with a histogram. Then we'll build a simple regression model and use it for forecasting.

Workfile: The Basic EViews Document

Start up a word processor, and you're handed a blank page to type on. Start up a spreadsheet program, and a grid of empty rows and columns is provided. Most programs hand you a blank "document" of one sort or another. When you fire up EViews— no document—just an empty window with a friendly "Welcome to EViews" message at the bottom.

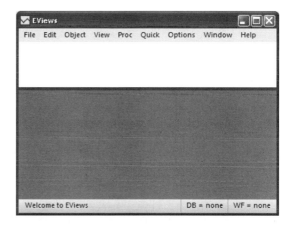

Because there aren't any visual clues on the opening screen, setting up a new document in EViews sometimes bewilders the new user. While word processor documents can start life as a generic blank page, EViews documents—called "*workfiles*"—include information about the structure of your data and therefore are never generic. Consequently, creating an EViews workfile and entering data takes a couple of minutes, or least a couple of seconds, of explanation. In the next chapter we'll go through all the required steps to set up a workfile from scratch.

Being impatient to get started, let's take the quick solution and load an existing workfile. If you're working on the computer while reading, you may want to load the workfile "nysevolume.wf1" using the menu steps **File/Open/EViews Workfile...** as pictured on the next page.

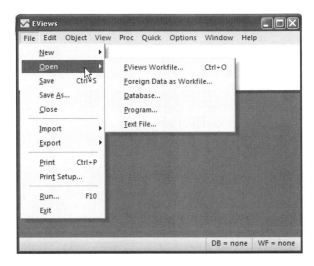

Hint: All the files used in this book are available on the web at www.eviews.com.

Now that a workfile's loaded EViews looks like this.

Our workfile contains information about quarterly average daily trading volume on the New York Stock Exchange (NYSE). There's quite a bit of information, with over 400 observations taken across more than a century. The icon ☑ indicates a data series stored in the workfile.

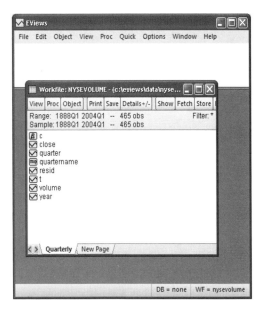

Viewing an individual series

If you double-click on the series VOLUME in the workfile window you'll get a first peek at the data.

Right now we're looking at the spreadsheet view of the series VOLUME. The spreadsheet view shows the numbers stored in the series. On average in the first quarter of 1888, 159,006 shares were traded on the NYSE. (The numbers for VOLUME were recorded in millions.) Interesting, but perhaps a little outdated for understanding today's market?

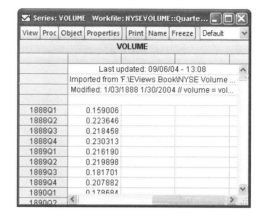

Scroll down to the bottom of the window to see the latest datum in the series. 1.67 billion shares were traded on an average day in the first quarter of 2004. Quite a change!

The more ways we can view our data the better. EViews provides a collection of "Views" for each type of object that can appear in a workfile. ("Object" is a computer science buzz word meaning "thingie".) The figures above are examples of the spreadsheet view, which lets us see the number for VOLUME at each date.

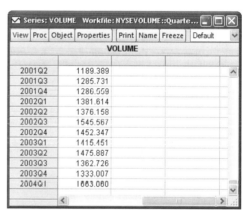

Another way to think about data is by looking at summary statistics. In fact, some kind of summary statistic is pretty much necessary in this kind of situation; we can't hope to learn much from staring at raw data when we have 400 plus numbers. To look at summary statistics for a series press the [View] button and choose **Descriptive Statistics & Tests/Histogram and Stats**.

Here, we see a histogram, which describes how often different values of VOLUME

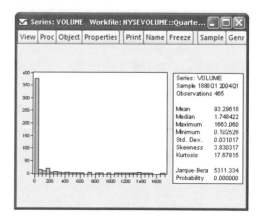

occurred. Most periods trading is light. Heavy trading volume— say over a billion shares— happened much less frequently.

To the right of the histogram we see a variety of summary statistics for the data. The average (mean) volume was just over 93 million shares, while the median volume was 1.75 million. The largest recorded trading volume was over 1.6 billion and the smallest was just over 100,000.

Now we've looked at two different views (**Spreadsheet** and **Histogram and Stats**) of a series (VOLUME). We've learned that trading volume on the NYSE is enormously variable. Can we say something more systematic, explaining when trading volume is likely to be high versus low? A starting theory for building a model of trading volume is that trading volume grows over time. Underlying this idea of growth over time is some sense that the financial sector of the economy is far larger than it was in the past.

Let's create a line graph to give us a visual picture of the relation between volume and time. Hit the ⸢View⸥ button again: this time choosing **Graph...** and selecting **Line & Symbol** on the left-hand side of the dialog under **Graph Type**. EViews graphs the date on the horizontal axis and the value of VOLUME on the vertical. Unsurprisingly perhaps, the most important descriptive aspect of our data is that volume is a heck of a lot bigger than it used to be!

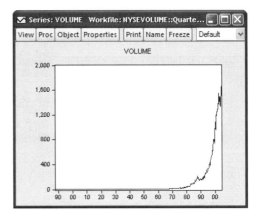

Looking at different samples

We've learned that in the early 21st century NYSE volume is many orders of magnitude greater than it was at the close of the 19th. In retrospect, the picture isn't surprising given how much the economy has grown over this period. Trading volume has grown enormously over more than a century; it's grown so much, in fact, that numbers from the early years are barely visible on the graph. Let's try a couple of different approaches to getting a clearer picture.

As a first pass, we'll look at only the last three years or so of data. To limit what we see to this period, we need to change the sample.

Click on the [Sample] button to get the dialog box shown to the right. The upper field, marked **Sample range pairs (or sample object to copy)**, indicates that all observations are being used. Replace "@all" with the beginning and ending dates we want. In this case use "2001q1" for the first date, a space to separate the dates, and the special code "@last" to pick up the last date available in the workfile. When you've changed the **Sample** dialog as shown in the second figure, hit [OK] .

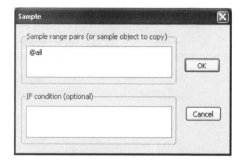

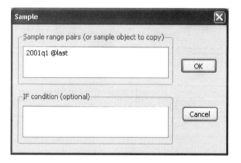

Hint: Ranges of dates in EViews are specified in pairs, so "2001q1 @last" means all dates starting with the first quarter of 2001 and ending with the last date in the workfile. EViews accepts a variety of conventions for writing a particular date. "2001:1" means the first period of 2001 and "2001q1" more specifically means the first quarter of 2001. Since the periods in our data are quarterly, the two are equivalent.

The **Line Graph** view changes to reflect the new sample. Note how the date scaling on the horizontal axis has changed. Previously we could fit only one label for each decade. This close up view gives a label every six months. For example, "03Q3" means year 2003, third quarter, which is to say, July-September 2003. Because the sample is so much more homogenous, we can now see lots of short-run up and down spikes.

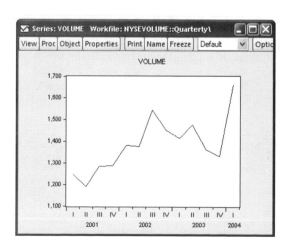

Remember: when we changed the sample on the view, we have *not* changed the underlying data, just the portion of the data that we're viewing at the moment. The complete set of data remains intact, ready for us to use any time we'd like.

Hint: The new sample applies to all our work until we change it again, not just this one graph. Note the change in the **Sample:** line of the workfile window.

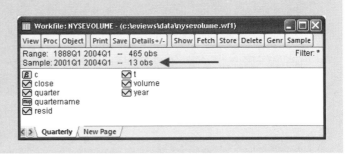

Generating a new series

Let's turn to another approach to thinking about trading volume. Our first line graph (before we shortened the sample) presented a picture which looks a lot like exponential growth over time. A standard trick for dealing with exponential growth is to look at the logarithm of a variable, relying on the identity $y = e^{gt} \Leftrightarrow \log y = gt$. In order to look at the trend in the log instead of in the level, we'll create a new variable named LOGVOL which equals the log of VOLUME. This can be done either with a dialog or by typing a command. We'll do the former first. Choose the menu item **Quick/Generate Series**... to bring up a dialog box. In the upper field, type "logvol = log(volume)". Notice that in the lower field the sample is still set to use only the 21st century part of our data. This matters, as we'll see in a moment.

The workfile window now has a new object, ☑ logvol .

Double-click ☑ logvol and then scroll the window so
that the beginning of 2000 is at the top. You'll see a
window looking something like the one shown here.

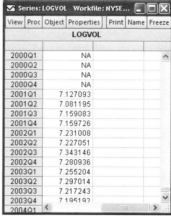

Starting in 2001 we see numbers. Before 2001, only the
letters "NA". There are two lessons here:

- EViews operates only on data in the current sample.

  When we created LOGVOL the sample began in
  2001. No values were generated for earlier dates.

- EViews marks data that are *not available* with the
  symbol NA.

  Since we didn't generate any values for the early
  years for LOGVOL, there aren't any values available. Hence the NA symbols.

Since we're trying to look at all the available data, we want to
change the sample to include, well the whole sample. One way
to do this is to use the menu selection **Quick/Sample**....
Another way to change the sample is to double-click on the
sample line in the upper pane of the workfile window—right
where the arrow's pointing in the picture on the right.

To illustrate another alternative, we'll type our first command.

The workfile window and the series window appear in the
lower section of the master EViews window. The upper area is
reserved for typing commands, and, not surprisingly, is called
the *command pane*. The command smpl is used to set the sample; the keyword @all signals EViews to use all available data in the current sample. Type the command:

    smpl @all

in the command pane and end with the **Enter** key.

Hint: Almost everything in EViews can be done either by typing commands or by
choosing a menu item. The choice is a matter of personal preference.

You can see that the sample in the workfile window has changed back to 1888Q1
through 2004Q1.

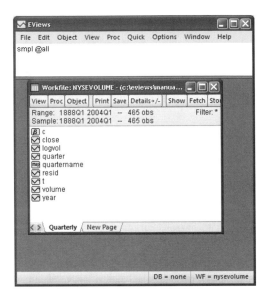

Historical hint: Ever wonder why so many computer commands are limited to four letters? Back in the early days of computing, several widely used computers stored characters "four bytes to the word." It was convenient to manipulate data a "word" at a
time. Hence the four letter limit and commands spelled like "smpl".

Now that you've set the sample to include all the data, let's generate LOGVOL again, this
time from the command line. Type:

```
series logvol = log(volume)
```

in the command pane and hit **Enter**. (This is the last time I'll nag you about hitting the
Enter key. I promise.)

Again double-click on LOGVOL to check that we now have all our data. Then use the **View** menu to choose **View/Graph...** and select **Line** graph. The line graph for LOGVOL—the logarithm of our original VOLUME variable—appears. What we see is not quite a straight line, but it's a lot closer to a straight line—and a lot easier to look at—than our graph of the original VOLUME variable.

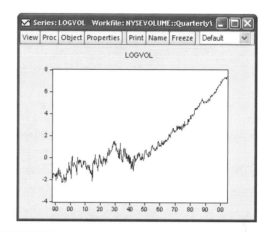

> Hint: Menu items, both in the menu bar at the top of the screen and menus chosen from the button bar, change to reflect the contents of the currently active window. If the menu items differ from those you expect to see, the odds are that you aren't looking at the active window. Click on the desired window to be sure it's the active window.

We might conclude from looking at our LOGVOL line graph that NYSE volume rises at a more or less constant percentage growth rate in the long run, with a lot of short-run fluctuation. Or perhaps the picture is better represented by slow growth in the early years, a drop in volume during the Great Depression (starting around 1929), and faster growth in the post-War era. We'll leave the substantive question as a possibility for future thought and turn now to building a regression model and making a forecast of future trading volume.

Looking at a pair of series together

Our line graph goes quite far in giving us a qualitative understanding of the behavior of volume over time. For a quantitative understanding, we'd like to put some numbers to the upward trending picture of LOGVOL. If we have a variable t representing time (0, 1, 2, 3...), then we can represent the idea of an upward trend with the algebraic model:

$$\log(volume_t) = \alpha + \beta t$$

where the coefficient β gives the quarterly increase in LOGVOL.

To get started we need to create the variable t. In the command pane at the top of the EViews screen type:

```
series t = @trend
```

"@TREND" is one of the many functions built into EViews for manipulating data. Double-click on ☑t and you'll see something like the screen shown.

Since we want to think about how volume behaves over time, we want to look at the variables T and LOGVOL together. In EViews a collection of series dealt with together is called a *Group*. To create a group including T and LOGVOL, first click on ☑t. Now, while holding down the Ctrl-key, click on ☑ logvol. Then right-click highlighting **Open**, bringing up the context menu as shown and choose **as Group**.

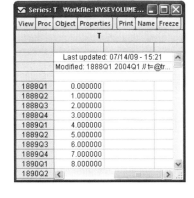

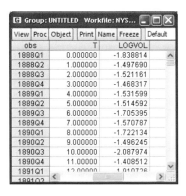

The group shows time and log volume, that is, the series T and LOGVOL, together. Just as there are multiple ways to view a series, there are also a number of group views. Here's the spreadsheet view.

Looking at a spreadsheet of a group with two series leaves us in the same situation we were in earlier with a spreadsheet view of a single series: too many numbers. A good way to look for a relationship between two series is the scatter diagram. Click on the View button and choose **Graph...**. Then select **Scatter** as the **Graph Type** on the left-hand side of the dialog that pops up. To add a regression line, select **Regression line** from the **Fit lines** dropdown menu. The default options for a regression line are fine, so hit OK to dismiss the dialog.

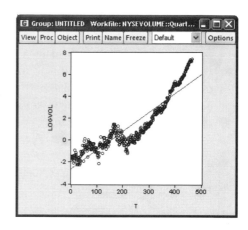

We can see that the straight line gives a good rough description of how log volume moves over time, even though the line doesn't hit very many points exactly.

The equation for the plotted line can be written algebraically as $y - \hat{\alpha} + \hat{\beta} t$. $\hat{\alpha}$ is the intercept estimated by the computer and $\hat{\beta}$ is the estimated slope. Just looking at the plot, we can see that the intercept is roughly -2.5. When $t = 400$, LOGVOL looks to be about 4. Reaching back—possibly to junior high school—for the formula for the slope gives us an approximation for $\hat{\beta}$.

$$\hat{\beta} \approx \frac{4 - (-2.5)}{400 - 0} = 0.01625$$

An eyeball approximation is that LOGVOL rises sixteen thousandths—a bit over a percent and a half—each quarter.

Estimating your first regression in EViews

The line on the scatter diagram is called a *regression line*. Obviously the computer knew the parameters $\hat{\alpha}$ and $\hat{\beta}$ when it drew the line, so backing the parameters out by eye may bring back fond memories, but otherwise is unnecessarily convoluted. Instead, we turn now to regression analysis, the most important tool of econometrics.

You can "run a regression" either by using a menu and dialog or by typing a command. Let's try both, starting with the menu and dialog method. Pick the menu item **Quick/Estimate Equation...** at the top of the EViews window. Then in the upper field type "logvol c t".

Alternatively, type in the EViews command pane:

```
ls logvol c t
```

as shown below.

In EViews you specify a regression with the `ls` command followed by a list of variables. ("LS" is the name for the EViews command to estimate an ordinary Least Squares regression.) The first variable is the *dependent variable*, the variable we'd like to explain—LOGVOL in this case. The rest of the list gives the *independent variables*, which are used to predict the dependent variable.

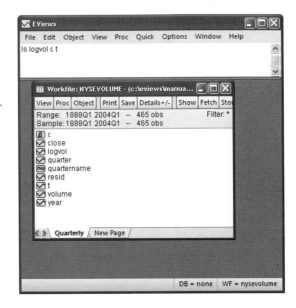

Hint: Sometimes the dependent variable is called the "left-hand side" variable and the independent variables are called the "right-hand side" variables. The terminology reflects the convention that the dependent variable is written to the left of the equal sign and the independent variables appear to the right, as, for example, in

$$\log(volume_t) = \alpha + \beta t.$$

Whoa a minute. "LOGVOL" is the variable we created with the logarithm of volume, and "T" is the variable we created with a time trend. But where does the "C" in the command come from? "C" is a special keyword signaling EViews to estimate an intercept. The coefficient on the "variable" C is $\hat{\alpha}$, just as the coefficient on the variable T is $\hat{\beta}$.

Whether you use the menu or type a command, EViews pops up with regression results.

EViews has estimated the intercept $\hat{\alpha} = -2.629649$ and the slope $\hat{\beta} = 0.017278$. Note that our eyeballing wasn't far off!

Equation: UNTITLED   Workfile: NYSEVOLUME::Quarterly\

View | Proc | Object | | Print | Name | Freeze | | Estimate | Forecast | Stats | Resids

Dependent Variable: LOGVOL
Method: Least Squares
Date: 07/14/09   Time: 15:31
Sample: 1888Q1 2004Q1
Included observations: 465

Variable	Coefficient	Std. Error	t-Statistic	Prob.
C	-2.629649	0.089576	-29.35656	0.0000
T	0.017278	0.000334	51.70045	0.0000

R-squared	0.852357	Mean dependent var		1.378867
Adjusted R-squared	0.852038	S.D. dependent var		2.514860
S.E. of regression	0.967362	Akaike info criterion		2.775804
Sum squared resid	433.2706	Schwarz criterion		2.793620
Log likelihood	-643.3745	Hannan-Quinn criter.		2.782816
F-statistic	2672.937	Durbin-Watson stat		0.095469
Prob(F-statistic)	0.000000			

We've estimated an equation explaining LOGVOL that reads:

$$LOGVOL = -2.629649 + 0.017278t$$

Having seen the picture of the scatter diagram on page 13, we know this line does a decent job of summarizing $\log(volume)$ over more than a century. On the other hand, it's not true that in each and every quarter LOGVOL equals $-2.629649 + 0.017278t$, which is what the equation suggests. In some quarters volume was higher and in some the volume was lower. In regression analysis the amount by which the right-hand side of the equation misses the dependent variable is called the *residual*. Calling the residual e ("e" stands for "error") we can write an equation that really is valid in each and every quarter:

$$LOGVOL = -2.629649 + 0.017278t + e$$

Since the residual is the part of the equation that's left over after we've explained as much as possible with the right-hand side variables, one approach to getting a better fitting equation is to look for patterns in the residuals. EViews provides several handy tools for this task which we'll talk about later in the book. Let's do something really easy to start the exploration.

Just as there are multiple ways to view series and groups, equations also come with a variety of built in views. In the equation window choose the [View] button and pick **Actual, Fitted, Residual/Actual, Fitted, Residual Graph.** The view shifts from numbers to a picture.

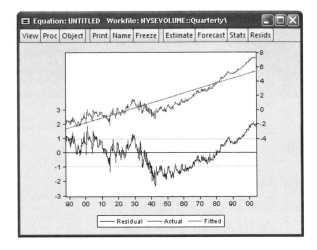

There are lots of details on this chart. Notice the two different vertical axes, marked on both the left and right sides of the graph, and the three different series that appear. The horizontal axis shows the date. The actual values of the left-hand side variable—called "Actual"—and the values predicted by the right-hand side—called "Fitted"—appear in the upper part of the graph. In other words, the thick upper "line" marked "Actual" is $\log(volume)$ and the straight line marked "Fitted" is $-2.629649 + 0.017278t$.

Actual and Fitted are plotted along the vertical axis marked on the right side of the graph; fitted values rising roughly from -2 to 8. Residual, plotted in the lower portion of the graph, uses the legend on the left hand vertical axis.

Whether we look at the top or bottom we see that the fitted line goes smack though the middle of $\log(volume)$ in the early part of the sample, but then the fitted value is above the actual data from about 1930 through 1980 and then too low again in the last years of the sample. If we could get an equation with some upward curvature perhaps we could do a better job of matching up with the data. One way to specify a curve is with a quadratic equation such as:

$$\log(volume_t) = \alpha + \beta_1 t + \beta_2 t^2 + e$$

For this equation we need a squared time trend. As in most computer programs, EViews uses the caret, "^", for exponentiation. In the command pane type:

```
series tsqr = t^2
```

To see that this does give us a bit of a curve, double-click ☑ tsqr. Then in the series window choose **View/Graph...** and select **Line** to see a plot showing a reassuring upward curve.

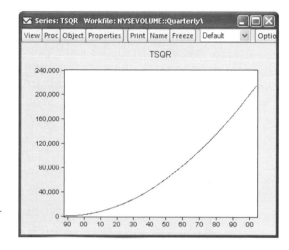

Close the equation window and any series windows that are cluttering the screen. (Don't close the workfile window.)

Now let's estimate a regression including t^2 to see if we can do a better job of matching the data. EViews is generally quite happy to let you use a mathematical expression right in the LS command, rather than having to first generate a variable under a new name. To illustrate this capability type in the command pane:

```
ls log(volume) c t tsqr
```

We've typed in "log(volume)" instead of the series name LOGVOL, and could have typed "t^2" instead of tsqr: thus illustrating that you can use either a series name or an algebraic expression in a regression command.

EViews provides estimates for all three coefficients, $\hat{\alpha}$, $\hat{\beta}_1$, and $\hat{\beta}_2$.

Has adding t^2 to the equation given a better fit? Let's take a look at the residuals for this new equation. Click **View/Actual, Fitted, Residual/Actual, Fitted, Residual Graph** again. The fitted line now does a much nicer job of matching the long run characteristics of $\log(volume)$. In particular, the residuals over the last several decades are now flat rather than trending strongly upward. This new equation is noticeably better at fitting recent data.

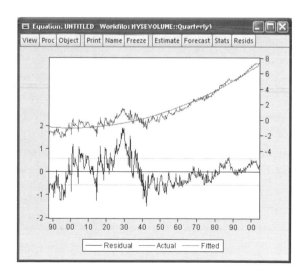

Saving your work

Quite satisfactory, but this is getting to be
thirsty work. Before we take a break, let's save
our equation in the workfile. Hit the Name button on the equation window. In the upper field
type a meaningful name.

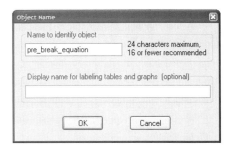

Hint: Spaces aren't allowed when naming an object in EViews.

Prior to this step the title bar of the equation window read "Equation: untitled." Using the
Name button changed two things: the equation now has a name which appears in the title
bar, and more importantly, the equation object is stored in the workfile. You can see these
changes below. If you like, close the equation window and then double-click on
pre_break_equation to re-open the equation. But don't take the break quite yet!

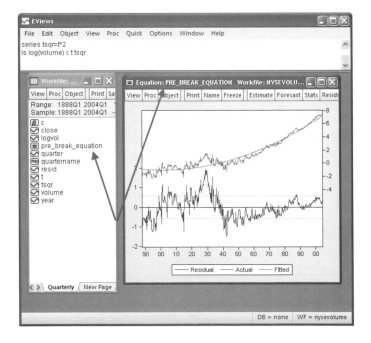

Before leaving the computer, click on the workfile window. Use the **File** menu choice **File/Save As...** to save the workfile on the disk.

Now would be a good time to take a break. In fact, take a few minutes and indulge in your favorite beverage.

Back so soon? If your computer froze while you were gone you can start up EViews and use **File/Open/EViews Workfile...** to reload the workfile you saved before the break.

Your computer didn't freeze, did it? (But then, you probably didn't really take a break either.) This is the spot in which authors enjoin you to save your work often. The truth is, EViews is remarkably stable software. It certainly crashes less often than your typical word processor. So, yes, you should save your workfile to disk as a safety measure since it's easy, but there's a different reason that we're emphasizing saving your workfile.

EViews doesn't have an Undo feature.

As you work you make changes to the data in the workfile. Sometimes you find you've gone up a blind alley and would like to back out. Since there is no Undo feature, we have to substitute by doing **Save As...** frequently. If you like, save files as "foo1.wf1", "foo2.wf1", *etc.* If you find you've made changes to the workfile in memory that you now regret you can "backup" by loading in "foo1.wf1".

You can also hit the **Save** button on the workfile window to save a copy of the workfile to disk. This is a few keystrokes easier than **Save As...**. But while **Save** protects you from computer failure, it doesn't substitute for an Undo feature. Instead it copies the current workfile in memory—including all the changes you've made—on top of the version stored on disk.

> Pedantic note: EViews does have an Undo item in the usual place on the Edit menu. It works when you're typing text. It doesn't Undo changes to the workfile.

Forecasting

We have a regression equation that gives a good explanation of $\log(volume)$. Let's use this equation to forecast NYSE volume. Hit the Forecast button on the equation window to open the forecast dialog.

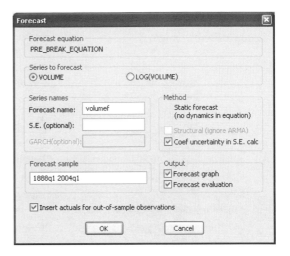

Notice that we have a choice of forecasting either volume or $\log(volume)$. (When you use a function as a dependent variable, EViews offers the choice of forecasting either the function or the underlying variable.) The one we actually care about is volume—taking logs was just a trick to get a better statistical model. Leave the dialog set to forecast volume. Uncheck **Forecast graph**, **Forecast evaluation**, and **Insert actuals for out-of-sample observations**. In the **Forecast sample** field enter "2001q1 2004q1". Your dialog should look something like the one shown.

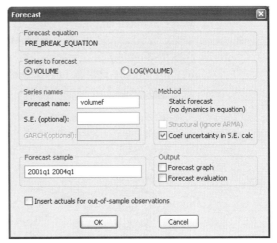

EViews creates a series of forecast values for volume, storing them in the series VOLUMEF, which now appears in the workfile window. Double-click on ☑ volumef . Choose **View/Graph...** in the VOLUMEF window and select **Line** in the dialog to see the forecast values.

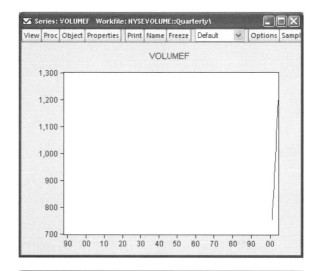

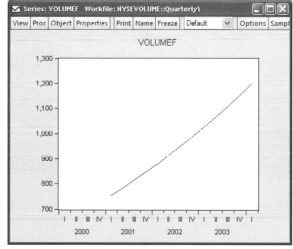

The first thing you'll notice is that nothing shows up on most of the plot. We asked EViews to start the forecast in January 2001 and that's what EViews did, so there is no forecast for most of our historical period. Click the [Sample] button and enter "2000 @LAST" in the upper field of the **Sample** dialog. The graph snaps to a close up view of the last few years.

You have a volume forecast. NYSE volume is forecast to rise over the forecast period from about 750 million shares to nearly 1.2 billion. Mission accomplished.

What's Ahead

This chapter's been a quick stroll through EViews, just enough—we hope—to whet your appetite. You can continue walking through the chapters in order, but skipping around is fine too. If you'll be mostly using EViews files prepared by others, you might proceed to Chapter 3, "Getting the Most from Least Squares," to dive right into regressions; to Chapter 7, "Look At Your Data," for both simple and advanced techniques for describing your data, or to Chapter 5, "Picture This!," if it's graphs and plots you're after. If you like the more orderly approach, continue on to the next chapter where we'll start the adventure of setting up your own workfile and entering your own data.

Now it's time to take a break for real.

Chapter 2. EViews—Meet Data

When you embark on an econometric journey, your first step will be to bring your data into EViews. In this chapter we talk about a variety of methods for getting this journey started on the right foot.

Unlike the blank piece of paper that appears (metaphorically speaking) when you fire up a word processor or the empty spreadsheet provided by a spreadsheet program, the basic EViews document—the workfile—requires just a little bit of structuring information. We begin by talking about how to set up a workfile. Next we turn to manual entry, typing data by hand. While typing data is sometimes necessary, it's awfully nice when we can just transfer the data in from another program. So a good part of the chapter is devoted to data import.

To get started, here's an excerpt from the file "AcadSalaries.wf1". This file, available on the EViews website, excerpts data from a September 1994 article in *Academe*, the journal of the American Association of University Professors. The data give information from a survey of salaries in a number of academic disciplines. The excerpt in *Table 1: Academic Salary Data Excerpt* shows average academic salaries and corresponding salaries outside of academics.

Table 1: Academic Salary Data Excerpt

OBS	DISCIPLINE	SALARY	NONACADSAL
1	Dentistry	44,214	40,005
2	Medicine	43,160	50,005
3	Law	40,670	30,518
4	Agriculture	36,879	31,063
5	Engineering	35,694	35,133
6	Geology	33,206	33,602
7	Chemistry	33,069	32,489
8	Physics	32,925	33,434
9	Life Sciences	32,605	30,500
10	Economics	32,179	37,052
...	...	...	...
28	Library Science	23,658	15,980

The Structure of Data and the Structure of a Workfile

Look at *Table 1: Academic Salary Data Excerpt* .

First thing to notice: data come arranged in rows and columns. Every column holds one series of data; for example, the values of SALARY for every discipline. Every row holds one observation; an example being the value of SALARY, NONACADSAL, and the name of the discipline for "dentistry." When data come arranged in a neat rectangle, as it does here, statisticians call the arrangement a "data rectangle."

> Hint: When thinking of an econometric model, a data series is often just called a "variable."

Second thing to notice: the observations (rows) come in order. In the column marked "obs" the observations are numbered 1, 2, 3, 4...28. The observation numbers are sometimes called, well, "observation numbers." Sometimes the entire set of observation numbers is called an "identifier" or an "id series." When appropriate, dates are used in place of plain numbers.

> Hint: Series (columns) don't have any inherent order, but observation numbers (rows) do. SALARY is neither before nor after DISCIPLINE in any important sense. In contrast, 2 really is the number after 1.

EViews needs to know how observations are numbered. When you set up a workfile, the first thing you need to do is tell EViews how the identifier of your data is structured: monthly, annual, just numbered 1, 2, 3, …, *etc.* Your second task is to tell EViews the range your observations take: January 1888 through January 2004, 1939 through 1944, 1 through 28, *etc.*

And that's all you need to know.

> Hint: Every variable in an EViews workfile shares a common identifier series. You can't have one variable that's measured in January, February, and March and a different variable that's measured in the chocolate mixing bowl, the vanilla mixing bowl, and the mocha mixing bowl.
>
> Subhint: Well, yes actually, you can. EViews has quite sophisticated capabilities for handling both mixed frequency data and panel data. These are covered later in the book.

Creating a New Workfile

Open EViews and use the menu to choose **File/New/Workfile...** The **Workfile Create** dialog pops up.

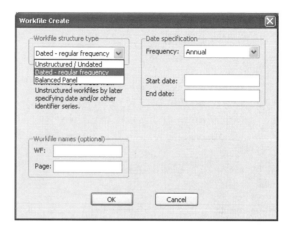

Hint: Alternatively, you can type

```
wfcreate
```

in the command pane to bring up the same dialog.

You'll notice in the dialog that EViews defaults to "Dated – regular frequency" and "Annual." However, the data shown in *Table 1: Academic Salary Data Excerpt* are just numbered sequentially. They aren't dated.

Choosing the **Workfile structure type** dropdown menu offers three choices:

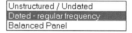

Hint: Changing the type of workfile structure can be mildly inconvenient, so it pays to think a little about this decision. In contrast, simply increasing or decreasing the range of observations in the workfile is quite easy.

Our data are **Unstructured/Undated**. Select this option. Later in this chapter we'll discuss **Dated – regular frequency**. (**Balanced Panel** is deferred to Chapter 11, "Panel—What's My Line?.")

Hint: Alternatively, we can enter

```
wfcreate u
```

in the command pane.

Unstructured/Undated instructs EViews to number the observations from 1 through however-many-observations-you-have. In our example we have 28 observations. Enter "28" in the field marked "**Observations:**" If you'd like to give your workfile a name you can enter the name in the "**WF:**" field at the lower right. You can also name the workfile when you save it, so giving a name now or later is purely a matter of personal preference.

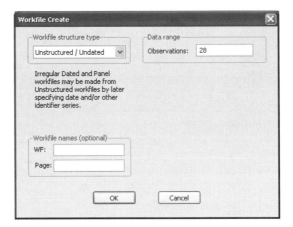

Hit [OK] and the workfile is created for you.

Hint: If you like, the workfile can be created with the single command

```
wfcreate u 28
```

Deconstructing the Workfile

There's no data yet, but let's dissect what EViews starts you off with. The initial workfile window looks something like the picture to the right.

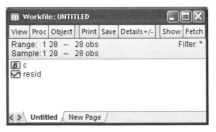

The title bar shows the name of the workfile. Since we didn't enter a name for the workfile in the dialog, EViews uses "UNTITLED" in the title bar.

The workfile window has buttons at the top and tabs at the bottom. The buttons provide menus linked to each EViews window type. The tabs mark *pages*, essentially workfiles within a workfile. We'll come back to pages in Chapter 9, "Page After Page After Page"; they're particularly useful for holding sets of data with different indices.

Let's look at the main window area, which is divided into a upper pane holding information about the workfile and a lower pane displaying information about the objects—series, equations, *etc.*—that are held in the workfile.

Range tells you the identifying numbers or dates of the first and last observation in the workfile—1 and 28 in this example—as well as the count of the number of observations. **Sample** describes the subset of the observations range being used for current operations. Since all we've done so far is to set up a workfile with 28 observations, both **Range** and **Sample** are telling us that we have 28 observations. (Later we'll see how to change the number of observations in the workfile by double-clicking on **Range,** and how to change the sample by double-clicking on **Sample**.)

Display Filter is used to control which objects are displayed in the workfile window. **Display Filter** is useful if you have hundreds of objects: Otherwise it's safely ignored.

Let's move to the lower panel. Our brand new workfile comes with two objects preloaded: ☑ resid and β c . The series RESID is designated specially to hold the residuals from the last regression, or other statistical estimation. (See Chapter 3, "Getting the Most from Least Squares" for a discussion of residuals.) Since we have not yet run an estimation procedure, the RESID series is empty, *i.e.*, all values are set to NA.

An EViews workfile holds a collection of objects, each kind of object designated by its own icon. Far and away the most important object is the series (icon ☑), because that's where our data are stored. You'll have noted that the object C has a different icon, a Greek letter β . Instead of a data series, C holds values of coefficients. Right now C is filled with zeros, but if you ran a regression and then double-clicked on C you would find it had been filled with estimated coefficients from the last regression.

Time to Type

One Series at a Time

We sit with an empty workfile. How to bring in the data? The easiest way to bring data in is to import data that someone else has already entered into a computer file. But let's assume that we're going to type the data in from scratch. *Table 1: Academic Salary Data Excerpt* displays three variables. You have a choice of entering one variable at a time or entering several in a table format. We'll illustrate both methods.

Suppose first we're going to enter one series at a time, starting with NONACADSAL. We want to create a new series and then fill in the appropriate values. The trick is to open a window with an empty series (and then fill it up). There are a bunch of ways to get the desired window to pop open.

These two methods pop open an Untitled series:

- Type the command "series" in the command pane.

- Use the menu commands **Object/New/Series**

These two methods create a series named NONACADSAL and place it in the workfile:

- Type the command "series nonacadsal" in the command window.

- Use the menu commands **Object/New/Series** and then enter NONACADSAL in the **Name for object** field.

The latter two methods place ☑ nonacadsal in the workfile. Double-click to open a series window. In contrast, the former two methods open a window automatically, but don't name it. These methods open an untitled series window.

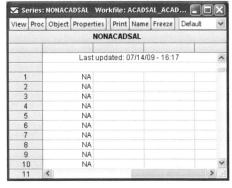

To name the untitled series, click on the [Name] button and enter NONACADSAL.

- EViews doesn't care about capitalization of names. NONACADSAL and nonacadsal are the same thing.

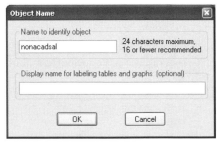

Hint: Naming a series (or other object) enters it in the workfile at the same time it attaches a moniker. In contrast, Untitled windows are not kept in the workfile. If you close an Untitled window: Poof! It's gone. The key to remember is that named objects are saved and that Untitled ones aren't. This design lets you try out things without cluttering the workfile.

Related hint: You can use the EViews menu item **Options/General Options/Windows/Window Behavior** to control whether you get a warning before closing an Untitled window. See Chapter 18, "Optional Ending."

We're ready to type numbers. But there's a trick to entering your data. To protect against accidents, EViews locks the window so that it can't be edited. To unlock, click on the `Edit+/-` button. Unlocked windows, as shown below for example, have an edit field just below the button bar. One way to know that a window is locked against editing is to observe the absence of the edit field. Alternatively, if you start typing and nothing happens, you'll remember that you meant to click on the `Edit+/-` button—at least that's what usually happens to the author.

Initially all the entries in the window are NA, for not available. Click on the cell just to the right of the `1` and type the first data point for nonacademic salaries, 40005. Hit **Enter** to complete the entry.

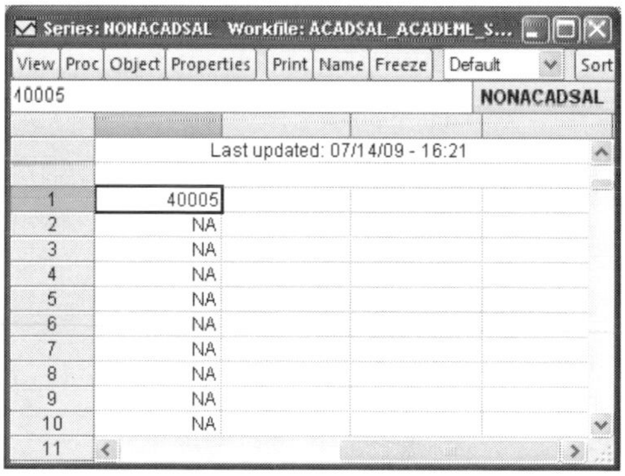

Enter the rest of the data displayed at the beginning of the chapter. You can use all the usual arrow and tab keys as well as the mouse to move around. In addition, when a cell is selected you can edit its contents in the edit field in the upper left of the window.

Hint for the terminally obedient: For goodness sakes, don't really enter all the data at the beginning of the chapter. You'll be bored out of your mind. Just type in a few numbers until you're comfortable moving around in the window.

Label View

We know that EViews provides several
different views for looking at a series. We
enter data in the spreadsheet view and if
we need to make a change we can come
back to the spreadsheet view to edit
existing data. Use the [View] button to
reach the label view where space is provided for you to enter a description,
source, *etc.*

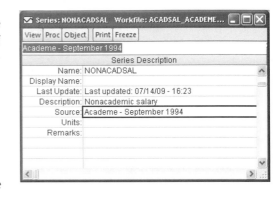

EViews automatically fills in the name
and date the series was last updated. The
other fields are optional. EViews uses the
Display Name for labeling output, so it's well worth filling out this field. Make the label
long enough to be meaningful, but short enough to fit in scarce space on a graph legend.
EViews will occasionally make an entry in the **Remarks:** field. When you start making
transformations to a series, a **History:** field is added with notes on the last ten or so
changes.

> Hint: It's worth the trouble to add as much documentation as possible in the series
> label. Later, you'll be glad you did.

Typing a Table at a Time

Now let's turn to entering data in the form of a table. As an example, we'll enter the name of
the academic discipline and the academic salary together. We begin with the same choice—
do we name the series before or after we open the window? If you like to name first, do the
following:

- Type the following commands in the command window:

    ```
    series salary
    alpha discipline
    ```

- Select DISCIPLINE and then SALARY in the workfile window (hold down the Ctrl key
  to select both series), double-click and choose **Open Group** to open a group window.

> Hint: Series in a group window are displayed from left to right in the same order as
> you click on them in the workfile window.

Note that the series DISCIPLINE is displayed with the abc icon to signal a series holding alphabetic data, as contrasted with the ☑ icon for ordinary numeric series.

> Hint: You can name a group and store it in the workfile just as you can with a series. Internally, a group is a list of series names. It's *not* a separate copy of the data. A series can be a member of as many different groups as you like.

If you like to open a window before creating a series, do the following:

- Use the menu **Quick/Empty Group (Edit Series)**. When the window opens scroll up one line. Then type DISCIPLINE in the cell next to the cell marked obs.

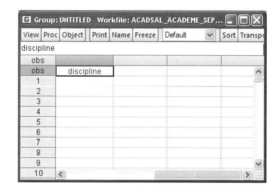

A dialog pops up so that you can tell what sort of series this is going to be.

Since DISCIPLINE is text rather than numbers, choose **Alpha series**. EViews initializes DISCIPLINE with blank cells.

Move one cell to the right of DISCIPLINE and enter SALARY, this time using the radio button to indicate a numeric series. EViews fills out the series with NAs.

> Hint: EViews uses NA to indicate "not available" for numeric series and just an empty string for a "not available" alpha value. The latter explains why the observations for DISCIPLINE are blank.

Click the ⸢Edit+/-⸥ button and type away. When editing a group window, the **Enter** key moves across the row rather than down a column. This lets you enter a table of data an observation at a time rather than one variable after the other; the observation at a time technique is frequently more convenient.

> Hint: To change the left-to-right order of series in a group use the menu **View/Group Members**. You'll see a list of series in the group. Edit the text—cut-and-paste is useful here—re-arranging the names into the desired order and click ⸢UpdateGroup⸥ to accept the changes. Alternatively, there's no law against closing the group window and opening a new one. Sometimes that's faster.

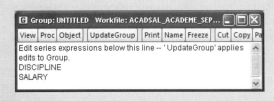

Identity Noncrisis

An important side effect of thinking of our data as being arranged in a rectangle is that each row has an *observation number* that identifies each observation. In a group window as above, or in a series window, the *id series* is called "obs" and appears on the left-hand side of the window. Obs isn't really a series, in that you can't access it or manipulate it. It serves to give a name to each observation.

When we set up an **Unstructured/Undated** workfile, EViews just numbers the observations 1, 2, 3, *etc.* (In dated workfiles, see below, dates are used for ids rather than sequence numbers.) Rather than calling data for dentistry "observation 1" and data for medicine "observation 2," it might be a lot more meaningful to label them "dentistry" and "medicine." EViews lets us specify that one of the existing series—obviously DISCIPLINE is the sensible choice—should be used as the id series.

Changing the id series requires "restructuring" the workfile. This is no big deal: "restructuring" amounts essentially to telling EViews to use an id series. Double-click on **Range** in the upper pane of the workfile window or choose the menu item **Proc/Structure/Resize Current Page**.... Then choose **Undated with ID series** and fill in the series you want used for the id, as illustrated here.

You'll notice that the **Range** field in the workfile window is now marked "(indexed)."

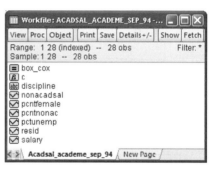

Now if we look at a spreadsheet view of SALARY the rows are labeled with DISCIPLINE in place of an uninformative observation number.

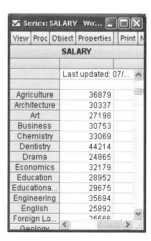

Hint: If you want to be able to see more or less of the id series in the left-hand column, just grab the column divider and drag it over to the right. All column widths are adjustable in the same way.

Counting Hint: If you want to add the observation number to the label right-click and select **ObsID** + /-. To return to the original display, just do it again.

	SALARY
Agriculture	36879
Architecture	30337
Art	27198
Business	30753
Chemistry	33069
Dentistry	44214
Drama	24865
Economics	32179
Education	28952
Educationa...	29675
Engineering	35694
English	25892
Foreign La...	25566
Geology	

Dated Series

Let's set aside our academic salary example for a bit and talk about more options for the identification series and the parallel options for structuring a workfile.

EViews comes with a rich, built-in knowledge of the calendar. Lots of data—lots and lots of data—is dated at regular intervals. Observations are taken annually, quarterly, monthly, *etc.* EViews understands a variety of such *frequencies*. The only difference between creating an undated workfile and a dated workfile is that for an undated workfile you enter the total number of observations, while for a dated workfile you provide a beginning date and an ending date.

Hint: Even when data are measured at regular intervals, measurements are sometimes missing. Not a problem, just leave missing measurements marked NA.

Let's create a couple of workfiles for practice. As a first example, let's make an annual workfile for the Roosevelt years (Franklin, not Teddy). Use the menu command **File/New/Workfile...** to bring up the **Workfile Create** dialog. Fill in the fields as shown.

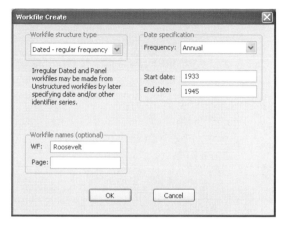

Note that when the workfile window pops open, **Range** shows 1933 to 1945 and that there are 13 observations in the workfile.

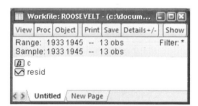

A second example. Most national income accounting macro data for the United States is available on a quarterly basis starting in 1947. To set up a quarterly workfile use **File/New/Workfile...** and change the drop down menu **Date Specification/Frequency:** to **Quarterly**. A new issue arises: what are the formats for specifying dates? Rules for date formats are one of those boring-but-necessary details that we'll put off 'til a boring-but-necessary appendix at the end of the chapter.

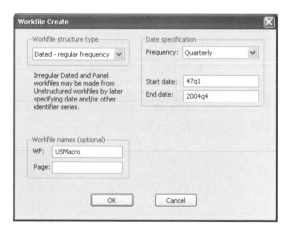

Why add a date structure to a workfile? One minor reason is that it saves you the trouble of figuring out that 1947q1 through 2004q4 includes exactly 232 observations. There are two more important reasons:

- An understanding of the calendar is built into many operations, so it pays to tell EViews how your information is dated. Two examples that we'll look at later: EViews will convert between monthly and quarterly data, and will compute elapsed time between two observations in order to compute annualized rates of return.

- EViews uses the id series to label all sorts of stuff, from series windows for editing data, through graphs of variables over time, to recording the sample used for statistical estimation.

Notice how much easier it is to edit data with a meaningful date label (right) and how much more meaning you get out of a plot with the x-axis labeled with a date rather than just an arbitrary observation number (below).

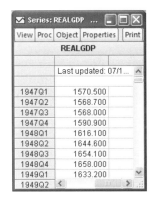

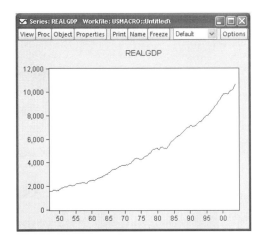

Tips for dating: In addition to the Annual and Quarterly frequencies that we've seen, EViews offers a wide range of built-in dated regular frequencies for those of you with dated data: (**Multi-year, Annual, Semi-annual, Quarterly, Monthly, Bimonthly, Fortnight, Ten-day, Weekly, Daily - 5 day week, Daily - 7 day week, Daily - custom week, Intraday**), and a special frequency (**Integer date**) which is a generalization of **Unstructured/Undated**.

(The Daily – 5 day week and intra-day frequencies are especially useful for Wall Street data; the Daily – 7 day for keeping track of graduate student work hours.)

Dated Irregular

The Dated Irregular workfile structure stands in between the Dated – Regular Frequency and the Unstructured/Undated structures. Each observation has a date attached, but the observations need not be evenly spaced in time. This sort of arrangement is especially useful for financial data, where quotes are available on some days but not on others.

You can't create a dated irregular structure from the **Workfile Create** dialog. Instead, you read the data into one of the available structures and then restructure the workfile. For example, the workfile "Russell3000Regular.wf1" holds Daily – 5 day week data. A small excerpt is shown to the right.

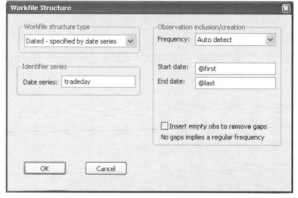

To change this to Dated-irregular, double-click on **Range** in the workfile window or choose **Proc/Structure/Resize Current Page**... to bring up the **Workfile structure** dialog. Pick **Dated-specified by date series**. Enter the name of the series containing observation dates in the **Identifier series** field.

Notice that after restructuring, November 26, 1987 (which was previously shown as NA) has disappeared from the data set.

Hint: Date functions work as expected in Dated – irregular workfiles. However, lags pick up the preceding observation (as in unstructured workfiles), not the preceding date (as in regular dated workfiles). In our original file, one lag of 11/27/1987 was 11/26/1987, which happened to be NA. In our new file, one lag of 11/27/1987 is 11/25/1987.

The Import Business

Once you've created an empty workfile, you can turn to filling it up with your data.

Frankly, the easiest way to get data into EViews is to start with data that someone else has already entered into a computer file. EViews is *very* clever about reading data in a variety of formats.

Let's go back to the academic salary example to go over some methods of bringing in data that's already on the computer. EViews provides three different methods for loading data from a "foreign" file:

- **File/Open/Foreign Data as Workfile...** translates any of a number of file formats into an EViews workfile.

- You can set up a workfile as we've done above and then use **File/Import** to bring in data from a spreadsheet program or text file (plus a couple of other specialized formats).

- You can use the standard Windows copy/paste commands to transfer data between a Series window or a Group window and another program. EViews is quite smart about interpreting the material you're pasting.

If most of your data comes from a single source, using **File/Open/Foreign Data as Workfile...** is far and away the easiest method. If you're cobbling together data from multiple sources, try using **File/Open/Foreign Data as Workfile...** on the most complicated file and then using **File/Import** or copy/paste to add from the other sources one at a time.

EViews is a fluent reader of many foreign file formats. Let's walk through examples of several of the most common.

Make It Slightly Easier Hint: Instead of choosing the menu **File/Open/Foreign Data as Workfile…** right click in any empty space inside EViews (not in the command pane or inside an open window) and choose **Open/Foreign Data as Workfile….**

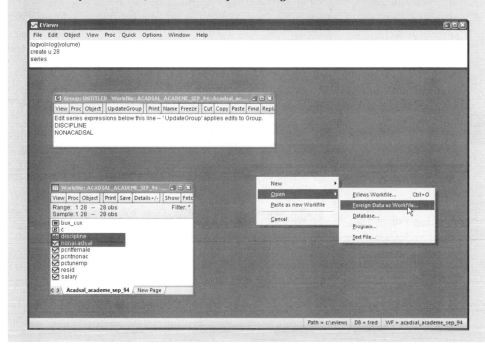

Make It Really Easy Hint: Just drag-and-drop any data file onto an empty space inside EViews. If EViews understands the data in the file, the file will pop open, ready to read. (You may have to answer a couple of questions first.)

An Excel-lent Import Source

The second-lowest common denominator file format is a Microsoft Excel spreadsheet. Here's an excerpt of "academic salaries by discipline.xls" (available on the EViews website).

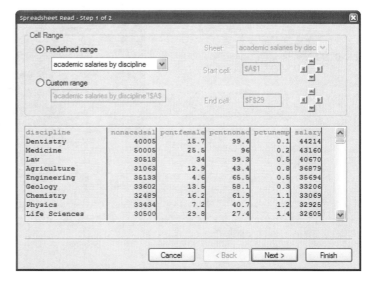

Note that variable names are conveniently provided in the first row of the file.

Use **File/Open/Foreign Data as Workfile...** and point to the desired Excel file. EViews does a quick analysis of the Excel file and opens the **Spreadsheet read** dialog.

The **Spreadsheet read** dialog displays lots of options, but most of the time if you just hit [Finish] EViews will correctly guess what you want done. Note, for example, that EViews has figured out that the first line holds variable names rather than data. To see what EViews is planning, and make adjustments if needed, hit [Next >] .

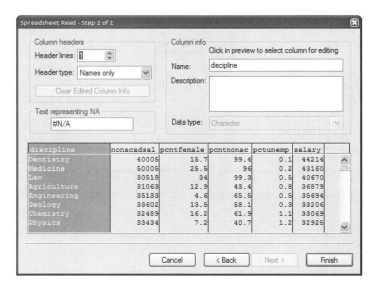

You can click in each column to change the series name or enter a description for the series. In our example EViews has correctly analyzed the file, so we can just hit [Finish] and EViews generates our workfile.

EViews' intuition is pretty good when it comes to reading Excel files, so frequently the first step is also the [Finish] step. Sometimes, though, we have to lend a hand. The file "Treasury_Interest_Rates.xls" (on the EViews web site) provides a few examples. If you drag-and-drop "Treasury_Interest_Rates.xls" onto EViews, the **Spreadsheet read**

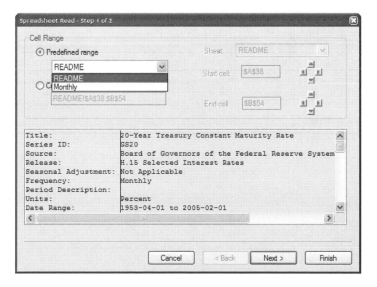

dialog opens to let us choose which sheet to read from the file. It so happens we want the second sheet, "Monthly," which we can choose in the **Predefined range** dropdown.

Hint: EViews examines your spreadsheet and generally makes a pretty intelligent guess about which part of the spreadsheet you'd like read. You can also set the range manually in the **Spreadsheet read** dialog. You'll find it saves time if you define a named range demarcating your data in Excel. In this way, you need only select the named range when EViews reads in the spreadsheet.

The controls in the upper left hand corner of the second **Spreadsheet read** dialog provide a number of options for customizing how EViews interprets the Excel spreadsheet. Which option you need depends on how your file is structured. Here's one example.

An excerpt from our Excel file is shown to the right. This particular file has a description of each variable in the first row and the name of the variable in the second row. Since the default assumption is that only the variable name is present, this won't do. We need to provide more information.

	A	F	G
1		3-Month Treasury Bill: Secondary Market Rate, Percent, Month	6-Month Tre
2	DATE	TB3MS	TB6MS
3	1934-01-01		0.72
4	1934-02-01		0.62
5	1934-03-01		0.24
6	1934-04-01		0.15
7	1934-05-01		0.16
8	1934-06-01		0.15
9	1934-07-01		0.15
10	1934-08-01		0.19
11	1934-09-01		0.21
12	1934-10-01		0.27
13	1934-11-01		0.25
14	1934-12-01		0.23
15	1935-01-01		0.20
16	1935-02-01		0.19
17	1935-03-01		0.15
18	1935-04-01		0.15

Treasury_Interest_Rates.xls [Read-Only] — README \ **Monthly**

The **Header type:** dropdown gives options that can handle most common file arrangements. In this case, choose **Names in last line** and away we go. (**Names in last line** means the names are at the end of the header information, right before the data begins—a pretty common arrangement.)

Names only
Descriptions only
Names in first line
Names in last line
Ignore header lines

Hint: There's no harm in trying out EViews' first guess. If the results aren't what you're looking for, throw them out, re-open the file, and set the controls the way you want in the **Spreadsheet read** dialog.

Being Date Savvy

It's not at all unusual for a data file to include the date of each observation. EViews does a surprisingly good job of guessing that a particular column of data consists of dates that ought to be used as identifiers in the workfile.

Here's an excerpt from an Excel file, "NZ Unemployment.xls", downloaded from Statistics New Zealand. The data are quarterly unemployment, but note that each observation is labeled with the last month of the quarter and the year, not with a quarter number. What's more, the data runs "backwards," with the most recent observation coming first.

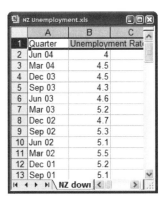

Drop-and-drag this file onto EViews and EViews will not only figure out that it's quarterly data, it'll also re-sort the data into the right order, so that it looks like the data shown to the right.

While EViews won't always figure out the "intent" of dates in a file, it gets it right quite frequently—so it's worth a try. By the way, this works with many formats of input files, not just Excel.

Reading the Great Texts

If the second-lowest common denominator file format is a Microsoft Excel spreadsheet, what's the lowest common denominator file format? A plain text file of course!

Hint: "Text" data and files are variously described as "text," "ASCII," "alpha," "alphanumeric," or "character." Sometimes the file extension "csv" is used for text data where data values are separated by commas.

Tab delimited

Here's an excerpt from "academic salaries by discipline.txt", available at the usual website.

```
 1 discipline» nonacadsal» pcntfemale» pcntnonac»  pctunemp»    salary¶
 2 Dentistry»  40005»  15.7»   99.4»   0.1»44214¶
 3 Medicine»   50005»  25.5»   96.0»   0.2»43160¶
 4 Law»30518»  34.0»   99.3»   0.5»40670¶
 5 Agriculture»31063»  12.9»   43.4»   0.8»36879¶
 6 Engineering»35133»  4.6»65.5»   0.5»35694¶
 7 Geology»33602»  13.5»   58.1»   0.3»33206¶
 8 Chemistry»  32489»  16.2»   61.9»   1.1»33069¶
 9 Physics»33434»  7.2»40.7»   1.2»32925¶
10 Life·Sciences»  30500»  29.8»   27.4»   1.4»32605¶
11 Economics»  37052»  14.8»   34.2»   0.3»32179¶
12 Philosophy» 18500»  23.1»   17.1»   1.8»31430¶
13 History»21113»  30.5»   20.5»   1.5»31276¶
```

As displayed, the symbol "»" represents a tab character, the raised dot, "·", denotes a space, and the paragraph mark "¶" marks the end of a line. EViews interprets the tab character as separating one datum from the next, and displays the text lined up in columns.

The data in "academic salaries by discipline.txt" lines up pretty much the same way as did the same data in the Excel file we looked at above. To pull text data directly into an workfile use **File/Open/Foreign Data as Workfile…** and point to the appropriate text file. (You don't want **File/Open/Text File…**, that's for bringing a file in as text, not for converting the text to an EViews workfile.)

EViews pops up with the **ASCII Read** dialog.

EViews has analyzed our text file and made a judgment call about how to interpret the data. A quick glance shows that EViews has hit it spot on, so we can just hit

[Finish]   and we'll have our workfile.

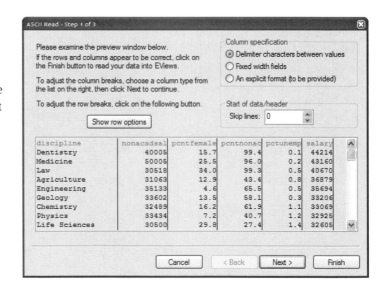

Text files aren't always this easy to interpret. When EViews reads in a line it has to decide which information goes with which variable. In this example, data are separated by tabs. When EViews finds a tab it knows it's done reading the current datum. In this context a tab is called a "*delimiter*" because it marks de limit, or de boundary, of a column. EViews has a built-in facility for using tabs or spaces for delimiters and also allows you to customize the choice of delimiter. (These choices are found by hitting [Next >] in the **ASCII Read** dialog.)

> Hint: If you have a choice, get your data tab delimited. Life is better with tab.

Space delimited

The most common format for text data is probably "space delimited." That just means there are one or more spaces between data fields. It's common because it's natural to us human types to find spaces between words. (At least for most modern western languages.) So this seems an ideal way to arrange data for the computer to read – and for the most part it works fine. But consider the line:

```
10 Life·Sciences»  30500»  29.8»   27.4»   1.4»32605¶
```

Is the value for the second variable "30500," or is it "Sciences?" We know the intended answer is the former because we understand the context. But if you tell EViews that your data are separated by spaces, it's going to believe you—and there *is* a space between "Life" and "Sciences."

If you have complete control of the text file, either because you create it or because you can edit it by hand, you can mark off a single text string by placing it between quotes. For example, put "Life Sciences" between quotes. EViews will treat quoted material as one long string, which is what we want in this case.

The inverse problem happens with space delimited data when a data item is missing. If a column is left blank for a particular observation we humans assume there is a number missing. EViews will just see the blank
```
1···2···3¶
4·······6¶
```
space as part of the delimiter. So while we understand that the text excerpt to the right should be interpreted as "1, 2, 3" for the first observation and "4, NA, 6" for the second observation, all EViews sees is a long, white space between the 4 and the 6 and interprets the data as "1, 2, 3" followed by "4, 6, NA". If the data are arranged in fixed columns, as is the case in this excerpt, try the **Fixed width fields** option described in the next section.

Fixed width fields

Another very popular format, especially with older data, is to skip the issue of delimiters entirely and put each data field in fixed columns. DIS-CIPLINE might be in columns 1 through 18, NONACADSAL in columns 19 through 360, *etc.* If you choose the

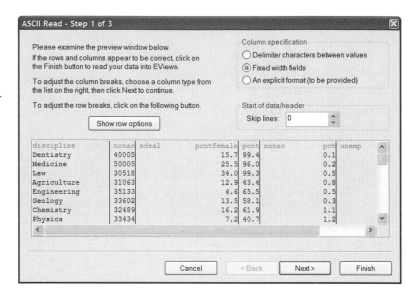

radio button **Fixed width fields** in the **ASCII Read** dialog, EViews will show you its best guess as to where fields end.

In this example, EViews' guess isn't quite right. Hit Next > so that you can drag the column dividers to the right locations.

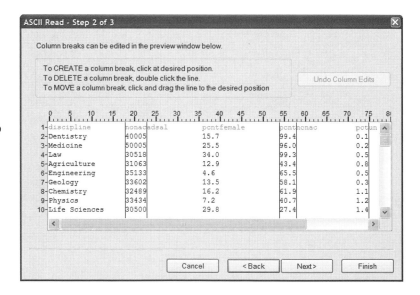

Now manually adjust the columns. After you have the column boundaries where they belong, hit Finish .

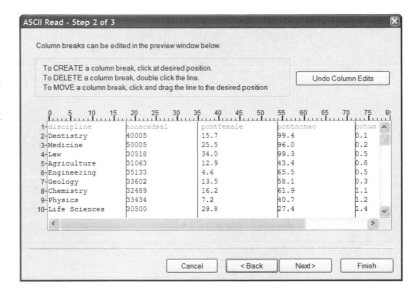

Hint: Telling EViews to use fixed column locations for each series replaces the use of delimiters. This can get around the missing number problem described above. Similarly, it can solve the problem of alpha observations that include spaces that would be mistaken for delimiters.

Explicit format

EViews provides a third, very powerful option for describing the layout of data. You can provide an **Explicit Format** which can be specified in EViews notation, or using notation from either of two widely used computer languages: Fortran format notation or C scanf notation. (See the *User's Guide* for more information.)

EViews reads about two dozen other file formats, including files from many popular statistics packages. EViews does an excellent job of reading these formats while preserving labeling information. So if you are given data from Stata, TSP, SPSS, SAS, *etc.*, try reading the data directly using **File/Open/Foreign Data as Workfile...**. (See the *User's Guide* for more information about this too.)

Hint: The counterpart to **File/Open/Foreign Data as Workfile...** is **File/SaveAs...** A wide variety of file formats are accessible in the **Save as type:** drop down menu, part of which is shown to the right.

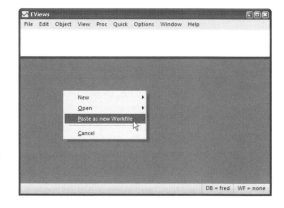

Coming in from the clipboard

Another useful option is to use **Copy/Paste**. For example, some web sites load data right onto the clipboard. EViews is happy to create a new work-file from the contents of the clipboard. Right-click on any blank spot in the lower EViews pane and then choose **Paste as new Workfile**. EViews will try to use the top row of data for series names. If that doesn't work out, EViews will name the series SERIES01, SERIES02, *etc.*, in which case you may want to rename the series to something more meaningful.

To rename a series, select the series in the work-file window, right-click and choose **Rename....** Fill out the dialog with the new name. You can enter a **Display Name** here as well.

Reading From the Web

EViews is just as happy to read a file from the web as it is to read a file from your disk. Although you can't browse the web within EViews the way you can browse your disk, you can enter a url (*i.e.*, a web address) in the open file dialog.

For example, my friend Fred posts data on the 1-Year Treasury Constant Maturity Rate at "http://research.stlouis-fed.org/fred2/data/WGS1YR.txt". In Internet Explorer, the data looks like the picture to the right.

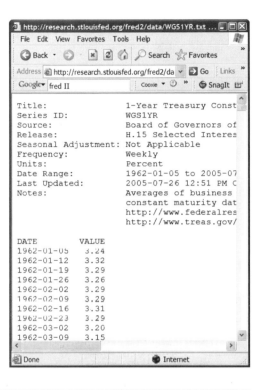

Choose **File/Open/Foreign Data as Workfile...** and enter the url in the **File name:** field. Often, the easiest way to grab a url is to copy it from the address bar of the web browser.

EViews does its usual nice job of interpreting the data.

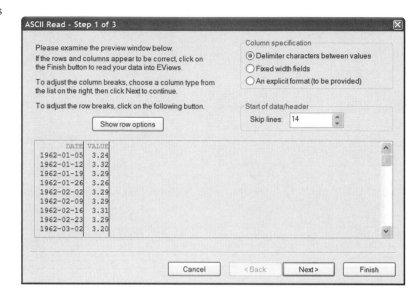

Hint: Sometimes the Open dialog remains open for what seems like a long time while EViews processes the data from the web. Be patient.

Reading HTML

The file above is a standard text file which happens to reside on the web. More commonly, files on the web are stored in HTML format. (HTML files can be stored on your local disk as well, of course.) HTML files generally contain large amounts of formatting information which is invisible when displayed in a web browser. EViews tries to work around this formatting information by looking for data presented using the HTML "table" format. If an HTML file doesn't read smoothly, it's likely that the data has been formatted to look nice when displayed, but that the table format wasn't used.

Reading Is Funkadelic

Clever as EViews is at interpreting data, it's not as smart as you are. We've seen that the dialogs include a *large* number of manual customization features. We've discussed some cases where automatic recognition doesn't work. Here's a more inclusive—but by no means exhaustive—list of issues. Most of the time you can use the customization features to read data with these problems:

1. Multi-line observations.

2. Streamed observations.

3. Fixed width, but undelimited, data.

4. Dates split across multiple columns, for example month in one column and year in another.

5. Multiple tables in one file.

6. Data in which one space is not a delimiter, but multiple spaces are.

7. Header lines that are interpreted as data.

Here are a couple of problems that you generally can't fix in the read dialog:

1. Variable length alphabetic data recognizable only by context.

2. Data where the format differs from one observation to another.

3. Dates that aren't in English. Verbum ianuarius non intellego.

Either read in the data the best you can and make corrections later, or re-arrange the data before you read it in.

> Hint: If your data are truly irregular, it's possible that reading it directly into EViews is just not a happening event. You may be better off lightly touching up the data organization in a text editor before bringing it into EViews.

Adding Data To An Existing Workfile—Or, Being Rectangular Doesn't Mean Being Inflexible

You have a workfile set up and you've populated it with data. How, you may ask, do I add more data? It helps to split this into two separate questions: How do I add more observations and how do I add more variables? In thinking about these questions, picture your data as being formed into a rectangle and then lengthening the rectangle from top to bottom (adding more observations) or widening the rectangle from left to right (adding more variables).

Pretend that our academic salary initially had only two variables (DISCIPLINE and SALARY) and five observations (workfile range "1 5"). We could picture the data as being in a rectangle with two columns and five rows:

Dentistry	44214
Medicine	43160
Law	40670
Agriculture	36879
Engineering	35694

We now discover a sixth observation: Geology with a salary of $33,206. Putting in the new observation takes two steps. First, we extend the workfile at the bottom. Next, we enter the new observation in the space we've created.

Double-click on **Range** in the upper pane of the workfile window or choose **Proc/Structure/Resize Current Page...** to bring up the workfile structure dialog. This dialog lets you change the range and/or the structure of the workfile. Be careful not to change the structure by accident. In our example we want an unstructured workfile with 6 observations, so the filled out dialog looks like this.

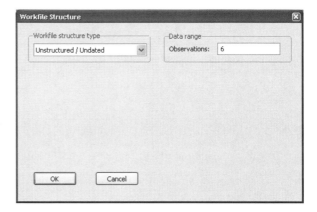

Open a group window containing DISCIPLINE and SALARY. You can see that a row with no data has been added at the bottom. SALARY is marked NA for "not available" and DISCIPLINE is an empty string. An empty string just looks like a blank entry in the table.

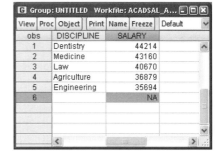

Now type in the new observation. It's okay for some of the new "entries" to be left as NA, just as there can be NAs in the existing data.

Copy/Paste

You could, of course, have added a thousand new observations just as easily as one. Typing 1,000 observations would be rather tedious though. In contrast, **Copy/Paste** isn't any harder for 1,000 observations than it is for one. Go to the computer file holding your data. Copy the data you wish to add, being sure that you've selected a rectangle of data. In EViews, open a group with the desired variables, select the empty rectangle at the bottom that you want to fill in, and choose **Paste**. EViews does a very smart job of interpreting the data you've copied and putting it in the right spot. But if you find that **Paste** doesn't do just what you want, try **Paste Special** which has extra options.

Sometimes the easiest way to combine observations from different sources is to read each source into a separate workfile, create a master workfile with a range large enough to hold all your data, and then manually copy from each small workfile into the master workfile. Suppose that our dentistry and medicine data originated in one source and law, agriculture, and engineering in another. We'd begin by reading our data into two separate workfiles, one with the first two observations and the other with the last three. Looking at an excerpt from the two separate files we'd see

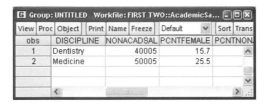

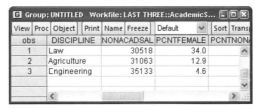

We want to extend the range of the first workfile and then copy in the data from the second. Select the workfile window for "First Two.wf1". Use **File/SaveAs** to change the name to "All Data". Now double-click on **Range** and change the range to 5 observations.

> Hint: **SaveAs** before changing range. This way an error doesn't mess up the original version of "First Two.wf1".

We need to be careful which workfile we're working in now. Select the workfile window for "Last Three.wf1". Hit the View button and **Select All (except C-Resid)**. Then open a group window, which will look more or less like the second window above. Select all the data by dragging the mouse. Then copy to the clipboard.

Click in "All Data.wf1" and open a group with all the series just as we did for "Last Three". Hit Edit+/-, highlight the last three rows, and paste. The data copied from "Last Three" replaced the NAs and we're done.

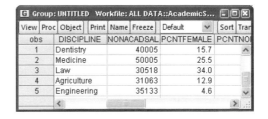

The same principle works with more than two data sources. Make your "all data" workfile big enough to hold all your data and then copy into the appropriate rows from each smaller workfile sequentially.

> Hint: Be careful that each group has all the series in the same order. EViews is just copying a rectangle of numbers. If you accidentally change the order of the series, EViews will accidentally scramble the data.

Expanding from the middle out

> *Question:* Can I insert observations in the middle of my file instead of at the end?
>
> *Response:* Nope.
>
> *Further Response:* Yep.

EViews expands a workfile by adding space for new observations at the end of the workfile range. Adding observations in the middle requires two steps. First, expand the workfile just as we've done above. Second, move observations down to the new bottom of the rectangle. To accomplish the latter, open a group including all series in the workfile, select the rows that should go to the bottom, and hit **Copy**. For example, to move Agriculture and Engineering to the bottom select the two rows as shown and select **Copy**.

Then, making certain that edit mode for the group is on, paste into rows at the bottom of the workfile.

Finally, clear out the area you copied from by selecting each cell in turn and hitting the **Delete** key.

> Hint: To prevent scrambling up the variables, be sure to move data for all your series at the same time.

> Hint: You can use the right-mouse menu item **Insert obs...** to move the data for you automatically.

Adding new variables

Adding a new variable (or variables) is relatively easy. Think of adding a blank column to the right of the data rectangle.

If the new variable is in an existing workfile—or if you can arrange to get it into one—adding the variable into the destination workfile is a cinch. EViews treats each series as a unified object containing data, frequency, sample, label, *etc.* Open the source workfile, select the series you want, and select **Copy**. Open the destination workfile and **Paste**. All done.

Suppose, for example, you have data on the clipboard that you want to add to an existing workfile. Use the **Paste as new Workfile** procedure we talked about earlier in the chapter to create a new workfile. Then **Copy/Paste** series from the new workfile into the desired destination workfile.

> Hint: In order to bring up the context menu with **Paste as new Workfile** be sure to right-click in the lower EViews pane in a blank area, *i.e.*, outside of any workfile window.

If the series you want to add isn't in an EViews workfile... well the truth is that the easiest thing to do may be to bring it into a workfile and then proceed as above.

One alternative is to use **File/Import**, which is designed to bring data into an existing work-file. **File/Import** is mostly helpful if the data are in a spreadsheet or a text file. It uses dialogs somewhat similar to the dialogs for **Spreadsheet Read** or **ASCII Read** from **File/Open/Foreign Data as Workfile...**

> Hint: **File/Open/Foreign Data as Workfile...** is more flexible than **File/Import**.

One more clipboard alternative makes you do more work, but gives you a good deal of manual control. Use the **Quick** menu at the top of the EViews menu bar for the command **Quick/Edit Group (Empty Series)**. As you might infer from the suggestive name, this brings up an empty group window all ready for you to enter data for one or more series. You can paste anywhere in the window. Essentially you are working in a spreadsheet view, giving you complete manual control over editing. This is handy when you only have part of a series or when you're gluing together data from different sources.

Among the Missing

Mostly, data are numbers. Sometimes, data are strings of text. Once in a while, data ain't...

In other words, sometimes you just don't know the value for a particular data point—so you mark it NA.

> Statistical hint: Frequently, the best thing to do with data you don't have is nothing at all. EViews' statistical procedures offer a variety of options, but the usual default is to omit NA observations from the analysis.

How do you tell EViews that a particular observation is not available? If you're entering data by typing or copy-and-paste, you don't have to tell EViews. EViews initializes data to NA. If you don't know a particular value, leave it out and it will remain marked NA.

The harder issue comes when you're reading data in from existing computer files. There are two separate issues you may have to deal with:

- How do you identify NA values to EViews?
- What if multiple values should be coded NA?

Reading NAs from a file

There are a couple of situations in which EViews identifies NAs for you automatically. First, if EViews comes across any nonnumeric text when it's looking for a number, EViews converts the text to NA. For example, the data string "1 NA 3" will be read as the number 1, an NA, and the number 2. The string "1 two 3" will be read the same way—there's nothing magic about the letters "NA" when they appear in an external file. Second, EViews will usually pick up correctly any missing data codes from binary files created by other statistical programs.

If you have a text file (or an Excel file) which has been coded with a numerical value for NA—"-999" and "0" are common examples—you can tell EViews to translate these into NA by filling out the field **Text representing NA** in the dialog used to read in the data. EViews allows only one value to be automatically translated this way.

Reading alpha series with missing values is slightly more problematic, because any string of characters might be a legitimate value. Maybe the characters "NA" are an abbreviation for North America! For an alpha series, you must explicitly specify the string used to represent missing data in the **Text representing NA** field.

Handling multiple missing codes

Some statistical programs allow multiple values to be considered missing. Others, EViews being a singular example, permit only one code for missing values. Suppose that for some variable, call it X, the values -9, -99, and -999 are all suppose to represent missing data. The way to handle this in EViews is to read the data in without specifying any values as missing, and then to recode the data. In this example, this could be done by choosing **Quick/Generate Series…** and then using the **Generate Series by Equation** dialog to set the sample to include just those values of x that you want recoded to NA.

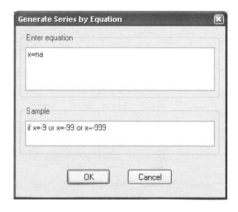

If you prefer, you can accomplish the same task with the recode command, as in:

```
x=@recode(x=-9 or x=-99 or x=-999, NA, x)
```

If the logical condition in the first argument of @recode is true (X is missing, in this example), the value of @recode is the second argument (NA), otherwise it's the third argument (X).

> Hint: It might be wiser to make a new series, say XRECODE, rather than change X itself. This leaves open the option to treat the different missing codes differently at a later date. If you change X, there's no way later to recover the distinct -9, -99, and -999 codes.

Quick Review

The easiest way to get data into EViews is to read it in from an existing data file. EViews does a great job of interpreting data from spreadsheet and text files, as well as reading files created by other statistical programs.

Whether reading from a file or typing your data directly into an EViews spreadsheet, think of the data as being arranged in a rectangle—observations are rows and series are columns.

Appendix: Having A Good Time With Your Date

EViews uses dates in quite a few places. Among the most important are:

- Labeling graphs and other output.
- Specifying samples.
- In data series.

Most of the time, you can specify a date in any reasonable looking way. The following commands all set up the same monthly workfile:

```
wfcreate m 1941m12 1942m1
wfcreate m 41:12 42:1
wfcreate m "december 1941" "january 1942"
```

Hint: If your date string includes spaces, put it in quotes.

Canadians and Americans, among others, write dates in the order month/day/year. Out of the box, EViews comes set up to follow this convention. You can change to the "European" convention of day/month/year by using the **Options/Dates & Frequency Conversion...** menu. You can also switch between the colon and frequency delimiter, *e.g.*, "41:12" versus "41m12".

Hint: Use frequency delimiters rather than the colon. "41q2 "always means the second quarter of 1941, while "41:2 "means the second quarter of 1941 when used in a quarterly workfile but means February 1941 in a monthly workfile.

Ambiguity is not your friend.

The most common use of dates as data is as the id series that appears under the **Obs** column in spreadsheet views and on the horizontal axis in many graphs. But nothing stops you from treating the values in any EViews series as dates. For example, one series might give the date a stock was bought and another series might give the date the same stock was sold. Internally, EViews stores dates as "date numbers"—the number of days since January 1, 0001AD according to the Gregorian proleptic (don't ask) calendar. For example, the series DATE, created with the command "series date = @date", looks like this.

Great for computers—not so great for humans. So EViews lets you change the display of a series containing date numbers. In a spreadsheet view, you can change the display by right-clicking on a column and choosing **Display format....** You can also open a series, hit the [Properties] button and change the **Numeric display** field to one of the date or time formats. Then more fields will appear to let you further customize the format. This looks a lot better.

EViews will also translate text strings into dates when doing an **ASCII Read**, and set the initial display of the series read to be a date format.

> Hint: Since dates are stored as numbers, you can do sensible date arithmetic. If the series DATEBOUGHT and DATESOLD hold the information suggested by their respective names, then:
>
>   series daysheld = datesold - datebought
>
> does just what it should.

So dates are pretty straightforward. Except when they're not. If you want more details, the *Command and Programming Reference* has a very nice 20+ page section for you.

Chapter 3. Getting the Most from Least Squares

Regression is the king of econometric tools. Regression's job is to find numerical values for theoretical parameters. In the simplest case this means telling us the slope and intercept of a line drawn through two dimensional data. But EViews tells us lots more than just slope and intercept. In this chapter you'll see how easy it is to get parameter estimates plus a large variety of auxiliary statistics.

We begin our exploration of EViews' regression tool with a quick look back at the NYSE volume data that we first saw in the opening chapter. Then we'll talk about how to instruct EViews to estimate a regression and how to read the information about each estimated coefficient from the EViews output. In addition to regression coefficients, EViews provides a great deal of summary information about each estimated equation. We'll walk through these items as well. We take a look at EViews' features for testing hypotheses about regression coefficients and conclude with a quick look at some of EViews' most important views of regression results.

Regression is a big subject. This chapter focuses on EViews' most important regression features. We postpone until later chapters various issues, including forecasting (Chapter 8, "Forecasting"), serial correlation (Chapter 13, "Serial Correlation—Friend or Foe?"), and heteroskedasticity and nonlinear regression (Chapter 14, "A Taste of Advanced Estimation").

A First Regression

Returning to our earlier examination of trend growth in the volume of stock trades, we start with a scatter diagram of the logarithm of volume plotted against time.

EViews has drawn a straight line—a regression line—through the cloud of points plotted with $\log(volume)$ on the vertical axis and time on the horizontal. The regression line can be written as an algebraic expression:

$$\log(volume_t) = \alpha + \beta t$$

Using EViews to estimate a regression lets us replace α and β with numbers

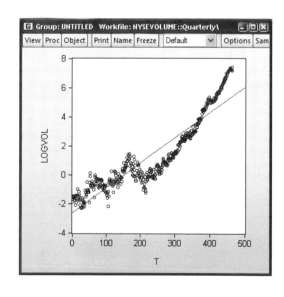

based on the data in the workfile. In a bit we'll see that EViews estimates the regression line to be:

$$\log(volume_t) = -2.629649 + 0.017278t$$

In other words, the intercept α is estimated to be -2.6 and the slope β is estimated to be 0.017.

Most data points in the scatter plot fall either above or below the regression line. For example, for observation 231 (which happens to be the first quarter of 1938) the actual trading volume was far below the predicted regression line.

In other words, the regression line contains errors which aren't accounted for in the estimated equation. It's standard to write a regression model to include a term u_t to account for these errors. (Econometrics texts sometimes use the Greek letter epsilon, ϵ, rather than u for the error term.) A complete equation can be written as:

$$\log(volume_t) = \alpha + \beta t + u_t$$

Regression is a statistical procedure. As such, regression analysis takes uncertainty into account. Along with an estimated value for each parameter (*e.g.*, $\hat{\beta} = 0.017$) we get:

- Measures of the accuracy of each of the estimated parameters and related information for computing hypothesis tests.

- Measures of how well the equation fits the data: How much is explained by the estimated values of α and β and how much remains unexplained.

- Diagnostics to check up on whether assumptions underlying the regression model seem satisfied by the data.

We're re-using the data from Chapter 1, "A Quick Walk Through" to illustrate the features of EViews' regression procedure. If you want to follow along on the computer, use the workfile "NYSEVOLUME" as shown.

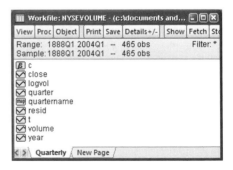

EViews allows you to run a regression either by creating an equation object or by typing commands in the command pane. We'll start with the former approach. Choose the menu command **Object/New Object…**. Pick **Equation** in the **New Object** dialog.

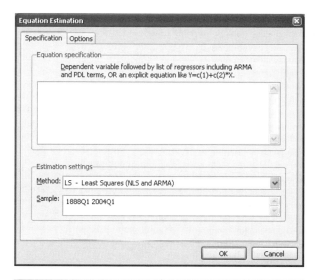

The empty equation window pops open with space to fill in the variables you want in the regression.

Regression equations are easily specified in EViews by a list in which the first variable is the *dependent* variable—the variable the regression is to explain, followed by a list of explanatory—or *independent*—variables. Because EViews allows an expression pretty much anywhere a variable is allowed, we can use either variable names or expressions in our regression specification. We want log($volume$) for our dependent variable and a time trend for our independent variable. Fill out the equation dialog by entering "log(volume) c @trend".

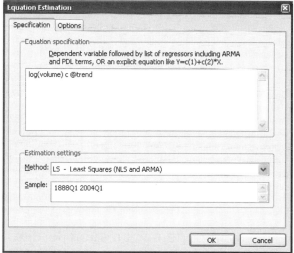

Hint: EViews tells one item in a list from another by looking for spaces between items. For this reason, spaces generally aren't allowed inside a single item. If you type:

```
log  (volume) c @trend
```

you'll get an error message.

Exception to the previous hint: When a text string is called for in a command, spaces are allowed inside paired quotes.

Reminder: The letter "C" in a regression specification notifies EViews to estimate an intercept—the parameter we called α above.

Hint: Another reminder: @trend is an EViews function to generate a time trend, 0, 1, 2, ….

Our regression results appear below:

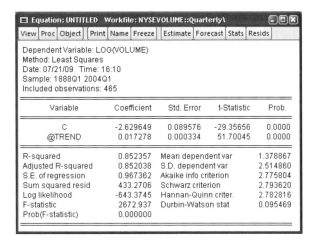

The Really Important Regression Results

There are 25 pieces of information displayed for this very simple regression. To sort out all the different goodies, we'll start by showing a couple of ways that the main results might be presented in a scientific paper. Then we'll discuss the remaining items one number at a time.

A favorite scientific convention for reporting the results of a single regression is display the estimated equation inline with standard errors placed below estimated coefficients, looking something like:

$$\log(volume_t) = \begin{array}{cc} -2.629649 & + \ 0.017278 \cdot t \ , \ ser = 0.967362, \ R^2 = 0.852357 \\ (0.089576) & (0.000334) \end{array}$$

> Hint: The dependent variable is also called the *left-hand side* variable and the independent variables are called the *right-hand side* variables. That's because when you write out the regression equation algebraically, as above, convention puts the dependent variable to the left of the equals sign and the independent variables to the right.

The convention for inline reporting works well for a single equation, but becomes unwieldy when you have more than one equation to report. Results from several related regressions might be displayed in a table, looking something like Table 2.

Table 2

	(1)	(2)
Intercept	-2.629649 (0.089576)	-0.106396 (0.045666)
t	0.017278 (0.000334)	-0.000736 (0.000417)
t^2	—	6.63E-06 (1.37E-06)
log(volume(-1))	—	0.868273 (0.022910)
ser	0.967362	0.289391
R^2	0.852357	0.986826

Column (2)? Don't worry, we'll come back to it later.

> Hint: Good scientific practice is to report only digits that are meaningful when displaying a number. We've printed far too many digits in both the inline display and in Table 2 so as to make it easy for you to match up the displayed numbers with the EViews output. From now on we'll be better behaved.

EViews regression output is divided into three panels. The top panel summarizes the input to the regression, the middle panel gives information about each regression coefficient, and the bottom panel provides summary statistics about the whole regression equation.

The most important elements of EViews regression output are the estimated regression coefficients and the statistics associated with each coefficient. We begin by linking up the numbers in the inline display—or equivalently column (1) of Table 2—with the EViews output shown earlier.

The names of the independent variables in the regression appear in the first column (labeled "Variable") in the EViews output, with the estimated regression coefficients appearing one column over to the right (labeled "Coefficient"). In econometrics texts, regression coefficients are commonly denoted with a Greek letter such as α or β or, occasionally, with a Roman b. In contrast, EViews presents you with the variable names; for example, "@TREND" rather than "β".

The third EViews column, labeled "Std. Error," gives the standard error associated with each regression coefficient. In the scientific reporting displays above, we've reported the standard error in parentheses directly below the associated coefficient. The standard error is a measure of uncertainty about the true value of the regression coefficient.

The standard error of the regression, abbreviated "*ser*," is the estimated standard deviation of the error terms, u_t. In the inline display, "*ser*=0.967362" appears to the right of the regression equation proper. EViews labels the *ser* as "S.E. of regression," reporting its value in the left column in the lower summary block.

Note that the third column of EViews regression output reports the standard error of the estimated coefficients while the summary block below reports the standard error of the regression. Don't confuse the two.

The final statistic in our scientific display is R^2. R^2 measures the overall fit of the regression line, in the sense of measuring how close the points are to the estimated regression line in the scatter plot. EViews computes R^2 as the fraction of the variance of the dependent variable explained by the regression. (See the *User's Guide* for the precise definition.) Loosely, $R^2 = 1$ means the regression fit the data perfectly and $R^2 = 0$ means the regression is no better than guessing the sample mean.

Hint: EViews will report a negative R^2 for a model which fits worse than a model consisting only of the sample mean.

The Pretty Important (But Not So Important As the Last Section's) Regression Results

We're usually most interested in the regression coefficients and the statistical information provided for each one, so let's continue along with the middle panel.

t-Tests and Stuff

All the stuff about individual coefficients is reported in the middle panel, a copy of which we've yanked out to examine on its own.

	Coefficient	Std. Error	t-Statistic	Prob.
C	-2.629649	0.089576	-29.35656	0.0000
@TREND	0.017278	0.000334	51.70045	0.0000

The column headed "t-Statistic" reports, not surprisingly, the *t*-statistic. Specifically, this is the *t*-statistic for the hypothesis that the coefficient in the same row equals zero. (It's computed as the ratio of the estimated coefficient to its standard error: *e.g.,* $51.7 = 0.017/0.00033$.)

Given that there are many potentially interesting hypotheses, why does EViews devote an entire column to testing that specific coefficients equal zero? The hypothesis that a coefficient equals zero is special, because if the coefficient does equal zero then the attached coefficient drops out of the equation. In other words, $\log(volume_t) = \alpha + 0 \times t + u_t$ is really the same as $\log(volume_t) = \alpha + u_t$, with the time trend not mattering at all.

> Foreshadowing hint: EViews automatically computes the test statistic against the hypothesis that a coefficient equals zero. We'll get to testing other coefficients in a minute, but if you want to leap ahead, look at the equation window menu **View/Coefficient Tests...**.

If the *t*-statistic reported in column four is larger than the *critical value* you choose for the test, the estimated coefficient is said to be "statistically significant." The critical value you pick depends primarily on the risk you're willing to take of mistakenly rejecting the null hypothesis (the technical term is the "size" of the test), and secondarily on the degrees of freedom for the test. The larger the risk you're willing to take, the smaller the critical value, and the more likely you are to find the coefficient "significant."

> Hint: EViews doesn't compute the degrees of freedom for you. That's probably because the computation is so easy it's not worth using scarce screen real estate. Degrees of freedom equals the number of observations (reported in the top panel on the output screen) less the number of parameters estimated (the number of rows in the middle panel). In our example, $df = 465 - 2 = 463$.

The textbook approach to hypothesis testing proceeds thusly:

1. Pick a size (the probability of mistakenly rejecting), say five percent.

2. Look up the critical value in a *t*-table for the specified size and degrees of freedom.

3. Compare the critical value to the *t*-statistic reported in column four. Find the variable to be "significant" if the *t*-statistic is greater than the critical value.

EViews lets you turn the process inside out by using the "*p*-value" reported in the right-most column, under the heading "Prob." EViews has worked the problem backwards and figured out what size would give you a critical value that would just match the *t*-statistic reported in column three. So if you are interested in a five percent test, you can reject if and only if the reported *p*-value is less than 0.05. Since the *p*-value is zero in our example, we'd reject the hypothesis of no trend at any size you'd like.

Obviously, that last sentence can't be literally true. EViews only reports *p*-values to four decimal places because no one ever cares about smaller probabilities. The *p*-value isn't literally 0.0000, but it's close enough for all practical purposes.

> Hint: *t*-statistics and *p*-values are different ways of looking at the same issue. A *t*-statistic of 2 corresponds (approximately) to a *p*-value of 0.05. In the old days you'd make the translation by looking at a "t-table" in the back of a statistics book. EViews just saves you some trouble by giving both *t*- and *p*-.

> Not-really-about-EViews-digression: Saying a coefficient is "significant" means there is statistical evidence that the coefficient differs from zero. That's not the same as saying the coefficient is "large" or that the variable is "important." "Large" and "important" depend on the substantive issue you're working on, not on statistics. For example, our estimate is that NYSE volume rises about one and one-half percent each quarter. We're very sure that the increase differs from zero—a statement about statistical significance, not importance.
>
> Consider two different views about what's "large." If you were planning a quarter ahead, it's hard to imagine that you need to worry about a change as small as one and one-half percent. On the other hand, one and one-half percent per quarter starts to add up over time. The estimated coefficient predicts volume will double each decade, so the estimated increase is certainly large enough to be important for long-run planning.

More Practical Advice On Reporting Results

Now you know the principles of how to read EViews' output in order to test whether a coefficient equals zero. Let's be less coy about common practice. When the *p*-value is under 0.05, econometricians say the variable is "significant" and when it's above 0.05 they say it's "insignificant." (Sometimes a variable with a *p*-value between 0.10 and 0.05 is said to be "weakly significant" and one with a *p*-value less than 0.01 is said to be "strongly significant.") This practice may or may not be wise, but wise or not it's what most people do.

We talked above about scientific conventions for reporting results and showed how to report results both inline and in a display table. In both cases standard errors appear in parentheses below the associated coefficient estimates. "Standard errors in parentheses" is really the first of two-and-a-half reporting conventions used in the statistical literature. The second convention places the t-statistics in the parentheses instead of standard errors. For example, we could have reported the results from EViews inline as

$$\log(volume_t) = \underset{(-29.35656)}{-2.629649} + \underset{(51.70045)}{0.017278 \cdot t} \ , \ ser = 0.967362, \ R^2 = 0.852357$$

Both conventions are in wide use. There's no way for the reader to know which one you're using—so you have to tell them. Include a comment or footnote: "Standard errors in parentheses" or "t-statistics in parentheses."

Fifty percent of economists report standard errors and fifty percent report t-statistics. The remainder report p-values, which is the final convention you'll want to know about.

Where Did This Output Come From Again?

The top panel of regression output, shown on the right, summarizes the setting for the regression.

Dependent Variable: LOG(VOLUME)
Method: Least Squares
Date: 07/21/09   Time: 16:10
Sample: 1888Q1 2004Q1
Included observations: 465

The last line, "Included observations," is obviously useful. It tells you how much data you have! And the next to last line identifies the sample to remind you which observations you're using.

Hint: EViews automatically excludes all observations in which any variable in the specification is NA (not available). The technical term for this exclusion rule is "listwise deletion."

Big (Digression) Hint: Automatic exclusion of NA observations can sometimes have surprising side effects. We'll use the data abstract at the right as an example.

obs	Y	X1	X2	X1(-1)	LOG(Y)
1	1.000000	5.000000	6.000000	NA	0.000000
2	2.000000	NA	9.000000	5.000000	0.693147
3	3.000000	10.00000	NA	NA	1.098612
4	4.000000	11.00000	12.00000	10.00000	1.386294
5	0.000000	13.00000	14.00000	11.00000	NA

Data are missing from observation 2 for X1 and from observation 3 for X2. A regression of Y on X1 would use observations 1, 3, 4, and 5. A regression of Y on X2 would use observations 1, 2, 4, and 5. A regression of Y on both X1 and X2 would use observations 1, 4, and 5. Notice that the fifth observation on Y is zero, which is perfectly valid, but that the fifth observation on log(Y) is NA. Since the logarithm of zero is undefined EViews inserts NA whenever it's asked to take the log of zero. A regression of log(Y) on both X1 and X2 would use only observations 1 and 4.

The variable, X1(-1), giving the previous period's values of X1, is missing both the first and third observation. The first value of X1(-1) is NA because the data from the observation before observation 1 doesn't exist. (There *is* no observation before the first one, eh?) The third observation is NA because it's the second observation for X1, and that one is NA. So while a regression of Y on X1 would use observations 1, 3, 4, and 5, a regression of Y on X1(-1) would use observations 2, 4, and 5.

Moral: When there's missing data, changing the variables specified in a regression can also inadvertently change the sample.

What's the use of the top three lines? It's nice to know the date and time, but EViews is rather ungainly to use as a wristwatch. More seriously, the top three lines are there so that when you look at the output you can remember what you were doing.

Dependent Variable: LOG(VOLUME)
Method: Least Squares
Date: 07/21/09   Time: 16:10
Sample: 1888Q1 2004Q1
Included observations: 465

"Dependent Variable" just reminds you what the regression was explaining— LOG(VOLUME) in this case.

"Method" reminds us which statistical procedure produced the output. EViews has dozens of statistical procedures built-in. The default procedure for estimating the parameters of an equation is "least squares."

The third line just reports the date and time EViews estimated the regression. It's surprising how handy that information can be a couple of months into a project, when you've forgotten in what order you were doing things.

Since we're talking about looking at output at a later date, this is a good time to digress on ways to save output for later. You can:

- Hit the Name button to save the equation in the workfile. The equation will appear in the workfile window marked with the ▤ icon. Then save the workfile.

> Hint: Before saving the file, switch to the equation's label view and write a note to remind yourself why you're using this equation.

- Hit the Print button.
- Spend output to a Rich Text Format (RTF) file, which can then be read directly by most word processors. Select **Redirect:** in the **Print** dialog and enter a file name in the **Filename:** field. As shown, you'll end up with results stored in the file "some results.rtf".

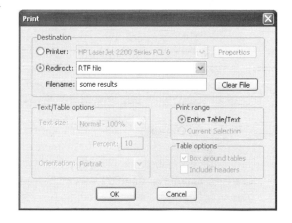

- Right-click and choose Select non-empty cells, or hit Ctrl A— it's the same thing. Copy and then paste into a word processor.

Freeze it

If you have output that you want to make sure won't ever change, even if you change the equation specification, hit Freeze. Freezing the equation makes a copy of the current view in the form of a table which is detached from the equation object. (The original equation is unaffected.) You can then Name this frozen table so that it will be saved in the workfile. See Chapter 17, "Odds and Ends."

Summary Regression Statistics

The bottom panel of the regression provides 12 summary statistics about the regression. We'll go over these statistics briefly, but leave technical details to your favorite econometrics text or the *User's Guide*.

R-squared	0.852357	Mean dependent var	1.378867
Adjusted R-squared	0.852038	S.D. dependent var	2.514860
S.E. of regression	0.967362	Akaike info criterion	2.775804
Sum squared resid	433.2706	Schwarz criterion	2.793620
Log likelihood	-643.3745	Hannan-Quinn criter.	2.782816
F-statistic	2672.937	Durbin-Watson stat	0.095469
Prob(F-statistic)	0.000000		

We've already talked about the two most important numbers, "R-squared" and "S.E. of regression." Our regression accounts for 85 percent of the variance in the dependent variable and the estimated standard deviation of the error term is 0.97. Five other elements, "Sum squared residuals," "Log likelihood," "Akaike info criterion," "Schwarz criterion," and "Hannan-Quinn criter." are used for making statistical comparisons between two different regressions. This means that they don't really help us learn anything about the regression we're working on; rather, these statistics are useful for deciding if one model is better than another. For the record, the sum of squared residuals is used in computing *F*-tests, the log likelihood is used for computing likelihood ratio tests, and the Akaike and Schwarz criteria are used in Bayesian model comparison.

The next two numbers, "Mean dependent var" and "S.D. dependent var," report the sample mean and standard deviation of the left hand side variable. These are the same numbers you'd get by asking for descriptive statistics on the left hand side variables, so long as you were using the sample used in the regression. (Remember: EViews will drop observations from the estimation sample if any of the left-hand side or right-hand side variables are NA—*i.e.*, missing.) The standard deviation of the dependent variable is much larger than the standard error of the regression, so our regression has explained most of the variance in log(volume)—which is exactly the story we got from looking at the R-squared.

Why use valuable screen space on numbers you could get elsewhere? Primarily as a safety check. A quick glance at the mean of the dependent variable guards against forgetting that you changed the units of measurement or that the sample used is somehow different from what you were expecting.

"Adjusted R-squared" makes an adjustment to the plain-old R^2 to take account of the number of right hand side variables in the regression. R^2 measures what fraction of the variation in the left hand side variable is explained by the regression. When you add another right hand side variable to a regression, R^2 always rises. (This is a numerical property of least squares.) The adjusted R^2, sometimes written $\overline{R}^2$, subtracts a small penalty for each additional variable added.

"F-statistic" and "Prob(F-statistic)" come as a pair and are used to test the hypothesis that none of the explanatory variables actually explain anything. Put more formally, the "*F*-statistic" computes the standard F-test of the joint hypothesis that all the coefficients, except the intercept, equal zero. "Prob(F-statistic)" displays the p-value corresponding to the reported F-statistic. In this example, there is essentially no chance at all that the coefficients of the right-hand side variables all equal zero.

> Parallel construction notice: The fourth and fifth columns in EViews regression output report the t-statistic and corresponding p-value for the hypothesis that the individual coefficient in the row equals zero. The F-statistic in the summary area is doing exactly the same test for all the coefficients (except the intercept) together.
>
> This example has only one such coefficient, so the t-statistic and the F-statistic test exactly the same hypothesis. Not coincidentally, the reported p-values are identical and the F- is exactly the square of the t-, $2672 = 51.7^2$.

Our final summary statistic is the "Durbin-Watson," the classic test statistic for serial correlation. A Durbin-Watson close to 2.0 is consistent with no serial correlation, while a number closer to 0 means there probably is serial correlation. The "DW," as the statistic is known, of 0.095 in this example is a very strong indicator of serial correlation.

EViews has extensive facilities both for testing for the presence of serial correlation and for correcting regressions when serial correlation exists. We'll look at the Durbin-Watson, as well as other tests for serial correlation and correction methods, later in the book. (See Chapter 13, "Serial Correlation—Friend or Foe?").

A Multiple Regression Is Simple Too

Traditionally, when teaching about regression, the simple regression is introduced first and then "multiple regression" is presented as a more advanced and more complicated technique. A simple regression uses an intercept and one explanatory variable on the right to explain the dependent variable. A multiple regression uses one or more explanatory variables. So a simple regression is just a special case of a multiple regression. In learning about a simple regression in this chapter you've learned all there is to know about multiple regression too.

Well, almost. The main addition with a multiple regression is that there are added right hand-side variables and therefore added rows of coefficients, standard errors, *etc.* The model we've used so far explains the log of NYSE volume as a linear function of time. Let's add two more variables, time-squared and lagged log(volume), hoping that time and time-squared will improve our ability to match the long-run trend and that lagged values of the dependent variable will help out with the short run.

In the last example, we entered the specification in the **Equation Estimation** dialog. I find it much easier to type the regression command directly into the command pane, although the method you use is strictly a matter of taste. The regression command is `ls` followed by the dependent variable, followed by a list of independent variables (using the special symbol "C" to signal EViews to include an intercept.) In this case, type:

```
ls log(volume) c @trend @trend^2 log(volume(-1))
```

and EViews brings up the multiple regression output shown to the right.

You already knew some of the numbers in this regression because they appeared in the second column in Table 1 on page 65. When you specify a multiple regression, EViews gives one row in the output for each independent variable.

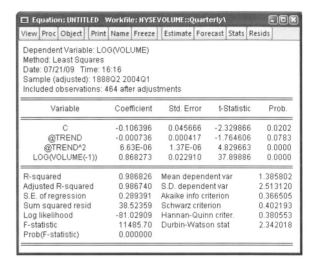

Hint: Most regression specifications include an intercept. Be sure to include "C" in the list of independent variables unless you're sure you don't want an intercept.

Hint: Did you notice that EViews reports one fewer observation in this regression than in the last, and that EViews changed the first date in the sample from the first to the second quarter of 1888? This is because the first data we can use for lagged volume, from second quarter 1888, is the (non-lagged) volume value from the first quarter. We can't compute lagged volume in the first quarter because that would require data from the last quarter of 1887, which is before the beginning of our workfile range.

Hypothesis Testing

We've already seen how to test that a single coefficient equals zero. Just use the reported t-statistic. For example, the t-statistic for lagged log(volume) is 37.89 with 460 degrees of freedom (464 observations minus 4 estimated coefficients). With EViews it's nearly as easy to test much more complex hypotheses.

Click the [View] button and choose **Coefficient Diagnostics/Wald – Coefficient Restrictions...** to bring up the dialog shown to the right.

In order to whip the **Wald Test** dialog into shape you need to know three things:

- EViews names coefficients C(1), C(2), C(3), *etc.*, numbering them in the order they appear in the regression. As an example, the coefficient on LOG(VOLUME(-1)) is C(4).

- You specify a hypothesis as an equation restricting the values of the coefficients in the regression. To test that the coefficient on LOG(VOLUME(-1)) equals zero, specify "C(4) = 0".

- If a hypothesis involves multiple restrictions, you enter multiple coefficient equations separated by commas.

Let's work through some examples, starting with the one we already know the answer to: Is the coefficient on LOG(VOLUME(-1)) significantly different from zero?

Hint: We know the results of this test already, because EViews computed the appropriate test statistic for us in its standard regression output.

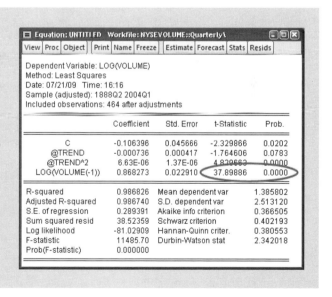

Complete the **Wald Test** dialog with C(4) = 0.

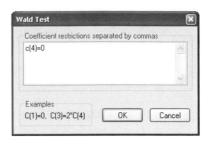

EViews gives the test results as shown to the right.

EViews always reports an *F*-statistic since the *F*- applies for both single and multiple restrictions. In cases with a single restriction, EViews will also show the *t*-statistic.

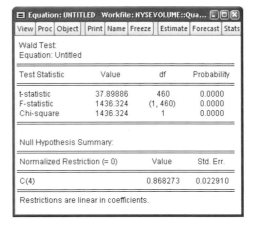

Hint: The *p*-value reported by EViews is computed for a two-tailed test. If you're interested in a one-tailed test, you'll have to look up the critical value for yourself.

Suppose we wanted to test whether the coefficient on LOG(VOLUME(-1)) equaled one rather than zero. Enter "c(4) = 1" to find the new test statistic.

So this hypothesis is also easily rejected.

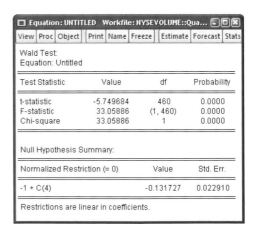

Econometric theory warning: If you've studied the advanced topic in econometric theory called the "unit root problem" you know that standard theory doesn't apply in this test (although the issue is harmless for this particular set of data). Take this as a reminder that you and EViews are a team, but you're the brains of the outfit. EViews will obediently do as it's told. It's up to you to choose the proper procedure.

EViews is happy to test a hypothesis involving multiple coefficients and nonlinear restrictions. To test that the sum of the first two coefficients equals the product of the sines of the second two coefficients (and to emphasize that EViews is perfectly happy to test a hypothesis that is complete nonsense) enter "$c(1) + c(2) = \sin(c(3)) + \sin(c(4))$".

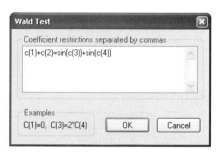

Not only is the hypothesis nonsense, apparently it's not true.

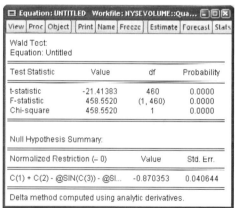

A good example of a hypothesis involving multiple restrictions is the hypothesis that there is no time trend, so the coefficients on both t and t^2 equal zero. Here's the **Wald Test** view after entering "c(2) = 0, c(3) = 0".

The hypothesis is rejected. Note that EViews correctly reports 2 degrees of freedom for the test statistic.

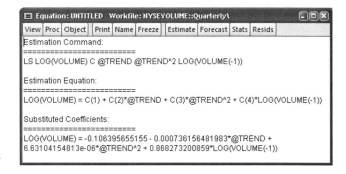

Representing

The **Representations** view, shown at the right, doesn't tell you anything you don't already know, but it provides useful reminders of the command used to generate the regression, the interpretation of the coefficient labels C(1), C(2), *etc.*, and the form of the equation written out with the estimated coefficients.

Hint: Okay, okay. Maybe you didn't really need the representations view as a reminder. The real value of this view is that you can copy the equation from this view and then paste it into your word processor, or into an EViews batch program, or even into Excel, where with a little judicious editing you can turn the equation into an Excel formula.

What's Left After You've Gotten the Most Out of Least Squares

Our regression equation does a pretty good job of explaining log(volume), but the explanation isn't perfect. What remains—the difference between the left-hand side variable and the value predicted by the right-hand side—is called the *residual*. EViews provides several tools to examine and use the residuals.

Peeking at the Residuals

The View **Actual, Fitted, Residual** provides several different ways to look at the residuals.

Actual,Fitted,Residual Table
Actual,Fitted,Residual Graph
Residual Graph
Standardized Residual Graph

Usually the best view to look at first is **Actual, Fitted, Residual/Actual, Fitted, Residual Graph** as illustrated by the graph shown here.

Three series are displayed. The residuals are plotted against the left vertical axis and both the actual (log(volume)) and fitted (predicted log(volume)) series are plotted against the vertical axis on the right. As it happens, because our fit is quite good and because we have so many observations, the fitted values nearly cover up the actual val-

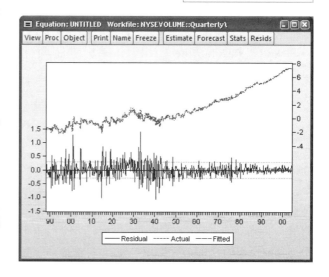

ues on the graph. But from the residuals it's easy to see two facts: our model fits better in the later part of the sample than in the earlier years—the residuals become smaller in absolute value—and there are a very small number of data points for which the fit is really terrible.

Points with really big positive or negative residuals are called *outliers*. In the plot to the right we see a small number of spikes which are much, much larger than the typical residual. We can get a close up on the residuals by choosing **Actual, Fitted, Residual/Residual Graph.**

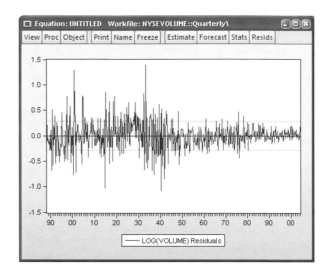

It might be interesting to look more carefully at specific numbers. Choose **Actual, Fitted, Residual/Actual, Fitted, Residual Table** for a look that includes numerical values.

You can see enormous residuals in the second quarter for 1933. The actual value looks out of line with the surrounding values. Perhaps this was a really unusual quarter on the NYSE, or maybe someone even wrote down the wrong numbers when putting the data together!

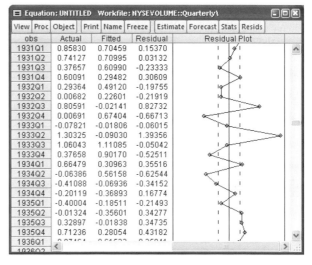

Grabbing the Residuals

Since there is one residual for each observation, you might want to put the residuals in a series for later analysis.

Fine. All done.

Without you doing anything, EViews stuffs the residuals into the special series ☑ resid after each estimation. You can use RESID just like any other series.

Resid Hint 1: That was a very slight fib. EViews won't let you include RESID as a series in an estimation command because the act of estimation changes the values stored in RESID.

Resid Hint 2: EViews replaces the values in RESID with new residuals after each estimation. If you want to keep a set, copy them into a new series as in:

```
series rememberresids = resid
```

before estimating anything else.

Resid Hint 3: You can store the residuals from an equation in a series with any name you like by using **Proc/Make Residual Series…** from the equation window.

Quick Review

To estimate a multiple regression, use the `ls` command followed first by the dependent variable and then by a list of independent variables. An equation window opens with estimated coefficients, information about the uncertainty attached to each estimate, and a set of summary statistics for the regression as a whole. Various other views make it easy to work with the residuals and to test hypotheses about the estimated coefficients.

In later chapters we turn to more advanced uses of least squares. Nonlinear estimation is covered, as are methods of dealing with serial correlation. And, predictably, we'll spend some time talking about forecasting.

Chapter 4. Data—The Transformational Experience

It's quite common to spend the greater part of a research project manipulating data, even though the exciting part is estimating models, testing hypotheses, and forecasting into the future. In EViews the basics of data transformation are quite simple. We begin this chapter with a look at standard algebraic manipulations. Then we take a look at the different kinds of data—numeric, alphabetic, *etc.*—that EViews understands. The chapter concludes with a look at some of EViews' more exotic data transformation functions.

Your Basic Elementary Algebra

The basics of data transformation in EViews can be learned in about two seconds. Suppose we have a series named ONE_SECOND that measures—in microseconds—the length of one second. (You can download the workfile "BasicAlgebra.wf1", from the EViews website.) To create a new EViews series measuring the length of two seconds, type in the command pane:

```
series two_seconds = one_second +
    one_second
```

Deconstructing Two Seconds Construction

The results of the command are shown to the right. They're just what one would expect. Let's deconstruct this terribly complicated example. The basic form of the command is:

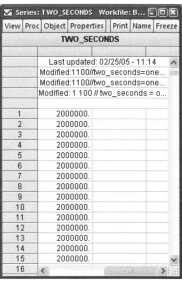

- the command name `series`, followed by a name for the new series, followed by an " = " sign, followed by an algebraic expression.

A number of EViews' "cultural values" are implicitly invoked here. Let's go though them one-by-one:

- Operations are performed on an entire series at a time.

  In other words, the addition is done for each observation at the same time. This is the general rule but we'll see two variants a little later, one involving lags and one involving samples.

- The " = " sign doesn't mean "equals," it means copy the values on the right into the series on the left.

  This is standard computer notation, although not what we learned " = " meant in school. Note that if the series on the left already exists, the values it contains are *replaced by those on the right*. This allows for both useful commands such as:

  ```
  series two_seconds = two_seconds/1000 'change units to milli-
      seconds
  ```

  and also for some really dumb ones:

  ```
  series two_seconds = two_seconds-two_seconds 'a really dumb
      command
  ```

Hint: EViews regards text following an apostrophe, "'", as a comment that isn't processed. "`'a really dumb command`" is a note for humans that EViews ignores.

Hint: There's no Undo command. Once you've replaced values in a series—they're gone! Moral: **Save** or **SaveAs** frequently so that if necessary you can load back a pre-mistake version of the workfile.

- The `series` command performs two logically separate operations. It declares a new *series object*, TWO_SECONDS. Then it fills in the values of the object by computing ONE_SECOND + ONE_SECOND

We could have used two commands instead of one:

```
series two_seconds
```

creates a series in the workfile named TWO_SECONDS initialized with NAs. We could then type:

```
two_seconds = one_second + one_second
```

Once a series has been created (or "declared," in computer-speak) the command name `series` is no longer required at the front of a data transformation line— although it doesn't do any harm.

Hint: EViews doesn't care about the capitalization of commands or series names.

Some Typing Issues

The command pane provides a scrollable record of commands you've typed. You can scroll back to see what you've done. You can also edit any line (including using copy-and-paste to help on the editing.) Hit Enter and EViews will copy the line containing the cursor to the bottom of the command pane and then execute the command.

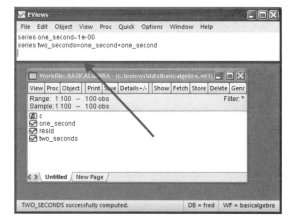

You may wish to use (CTRL + UP) to recall a list of previous commands in the order they were entered. The last command in the list will be entered in the command window. Holding down the CTRL key and pressing UP repeatedly will display the prior commands. Repeat until the desired command is recalled for editing and execution.

If you've been busy entering a lot of commands, you may press (CTRL + J) to examine a history of the last 30 commands. Use the UP and DOWN arrows to select the desired command and press ENTER, or double click on the desired command to add it to the command window. To close the history window without selecting a command, click elsewhere in the command window or press the Escape (ESC) key.

The size of the command pane is adjustable. Use the mouse to grab the separator at the bottom of the command pane and move it up or down as you please. You may also drag the command window to anywhere inside the EViews frame. Press F4 to toggle docking, or click on the command window, depress the right-mouse button and select **Toggle Command Docking**.

You can print the command pane by clicking anywhere in the pane and then choosing **File/Print**. Similarly, you can save the command pane to disk (default file name "command.log") by clicking anywhere in the pane and choosing **File/Save** or **File/SaveAs...**.

Some folks have a taste for using menus rather than typing commands. We could have created TWO_SECONDS with the menu **Quick/Generate Series...**. Using the menu and **Generate Series by Equation** dialog has the advantage that you can restrict the sample for this one operation without changing the workfile sample. (More on samples in the next section.) There's a small disadvantage in that, unlike when you type directly in the command pane, the equation doesn't appear in the command pane—so you're left without a visual record.

Deprecatory hint: Earlier versions of EViews used the command `genr` for what's now done with the distinct commands `series`, `alpha`, and `frml`. (We'll meet the latter two commands shortly.) `Genr` will still work even though the new commands are preferred. (Computer folks say an old feature has been "deprecated" when it's been replaced by something new, but the old feature continues to work.)

Obvious Operators

EViews uses all the usual arithmetic operators: " + ", "-", "*", "/", "^". Operations are done from left to right, except that exponentiation ("^") comes before multiplication ("*") and division, which come before addition and subtraction. Numbers are entered in the usual way, "123" or in scientific notation, "1.23e2".

Hint: If you aren't sure about the order of operations, (extra) parentheses do no harm.

EViews handles logic by representing TRUE with the number 1.0 and FALSE with the number 0. The comparison operators " > ", " < ", " = ", " > = " (greater than or equal), " < = " (less than or equal), and " < > " (not equal) all produce ones or zeros as answers.

> Hint: Notice that " = " is used both for comparison and as the assignment operator—context matters.

EViews also provides the logical operators `and`, `or`, and `not`. EViews evaluates arithmetic operators first, then comparisons, and finally logical operators.

> Hint: EViews generates a 1.0 as the result of a true comparison, but only 0 is considered to be FALSE. Any number other than 0 counts as TRUE. So the value of the expression 2 AND 3 is TRUE (*i.e.*, 1.0). (2 and 3 are both treated as TRUE by the AND operator.)

Using 1 and 0 for TRUE and FALSE sets up some incredibly convenient tricks because it means that multiplying a number by TRUE copies the number, while multiplying by FALSE gives nothing (uh, zero isn't really "nothing," but you know what we meant). For example, if the series ONE_2_3 and TWO_3_1 are as shown, then the command:

obs	ONE_2_3	TWO_3_1	BIGGER
1	1.000000	2.000000	2.000000
2	2.000000	3.000000	3.000000
3	3.000000	1.000000	3.000000
4	4.000000	NA	NA
5	5.000000	NA	NA
6	NA	NA	NA
7			

```
series bigger = (one_2_3>=two_3_1)*one_2_3 +
    (one_2_3<two_3_1)*two_3_1
```

picks out the values of ONE_2_3 when ONE_2_3 is larger than TWO_3_1 $(1 \times ONE\_2\_3 + 0 \times TWO\_3\_1)$ and the values of TWO_3_1 when TWO_3_1 is larger $(0 \times ONE\_2\_3 + 1 \times TWO\_3\_1)$.

> Na, Na, Na: EViews code for a number being not available is NA. Arithmetic and logical operations on NA always produce NA as the result, except for a few functions specially designed to translate NAs. NA is neither true nor false; it's NA.

The Lag Operator

Reflecting its time series origins a couple of decades back, EViews takes the order of observations seriously. In standard mathematical notation, we typically use subscripts to identify one observation in a vector. If the generic label for the current observation is y_t, then the previous observation is written y_{t-1} and the next observation is written y_{t+1}. When there isn't any risk of confusion, we sometimes drop the t. The three observations might be written y_{-1}, y, y_{+1}. Since typing subscripts is a nuisance, lags and leads are specified in EViews by following a series name with the lag in parentheses. For example, if we have a series named Y, then Y(-1) refers to the series lagged once; Y(-2) refers to the series lagged twice; and Y(1) refers to the series led by one.

As an illustration, the workfile "5Days.wf1" contains a series Y with NASDAQ opening prices for the first five weekdays of 2005. Looking at Tuesday's data you'll see that the value for Y(-1) is Monday's opening price and the value for Y(1) is

obs	DAYNAMES	Y	Y(-1)	Y(1)
1/03/2005	Monday	2184.750	NA	2158.310
1/04/2005	Tuesday	2158.310	2184.750	2102.900
1/05/2005	Wednesday	2102.900	2158.310	2098.510
1/06/2005	Thursday	2098.510	2102.900	2099.950
1/07/2005	Friday	2099.950	2098.510	NA

Wednesday's opening price. Y(-1) for Monday and Y(1) for Friday are both NA, because they represent unknown data—the opening price on the Friday before we started collecting data and the opening price on the Monday after we stopped collecting data, respectively.

The group shown above was created with the EViews command:

```
show daynames y y(-1) y(1)
```

If we wanted to compute the percentage change from the previous day, we could use the command:

```
series pct_change = 100*(y-y(-1))/y(-1)
```

> Hint: In a regularly dated workfile, "5Days.wf1" for example, one lag picks up data at $t-1$. In an undated or an irregularly dated workfile, one lag simply picks up the preceding observation—which may or may not have been measured one time period earlier.
>
> Put another way, in a workfile holding data for U.S. states in alphabetical order, one lag of Missouri is Mississippi.

The "Entire Series At A Time" Exception For Lags

A couple of pages back we told you that EViews operates on an entire series at a time. Lags are the first exception. When the expression on the right side of a series assignment includes lags, EViews processes the first observation, assigns the resulting value to the series on the left, and then processes the second observation, and so on. The order matters because the assignment for the first observation can affect the processing of the second observation. Consider the following EViews instructions, ignoring the smpl statements for the moment.

```
smpl @all
series y = 1
smpl @first+1 @last
y = y(-1) + .5
```

The first assignment statement sets all the observations of Y to 1. As a consequence of the second `smpl` statement (Smpl limits operations to a subset of the data; more on `smpl` in the section *Simple Sample Says*), the second assignment statement begins with the second observation, setting Y to the value of the first observation (Y(-1)) plus .5 (1.0 + 0.5). Then the statement sets the third observation of Y to the value of the second observation (Y(-1)) plus .5 (1.5 + 0.5). Contrast this with processing the entire series at a time, adding .5 to each original lagged observation (setting all values of Y to 1.5)—which is what EViews *does not* do.

	Y
1	1.000000
2	1.500000
3	2.000000
4	2.500000
5	3.000000
6	3.500000
7	4.000000
8	4.500000
9	5.000000
10	5.500000

Now we'll unignore the `smpl` statements. If we'd simply typed the commands:

```
series y = 1
y = y(-1) + .5
```

the first assignment would set all of Y to 1. But the second statement would begin by adding the value of the zero[th] observation (Y(-1))—oops, what zero[th] observation? Since there *is no* zero[th] observation, EViews would add NA to 0.5, setting the value of the first Y to NA. Next, EViews would add the first observation to 0.5, this time setting the second Y to NA + 0.5. We would have ended up with an entire series of NAs.

	Y
1	NA
2	NA
3	NA
4	NA
5	NA
6	NA
7	NA
8	NA
9	NA
10	NA

Our original use of `smpl` statements to avoided propagating NAs by having the first lagged value be the value of the first observation, which was 0—as we intended.

> Moral: When you use lagged variables in an equation, think carefully about whether the lags are picking up the observations you intend.

Functions Are Where It's @

EViews function names mostly begin with the symbol "@." There are a *lot* of functions which are documented in the *Command and Programming Reference*. We'll work through some of the more interesting ones below in the section *Relative Exotica*. Here, we look at the basics.

Several of the most often used functions have "reserved names," meaning these functions don't need the "@" sign and that the function names cannot be used as names for your data series. (Don't worry, if you accidentally specify a reserved name, EViews will squawk loudly.) To create a variable which is the logarithm of X, type:

```
series lnx = log(x)
```

> Hint: `log` means natural log. To quote Davidson and MacKinnon's *Econometric Theory and Methods*:
>
> > *In this book, all logarithms are natural logarithms....Some authors use "ln" to denote natural logarithms and "log" to denote base 10 logarithms. Since econometricians should never have any use for base 10 logarithms, we avoid this aesthetically displeasing notation.*

> Hint: If you insist on using base 10 logarithms use the `@log10` function. And for the rebels amongst us, there's even a `@logx` function for arbitrary base logarithms.

Other functions common enough that the "@" sign isn't needed include `abs(x)` for absolute value, `exp(x)` for e^x, and `d(x)` for the first difference (*i.e.,* $d(x)=x-x(-1)$). The function `sqr(x)` means $\sqrt{x}$, not x^2, for what are BASICally historical reasons (for squares, just use "^2").

EViews provides the expected pile of mathematical functions such as `@sin(x)`, `@cos(x)`, `@mean(x)`, `@median(x)`, `@max(x)`, `@var(x)`. All the functions take a series as an argument and produce a series as a result, but note that for some functions, such as `@mean(x)`, the output series holds the same value for every observation.

Random Numbers

EViews includes a wide variety of random number generators. (See *Statistical Functions*.) Three functions for generating random numbers that are worthy of special attention are `rnd` (uniform (0,1) random numbers), `nrnd` (standard normal random numbers), and `rndseed` (set a "seed" for random number generation). Officially, these functions are called "special expressions" rather than "functions."

Statistical programs generate "pseudo-random" rather than truly random numbers. The sequence of generated numbers look random, but if you start the sequence from a particular value the numbers that follow will always be the same. `Rndseed` is used to pick a starting point for the sequence. Give `rndseed` an arbitrary integer argument. Every time you use the *same* arbitrary argument, you'll get the same sequence of pseudo-random numbers. This lets you repeat an analysis involving random numbers and get the same results each time.

What if you want uniform random numbers distributed between limits other than 0 and 1 or normals with mean and variance different from 0 and 1? There's a simple trick for each of these. If x is distributed uniform(0,1), then $a + (b - a) \times x$ is distributed uniform(a, b). If x is distributed N(0,1), then $\mu + \sigma x$ is distributed $N(\mu, \sigma^2)$. The corresponding EViews commands (using 2 and 4.5 for a and b, and 3 and 5 for μ and σ) are:

```
series x = 2 + (4.5-2)*rnd
series x = 3 + 5*nrnd
```

Trends and Dates

The function `@trend` generates the sequence 0, 1, 2, 3,.... You can supply an optional date argument in which case the trend is adjusted to equal zero on the specified date. The results of `@trend(1979)` appear to the right.

The functions `@year`, `@quarter`, `@month`, and `@day` return the year, quarter, month, and day of the month respectively, for each observation. `@weekday` returns 1 through 7, where Monday is 1. For instance, a dummy (0/1) variable marking the postwar period could be coded:

```
series postwar = @year>1945
```

or a dummy variable used to check for the "January effect" (historically, U.S. stocks performed unusually well in January) could be coded:

```
series january = @month=1
```

The command:

```
show january @weekday=5
```

tells us both about January and about Fridays, as shown to the right.

If?

In place of the "if statement" of many programming languages, EViews has the `@recode(s,x,y)` function. If S is true for a particular observation, the value of `@recode` is X, otherwise the value is Y. For example, an alternative to the method presented earlier for choosing the larger observation between two series is:

```
series bigger =
   @recode(one_2_3>=two_3_1,
   one_2_3, two_3_1)
```

Not Available Functions

Ordinarily, any operation involving the value NA gives the result NA. Sometimes—particularly in making comparisons—this leads to unanticipated results. For example, you might think the comparison x=1 is true if X equals 1 and false otherwise. Nope. As the example shows, if X is NA then x=1 is not false, it's NA.

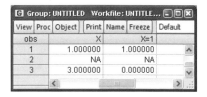

"A foolish consistency is the hobgoblin of little minds" hint: Logically, the result of the comparison x=na should always return NA in line with the rule that any operation involving an NA results in an NA. Logical perhaps, but useless. EViews favors common sense so this operation gives the desired result.

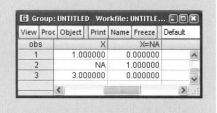

EViews includes a set of special functions to help out with handling NAs, notably @isna(X), @eqna(X,Y), and @nan(X,Y). @isna(X) is true if X is NA and false otherwise. @eqna(X,Y) is true if X equals Y, including NA values. @nan(X,Y) returns X unless X is NA, in which case it returns Y. For example, to recode NAs in X to -999 use X=@nan(X,-999).

Q: Can I define my own function?

A: No.

Auto-Series and Two Examples

Pretty much any place in EViews that calls for the name of a series, you can enter an expression instead. EViews calls these expressions *auto-series*.

Showing an expression

For example, to check on our use of @recode on page 91, you can enter an expression directly in a show command, thusly:

```
show one_2_3 two_3_1 @recode(one_2_3>=two_3_1, one_2_3, two_3_1)
```

Auto-series in a regression

Here's an example which illustrates the econometric theorem that a regression including a constant is equivalent to the same regression in deviations from means excluding the constant. We can use the random number generators to fabricate some "data":

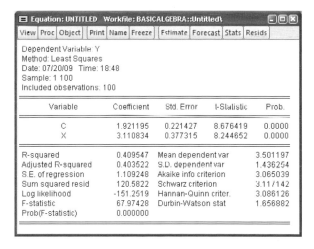

```
rndseed 54321

series x = rnd

series y = 2+3*x + nrnd
```

Then we can run the usual regression with:

```
ls y c x
```

The results are as expected: Both the intercept and slope are close to the values that we used in generating the data.

Now we can run the regression in deviations from means and, not incidentally, illustrate the use of auto-series:

```
ls y-@mean(y)
    x-@mean(x)
```

Group: UNTITLED Workfile: BASICALGEBRA::U...

View | Proc | Object | Print | Name | Freeze | Default | Sort

obs	ONE_2_3	TWO_3_1	@RECODE(...
1	1.000000	2.000000	2.000000
2	2.000000	3.000000	3.000000
3	3.000000	1.000000	3.000000
4	4.000000	NA	NA
5	5.000000	NA	NA
6	NA	NA	NA
7	NA	NA	NA

Equation: UNTITLED Workfile: BASICALGEBRA::Untitled\

View | Proc | Object | Print | Name | Freeze | Estimate | Forecast | Stats | Resids

Dependent Variable: Y
Method: Least Squares
Date: 07/20/09 Time: 18:48
Sample: 1 100
Included observations: 100

Variable	Coefficient	Std. Error	t-Statistic	Prob.
C	1.921195	0.221427	8.676419	0.0000
X	3.110834	0.377315	8.244652	0.0000

R-squared	0.409547	Mean dependent var	3.501197
Adjusted R-squared	0.403522	S.D. dependent var	1.436254
S.E. of regression	1.109248	Akaike info criterion	3.065039
Sum squared resid	120.5822	Schwarz criterion	3.117142
Log likelihood	-151.2519	Hannan-Quinn criter.	3.086126
F-statistic	67.97428	Durbin-Watson stat	1.656882
Prob(F-statistic)	0.000000		

Note that the output from this second regression is identical to the first (demonstrating the theorem but not having anything particular to do with EViews). You'll also see that EViews has expanded `@mean(y)` to `@mean(y, "1 100")`. We'll explain this expansion of the `@mean` function in just a bit.

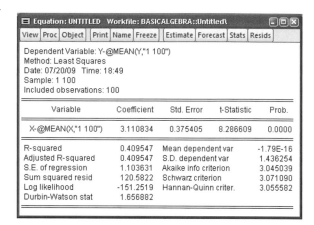

> Typographic hint: EViews thinks series are separated by spaces. This means that when using an auto-series it's important that there *not* be any spaces, unless the auto-series is enclosed in parentheses. In our example, EViews interprets `y-@mean(y)` as the deviation of Y from its mean, as we intended. If we had left a space before the minus sign, EViews would have thought we wanted Y to be the dependent variable and the first independent variable to be the negative of the mean of Y.

FRML and Named Auto-Series

Have a calculation that needs to be regularly redone as new data comes in, perhaps a calculation you do each month on freshly loaded data? Define a named *auto-series* for the calculation. When you load the fresh data, the named auto-series automatically reflects the new data.

Named auto-series are a cross between expressions used in a command (`y-@mean(y)`) and regular series (`series yyy = y-@mean(y)`). Since it's simple, we'll show you how to create a named auto-series and then talk about a couple of places where they're particularly useful.

Creation of a named auto-series is identical to the creation of an ordinary series, except that you use the command `frml` rather than `series`. To create a named auto-series equal to `y-@mean(y)` give the command:

```
frml y_less_mean = y-@mean(y)
```

The auto-series Y_LESS_MEAN is displayed in the workfile window with a variant of the ordinary series icon, ☑.

Hint: frml is a contraction of "formula."

To understand named auto-series, it helps to know what EViews is doing under the hood. For an ordinary series, EViews computes the values of the series and stores them in the workfile. For a named auto-series, EViews stores the formula you provide. Whenever the auto-series is referenced, EViews recalculates its values on the fly. A minor advantage of the auto-series is that it saves storage, since the values are computed as needed rather than always taking up room in memory.

The major advantage of named auto-series is that the values automatically update to reflect changes in values of series used in the formula. In the example above, if any of the data in Y changes, the values in Y_LESS_MEAN change automatically.

When we get to Chapter 8, "Forecasting," we'll learn about a special role that auto-series play in making forecasts.

Simple Sample Says

As you've no doubt gathered by now, the statement "Operations are performed on an entire series at a time" is a hair short of being true. The fuller version is:

- Operations are performed on all the elements of a series included in the current sample.

A sample is an EViews object which specifies which observations are to be included in operations. Effectively, you can think of a sample as a list of dates in a dated workfile, or a list of observation numbers in an undated workfile. Samples are used for operational control in two different places. The primary sample is the *workfile sample*. This sample provides the default control for all operations on series, by telling which observations to include. Specific commands occasionally allow specification of a secondary sample which over-rides the workfile sample.

When a workfile is first created, the sample includes all observations in the workfile. The current sample is shown in the upper pane of the workfile window. In this example, the workfile consists of five daily observations beginning on 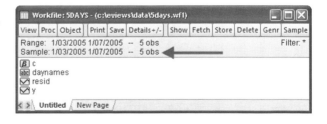 Monday, January 3, 2005 and ending on Friday, January 7, 2005.

Here's the key concept in specifying samples:

- Samples are specified as one or more pairs of beginning and ending dates.

In the illustration, the pair "1/03/2005 1/07/05" specifies the first and last dates of the sample.

> Hint: Above, we used the word "date." For an undated workfile, substitute "observation number." To pick out the first ten observations in an undated workfile use the pair "1 10."

To pick out Monday and Wednesday through Friday, specify the two pairs "1/03/2005 1/03/2005 1/05/2005 1/07/2005." Notice that we picked out a single date, Monday, with a pair that begins and ends on the same date.

EViews is clever about interpreting sample pairs as beginning and ending dates. In a daily workfile, specifying 2005m1 means January 1 if it begins a sample pair and January 31 if it ends a sample pair. As an example,

```
smpl 2005m1 2005m1
```

picks out all the dates in January 2005.

SMPLing the Sample

To set the sample, use the `smpl` command. (*Not* the related `sample` command, which we'll get to in a second.) The command format is the word `smpl`, followed by the sample you want used, as in:

```
smpl 1/03/2005 1/03/2005 1/05/2005 1/07/2005
```

If you prefer, the menu **Quick/Sample...** or the [Sample] button (which implements the `smpl` command, not the `sample` command) brings up the **Sample** dialog where you can also type in the sample. The dialog is initialized with the current sample for ease of editing.

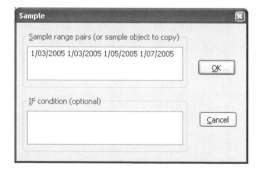

SMPL Keywords

Three special keywords help out in specifying date pairs. `@first` means the first date in the workfile. `@last` means the last date. `@all` means all dates in the workfile. So two equivalent commands are:

```
smpl @all
smpl @first @last
```

Arithmetic operations are allowed in specifying date pairs. For example, the second date in the workfile is @first+1. To specify the entire sample except the first observation use:

```
smpl @first+1 @last
```

The first ten and last ten observations in the workfile are picked by:

```
smpl @first @first+9 @last-9 @last
```

Smpl Splicing

You can take advantage of the fact that observations outside the current sample are unaffected by series operations to splice together a series with different values for different dates. For example, the commands:

```
smpl @all

series prewar = 1

smpl 1945m09 @last

prewar = 0

smpl @all
```

first create a series equal to 1.0 for all observations. Then it sets the later observations in the series to 0, leaving the pre-war values unchanged.

> Hint: It is a very common error to change the sample for a particular operation and then forget to restore it before proceeding to the next step. At least the author seems to do this regularly.

SMPLing If

A sample specification has two parts, both of which are optional. The first part, the one we've just discussed, is a list of starting and ending date pairs. The second part begins with the word "if" and is followed by a logical condition. The sample consists of the observations which are included in the pairs in the first part of the specification AND for which the logical condition following the "if" is true. (If no date pairs are given, @all is substituted for the first part.) We could pick out the last three weekdays with:

```
smpl if @weekday>=3 and @weekday<=5
```

We could pick out days in which the NASDAQ closed above 2,100 (remember that the series Y is the NASDAQ closing price) with:

```
smpl if y>2100
```

To select the days Monday and Wednesday through Friday in the first trading week of 2005, but only for those days where the NASDAQ closed above 2,100, type:

```
smpl 1/03/2005 1/03/2005 1/05/2005 1/07/2005 if y>2100
```

Sample SMPLs

Since the `smpl` command sets the sample, you won't be surprised to hear that the `sample` command sets smpls.

The `sample` command creates a new object which stores a smpl. In other words, while the `smpl` command changes the active sample, the `sample` command stores a sample specification for future use. Sample objects appear in the workfile marked with a ⬌ icon. Thus the command:

```
sample s1 1/03/2005 1/03/2005 1/05/2005 1/07/2005 if y>2100
```

stores ⬌ s1 in the workfile. You can later reuse the sample specification with the command:

```
smpl s1
```

remembering that the specification is evaluated when used, not when stored. In fact, there's an important general rule about the evaluation of sample specifications:

• The sample is re-evaluated every time EViews processes data.

The example at hand includes the clause "if y > 2100". Every time the values in Y change, the set of points included in the sample may change. For example, if you edit Y, changing an observation from 2200 to 2000, that observation drops out of sample S1.

Three Simple SAMPLE & SMPL Tricks

To save the current sample specification, give the command `sample` or use the menu **Object/New Object** and pick **Sample**. Either way, the **Sample** dialog opens with the current workfile sample as initial values. Immediately hit ⬐ OK ⬏ to save the current specification in the newly defined sample object.

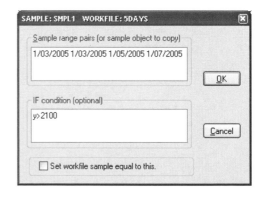

Remember that the "if clause" in a sample includes observations where the logical condition evaluates to TRUE (1) and excludes observations where the condition evaluates to False (0).

Hint: In a sample "if clause," NA counts as false.

Freezing the current sample

To "freeze" a sample, so that you can reuse the same observations later even if the variables in the sample specification change, first create a variable equal to 1 for every point in the current sample.

```
series sampledummy = 1
```

Then set up a new sample which selects those data points for which the new variable equals 1.

```
sample frozensample if sampledummy
```

Now any time you give the command:

```
smpl frozensample
```

you'll restore the sample you were using.

Creating dummy variables for selected dates

To create a dummy (zero/one) variable that equals one for certain dates and zero for others, first save a sample specification including the desired dates. Later you can include the sample in a series calculation, taking advantage of the fact that in such a calculation EViews evaluates the sample as 1 for points in the sample and 0 for points outside. Try deconstructing the following example.

```
sample s2 @first+1 @last if y-y(-1)
smpl @all
series sameyasprevious = y*s2 - 999*(1-s2)
```

Got it? The first line defines S2 as holding a sample specification including all observations for which Y equals its own lagged value. The second line sets the sample to include the entire workfile range. The third line creates a new series named SAMEYASPREVIOUS which equals Y if Y equals its own lagged value and -999 otherwise. The trick is that the sample S2 is treated as either a 1 or a 0 in the last line.

Nonsample SMPLs

Each workfile has a current sample which governs all operations on series—except when it doesn't. In other words, some operations and commands allow you to specify a sample which applies just to that one operation. For these operations, you write the sample specification just as you would in a `smpl` command. In some cases, the string defining the sample needs to be enclosed in quotes.

We've already seen one such example. The function `@mean` accepts a sample specification as an optional second argument. Following along from the preceding example, we could compute:

```
smpl @all
```

```
series overallmean = @mean(y)

series samplemean1 = @mean(y,s2)

series samplemean2 = @mean(y,"@first+1 @last if y=y(-1)")
```

OVERALLMEAN gives the mean of Y taken over all observations. SAMPLEMEAN1 takes the mean of those observations included in S2, as does SAMPLEMEAN2.

Data Types Plain and Fancy

Series hold either numbers or text. That's it.

Except that sometimes numbers aren't numbers, they're dates. And sometimes the numbers or text you see aren't there at all because you're looking at a value map instead. We'll start simply with numbers and text and then let the discussion get a teeny bit more complicated.

Numbers and Letters

As you know, the command `series` creates a new data series, each observation holding one number. Series icons are displayed with the series icon, ☑. EViews stores numbers with about 16 digits of accuracy, using what computer types call double precision.

> Computer hint: Computer arithmetic is not perfect. On very rare occasion, this matters.

> Data hint: Data measurement is not perfect. On occasion, this matters a lot.

Number Display

By default, EViews displays numbers in a format that's pretty easy to read. You can change the format for displaying a series through the **Properties** dialog of the spreadsheet view of the series. Check boxes let you use a thousands separator (commas are the default), put negative values in parentheses (often used for financial data), add a trailing "%" (doesn't change the value displayed, just adds the percent sign), or use a comma to separate the integer and decimal part of the number.

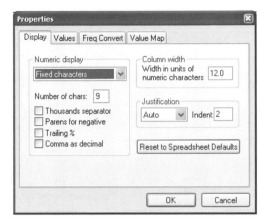

Hint: Click on a cell in the spreadsheet view to see a number displayed in full precision in the status line at the bottom of the EViews window.

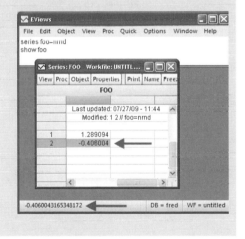

The **Numeric display** dropdown menu in the dialog provides options in addition to the default **Fixed characters**. **Significant digits** drops off trailing zeros after the decimal. Using **Fixed decimal,** you can pick how many places to show after the decimal. For example, you might choose two places after the decimal for data measured in dollars and cents. **Scientific notation** (sometimes called engineering notation) puts one digit in front of the decimal and includes a power of ten. For example, 12.05 would appear as 1.205E01. **Percentage** displays numbers as percentages, so 0.5 appears as 50.00. (To add a "%" symbol, check the **Trailing %** checkbox.) **Fraction** displays fractions rather than decimals. This can be especially useful for financial data in which prices were required to be rounded. For example, "10 1/8" rather than "10.125".

EViews saves any display changes you make in the series window **Properties** dialog **Display** tab and uses them whenever you display the series. Remember that the **Properties** dialog changes the way the number is displayed, not the underlying value of the number.

> Hint: To change the default display, use the menu **Options/Spreadsheet Defaults....** See Chapter 18, "Optional Ending."

Letters

EViews' second major data type is text data, stored in an *alpha* series displayed with the 🔤 icon. You create an alpha series by typing the command:

```
alpha aname
```

or using the **Object/New Object.../Series Alpha** menu.

Double-clicking an alpha series opens a spreadsheet view which you can edit just as you would a numeric series.

Hint: If you use text in the command line, be sure to enclose the text in quotes. For example,

```
alpha alphabet = "abc's"
```

To include a quote symbol in a string as part of a command, use a pair of quotes. To create a string consisting of a single double quote symbol write:

```
alpha singledoublequote = """"
```

Hint: Named auto-series defined using `frml` work for alpha series just as they do for numeric series.

Alpha series have two quirks that matter once in a great while. The first quirk is that the "not available" code for alpha series is the empty string, "", rather than NA. Visually, it's difficult to tell the difference between an empty string and a string holding nothing but one or more spaces. They both have a blank look about them.

The second quirk is that all alpha series in EViews share a maximum length. Strings with more than the maximum permitted characters are truncated. By default, 40 characters are permitted. While you can't change the truncation limit for an individual series, you can change the default through the

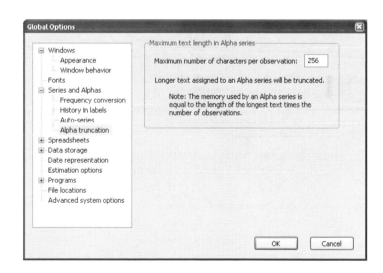

General Options/Series and Alphas/Alpha truncation dialog. And you should. Again, see Chapter 18, "Optional Ending."

String Functions

String functions are documented in the *Command and Programming Reference*. An example here gives a taste. The series STATE contains state names. Unfortunately, spellings vary.

Consider the following expressions:

```
show state state="Wash" @upper(state)="WASH"
    @upper(@left(state,2))="WA"
```

The group window shows the results of all three comparisons. 'state = "Wash"' is true for observations 1, 2, and 4 ("Wash"), but

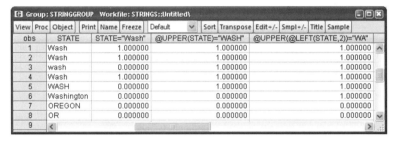

not for the third or fifth observation ("wash" and "WASH"), because upper and lower case letters are *not* equal. The next comparison uses the function @upper, which produces an uppercase version of a string, to pick up observations 1 through 5 by making the comparison using data converted to uppercase. Both upper and lower case are changed to upper case before the comparison is made.

Converting everything to upper or lower case before making comparisons is a useful trick, but doesn't help with fundamentally different spellings such as "Wash" and "Washington." For this particular set of data, all spellings of Washington begin with "wa" and the spelling of no other state begins with "wa." So various spellings can be picked out by looking only at the first two letters (in uppercase), which is what the function @left(state,2) does for us. (@left(a,n) picks out the first *n* letters of string *a*. EViews provides a comprehensive set of such functions. As we said above, see Appendix F of the *Command and Programming Reference*.)

> Embarrassing revelation: I once spent weeks on a consulting project producing wrong answers because I didn't realize "Washington" had been spelled about half a dozen different ways. The first few hundred observations that I checked visually all had the same spelling and I didn't think to check further.

There's no general procedure for comparing strings by meaning rather than spelling, although the @youknowwhatimeant function is eagerly awaited in a future release. In the meantime, the **One-Way Tabulation…** view (see Chapter 7, "Look At Your Data") gives a list of all the unique values of a series. This offers a quick check for various spellings for alpha series where a limited number of values are expected, as is true of state names. Uncheck the boxes in the **Tabulate Series** dialog except for **Show Count**.

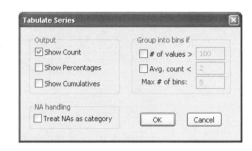

The view that pops up gives a nicely alphabetized list of spellings.

One more string function is very useful, but doesn't look like a function. When used between alpha series, " + " means concatenate. Thus the command

    ="a"+"b"+"c"

gives the string "abc".

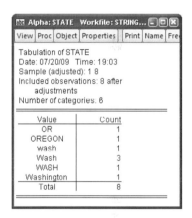

Tabulation of STATE
Date: 07/20/09   Time: 19:03
Sample (adjusted): 1 8
Included observations: 8 after
    adjustments
Number of categories: 6

Value	Count
OR	1
OREGON	1
wash	1
Wash	3
WASH	1
Washington	1
Total	8

Hint: Typing an equal sign followed by an expression turns EViews into a nice desk calculator. Results are shown in the status line at the bottom of the EViews window.

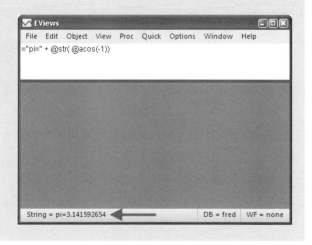

Can We Have A Date?

Technically, EViews doesn't have a "date type." Instead, EViews has a bunch of tools for interpreting numbers as dates. If all you do with dates is look at them, there's no need to understand what's underneath the hood. This section is for users who want to be able to manipulate date data.

The key to understanding EViews' representation of dates is to take things one day at a day:

- An observation in a "date series" is interpreted as the number of days since Monday, January 1, 0001 CE.

Date series are manipulated in three ways: you can control their display in spreadsheet views, you can convert back and forth between date numbers and their text representation, and you can perform date arithmetic.

Date Displays

Open a series T = 0, 0.5, 1, 1.5, 2,… and you get the standard spreadsheet view.

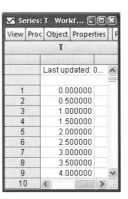

Use the Properties button to bring up the Properties dialog. Choose **Day-Time** to change the display to treat the numbers as dates showing both day and time.

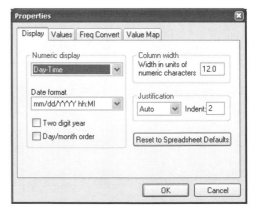

The display changes as shown to the right. Notice that fractional parts of numbers correspond to a fraction of a day. Thus 1.5 is 12 noon on the second day of the Common Era. Two **Day** and **Time** formats are also shown by way of illustration.

obs				
1	0.000000	1/1/0001 0:00	January 1, 0001	12:00:00.000 am
2	0.500000	1/1/0001 12:00	January 1, 0001	12:00:00.000 pm
3	1.000000	1/2/0001 0:00	January 2, 0001	12:00:00.000 am
4	1.500000	1/2/0001 12:00	January 2, 0001	12:00:00.000 pm
5	2.000000	1/3/0001 0:00	January 3, 0001	12:00:00.000 am
6	2.500000	1/3/0001 12:00	January 3, 0001	12:00:00.000 pm
7	3.000000	1/4/0001 0:00	January 4, 0001	12:00:00.000 am
8	3.500000	1/4/0001 12:00	January 4, 0001	12:00:00.000 pm
9	4.000000	1/5/0001 0:00	January 5, 0001	12:00:00.000 am
10				

The **Date format** dropdown menu provides a variety of date display formats.

```
mm/dd/YYYY hh:MI
mm/dd/YYYY hh:MI:SS
mm/dd/YY hh:MI:SS.SSS
mm/DD/YYYY HH:MI
mm/DD/YYYY HH:MI:SS
mm/DD/YY HH:MI:SS.SSS
YYYY-MM-DD HH:MI
YYYY-MM-DD HH:MI:SS
YY-MM-DD HH:MI:SS.SSS
```

Date to Text and Back Again

"January 1, 1999" is more easily understood by humans than is its date number representation, "729754." On the other hand, computers prefer to work with numbers. A variety of functions translate between numbers interpreted as dates and their text representation.

The function `@datestr(x[,fmt])` translates the number in X into a text string. A second optional argument specifies a format for the date. As examples, `@datestr(731946)` produces "1/1/2005"; `@datestr(731946,"Month dd, yyyy")` gives "January 1, 2005"; and `@datestr(731946,"ww")` produces a text string representation of the week number, "6." More date formats are discussed in the *User's Guide*.

The inverse of `@datestr` is `@dateval`, which converts a string into a date number. `@dateval` is particularly useful when you've read in text representing dates and want a numerical version of the dates so that you can manipulate them. The file "SPClose Text excerpt.txt" has the closing prices for the S&P 500 for the first few days of 2005. Reading this into EViews gives a numeric series for SP500CLOSE and an alpha series for CLOSE-DATE. The command:

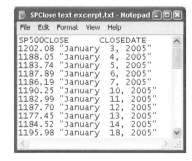

```
series tradedate = @dateval(closedate)
```

gives a numerical date series which is then available for further manipulation.

`@makedate` translates ordinary numbers into date numbers, for example `@makedate(1999, "yyyy")` returns 729754, the first day in 1999. The format strings used for the last argument of `@makedate` are also discussed in the *User's Guide*.

The workfile "SPClose2005.wf1" includes S&P 500 daily closing prices (SP500CLOSE) on a given YEAR, MONTH, and DAY. To convert the last three into a usable date series use the command:

```
series tradedatenum = @makedate(year,month,day,"yyyy mm dd")
```

To turn these into a series that looks like '"January 3, 2005"' (*etc.*), use the command:

```
alpha tradedate = """" + @datestr(tradedatenum,"Month dd, yyyy") +
    """"
```

In this command the four quotes in a row are interpreted as a quote opening a string (first quote), two quotes in a row which stand for one quote inside the string (middle two quotes), and a quote closing the string (last quote). It takes all four quotes to get one quote embedded in the string.

Date Manipulation Functions

Since dates are measured in days, you can add or subtract days by, unsurprisingly, adding or subtracting. For example, the function `@now` gives (the number representing) the current day and time, so `@now + 1` is the same time tomorrow.

The functions `@dateadd(date1,offset[,units_string])` and `@datediff(date1,offset[,units_string])` add and subtract dates, allowing for different units of time. The `units_string` argument specifies whether you want arithmetic to be done in days ("dd"), weeks ("ww"), *etc.* (See the *User's Guide* for information on "etc.") `@dateadd(@now,1,"dd")` is this time tomorrow, while `@dateadd(@date,1,"ww")` is this time on the same day next week.

Suppose we want to compute annualized returns for our 2005 S&P closing price data. We can compute the percentage change in price from one observation to the next with,

```
series pct_change = (sp500close-sp500close(-1))/sp500close(-1)
```

or with the equivalent built-in command `@pch`:

```
series pct_change = @pch(sp500close)
```

To annualize a daily return we could multiply by 365. (Or we could use the more precise formula that takes compounding into account, $(1 + pct\_change)^{365} - 1$). But some of our returns accumulated over a weekend, and arguably represent three days' earnings. Taking into account that the number of days between observations varies, we can annualize the return with:

```
series return = (365/@datediff(tradedatenum, tradedate-
    num(-1),"dd"))*pct_change
```

Let's take this apart. The expression '@datediff(tradedatenum, tradedatenum(-1),"dd")' returns the number of days between observations. Usually there's one day between observations, giving us 365/1. Over an ordinary weekend, the `datediff` function returns 3, so we annualize by multiplying by 365/3.

Note two things about annualized returns. First, typical daily returns imply very large annual rates of change. In fact, the annual rates are implausible. Second, we've captured not only weekends, but also the January 17th closing in honor of Dr. King.

obs	TRADEDATE	@DATEDIFF...	RETURN
1	1/3/2005	NA	NA
2	1/4/2005	1.000000	-426.01%
3	1/5/2005	1.000000	-132.41%
4	1/6/2005	1.000000	127.96%
5	1/7/2005	1.000000	-52.24%
6	1/10/2005	3.000000	41.64%
7	1/11/2005	1.000000	-222.63%
8	1/12/2005	1.000000	145.32%
9	1/13/2005	1.000000	-315.00%
10	1/14/2005	1.000000	219.16%
11	1/18/2005	4.000000	88.28%
12	1/19/2005	1.000000	-346.39%
13	1/20/2005	1.000000	-284.08%
14			

What Are Your Values?

The workfile "CPSMAR2004Extract.wf1" is a cross section of individuals from the Current Population Survey. The series FE codes a person's gender. As you will remember from early biology lessons, humans have two genders—0 and 1.

Some of us prefer to think of humans as male and female, rather than 0 and 1. EViews uses *value maps* to translate the appearance of codes into something more pleasant to read. The codes themselves are unchanged—it's their appearance that's improved.

To create a new value map named GENDER, use **Object/New Object.../ValMap** or type the command:

```
valmap gender
```

The ValMap editor view pops up showing two columns. Values (0 or 1 in this case) go on the left and the corresponding labels (male, female) go on the right. Two default mappings appear at the top: blanks and NAs are displayed unchanged.

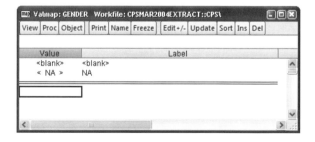

To fill out the value map, enter a list of codes on the left and labels on the right. When you close the valmap window, 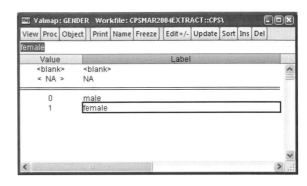 gender is stored in the workfile with an icon that says "map." (The values can be either numeric or text, and there's no harm in providing maps for values that aren't used.) To tell EViews to use the map just created, open the series FE, click the Properties button, choose the **Value Map** tab and type in GENDER.

Displayed FE now uses much friendlier labels.

Hint: If you want to see FE's underlying codes, switch the **display type** menu in the series spreadsheet view from **Default** to **Raw Data**.

EViews will use the new labels wherever possible. For example, the command:

```
ls lnwage ed @expand(fe)
```

which regresses a series containing $\log(wage)$ on education and a dummy variable for each gender produces nicely labeled output. (More on the @expand function under *Expand the Dummies*).

In fact, you can use the value labels in editing a series. (Be sure the **Display type** menu is set to **Default**.) EViews checks to see if an entry matches any of the labels in the value map. If so, the corresponding value is entered. If not, the new entry is used directly. As a consequence, you can use either the label or underlying code to enter a new value—so long as the underlying code hasn't been used to label some other value.

Equation: UNTITLED   Workfile: CPSMAR2004EXTRACT::CPS

View | Proc | Object | Print | Name | Freeze | Estimate | Forecast | Stats | Resids

Dependent Variable: LNWAGE
Method: Least Squares
Date: 07/21/09   Time: 15:24
Sample: 1 136879 IF HRSWK>0
Included observations: 99991

Variable	Coefficient	Std. Error	t-Statistic	Prob.
ED	0.135827	0.001060	128.1338	0.0000
FE=MALE	0.779365	0.014855	52.46510	0.0000
FE=FEMALE	0.444924	0.015081	29.50315	0.0000

R-squared	0.160927	Mean dependent var	2.458741
Adjusted R-squared	0.160911	S.D. dependent var	1.012580
S.E. of regression	0.927542	Akaike info criterion	2.687472
Sum squared resid	86023.01	Schwarz criterion	2.687757
Log likelihood	-134358.5	Hannan-Quinn criter.	2.687558
Durbin-Watson stat	1.819320		

Hint: Labels in the editor are case sensitive, *e.g.*, "male" translates to 0 but "Male" translates to NA.

Since a value map is just a translation from underlying code to appearance, you're free to use the same value map for multiple series. To help keep track of which series is using a given value map, the **Usage** view of a value map shows a list of all the series currently attached.

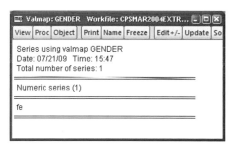

Valmap: GENDER   Workfile: CPSMAR2004EXTR...

View | Proc | Object | Print | Name | Freeze | Edit+/- | Update | So

Series using valmap GENDER
Date: 07/21/09   Time: 15:47
Total number of series: 1

Numeric series (1)

fe

Hint: EViews doesn't care what you use for a label. It will cheerfully let you label the number "0" with the value map "1". Don't. For further discussion, see *Origin of the Species*.

> Hint: If you load data created in another stat program that has its own version of value maps, EViews will create value maps and correctly hook them up to the relevant series. However, there's no general method using values in an alpha series as labels in a value map.

Many-To-One Mappings

Value maps can be used to group a range of codes for the *purpose of display*. Instead of a single value in the value map, enter a range in parentheses. For example "(-inf, 12)" specifies all values less than 12. Parentheses are used to specify open intervals, square brackets are used for closed intervals. So "(-inf, 12]" is all values less than or equal to 12.

The series ED in "CPSMAR2004Extract.wf1" measures education in years. We could use the value map shown to the right to group education into three displayed values.

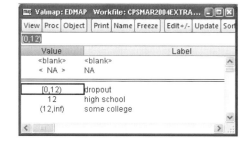

The many-to-one mapping is only for display purposes. If we analyze the data, all the underlying categories are still there. For example, here's a tabulation of ED. Everyone with less than a high school education is labeled "dropout," but they're still tabulated in separate categories according to the years of education they've had. That's why we see seven "dropout" rows on the right.

Tabulation of ED
Date: 07/21/09   Time: 16:02
Sample: 1 136879 IF HRSWK>0
Included observations: 106099
Number of categories: 12

Value	Count	Percent	Cumulative Count	Cumulative Percent
dropout	183	0.17	183	0.17
dropout	623	0.59	806	0.76
dropout	1457	1.37	2263	2.13
dropout	1232	1.16	3495	3.29
dropout	2003	1.89	5498	5.18
dropout	3145	2.96	8643	8.15
dropout	4037	3.80	12680	11.95
high school	32861	30.97	45541	42.92
some college	31162	29.37	76703	72.29
some college	19629	18.50	96332	90.79
some college	6896	6.50	103228	97.29
some college	2871	2.71	106099	100.00
Total	106099	100.00	106099	100.00

Relative Exotica

EViews has lots of functions for transforming data. You'll never need most of these functions, but the one you do need you'll need *bad*.

Stats-By

We met several data summary functions such as @mean above in the section *Functions Are Where It's @*. Sometimes one wants a summary statistic computed by group. We might want a series that assigned the mean education for women to women and the mean education for men to men. This is accomplished with the Stats-By family of functions: @meansby(x,y), @mediansby(x,y), *etc.* (See the *Command and Programming Reference* for more functions.) These functions summarize the data in X according to the groups in Y. (Optionally, a sample can be used as a third argument.) Thus the command:

```
show fe ed @meansby(ed,fe) @stdevsby(ed,fe)
```

shows gender and years of education followed by the mean and standard deviation of education for women if the individual is female, and the mean and standard deviation of education for men if the individual is male.

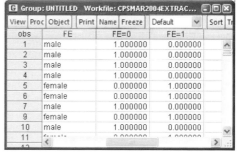

Expand the Dummies

The @expand function isn't really a data transformation function at all. Instead, @expand(x) creates a set of temporary series. One series is created for each unique value of X and the value of a given series is 1 for observations where X equals the corresponding value. For example, @expand(fe) creates two series in the command:

```
show fe @expand(fe)
```

If you give @expand more than one series as an argument, as in @expand(x,y,z), series are created for all possible combinations of the values of the series.

The primary use of @expand is as part of a regression specification, where it generates a complete set of dummy variables. Because it's often desirable to omit one series from the complete set, @expand can take an optional last argument, @dropfirst or @droplast. The former omits the first category from the set of series generated and the latter omits the last category. (For more detail, see the *Command and Programming Reference*).

`@expand` can also be used in algebraic expressions, with each resulting temporary series being inserted in the expression in turn. The command,

```
ls lnwage c ed*@expand(fe)
```

is equivalent to:

```
ls lnwage c ed*(fe=0) ed*(fe=1)
```

and estimates separate returns to education for men and women.

Statistical Functions

Uniform and standard normal random number generators were described earlier in the chapter. EViews supplies families of statistical functions organized according to specific probability distributions. A function name beginning with "@r" is a random number generator, a name beginning with "@d" evaluates the probability density function (also called the "pdf"), a name beginning with "@c" evaluates the cumulative distribution function (or "cdf"), and a name beginning with "@q" gives the quantile, or inverse cdf. In each case, the @-sign and initial letter are followed by the name of the distribution.

As an example, the name used for the uniform distribution is "unif." So `@runif(a,b)` generates random numbers distributed uniformly between A and B. (This means that `@rnd` is a synonym for `@runif(0,1)`.) We can make up an example with:

```
series x = @runif(0,2)

show x @dunif(x,0,2) @cunif(x,0,2) @qunif(@cunif(x,0,2),0,2)
```

which randomly resulted in the data shown to the right. The first column, X, is a random number randomly distributed between 0 and 2. The second column gives the pdf for X, which for this distribution always equals 0.5. The third column gives the cdf. Just for fun, the last column reports the inverse cdf of the cdf, which is the original X, just as it should be.

obs	X	@DUNIF(X,...	@CUNIF(X,...	@QUNIF(@...
1	1.848843	0.500000	0.924422	1.848843
2	1.040776	0.500000	0.520388	1.040776
3	0.723056	0.500000	0.361528	0.723056
4	1.827843	0.500000	0.913921	1.827843
5	1.377608	0.500000	0.688804	1.377608
6	1.390876	0.500000	0.695438	1.390876
7	1.845547	0.500000	0.922774	1.845547
9	1.868945	0.500000	0.934473	1.868945
10	1.898861	0.500000	0.949431	1.898861
11				

A variety of probability distributions are discussed in the *Command and Programming Reference*. Probably the most commonly used are "norm," for standard normal, and "tdist," for Student's *t*. Here are a few examples:

```
=@qtdist(.95, 30) = 1.69726

=@qtdist(0.05/2, 30) = -2.04227

=@qnorm(.025) = -1.95996
```

Quick Review

Data in EViews can be either numbers or text. A wide set of data manipulation functions are available. In particular, the "expected" set of algebraic manipulations all work as expected. You can use numbers to conveniently represent dates. EViews also provides control over the visual display of data. Value maps and display formats play a big role in data display. In particular, value maps let you see meaningful labels in place of arbitrary numerical codes.

Chapter 5. Picture This!

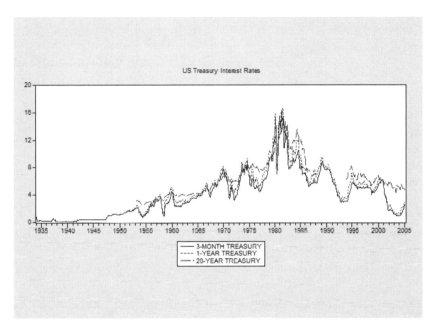

Interest rates over a wide spectrum of maturities—three months to 20 years—mostly move up and down together. Long term interest rates are usually, although not always, higher than short term interest rates. Long term interest rates also bounce around less than short term interest rates. One picture illustrates all this at a glance.

This chapter introduces EViews graphics. EViews can produce a wide variety of graphs, and making a good looking graph is trivial. EViews also offers a sophisticated set of customization options, so making a great looking graph isn't too hard either. In this chapter we focus on the kinds of graphs you can make, leaving most of the discussion of custom settings to Chapter 6, "Intimacy With Graphic Objects."

We start with a simple soup-to-nuts example, showing how we created the interest rate illustration above. This is followed by simpler examples illustrating, first, graph types for single series and, next, graph types for groups of series.

A Simple Soup-To-Nuts Graphing Example

The workfile "Treasury_Interest_Rates.wf1" contains monthly observations on interest rates with maturities from three months to 20 years. Multiple series are plotted together in the same way that EViews always analyzes multiple series together: as a group. To get started, create a group by selecting the three-month, one-year, and 20-year interest rate series, TM3, TY01, and TY20, with the mouse, opening them as a group, and then naming the group RATES_TO_GRAPH. (As a reminder, you select multiple series by holding down the Ctrl key.) Equivalently, type the command:

```
group rates_to_graph tm3 ty01 ty20
```

and then double-click
 rates_to_graph to open the group. The menu **View/Graph...** brings up the **Graph Options** dialog. This master dialog can be used to create a wide variety of graph types, and also provides entry for tuning a graph's appearance after it's created.

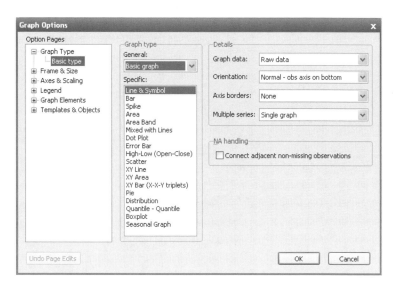

For now, hit OK to produce a simple line graph. This graph looks pretty good. You can print it out or copy it into a word processor and be on your merry way.

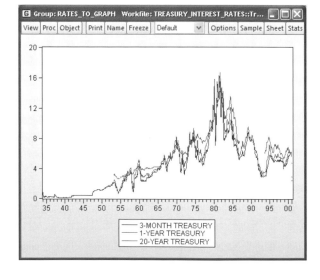

Hint: Where did those nice, long descriptive names in the legend come from? EViews automatically uses the DisplayName for each series in the legend, if the series has one. (See "Label View" on page 30 in Chapter 2, "EViews—Meet Data.") If there is no DisplayName, the name of the series is used instead.

Hint: If you hover your cursor over a data point on a line in the graph EViews will show you the observation label and value. If you hover over any other point inside the graph frame, EViews will display the values in the statusline located in the lower left-hand corner of your EViews window.

To Freeze Or Not To Freeze

Before adding any customizations, we have a choice to make about whether to *freeze* the graph. The group we're looking at right now is fundamentally a list of data series, which we happen to be looking at in a graphics view. If we change any of the underlying data, the change will be reflected in the picture. Same thing if we change the sample. For that matter, we can switch to a different graphics view or even a spreadsheet or statistical view. But a group view does have one shortcoming:

- When you close a group window or shift to another view, many customizations you've made on the graph disappear.

Freezing a graph view creates a new object—a *graph* object—which is independent from the original series or group you were looking at.

A graph object is fundamentally a picture that happens to have started life as a graphic view. You make a graph object by looking at a graphic view, as we are at the moment, and hitting the Freeze button.

A dialog opens, allowing you to choose how you want your new graph object to be tied to the underlying data. Selecting **Manual** or **Automatic** update will keep the graph object tied to the data in the series or group that it came from. When the data changes, the graph object will reflect the new values. To update the graph with any applicable changes, select **Automatic**. To control when the graph update occurs, select **Manual**. If you'd rather freeze the graph as a snapshot of its current state, select **Off**. Click [OK] to create the graph object.

Hint: If you select **Off** and then decide you'd like to relate the graph object to its underlying data again, you can always change your selection later in the master **Graph Options** dialog, in the **Graph Updating** section.

A new window opens with the same picture, but with "Graph" in the titlebar instead of "Group," and with a different set of buttons in the button bar. Named graph objects appear in the workfile window with a 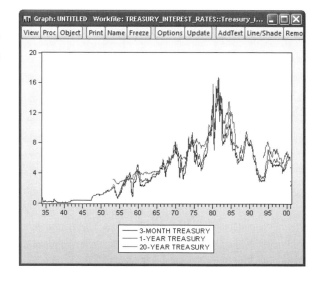 icon. An orange icon alerts us to a graph that will update with changes in the data, while a green icon indicates that updating is off.

Hint: Because a frozen graph with updating off is severed from the underlying data series, the options for changing from one type of graph to another (categorical graph, distribution plot, *etc.*) are limited. It's generally best to choose a graph type before freezing a graph if you intend to keep updating off.

Frozen graphs have two big advantages:

- Customizations are stored as part of the graph object, so they don't disappear.
- You can choose whether or not you want the graph to change every time the data or sample changes.

A good rule of thumb is that if you want any changes to a graph to last, freeze it.

Hint: To make a copy of a graph object, perhaps so you can try out new customizations without messing up the existing graph, click the Object button and choose **Copy Object....**, or press the Freeze button to create a graph object with updating turned off. A new, untitled graph window will open.

A Little Light Customization

To add the title "US Treasury Interest Rates," click the AddText button. Enter the title in the **Text for label** field and change **Position** to **Top**.

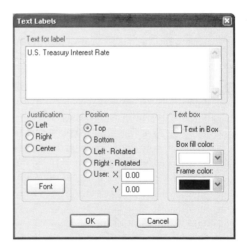

The graph now looks almost like the picture opening the chapter. The remaining difference is that all the series in this picture are drawn with solid lines, while the opening picture used a variety of solid, dashed, and dotted lines. (Actually, there's one other difference. The opening graph is stretched horizontally to make it look more dramatic. See *Frame & Size* in the next chapter.)

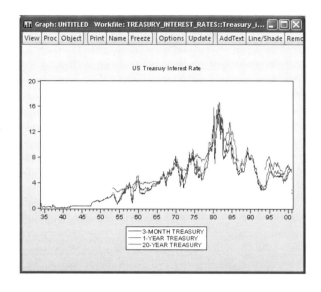

Hint: Unlike many customization options, AddText is only available after a graph has been frozen.

Whenever more than one series appears on a graph, the question arises as to how to visually distinguish one graphed line from another. The two methods are to use different colors and to use different line patterns. Different colors are much easier to distinguish—unless your output device only shows black and white!

Click the graph window's Options button. Initially, the dialog opens to the **Lines & Symbols** section. The default **Pattern use** is **Auto choice**, which uses solid lines when EViews renders the graph in color and patterned lines when EViews renders the graph in black and white. Using the **Auto choice**

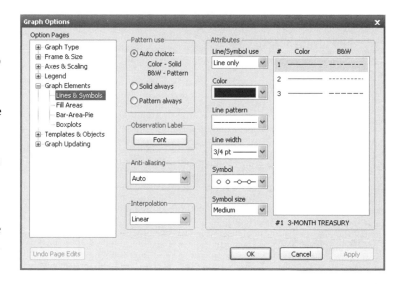

default, the graph appears in solid lines distinguished by colors on your display screen, but patterned black lines are used if you print from EViews to a monochrome printer.

This default is usually the right choice. But imagine that you're producing a graph for a document that some readers will read electronically, and therefore in color, while others will read in a book, and therefore in black and white. Our best compromise is to use color *and* line patterns. Readers of the electronic version will see the color, and readers in traditional media will be able to distinguish the lines by their patterns. Change the **Pattern use** radio button to **Pattern always**. (I'll do this for graphs later in the chapter without further ado.)

The default line patterns are solid, short dashes, and long dashes. Click on line 3 in the right side of the dialog to select the 20-year treasury rate. Then select the **Line pattern** dropdown menu, and change the pattern to the very long dashes appearing at the end of the list.

Click [OK] to see the third version of the graph, which is virtually identical to the one that opened the chapter.

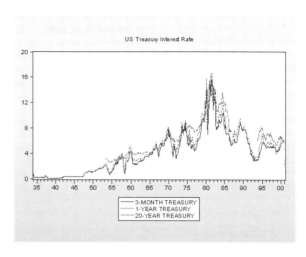

Graphic Auto-Tweaks

In making an aesthetically pleasing data graph, EViews hides the details of many complex calculations. Graphic output is tuned with many small tweaks to make the graph look "just right." In particular, well done graphics scale *nonlinearly*. In other words, if you double the picture size, picture elements don't simply grow to twice their original size. If you plan to print or publish a graphic, try to make it as close as possible to its final appearance while it's still inside EViews. Pay particular attention to color versus monochrome and to the ratio of height versus width.

As an example, we switched the graph above to be tall and skinny. (See *Frame & Size* in the next chapter.) Notice that EViews switched the tick labeling on both horizontal and vertical axes to keep the labeling looking pretty.

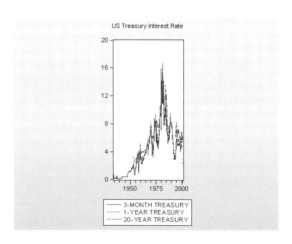

The aesthetic choices made by EViews involve complicated interactions between space, font sizes, and other factors. Although all the options can be controlled manually, it's generally best to trust EViews' judgment.

Print, Copy, Or Export

It's not hard to print a copy of a graph—just click the [Print] button. If you're sending to a color printer, check the **Print in Color** checkbox in the print dialog.

To make a copy of a graph object inside an EViews workfile, use **Object/Copy Object...**, or copy and paste the object in the workfile window. To make an external copy, you can either copy-and-paste or save the graph as a file on disk.

Graph Copy-and-Paste

With the graph window active, you copy the graph onto the clipboard by hitting the `Proc` button and choosing **Copy...**, or by choosing **Copy...** from the right-click menu, or with the usual Ctrl-C. (Depending on the global option you've chosen (see Chapter 18, "Optional Ending"), you may see a **Graph Metafile** dialog which offers a few options controlling how the picture is copied.) Then paste into your favorite graphics program or word processor. EViews pictures are editable, so a certain amount of touch-up can be done in the destination program.

> Hint: Copying a graph object in the workfile window is different from copying from a graph window. The latter puts a picture on the clipboard that can be pasted into another program. The former copies the internal representation of the graph which can only be pasted into an EViews workfile. The picture you want won't show up on the clipboard.

Exporting options are covered in some detail in Chapter 6, "Intimacy With Graphic Objects," but two options are used frequently enough that we mention them now.

By default, EViews copies in color. If the graph's final destination is black-and-white, it's generally better to take a monochrome copy out of EViews, because EViews makes different choices for line styles and backgrounds when it renders in monochrome.

The picture placed on the clipboard is provided as an *enhanced metafile*, or EMF, by default. While this is the best all-around choice, some graphics and typesetting programs prefer *encapsulated postscript*, or EPS. This is particularly true for LaTeX and some desktop publishing programs. Although EViews won't put an EPS picture on the clipboard, it will save a file in EPS format using **Proc/Save graph to disk...** as described in the next section.

> Hint: It's best to do as much graph editing as possible inside EViews—before exporting—so that EViews has a chance to "touch-up" the final picture. See *Graphic Auto-Tweaks* above.

Graph Save To Disk

The alternative to copy-and-paste is to save a graph as a disk file. Choose **Save to disk...** either from the [Proc] button or the right-click menu to bring up the **Graphics File Save** dialog. From here you can choose a file format (including EMF, EPS, GIF, JPEG, PNG, and BMP), whether or not to use color, and whether or not to make the background of the graph transparent. You can also adjust the picture size and, of course, pick a location on the disk to save the file.

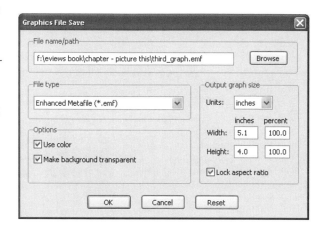

Hint: There isn't any way to read a graphic file into EViews, nor can you paste a picture from the clipboard into an EViews object.

A Graphic Description of the Creative Process

Graph creation involves four basic choices:

- What specific graph type should be used to display information? Line graph? Scatter plot? Something more esoteric perhaps?

- Do you want to graph your raw data, or are you looking to graph summary statistics such as mean or standard deviation?

- Do want a "basic" or a "categorical" graph, the latter graph type displaying your data with observations split up into categories specified by one or more control variables? For example, you might compare wage and salary data for unionized and non-unionized workers.

- If more than one group of data is being graphed, i.e. multiple series or multiple categories, how would you like them visually arrayed? Multiple graphs? All in one graph?

While it's helpful to think of these as four independent choices, there is some interaction among them. For example, the number of series in the window determines the choices of graph types that are available. (A scatter diagram requires (at least!) two series, right?) The **Graph Options** dialog adjusts itself to display options sensible for the data at hand.

Stressing out: Making a graph is starting to sound awfully complicated.

Hakuna matata: Probably half the graphs ever produced in EViews are line graphs. As you've already seen this requires you to:

1. Open a window with desired data.

2. Choose **Graph...** from the **View** menu.

3. Click OK .

Thinking about the four basic choices in graph creation is a useful organizing principle, but the truth is most graphs are made with a couple of mouse clicks and where to click is usu-

> Single graph
> Stack in single graph
> Multiple graphs

ally pretty obvious. We've been showing our interest rate data in a single graph as a useful way to show that interest rates of different maturities largely move together. To show each series separately, set the **Multiple series:** dropdown menu to **Multiple graphs**. Presto!

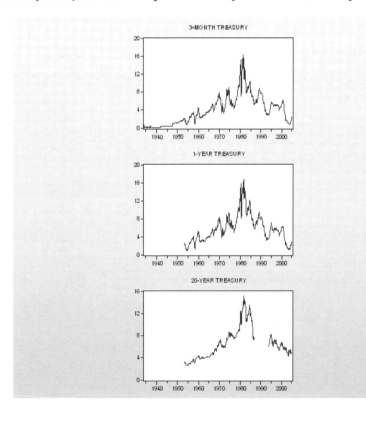

Or suppose we wanted a scatter plot of long rates against the short (3-month) rate? Just choose the **Scatter** and accept the defaults settings.

to display the scatterplots:

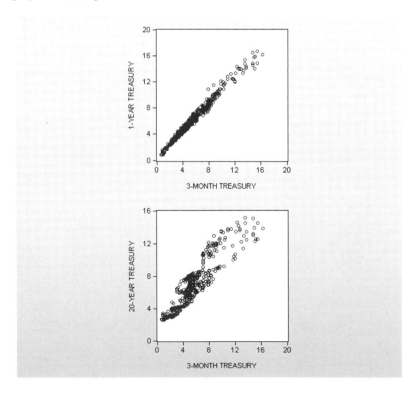

But here's my favorite one-click wonder: Change the **Graph type** back to **Line & Symbol** and then with a single click, change **Graph data:** to **Means**:

The graph now flicks from raw data to a particularly interesting summary. Instead of a line graph for each series, EViews plots the mean for each series and connects the means with a line. This view of interest rates, called an *average yield curve*, shows at a glance that long term interest rates are typically higher than short-term rates, with 20-year bonds paying on average about 2.5 percentage points more than 3-month bonds.

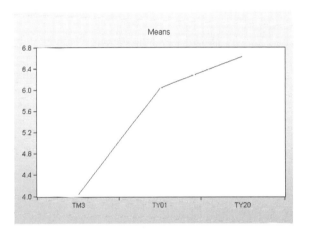

Financial econometrics visualization alert: This average yield curve worked out neatly because the series in the group "just happened to be" ordered from short maturity to long maturity. If we'd chosen a different order for the series, the line connecting the means wouldn't have been meaningful. As is, the scaling on the horizontal axis is a little misleading. We probably think of the one-year rate as being close to the 3-month rate, not halfway between the 3-month and 20-year rates.

My favorite two-click wonder takes the previous graph and adds a click on **Bar** to give us this version of the same summary information.

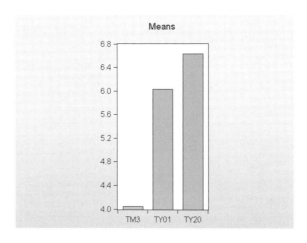

Picture One Series

Our soup-to-nuts example graphed three interest rates together. Now we step back and for the sake of simplicity look at the various graphic views available for a single series, all of which are available by opening a series window and choosing **View/Graph...**. All these graph types are available for Groups as well, as are additional types discussed in *Group Graphics* below.

Line Graph (…and Dot Plots)

A series line graph is just like the group line graph we saw above, except it only shows a single series. The line graph plots the value of the series on the vertical axis against the date on the horizontal axis.

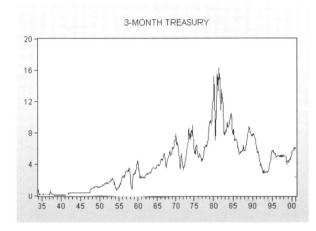

An EViews **Dot Plot** is a line graph with the lines replaced with little circles. Series in a dot plot are indented a little to improve their visual appearance.

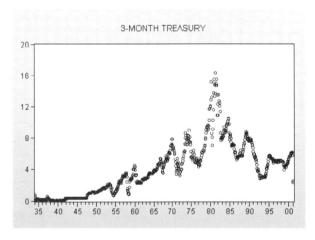

Area Graph

An area graph is a line graph with the area underneath the line filled in. The same information is displayed in line and area graphs, but area graphs give a sense that higher values are "bigger." Interest rates are probably better depicted as line graphs. In contrast, an area graph of the federal debt held by the public emphasizes that the U.S. national debt is one whole heck of a lot more than it used to be.

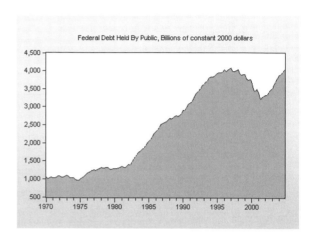

Bar Graph

A bar graph represents the height of each point with a vertical bar. This is a great format for displaying a small number of observations; and a crummy format for displaying large numbers of observations. The figure to the right shows federal debt for the first observation in each decade. Note that EViews has drawn vertical lines to indicate breaks in the sample.

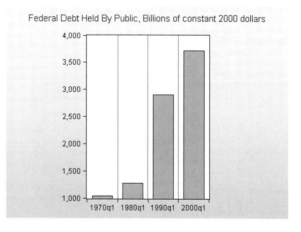

Bar labels can be added with the click of a radio button in the **Fill Areas** tab of the **Graph Options** dialog. An example is shown to the right. Note that we have also used the options page to add a neat fade effect to the bars.

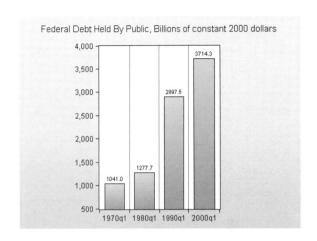

Spike Graph

A spike graph is just like a bar graph—only with really skinny bars. It's especially useful when you have too many categories to display neatly with a bar graph. Here's a version of our debt graph, using spikes to show the first quarter of each year with padding for excluded obs.

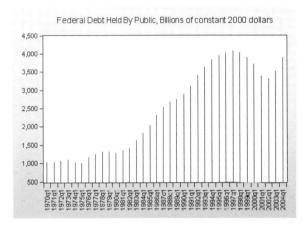

Seasonal Graphs

The standard line graph to the right shows U.S. retail and food service sales over a dozen years. Notice the regular spikes. How fast can you say "Christmas?"

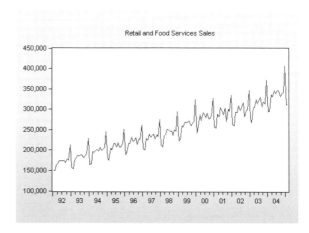

Change the **Graph type** to **Seasonal** and the right-hand side of the **Graph Option** dialog changes to give you choices of two kinds of seasonal graphs.

Paneled lines & means draws one line graph for each season, and also puts in a horizontal line to mark the seasonal mean. Since our retail sales data ("Retail Sales.wf1") is in a monthly workfile, that means twelve lines.

Using a **Paneled lines & means** graph it's easy to see that December sales are relatively high and that sales in January and February are typically low.

Multiple overlayed lines graphs also provide one line for each season, but use a common date axis. For our retail sales data, the **Multiple overlayed lines** graph does a particularly good job of showing how December (higher) and January and February (lower) compare to the remaining months.

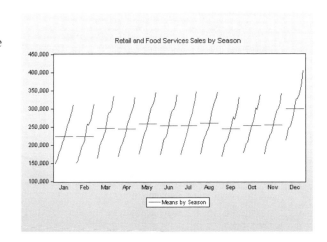

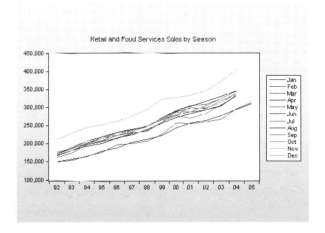

Distribution, Quantile-Quantile, and Boxplots

Distribution graphs, quantile-quantile plots, and boxplots provide pictures of the statistical distribution of the data, rather than plotting the observations directly. (A histogram is probably the most familiar example.) These graphs are discussed in Chapter 7, "Look At Your Data", on page 193.

Axis Borders

Even though discussion of distribution graphs awaits Chapter 7, we'll sneak in one marginal comment. EViews lets you decorate the axes of most graphs with small histograms or other distribution graphs by using the **Axis borders:** menu. This is a great technique for looking at raw data and distribution information together.

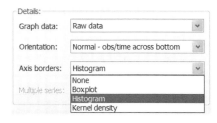

The graph to the right has a histogram added to the line graph for the 3-month Treasury bill rate. The histogram provides a reminder that interest rates were close to zero for much of our sample. The line graph reveals that these extremely low rates were a phenomenon of the Great Depression and World War II.

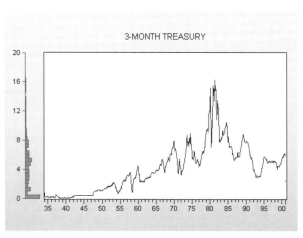

Group Graphics

Any graph type applicable to a single series can also be used to graph all the series in a Group. EViews' default setting is to plot the series in a single graph, as in our interest rate example. As you saw earlier you can switch the **Multiple series:** field in Graph Options to **Multiple graphs** to get one series per graph.

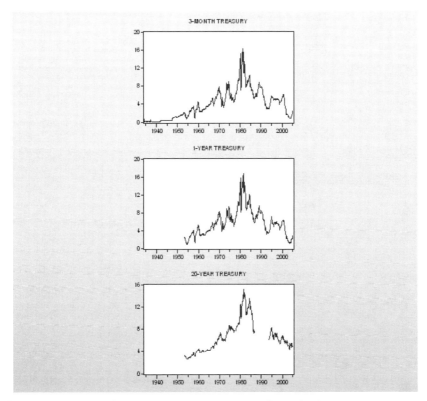

Each of the graphs in the window is a separate graphic sub-object. You can set options for the graphs individually or all together. You can also grab the graphs with the mouse and drag them around to re-arrange their locations in the window.

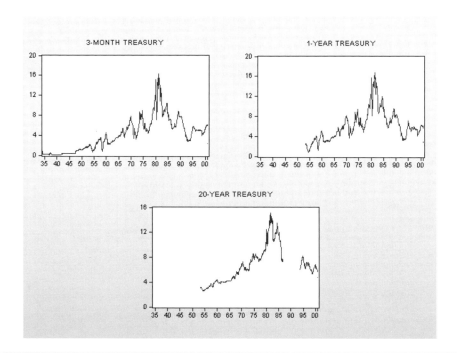

Hint: If you prefer, EViews can auto-arrange the individual graphs into neat rows and columns. Right-click on the graph window and choose **Position and align graphs...**

Stack ´Em High

Several graph types let you "stack" multiple series, which is sort of like adding the data values in the series vertically. The first series is plotted in the usual way. The second is plotted as the sum of the first and the second series. The third as the sum of the first three series. And so forth. Here's an ordinary bar graph (from the workfile "consumption sectors.wf1") showing the various pieces of U.S. consumption in 1999.

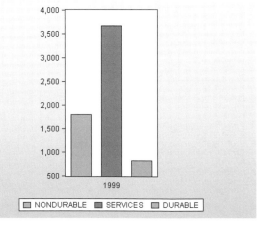

Using the **Multiple series:** field to tell EViews to **Stack in single graph** gives a better sense of how much total consumption was, as well as packing in the information while using less space. Several graph types provide this kind of stacking option.

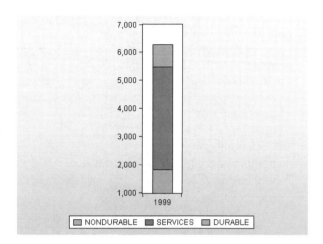

Other than deciding on window arrangements, **Line**, **Area**, **Bar**, and **Spike** graphs are the same for a group as for a series, except that you get one line (set of bars, *etc.*) for each series in the group. So we won't discuss these further.

Left and Right Axes in Group Line Graphs

Well, truth-be-told, there's one element of group line graphs that *is* worth discussing. The line graph to the right (from "Output_and_Unemployment.wf 1") shows real GDP and the civilian unemployment rate. The first thing you'll notice about this graph is that it's completely useless. GDP and unemployment have different units of measurement, GDP being measured in billions of 2000 dollars and unemployment in percentage points. The former scale is so

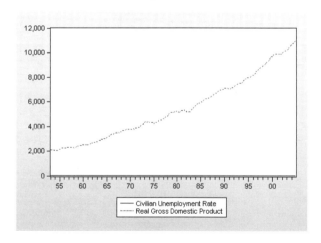

much larger than the latter scale, that unemployment is all but invisible.

Since the two series have different units of measurement, we need two vertical axes so that each series can be associated with meaningful units. Click the Options button and switch to the **Axes & Scaling** group. Select series 2 (Real GDP) in the **Series axis assignment** field and click on the **Right** radio button.

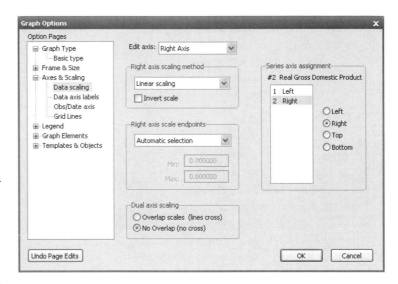

Now we have a meaningful graph. We can see that GDP is strongly trended while unemployment isn't. We can also see something of an inverse relation between bumps in GDP and unemployment.

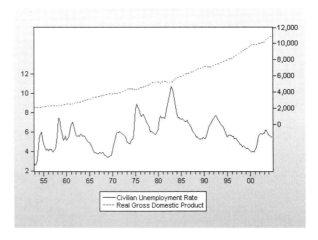

One more option is immediately relevant. Return to the **Axes/Scales** tab and click **Overlap** (lines cross) in the **Vertical axes labels** field.

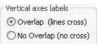

The **Overlap** option—this will not come as a great surprise—allows the lines to overlap. Since the lines "share" the vertical space, they're each a little easier to read. The downside is that the viewer's attention may be drawn to the line crossings, which for these series aren't meaningful.

Now let's take a look at some graph types that apply only when there's more than one series.

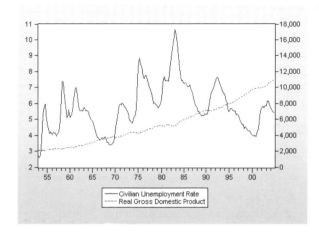

Area Band

Area Band plots a band using pairs of series by filling in the area between the two sets of values. Band graphs are most often used to display forecast bands or error bands around forecasts.

EViews will construct bands from successive pairs of series in the group. If there is an odd number of series in the group, the final series will, by default, be plotted as a line.

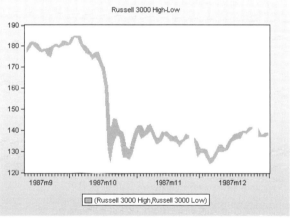

The example here shows high and low prices for the Russell 3000 (a very broad index of U.S. stocks) in the later part of 1987.

Mixed With Lines

Mixed with Lines plots the first series in a group as an Area, Bar, or Spike graph (your choice) and the remaining series as lines. We've used this feature to put the U.S. national debt and GDP together in one picture. Note that we've used both left and right axes for labels. Note too how nicely mixing an Area and a Line graph illustrates that debt dropped dramatically in the second Clinton administration and rebounded in the first Bush administration, even while GDP growth was relatively steady.

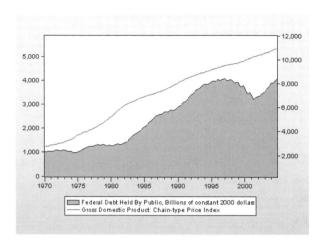

High-Low — High-Low-Open-Close Graphs

High-Low graphs take observations from pairs of series and draw vertical lines connecting each pair, placing the value from the first series at the top and the value from the second series at the bottom. The most common use of the **High-Low** graph is to show opening and closing prices for a stock or other traded good, but these graphs are nifty any time you want to display a range of values at each date. The example here shows high and low prices for the Russell 3000

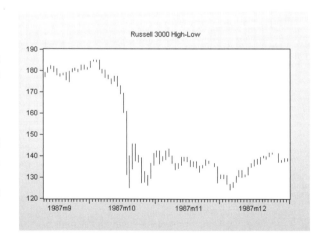

in the later part of 1987 ("Russell3000.wf1"). October 19th really stands out, doesn't it!

Hint: The legend isn't displayed on **High-Low** graphs, so be sure to include your own label using the AddText button as we have here.

High-Low graphs' display of pairs extends to display of triples or quadruples. The first two series in the group mark the top and bottom of the vertical bar, respectively. If there are three series (perhaps the third series represents closing prices), values from the third series are shown with a right facing horizontal bar. If there's a fourth series, then it's shown with a right-facing horizontal bar (perhaps representing closing prices) and the third series gets the left-facing bar.

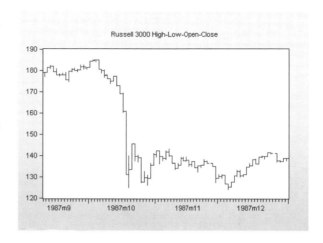

These graphs carry a lot of information. They're probably most effective when limited to a small number of data points. The version shown to the right covers two weeks, whereas the previous graph had four months of data. This shorter graph does a better job of showing market behavior in the period right around the 1987 stock market crash.

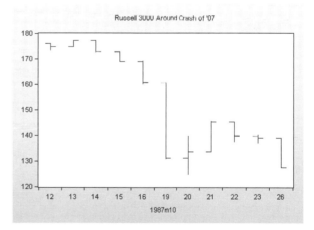

Orderly hint: The order in which the series appear in the group matters for the **High-Low** graph. EViews puts series in the same order as you select them in the workfile window, but the order is easily re-arranged by choosing the **Group Members** view and manually editing the list. This is true for any group, but it's especially important for graphs such as the **High-Low** graph, where the order of the series affects their interpretation.

Be sure to click the [UpdateGroup] button when you're done re-arranging.

Error Bar Graphs

Error bar graphs are similar to High-Low graphs in that pairs of observations from the first two series are used to mark the high and low values of vertical lines. They're slightly different in that error bar graphs have small horizontal caps drawn at the top and bottom of each line. When there's a third series, its value is marked by placing a symbol on the vertical line. Such triplet error bar graphs are commonly used for showing point estimates together with confidence bands, for example, after forecasting a series.

> Hint: Use an error bar graph whenever you want to draw primary attention to a central point (the third series) and secondary attention to a range.

As an example, we estimated log(GDP) as a function of unemployment and a time trend, and then used EViews' forecasting feature to put the forecast values of GDP in the series GDPC96F and the forecast standard errors in GDPC96SE.

Dependent Variable: LOG(GDPC96)
Method: Least Squares
Date: 07/20/09   Time: 17:32
Sample: 1953Q1 2004Q4
Included observations: 208

Variable	Coefficient	Std. Error	t-Statistic	Prob.
C	7.677407	0.010145	756.7322	0.0000
@TREND	0.008209	4.18E-05	196.5536	0.0000
UNRATE	-0.007804	0.001701	-4.588521	0.0000

R-squared	0.994911	Mean dependent var	8.482038
Adjusted R-squared	0.994861	S.D. dependent var	0.493033
S.E. of regression	0.035344	Akaike info criterion	-3.833036
Sum squared resid	0.256091	Schwarz criterion	-3.784898
Log likelihood	401.6357	Hannan-Quinn criter.	-3.813571
F-statistic	20037.14	Durbin-Watson stat	0.046350
Prob(F-statistic)	0.000000		

The command

```
show gdpc96f+1.96*gdpc96se gdpc96f-1.96*gdpc96se gdpc96f
```

opened a group window which we then switched to an **Error Bar** graph. (We added the title manually.)

Of course, EViews can also produce forecast graphs with confidence intervals automatically. See Chapter 8, "Forecasting."

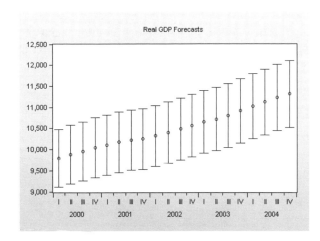

Scatter Plots

Scatter plots are used for looking at the relation between two—or more—variables. We'll use data on undergraduate grades and LSAT scores for applicants to the University of Washington law school to illustrate scatter plots ("Law 98.wf1").

Simple Scatter

At the default settings, **Scatter** creates a scatter plot using the first series in the group for X-axis values and the second series for the Y-axis. While there's a tendency for higher undergraduate grades to be associated with higher LSAT scores, as shown on the graph to the right, the relationship certainly isn't a very strong one. (If there were a really strong relationship, law schools wouldn't need to look at both grades and test scores.)

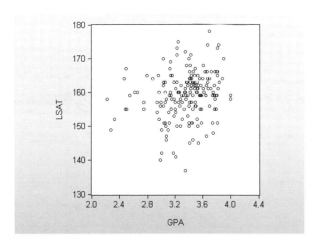

Hint: Scatter plots don't give good visuals when there are too many observations. The plots tend to get too "busy" to discern patterns. Additionally, scatter plots with very large numbers of observations can take a very, very long time to render when the graphs are copied outside of EViews.

Scatter with Regression

EViews offers several options for fitting a line or curve to the data in a scatter plot in the **Fit Lines** menu. **Regression Line** is the one most commonly used. (To learn about the other options see the *User's Guide.*)

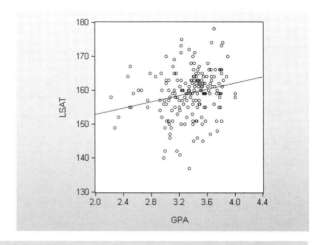

As you might expect, **Regression Line** adds a least squares regression line to the scatter plot we've just seen.

Hint: The equation for the line shown is, of course, the equation estimated by the command

```
ls lsat c gpa
```

If you want to fit the line to transformed data, using logs for example, choose Options to bring up the **Scatterplot Customize** dialog to choose from a variety of transformations.

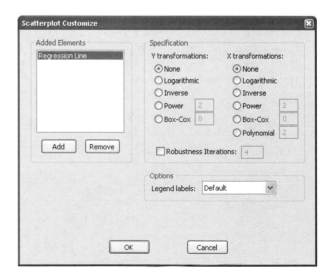

Hint: Changing the axis scales to logarithmic is different than drawing the fitted line using logs in the **Scatterplot Customize** dialog. The former changes the display of the scattered points while the latter changes how the line is drawn. Changing the axis scales is covered in Chapter 6, "Intimacy With Graphic Objects."

Multiple Scatters

If the group has more than two series, EViews presents a number of choices in the **Multiple series:** field of the **Graph Options** dialog. The default is to add more scatterings to the plot using the third series versus the first, the fourth series versus the first, and so on. Alternatively, choosing **Multiple graphs - First vs. All** puts each scatter in its own plot. You can also see all the possible pairs of series in the group in individual scatter plots by choosing **Scatterplot matrix.** It's clear that the 3-month rate is more closely related to the 1-year rate than it is to the 20-year rate. Not surprising, of course.

| Single graph - First vs. All |
| Single graph - Stacked |
| Multiple graphs - First vs. All |
| Scatterplot matrix |
| Lower triangular matrix |

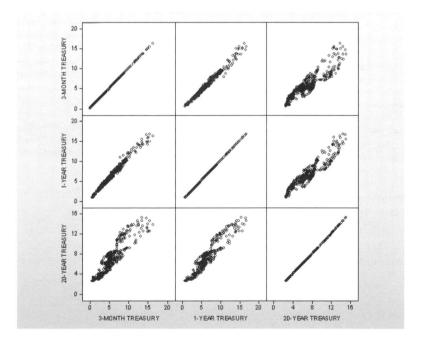

Where **Scatterplot matrix** gives each series a turn on both horizontal and vertical axes, **Lower triangular matrix** shows a single orientation for each pair.

If you have four or more series in a group, **Scatter** adds the choice **Multiple Graphs - XY Pairs** which plots a scatter of the second series (on the vertical axis) versus the first series (on the horizontal axis), the fourth series versus the third series, and so forth. Contrast with **Multiple graphs - First vs. All**, which uses the first series for the horizontal axis and places all the remaining series on the vertical axis.

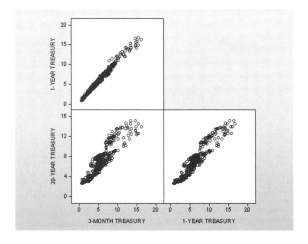

Togetherness of the First Sort

Scatter plots (XY Line plots too) have a special feature by which you can include multiple fitted lines on one scatter plot. We'll use this feature to illustrate what happens when you misspecify the functional form in a regression.

First, we'll generate some artificial data:

```
workfile u 100
series x = rnd
series log(y) = 2+3*x+rnd
```

Now we'll make a scatter plot and have EViews put in the standard (misspecified) linear regression line. Notice the predominance of positive errors for both low and high values of X.

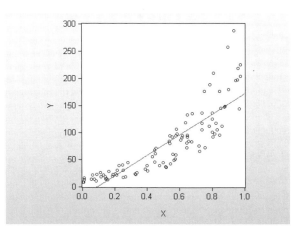

Clever observation: Did you notice that EViews cleverly solved for Y even though we specified log(Y) on the left of the series command?

To add a second fitted line, click the Options button in the **Details:** field to bring up the **Scatterplot Customize** dialog. Click Add for a new regression line, this one using a log transformation on the Y variable.

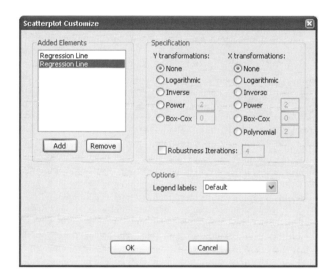

Using the right specification sure fits the data a lot better!

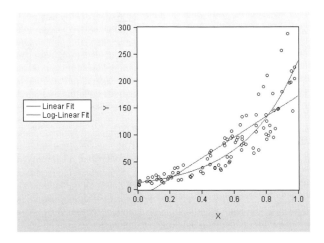

Scatter Plots and Distributions

Scatter plots help us understand the joint distribution of two variables, answering questions such as: "If variable one is high, is variable two likely to be high as well?" We can add information about the marginal distributions of each variable by turning on **Axis borders**. We can also add confidence ellipses through the **Fit lines:** menu and the Options button. Here we've added histograms to the axes in our law school admission example, as well as two confidence

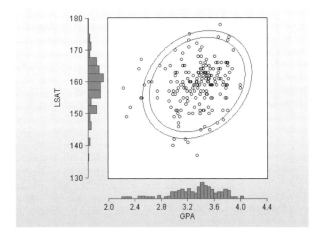

ellipses. The confidence ellipses enclose areas that would contain 90 percent and 95 percent, respectively, of the sample if the sample was drawn from a normal distribution. Of course, as you can see from the histograms, the data are not drawn from a normal distribution.

XY Line and XY Area Graphs

XY Line graphs are really just scatter plots where the consecutive points are connected, and **XY Area** graphs are XY Line graphs with the area below the line filled in. Contrast a scatter diagram (shown right) of inflation versus unemployment ("Output_and_Unemployment.wf1") from 1959 through 1979 with the same data shown with connecting lines (shown next).

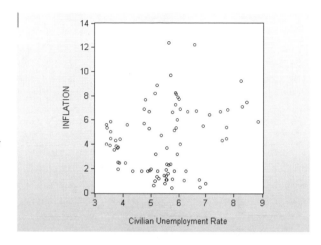

The connecting lines give a much clearer hint that we're seeing a series of negatively sloped, relatively flat lines that are moving up over time.

Let's try a little trick for displaying pre-1970 and 1970's inflation separately on the same graph. By making separate series for inflation in different periods, we can exploit the ability of XY Line graphs to show multiple pairs. We create our series with the commands:

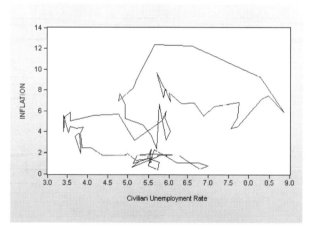

```
smpl 59 69
series inf_early = inflation
smpl 70 79
series inf_late = inflation
smpl 59 79
```

The series INF_EARLY has inflation from 1959 through 1969 and NAs elsewhere. Similarly, INF_LATE is NA except for 1970 through 1979. Now we open a group with the unemployment rate as the first series and INF_EARLY and INF_LATE as the second and third series. We can exploit the fact that EViews doesn't plot observations with NA values to get a very nice looking **XY Line** graph.

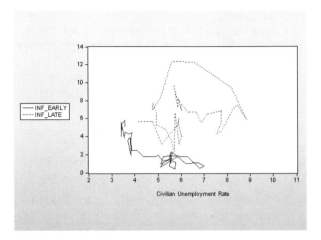

Obscure graph type hint: The graph type **XY Bar (X-X-Y triplets)** lets you draw bar graphs semi-manually. Vertical bars are drawn with the left edge specified by the first series, the right edge specified by the second series, and the height given by the third series.

Pie Graphs

Pie graphs don't fit neatly into the EViews model of treating a series as the relevant object. The **Pie Graph** command produces one pie for each observation. The observation value for each series is converted into one slice of the pie, with the size of the slice representing the observation value of one series relative to the same period's observation for the other series. For example, if there are three series with values π, π, and 2π, the first two slices will each take up one quarter of the pie and the third slice will occupy the remaining half.

Here's a simple pie chart ("consumption sectors.wf1") showing the relative sizes of the consumption of durables, nondurables, and services in the United States in 1959 and 1999. (We've turned on **Label Pies** in the **Bar-Area-Pie** section of the **Graph Elements** group in the **Graph Options** dialog.) It's easy to see here the dramatic increase in the size of the service sector.

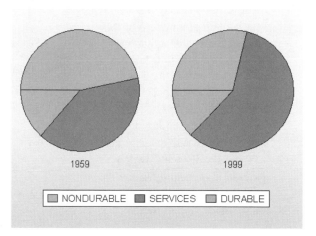

Hint: In case you were wondering, there's no way to automatically label individual slices.

Most EViews graphs render pretty nicely in monochrome, even if you've created the graphs in color. Pie graphs don't make out quite so nicely, so you'll want to do a little more customization for black and white images. The aesthetic problem is that pie graphs have large filled in areas right next to each other. Colors distinguish; in monochrome, adjacent filled areas don't look so good. (If you have access to both the black and white printed version of this book and the electronic, color version, compare the appearance of the pie chart above. Color looks a lot better.)

The solution is further complicated because there are two ways to get a monochrome graph out of EViews. You can tell EViews to render it without color by unchecking **Use Color** in the appropriate **Save** or **Copy** dialogs, or by sending it directly to a monochrome printer. When EViews knows that it's rendering in black and white, it does a decent job of picking grey scales. Alternatively, you can copy the image in color into another program and then let the other program render it the best it can.

If you want to use color but still get acceptable monochrome renderings, change the colors in the **Fill Areas** section in the **Graph Elements** group of the **Graph Options** dialog to ones with different "darkness levels." Here we've used blue, pink, and white. You can also select different **Grey shade** levels, which operate independently of the color choice when EViews renders in black and white.

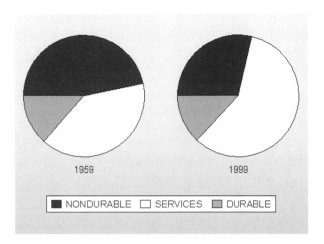

Hint: The same issue arises in any graph with adjacent filled areas. You can use the same trick in any graph.

Let's Look At This From Another Angle

To twist a graph on it's side, choose **Rotated - obs axis on left** in the **Orientation** combo of the **Graph Type dialog**. Below is a rotated version of the bar graph we saw on page 138.

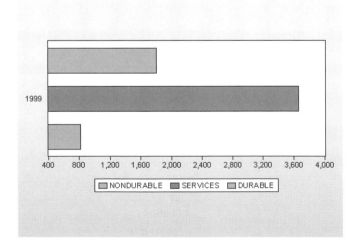

Hint: **Rotated** only works for some graph types. For types where it doesn't, the **Rotated** option won't appear.

Hint: Frozen graphs with updating off don't rotate.

Continuing hint: But if you wish, you can accomplish the same thing by going to the **Axes & Scaling** section and reassigning the series manually.

To Summarize

To visually summarize your data, change the **Graph data:** dropdown in the **Details:** field to a summary statistic of your choice. For example, here's a bar graph showing the median level of wages and salaries for U.S. workers in 2004 ("cpsmar2004extract.wf1").

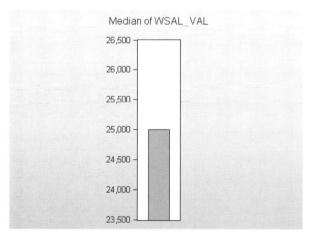

Pretty boring, eh? Even if you're fascinated by wage distributions, that's a pretty boring graph. All the choices other than **Raw data** produce a single summary statistic for each group of data. If all you have is one series, there's only one number to plot. Plotting summary statistics gets interesting when you compare statistics for different groups of data. We saw this in the comparison of the means of three different interest rate series in the plot of the average yield curve on page 129. We'll see examples where the groups of data represent different categories in the next section.

Hint: As a general rule, different groups of data summarized in a single plot need to be *commensurable*, meaning they should all have the same units of measurement. Our three interest series are all measured in percent per annum. In contrast, even though GDP and unemployment are both indicators of economic activity, it makes no sense to compare a mean measured in billions of dollars per year with a mean measured in percentage points.

Hint: **Details** only works for some graph types. For types where it doesn't, the **Details** option won't appear.

Categorical Graphs

So far, all our graphs have produced one plot per series. EViews can also display plots of series broken down by one or more categories. This is a great tool for getting an idea of how one variable affects another. Categorical graphs work for both raw data and summary statistics and pretty much all the graph types available under **Basic graph** are also available under **Categorical graph**.

```
Basic graph
Categorical graph
```

For example, a bar graph of median wages isn't nearly so interesting as is a graph comparing wages for union and nonunion workers. Union workers get paid more. (But you knew that.)

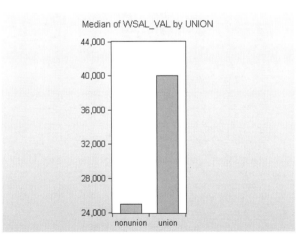

Median of WSAL_VAL by UNION

Junk graphics alert: The graph appears to show that union workers are paid *enormously* more than are non-union workers. In generating a visually appealing graph, EViews selected a lower limit of 24,000 for the vertical axis. Union wages are about 60 percent higher than non-union wages. But the union bar is about 10 times as large. The visual impression is very misleading. We'll fix this in Chapter 6, page 184.

Factoring out the categories

EViews allows multiple categorical variables, each with multiple categories. This can mean lots and lots of individual plots. EViews uses the **Factors - series defining categories** field to sort out which variables place plots within a graph and which place plots across graphs. For the graph above, we put UNION in the **Within graph:** box. This told EViews to place the bars for all the categories of UNION ("nonunion" and "union") within the same graph.

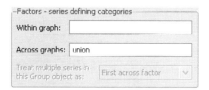

In contrast, if we'd entered UNION in the **Across graphs:** box EViews would have spread the bars across plots, so that each UNION category appears separately—as below.

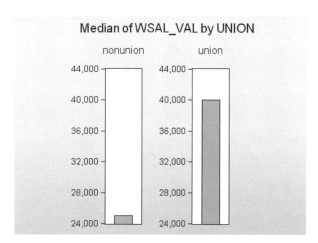

Splitting up wages by gender as well as union membership, we have four plots with numerous arrangement possibilities. If we make "UNION FE" the within factors (FE codes gender), we get the plot shown below.

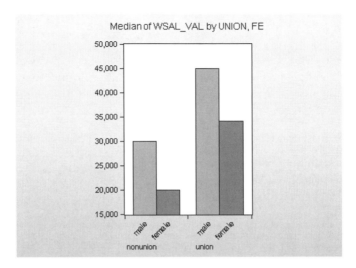

Note that the first categorical variable listed becomes the major grouping control. Switch the within order to "FE UNION" and EViews switches the ordering in the graph as shown below.

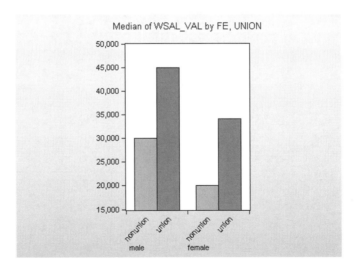

Hint: The graphs give identical information, but the first graph gives visual emphasis to the fact that men are paid more than women whether they're union or non-union. The second graph emphasized the union wage premium for both genders.

If we move the variable FE to the **Across** field, EViews splits the graph across separate plots for each gender.

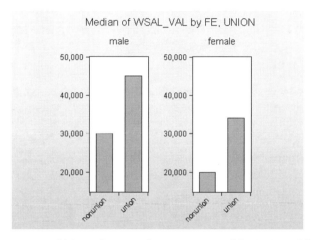

You can use as many within and across factors as you wish. We've added "highest degree received" to the across factor in this graph.

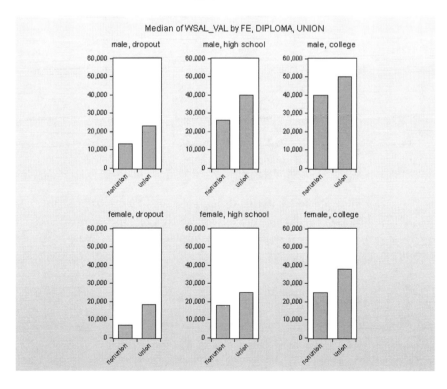

Hint: EViews will produce graphs with as complex a factor structure as you'd like. That doesn't make complex structures a good idea. Anything much more complicated than the graph above starts to get too complicated to convey a clear visual message.

Multiple Series as Factors

Having multiple series in a graph is sort of like having multiple categories for a single series, in that there's more than one group of data to graph. EViews recognizes this. Use the **Treat multiple series in this Group object as:** menu to treat the series (the series in this group were WSAL_VAL and HRSWK) as a factor.

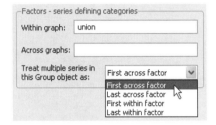

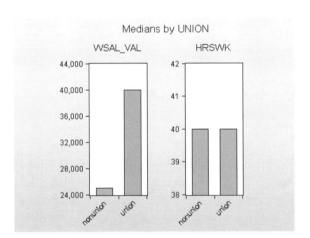

If we'd set **Treat multiple series in this Group object as: First within factor** both WSAL_VAL and HRSWK would appear in the same plot, as shown below. Because of the difference in scales for the two series, **First within factor** wouldn't be a sensible choice for this application.

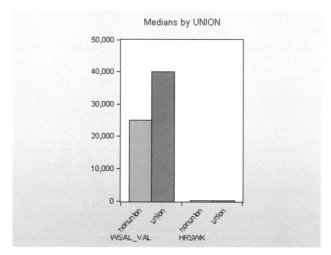

Polishing Factor Layouts

For categorical graphs, the **Graph Type** group on the left-hand side of the dialog includes a **Categorical options** section with a number of fine-tuning options. We discuss the most used options here, leaving the rest to your experimentation (and to the *User's Guide*).

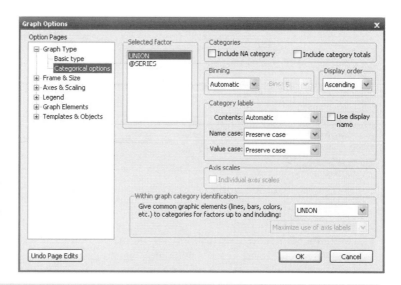

Hint: Categorical options aren't available on frozen graphs if updating is disabled.

Distinguishing Factors

In the graph depicted earlier, all the bars are a single color and pattern. Contrast the graph to the graph shown below, where "union" bars are shown in solid red and "nonunion bars" come in cross-hatched blue. Turning on **Within graph category identification** instructs EViews to add visual distinction to the within graph elements. We've done this to change the color in the graph to the right by changing **Within graph category identification** from **none** to **UNION**.

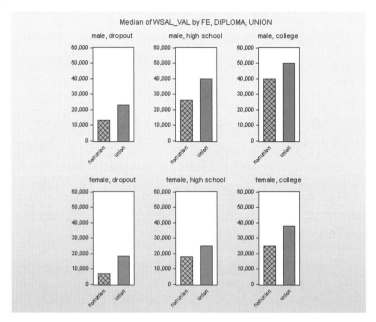

EViews interprets "add visual distinction" for this graph as assigning a unique color for each within category. This choice is ideal when the graph is presented in color, but we wanted clear visual distinction for a monochrome version as well. So we added the cross-hatching manually. To see how, see *Fill Areas* in the next chapter.

More Polish

Two more items are worthy of quick mention. The first item is that you can direct EViews to maximize the use of either axis labels or legends. Axis labels are generally better than using a legend, but sometimes they just take up too much room. The graph above maximized label use. Here's the same graph maximizing legend use. In this example neither graph is hard to understand nor terribly crowded, so which one is better mostly depends on your taste.

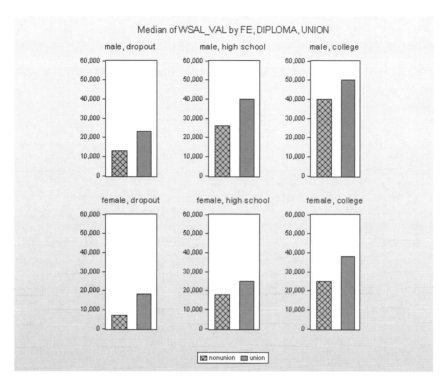

Median of WSAL_VAL by FE, DIPLOMA, UNION

The second item worth knowing about this dialog is that it uses @series as a special keyword. You can see an example in the dialog on page 161. When a graph has multiple series, EViews will treat data coming from one series versus another analogously with data within a series coming from one category versus another. In other words, the list of series can be treated like an artificial categorical variable for arranging graph layouts. (Just as we saw in *Multiple Series as Factors*.) The keyword @series is used to identify the list of series in the graph.

Togetherness of the Second Sort

At this point you know lots of ways to create graphs. Graphs, however created, are easily combined into a new, single graph.

Hint: Remember that a graph view of a series or group isn't a graph object. A graph object, distinguished by the 🔳 icon, is most commonly created by *freezing* a graph view.

Select the graph objects you want to combine just as you would select series for a group, or use the `show` command, as in:

```
show tm3_ty01 tm3_ty20
```

where `tm3_ty01 tm3_ty20` are names of graphs stored in the workfile, to open a new graph object.

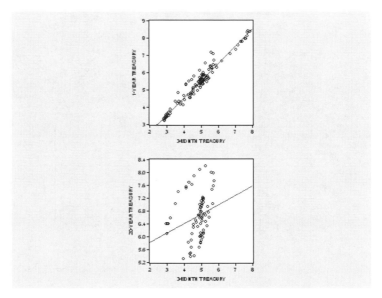

Using the mouse, you can re-arrange the position of the subgraphs within the overall graph window. This allows you to produce some very interesting effects. For example, if you have two graphs with identical axes, you can superimpose one on the other.

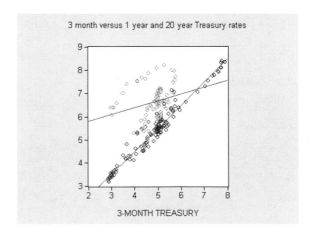

You'll note that this last picture has been messed with some: colors, titles, and axes have changed. Such messing around techniques are covered in Chapter 6, "Intimacy With Graphic Objects."

Quick Review and Look Ahead

EViews makes visually pleasing graphs quite easily. All you need do is open a series or a group and choose from the wide variety of graph types available. A variety of summary statistics can be graphed as easily as raw data. You can also have EViews make individual plots for data falling into different categories. Customizing graphs by adding text or changing colors is similarly easy.

If your visual needs have been satisfied, then this chapter is all you need to know about graphics. If more control is your style, then the next chapter will make you very happy.

Chapter 6. Intimacy With Graphic Objects

EViews does a masterful job of creating aesthetically pleasing graphs. But sometimes you want to tweak the picture to get it "just so," choosing custom labeling, axes, colors, *etc*. In this chapter we get close-up and intimate with EViews graphics.

We organize our tweaking exploration around four buttons in the graph window: AddText , Line/Shade , Template , and Options , ordered from easiest to most sophisticated. This last button, Options , brings up the **Graph Options** dialog, which itself has well over a dozen sections.

If you prefer, you can reach the same features by right-clicking anywhere in the graph window and choosing from the context menu. The same menu pops up if you click on the Proc button.

Copy to clipboard...	Ctrl+C
Options...	
Add text...	
Add single lines & shading...	
Templates...	
Sort...	
Remove selected	
Save graph to disk...	

Hint: Double-click on almost anything in a graphics window and the appropriate dialog will pop open, presenting you with the options available for fine-tuning.

Hint: Double-click on nothing in a graphics window (i.e. in a blank spot) and the **Graph Options** dialog will pop open. This is probably the easiest way to reach all the fine-tuning options.

Hint: Single-click on almost any thing in a graphics window and hit the **Delete** key to make the thing disappear. Be careful—there's no undo and no "Are you sure?" alert.

To Freeze Or Not To Freeze Redux

You'll remember from the last chapter that a graph in a series or group window can be *frozen* to create a graph window. Freezing can be done with updating turned on or updating turned off; freezing with updating turned off severs the graph from the original data.

In general, it's better to freeze a graph before fine tuning. One option discussed in the current chapter, sorting, is only available after freezing with updating turned off. On the other hand, some functions that you might think of as fine tuning EViews regards as part of the graph creation process. Adding axis borders is one example. These don't work once a graph is frozen with updating turned off.

Hint: I find it convenient to freeze a graph before fine tuning, but to leave the original series or group window open until I'm sure I won't need to make any changes that don't work on completely frozen graphs. Alternately, you can freeze the graph with updating turned on, and make desired changes. If you'd like, you can then copy the result or turn updating off once you are certain that you are done.

Hint: To make side-by-side comparisons of different visual representations of a given set of data, you have to freeze at least one window because you can only have a single view open of a series or group. Freezing creates a new graph object, detached from the original view.

A Touch of Text

Since adding text is the easiest touch-up, we'll start there.

Hint: As you know, you must freeze a graph before you can add text to it.

Clicking AddText opens the **Text Labels** dialog. Enter the desired text, pick a location, and hit OK . Note that the **Enter** key is intentionally *not* mapped to the OK button, so that you can enter multi-line labels by ending lines with **Enter**.

The options on the dialog mean pretty much just what they say. **Justification** lets you specify left, right, or center justification when there are multiple lines in a single label.

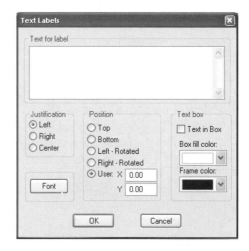

The Font button opens the **Font/Color** dialog which has pretty standard options. The checkbox **Text in Box,** and the **Box fill color:** and **Frame color:** dropdowns are also used in the obvious way.

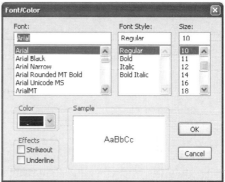

The **Position** field is worth a comment or two. **Left-Rotated** and **Right-Rotated** tilt text 90 degrees so. The default position, **User:**, sticks the text inside the frame of the graph itself. The location is measured in "virtual inches" (see *"Frame & Size"* on page 181) with positive numbers moving down and to the right. Frankly, sometimes it's easiest to just stick the text any old place and then use the mouse to re-position it.

The figure to the right shows labels in a variety of positions. Take note that the default positioning is **User:**. You'll probably find yourself most often adding text to put a title on the top or bottom of the graph. Since EViews frequently sticks a legend at the bottom of the graph, you may find it best to place the title at the top.

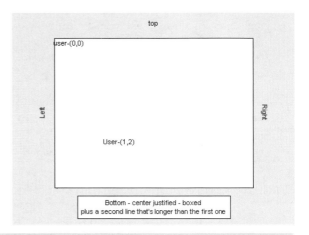

Hint: The six custom text items in the illustration were added by clicking AddText six times.

EViews goes to a *lot* of trouble to make text look nice. Each letter is carefully placed for the best appearance. A side effect of this extra care is that other programs may have trouble editing text included inside graphs copied-and-pasted from EViews. Sometimes trouble can be avoided, or at least mitigated, by changing the graphics default through the menu **Options/Graphics Defaults...**, clicking the **Exporting** section and setting **Text labels** to **Keep label as a single block of text so that it can be edited in other programs**. Unfortunately, even this isn't guaranteed to work with one very popular Word processing program. The moral is: *try to completely polish your graphic in EViews before exporting it.*

Hint: The **Text Labels** dialog is for the text *you* add to the graphic. Text placed by EViews, such as legends and axis labels, is adjusted through the **Graph Options** dialog. Uh, except for the occasional automatically generated title, which *is* tweaked through **Text Labels**. Not to worry, double-click on text and the appropriate dialog opens.

Shady Areas and No-Worry Lines

Adding shaded areas or vertical or horizontal lines to graphs is a very effective way of focusing your audience's attention on specific aspects of a plot. The Line/Shade button brings up the **Lines & Shading** dialog, which is used to place both lines and shades.

Shades

Beginning in 1942 and ending with the March 4, 1951 Treasury-Federal Reserve Accord, the Federal Reserve kept interest rates low in support of the American war effort. We can use shading to highlight interest rates during this period. Define a shaded area by entering **Left** and **Right** observations in the **Position** field of the **Lines & Shading** dialog.

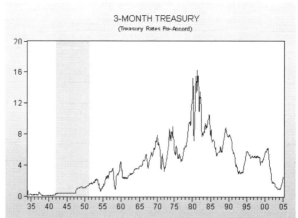

Hint: To put in multiple shaded areas, use Line/Shade repeatedly.

Hint: The **Apply color to all vertical shaded areas** checkbox lets you change the color of all the vertical shades on a graph with one command. This checkbox morphs according to the type of line or shade selected. For example, if you've set the combo for **Orientation** to **Horizontal - left axis**, the checkbox reads **Apply color, pattern, & width to all left scale lines**.

Shading can also be applied horizontally. After the Bretton Woods agreement on exchange rates broke down, a number of European countries agreed to keep their exchange rates from rising or falling more than 2.25 percent. Sometimes this worked and sometimes it didn't. Shading visually highlights a band of the appropriate width for the Belgian/Dutch exchange rate in the figure to the right.

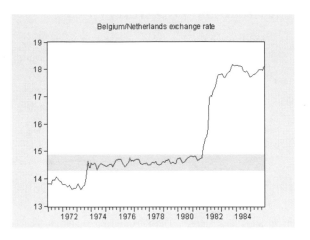

Lines

Adding a vertical or horizontal line, or lines, to a graph draws the viewer's eyes to distinguishing features. For example, long term interest rates are usually higher than short term interest rates. (This goes by the term called "normal backwardation," in case you were wondering.) The reverse relation is sometimes thought to signal that a recession is likely. Here's a graph that shows the difference between the one year and three month interest rates.

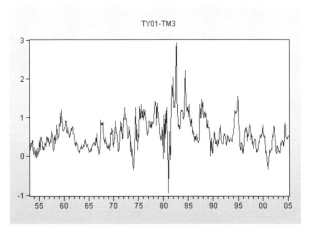

Use Line/Shade to add a horizontal line at zero, as shown.

In the revised figure it's much easier to see how rare it is for the longer term rate to dip below the short rate.

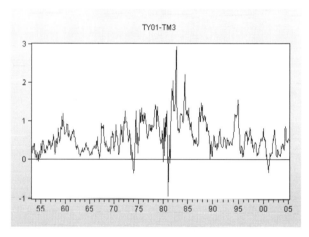

Templates for Success

What's really useful is to see how the difference between long and short term interest rates compares to (shaded) periods of recession. Periods in which the long rate dips below the short rate *are* associated with recessions. On the other hand, there have been a number of recessions in which this didn't happen.

In fact, adding shading for recessions has become something of a

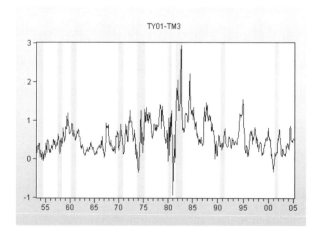

standard in the display of U.S. macro time series data. Including shades for the NBER recession dates is so easy that you may want to make it a regular practice. Just use the Line/Shade button for each of the 32 recessions identified by the NBER.

You don't really want to re-enter the same 32 sets of shade dates every time you draw a graph, do you? *Templates* to the rescue!

A template is nothing more than a graphic object from which you can copy option settings into another graph. Open the graph *sans* shades and click Template . (You may need to widen the graph window to see this button on the far right.) The **Graph Options**

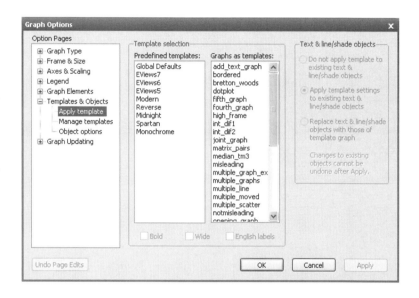

dialog opens to the **Templates & Objects** section. I *once* made a graph with the NBER recessions marked as shades, and saved that graph in the workfile with the name RECESSIONS. Choosing RECESSIONS, in the **Graphs as templates:** scroll area, makes available all the graphic options—including shade bands—for copying into the current graph.

> Hint: When you select a template, an alert pops open to remind you that *all* the options in *all* the various **Graph Options** sections will be changed.

> Hint: The list in **Graphs as templates:** shows graphs in the current workfile. If the template graph is in another workfile, it's easy enough to copy it and then paste it into the current workfile.

Once you hit the Apply button all the basic graphic elements are copied into the current graph, with the exception of text, line, and shade objects. Note in particular that legend options, but not legend text, will be replaced.

Hint: Applying a template can make a lot of changes, and there's no undo once you exit the dialog. It can pay to use **Object/Copy Object...** to duplicate the graph before making changes. Then try out the template on the fresh copy.

Text, lines, and shades in templates

Radio buttons offer three options for how text, line, and shade objects are copied.

Do not apply means *don't* copy these objects from the template. Use this setting to change everything except text, line, and shades to the styles in the template. Any text, line, or shade objects you add subsequent to the choice of template *will* use the template settings.

Apply template settings to existing uses the template styles for both existing and future text, line, and shades.

Text & line/shade objects

○ Do not apply template to existing text & line/shade objects

⊙ Apply template settings to existing text & line/shade objects

○ Replace text & line/shade objects with those of template graph

Changes to existing objects cannot be undone after Apply.

Replace text & line/shade wipes out existing text, line, and shade objects and then copies these objects in from the template. In the previous figure, we manually re-entered the zero line after the recession shading was applied from the template. This was necessary because the template didn't have a zero line, and all lines get replaced.

Hint: If you regularly shade graphs to show periods of recession—something commonly done in macroeconomics—make a template with recession periods shaded and then use **Replace text & line/shade** to copy the shaded areas onto new graphs.

Hint: Nope, there's no way to copy text, line or shade objects from the template without replacing the existing ones.

Bold, wide, and English labels in templates

You will also be given the choice of applying the **Bold**, **Wide**, or **English labels** modifiers. **Bold** modifies the template settings so that lines and symbols are bolder (thicker, and larger) and adjusts other characteristics of the graph, such as the frame, to match, **Wide** changes the aspect ratio of the graph so that the horizontal to vertical ratio is increased, and **English labels** modifier changes the settings for auto labeling the date axis so that labels that use month formatting will default to English month names ("Jan", "Feb", "Mar" instead of "M1", "M2", "M3").

Predefined Templates

EViews comes with a set of predefined templates that
provide attractive looking graphic styles. These appear
on the left in the **Template selection** field.

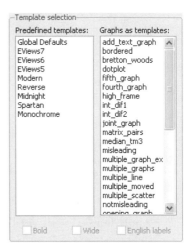

You can add any
graph you like to
the predefined
list so that it will
be globally avail-
able by going to
the **Manage
templates** page
of the **Templates
& Objects** sec-
tion. Then use
the dialog to add
the graph to the
**Predefined tem-
plates** list. Note
that predefined
templates don't

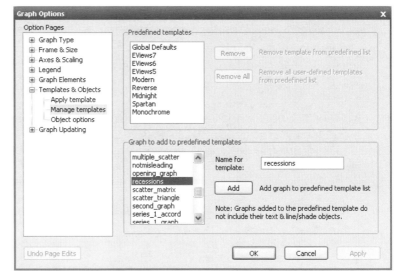

include text or lines/shades from the original graph.

You can make any template the default for all new graphs by going to the **Options/Graphics
Defaults...** menu and then choosing the desired template from the **Apply template** page.

Work around hint: Since predefined templates don't include line/shades, you can't just add the Recessions graph to the **Predefined template** list and have recession shading globally available. Hence, the hint on page 174 about copy-and-pasting a graph that you wish to use as a template.

Your Data Another Sorta Way

You can sort a spreadsheet view. (See *Sorting Things Out* in Chapter 7, "Look At Your Data.") You can also sort the data in a frozen graph. Choose **Sort...** from the Proc button or the right-click menu.

Hint: As mentioned earlier, you must freeze a graph before you sort it. **Sort...** re-arranges the data, so if you try to sort a histogram or other plot where sorting isn't sen-sible—EViews sensibly doesn't do anything.

In addition to being able to sort according to the values in as many as three of your data series, you can sort according the value of observation labels.

Give A Graph A Fair Break

If there's a break in your sample, how would you like that break to be displayed in a graph? EViews offers three options in the **Graph Options** dialog. In order to have something simple for an illustration, we've created a series 1, 2, 3, 4, 5 and then set the sample with `smpl 1 2 4 5`, so the middle observation is missing.

- **Drop excluded obs** deletes the missing part of the sample from the x-axis. Notice that it looks like the distance between 2 and 4 is the same as the distance between 1 and 2 or 4 and 5. This makes sense if the x-coordinates are *ordinal*, but isn't so good if they're *cardinal*. In other words, dropping part of the x-axis works if the measurements are things like "strongly agree," "agree", "indifferent," but doesn't work so well for measurements like "1 mile from the Eiffel Tower," "2 miles from the Eiffel Tower," *etc.*

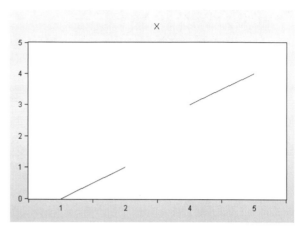

- **Pad excluded obs** leaves in the part of the x-axis for which data are missing. It's better for cardinal ordinates.

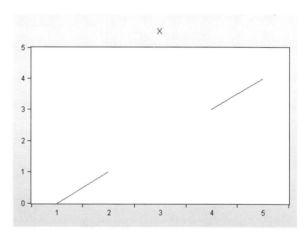

- **Segment with lines** is a stronger version of **Drop excluded**, deleting more of the missing x-axis, with an added vertical lines to show the break points. **Segment with lines** is the most "intellectually honest" display, because it makes sure everyone knows where breaks in the sample occur. The two disadvantages are that it's not always the most aesthetically pleasing picture (especially if there are lots of breaks) and that the vertical line draws attention to the sample break, which

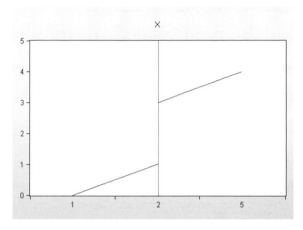

may or may not be a particularly interesting part of the data.

Hint: Checking **Connect adjacent** for either of the first two choices connects points on either side of the sample break. This frequently makes for a nicer looking picture, but can be misleading if it appears to report data that isn't there.

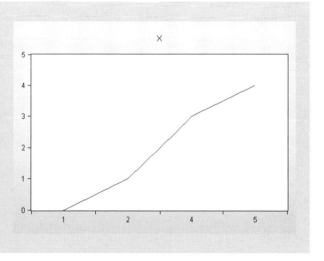

Hint: You control whether lines are connected over NAs with the **NA Handling** option. You can also use the broken sample options by including `not @isna(x)` in the `if` part of your `smpl` statement.

NA handling

☐ Connect adjacent non-missing observations

Options, Options, Options

There are lots of options for fine-tuning the appearance of your graphs. The **Graph Options** dialog has seven sections, each broken into pages filled with their own collection of details you can change. Many of the options are obvious—clicking a button marked [Font] lets you mess with the font, right? In this section, we touch on the most important touch-ups.

The Command Line Option

Every option that can be set through dialogs can also be set by typing commands in the command pane. In general, it's a lot easier to use the dialogs. The command line approach can be advantageous when you want to set the same options over and over. If the techniques covered in *Templates for Success*, above, and *The Impact of Globalization on Intimate Graphic Activity*, below, aren't powerful enough, take a look at the *Command and Programming Reference*.

Now, back to our discussion of tweaking–by–dialog.

Graph Type

From the **Graph Type** section you can change from one type of graph to another. The only graph types that appear are those that are permissible. For example, if you're looking at a single series you won't be offered a scatterplot.

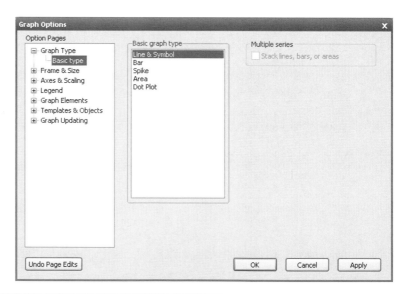

Hint: The **Basic type** page for a frozen graph that has updating off offers a limited set of options, typically far fewer than are available for a graphical view of a series or group.

Frame & Size

The **Frame & Size** section is the place for setting options that are essentially unrelated to the data being graphed. The **Color & Border** page lets you set specifications for the frame itself. On the left you can set colors for the area inside the frame (**Frame fill:**) and the area outside

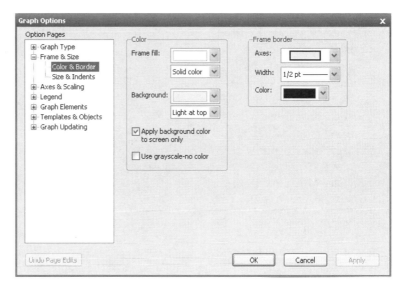

the frame (**Background:**). On the right you can set aspects of the frame border, even eliminating the border entirely if you wish.

The **Size & Indents** page of the **Frame & Size** section lets you set a margin for the graph inside the frame.

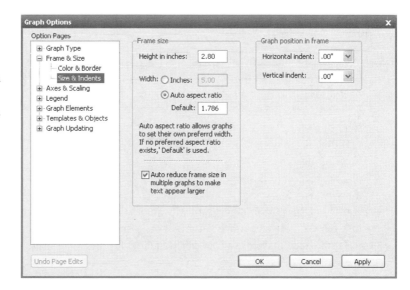

The left side of the **Size & Indents** page lets you set the **Frame size**— except that the frame size on the screen doesn't change. What this field really lets you choose is the *shape* of the frame (sometimes called the *aspect ratio*), within the size of the existing window. So if you choose 2 inches high and 8 inches wide, you get a really wide frame. (You can also change the aspect ratio of the graph by click-and-dragging the bottom or right edges of the graph.)

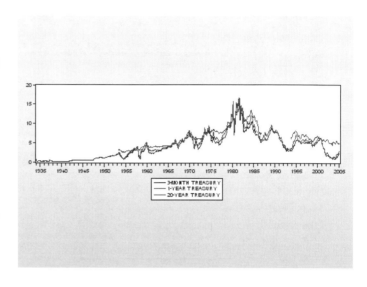

In contrast, choosing 4 inches high and 3 inches wide gives a high and narrow frame.

The frame shape is measured in "virtual inches." What's really being determined is the width-to-height ratio and the font size relative to the frame size. In addition, these virtual inches are used as the units of measurement for placing text, determining margins, *etc.* So if you

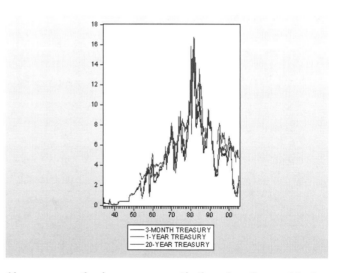

want to "User position" text half way across the frame you specify the x location as 4 inches in a $8'' \times 2''$ and 1.5 inches in a $3'' \times 4''$ frame. One consequence of this is that changing the frame size may cause user positioned text to re-locate itself.

Axes & Scaling

You may find that you visit the **Axes & Scaling** section frequently. Its features are both useful and very easy to use.

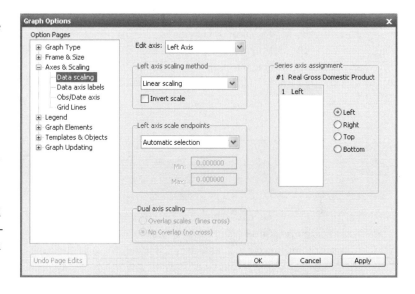

Assigning series to axes

The **Series axis assignment** field on the **Data scaling** page lets you assign each series to either the left or right axis with a radio button click (or to the top and bottom axes for X-Y Graphs). This is especially important when graphing series with different units of measurement. (See "Left and Right Axes in Group Line Graphs" on page 139 in Chapter 5, "Picture This!")

The **Edit axis** menu controls whether the fields below apply to the left, right, bottom or top axis. Switching the axis in the menu changes the fields in the dialog.

Left and right axes

For axes scaled numerically, the **scaling method** dropdown lets you pick between the standard linear scale, a linear scale that's guaranteed to include zero, a log scale, and normalized data. This last scale marks the mean of the data as zero and makes one vertical unit equivalent to one standard deviation.

Hint: Most often it's the vertical axes that have numerical scaling, dates being shown on the bottom. But sometimes, scatterplots are an example, numerical scales appear on the x-axis.

The log scale is especially useful for data that exhibits roughly constant percentage growth. As an example, here's a plot of U.S. real GDP. By plotting on a log scale, we see a nice, more-or-less straight line.

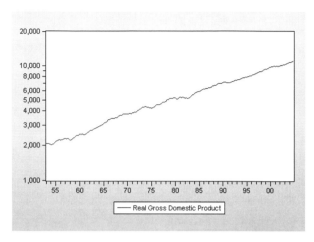

For the two vertical axes, the **Axis scale endpoints** dropdown has choices for automatic, data minimum and maximum, and user specified. Most of the time the automatic choice is fine, but once in a while you may prefer to change the scale.

Honest graph alert: In Chapter 5, page 156, we saw a bar graph comparing wages of union and non-union workers. **Automatic selection** chose a pretty, but substantively question-able endpoint for the y-axis. Here's a better ver-sion, where we've **User specified** a lower limit of zero.

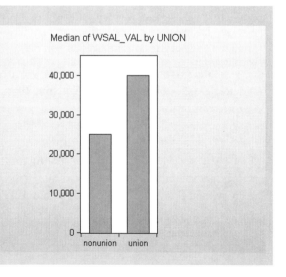

In addition, on the **Data axis labels** page, the **Data units & label format** section allows you to label your axis using scaled units or if you wish to customize the formatting of your labels.

The **Ticks** dropdown provides the obvious set of choices for display-ing—or not displaying—tick marks on the axes.

Top and Bottom Axes

The choices for marking the top and bottom axes vary depending on whether the horizontal scale displays numbers, in which case the choices are essentially the same as the ones we've just seen, or if—as is more common— the bottom scale shows dates. In the latter situation, the choices

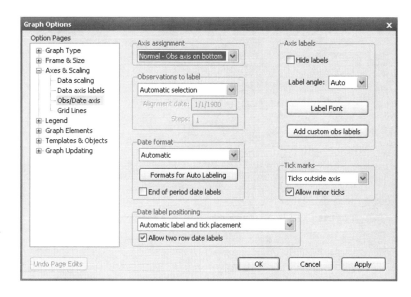

are the ones appropriate to dates and the exact choices depend on the frequency of the workfile. Options for the date scale can be found on the **Obs/Date axis** page.

The **Date format** dropdown provides a variety of fairly self-explanatory choices, including **Custom** for when you want to roll your own. (See the *User's Guide.*)

Observations to label similarly provides both a selection of built-in and custom options.

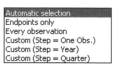

Hint: Just as numerical scales sometimes appear on the horizontal axes, dates sometimes appear on the vertical, rotated graphs are a notable example. The appropriate marking options work as you would expect.

You can cause grid lines to be displayed from the **Grid Lines** page. The **Obs/Date axis grid lines** field lets you customize the interval of grid lines for the date axis.

Legend

The **Legend** sec-
tion controls a
number of
options, the most
useful of which
is editing **Legend
entries**. Gener-
ally a series' **Dis-
play Name** (you
can edit the dis-
play name from
the series label
view) is used to
identify the
series in the leg-
end. If the series
doesn't have a
Display Name,

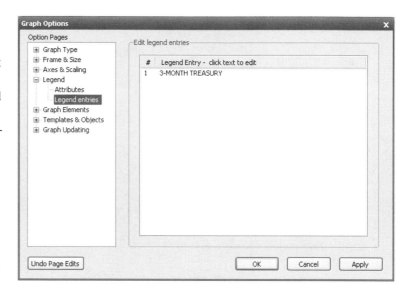

the series name itself is used. Either way, this is the spot for you to edit the legend text.

On the **Attributes** page, the **Legend Columns** entry on the left side determines how many
columns are used in the legend. The default "Auto" (automatic) lets EViews use its judgment. Alternatively, select 1, 2, 3, *etc.* to specify the number of columns.

Legend Aesthetics

Setting the text for the legend
sometimes presents a trade-off
between aesthetics and information. The longer the text, the
more information you can cram
in. But shorter legends generally
look better. Here's a graph with
a moderately long legend.

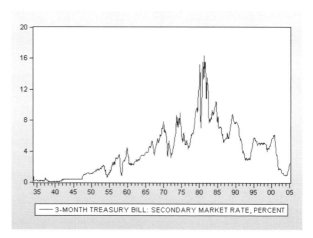

Rule of thumb: the legend should be shorter than the frame.

Here's the same graph with shorter legend text. This graph looks better, at the cost of dropping the information that the rate quotes come from the secondary market. In general, detailed information is probably better in a footnote or figure caption. But the choice, of course, is yours.

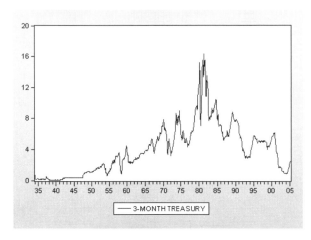

Graph Elements

The **Graph Elements** section contains options for specific graph types.

Lines & Symbols

The **Attributes** field on the right in the **Lines & Symbols** page is the place to pick colors and patterns for the lines and symbols for each series. Click on the numbered lines at the far right to select the series to adjust. (Note that the legend label, "3-MONTH TREASURY," appears at the bottom of the **Attributes** field to identify the selected series.) The provided drop down menu lets you choose whether to use a line, a symbol, or both, for each series.

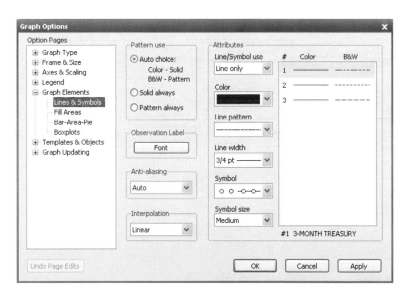

The right-most field displays the representation for each series, showing how the series will be rendered in color and how it will be rendered in black and white. The default pattern uses the colors shown in the **Color** column of the **Attributes** field for color rendering and the line patterns shown under **B&W** for black and white rendering. The **Pattern use** radio button on the left side of the page specifies whether to use the default (**Auto choice:**) or force all rendering to solid or all to pattern. (See the discussion under *A Little Light Customization* in Chapter 5, "Picture This!")

Two rules to remember:

- Multiple colors are *much* better than patterns in helping the viewer distinguish different series in a graph.

- Multiple colors are not so great if the graph is printed in black and white.

Fill Areas

The **Fill Areas** page does the same job for filled in areas—in bar graphs for example—that the **Lines & Symbols** page does for lines.

In addition, the **Bar-Area-Pie** page is the place to control labeling, outlining, and spacing of filled areas.

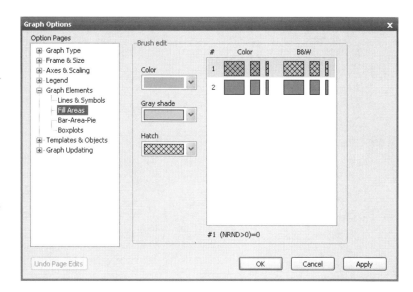

In *Distinguishing Factors* in the previous chapter we used **Within graph category identification** to have EViews automatically select visually distinct colors for different graph elements. EViews' automatic selection produced the graph below.

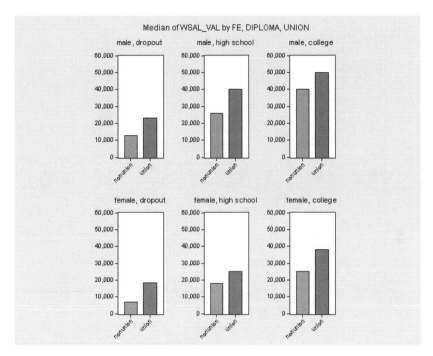

Using the **Fill Areas** page to set hatching for the first "series" (the dialog says "series," even though the bars are really categories of a single series) produces the more visually distinctive version shown here.

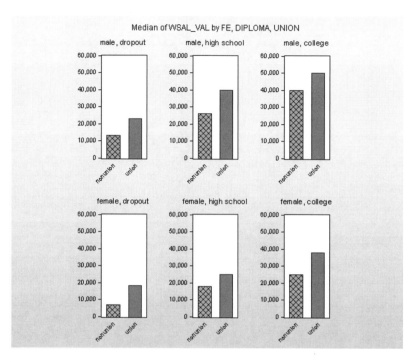

Boxplots

The **BoxPlots**
page offers lots
of options for
deciding which
elements to
include in your
boxplot, as well
as color and
other appear-
ance controls for
these elements.
For a light
review of the
various ele-
ments, see *Box-*
plots in
Chapter 7, "Look
At Your Data." For more information, see the *User's Guide.*

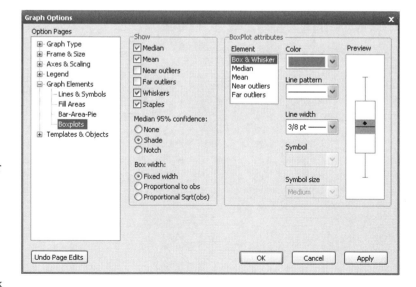

Objects

The **Object options** page controls the style, but not the content, for lines, shading, and text objects. You can set the style for a given object directly in the **Text Labels** and **Lines & Shading** dialogs. The **Object options** page lets you set the default styles for any new objects

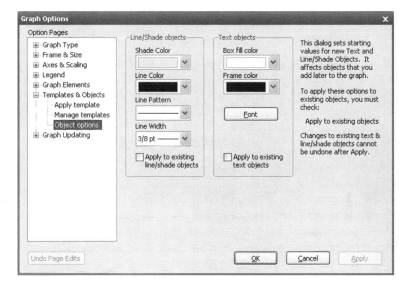

in the graph at hand. You can also change the styles for existing objects in the graph by checking the relevant **Apply to existing** box.

Graph Updating

The **Graph Updating** section lets you specify if you would like your graph to update with changes in the underlying data. If you select **Manual** or **Automatic** the bottom half of the page becomes active, where you may specify the update sample.

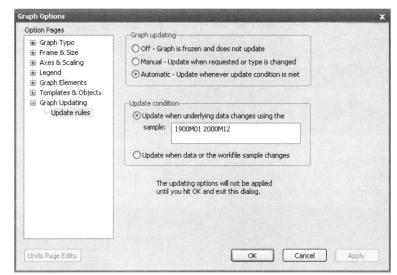

The Impact of Globalization on Intimate Graphic Activity

If you do lots of similar graphs, you aren't going to want to set the same options over and over and over and over. Templates help some. You can also set global default options through the menu **Options/Graphic Defaults…**, which brings up a **Graph Options** dialog with essentially the same sections we've seen already. Changes made here become the initial settings for all future graphs.

Exporting

The global **Graph Options** dialog has an extra section— **Exporting**. Make changes here to control the defaults for exporting graphics to other programs. If you always want to use the same exporting options, uncheck **Display options dialog on all copy operations** to save a second here and there.

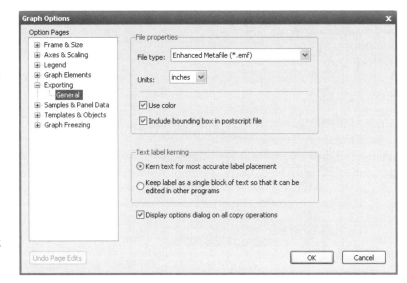

Quick Review?

Basically, EViews has a gazillion options for getting up-close and personal with graphics. Fortunately, you rarely need this level of detail because EViews has sound artistic sensibilities. Nonetheless, when there's a customization you do need, it's probably available.

Chapter 7. Look At Your Data

Data description precedes data analysis. Failure to carefully examine your data can lead to what experienced statisticians describe with the phrase "a boo boo."

True story. I was involved in a project to analyze admissions data from the University of Washington law school. (An extract of the data, "UWLaw98.wf1", can be found on the EViews website.) Some of my early results were really, *really* strange. After hours of frustration I did the sensible thing and went and asked my wife's advice. She told me:

Look at your data!

So I quickly pulled up a histogram of the applicants' grade point averages (GPA). Notice the one little data point all by its lonesome way off to the right? According to the summary table, the highest recorded GPA was 39. Since GPAs in American colleges are generally on a 4.0 scale, it's a pretty good bet that a decimal point was omitted somewhere.

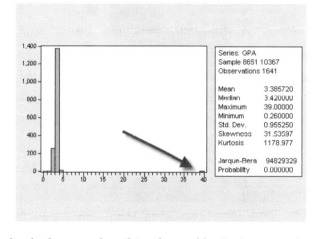

In this chapter we'll walk through a number of techniques for looking at your data. Since the border between describing data and beginning an analysis can be fuzzy, some of the topics covered here are useful in data analysis as well. Our discussion is split into univariate (describing one variable at a time) and multivariate (describing several variables jointly). Maybe it's easier to think of descriptive views of series and descriptive views of groups.

Hint: Two important data descriptive techniques are covered elsewhere. Graphing techniques are explored in Chapter 5, "Picture This!" And while one of the very best techniques for looking at your data is to open a spreadsheet view and then look at it, this doesn't require any instructions—so past this reminder-sentence we won't give any…except for one little trick in the next section.

Reminder Hint: Don't forget that you can hover your cursor over points in a graph to display observation labels and values.

Sorting Things Out

As you know, you can open a spreadsheet view of a series or a group of series to get a visual display. For example, the spreadsheet view of GPA is shown to the right. Observations appear in order.

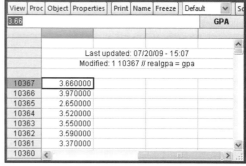

Push the [Sort] button to bring up the **Sort Order** dialog, which gives you the option of sorting by either observation number or the value of GPA. You can sort in either Ascending (low-to-high) or Descending (high-to-low) order.

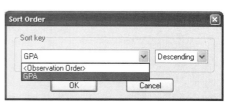

By sorting according to GPA, we can instantly see where the problem value is located.

More generally, the **Sort Order** dialog for groups lets you sort using up to three series to order the observations.

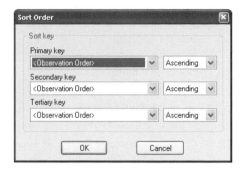

Hint: Sorting changes the order in which the data is visually displayed. The actual order in the workfile remains unchanged, so analysis is not affected. To restore the appearance to its original order, sort using **Observation Order** and **Ascending**.

Describing Series—Just The Facts Please

Open a series and click the [View] button. The dropdown menu shows the tools available for looking at the series. We begin with the basic descriptive statistics.

Stats Panel from Histogram and Stats

Histograms and basic statistics are generated through the **Descriptive Statistics & Tests/Histogram and Stats** menu item. The data used for computing descriptive statistics is, as always, restricted to the current sample. Let's first eliminate reported grades that are almost certainly data errors.

```
smpl if gpa>1 and gpa<5
```

As you can see, **Histogram and Stats** produces a histogram on the left and a panel of descriptive statistics on the right. Let's start with the latter, coming back to the picture part later.

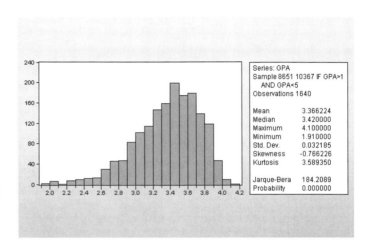

The top of the statistics panel gives the sample in effect when the report was made and the number of observations. If you compare this report with the one at the beginning of the chapter, you might note that the `smpl if` command cut out two observations. Comparing the maximum and minimum between the two reports, we can deduce that one GPA of 39 and one GPA of .26 was eliminated.

Was it a good idea to eliminate these two observations? This question can't be answered by statistical analysis—you need to apply subject area knowledge. In this case, we might have chosen instead to "correct" the data by changing 39 to 3.9 and .26 to 2.6. (Although, one is left with the nagging question of whether there might really have been an applicant with a 0.26 GPA.) When we eliminated two grade observations by changing the sample, we also cut out data for other series for these two individuals. Their state of residence or LSAT scores might still be of interest, for example. There's no right or wrong about this "side effect." You just want to be aware that it's happening.

> Hint: If you want to eliminate data errors for one series without affecting which observations are used for other series in an analysis, change the erroneous values to NA instead of cutting them out of the sample.

The remainder of the statistics panel reports characteristics of the data sample, mean, median, *etc.*

Export Hint: If you double-click on the statistics panel, the **Text Labels** dialog opens. This is the place to manipulate the text display. (See Chapter 5, "Picture This!") You can also **Edit/Copy** the text in the statistics panel and then paste the text into your word processor.

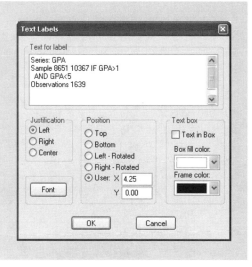

The statistic at the bottom of the panel, the Jarque-Bera, tests the hypothesis that the sample is drawn from a normal distribution. The statistic marked "Probability" is the p-value associated with the Jarque-Bera. In this example, with a p-value of 0.000, the report is that it is extremely unlikely that the data follows a normal distribution.

Hint: There are relatively few places in econometrics where normality of the data is important. In particular, there is no requirement that the variables in a regression be normally distributed. I don't know where this myth comes from.

One-Way

To look at the complete distribution of a series use **One-Way Tabulation…**, which lets you **Tabulate Series**. Initially, it's best to uncheck both **Group into bins if** checkboxes. Eliminating binning ensures that we see a complete list of every value appearing in the series from low to high, as well as a count and cumulative count of the number of observations taken by each value.

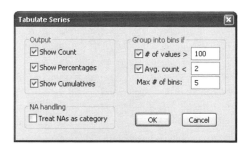

Tabulation of GPA provides lots of information. It also illustrates a common problem—too many categories.

This is why the **Tabulate Series** dialog defaults provides binning control.

Binning Control

The **Group into bins if** field is a three-part control over grouping individual values into bins. Checking **# of values** tells EViews to create bins if there are more than the specified number of values and checking **Avg. count** means to create bins if the average count in a category is less than specified. **Max # of bins**, not surprisingly, sets the maximum number of bins. Sometimes you need to play around with these options to get the tabulation that best fits your needs.

As an example, here's a GPA tabulation that shows broad categories. It's now easy to see that 15 percent of applicants had below a 3.0 average and 10 applicants, 0.61 percent of the applicant pool, did report GPAs above 4.0.

Tabulation of GPA
Date: 12/06/06 Time: 14:15
Sample: 8651 10367 IF (GPA>1 AND GPA<5 AND LSAT>100)
Included observations: 1638
Number of categories: 177

Value	Count	Percent	Cumulative Count	Cumulative Percent
1.910000	1	0.06	1	0.06
1.980000	1	0.06	2	0.12
2.000000	1	0.06	3	0.18
2.010000	1	0.06	4	0.24
2.060000	2	0.12	6	0.37
2.070000	1	0.06	7	0.43
2.080000	1	0.06	8	0.49
2.190000	1	0.06	9	0.55
2.210000	1	0.06	10	0.61
2.230000	2	0.12	12	0.73
2.240000	3	0.18	15	0.92
2.280000	1	0.06	16	0.98
2.300000	1	0.06	17	1.04
2.310000	1	0.06	18	1.10
2.320000	3	0.18	21	1.28
2.330000	1	0.06	22	1.34
2.350000	1	0.06	23	1.40
2.370000	1	0.06	24	1.47
2.380000	1	0.06	25	1.53
2.390000	1	0.06	26	1.59
2.410000	2	0.12	28	1.71
2.440000	1	0.06	29	1.77
2.450000	2	0.12	31	1.89
2.460000	1	0.06	32	1.95
2.470000	2	0.12	34	2.08
2.480000	2	0.12	36	2.20
2.490000	2	0.12	38	2.32

Tabulation of GPA
Date: 03/29/05 Time: 15:27
Sample: 8651 10367 IF GPA>1 AND GPA<5
Included observations: 1639
Number of categories: 4

Value	Count	Percent	Cumulative Count	Cumulative Percent
[1, 2)	2	0.12	2	0.12
[2, 3)	253	15.44	255	15.56
[3, 4)	1374	83.83	1629	99.39
[4, 5)	10	0.61	1639	100.00
Total	1639	100.00	1639	100.00

Stats Table

The menu **Descriptive Statistics/Stats Table** creates a table with pretty much the same information as is found in the statistics panel of **Histogram and Statistics**. This table format has the advantage that it's easier to copy-and-paste into your word processor or spreadsheet program.

	GPA
Mean	3.365898
Median	3.420000
Maximum	4.100000
Minimum	1.910000
Std. Dev.	0.364573
Skewness	-0.766733
Kurtosis	3.591009
Jarque-Bera	184.4428
Probability	0.000000
Sum	5516.707
Sum Sq. Dev.	217.7117
Observations	1639

Stats By Classification

A common first step on the road from data description to data analysis is asking whether the basic series statistics differ for sub-groups of the population. Clicking **Descriptive Statistics/Stats by Classification...** brings up the **Statistics By Classification** dialog. You'll see a field called **Series/Group for classify** smack in the upper center of the dialog. Enter one or more series (or groups) here, hit ⌐ OK ⌐, and you get summary

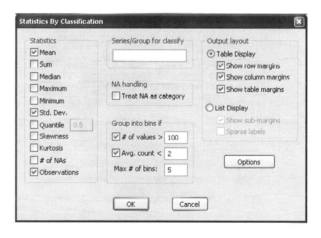

statistics computed for all the distinct combinations of values of the classifying series.

Here's a simple example. In our workfile, the variable WASH equals one for Washington State residents and zero for everyone else. Using WASH as the classifying variable gives the results shown to the right. About 60 percent of applications (1028 out of 1639) were from out of the state, and the out of state applicants averaged a slightly higher GPA.

Descriptive Statistics for GPA
Categorized by values of WASH
Date: 03/27/05 Time: 15:16
Sample: 8651 10367 IF GPA>1 AND GPA<5
Included observations: 1639

WASH	Mean	Std. Dev.	Obs.
0	3.386349	0.361168	1028
1	3.331489	0.367968	611
All	3.365898	0.364573	1639

If we wanted to see the effect of state *and* having a relatively high LSAT score (Law School Admission Test), we could fill out the **Series/Group for classify** field with both WASH and LSAT > 160.

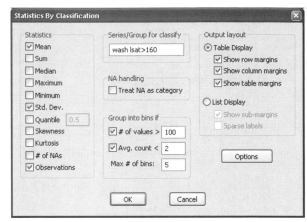

Now we get a table showing mean, standard deviation, and the number of observations for all four combinations of Washington resident/not resident and high/low LSAT. The list of statistics reported appears in the upper left-hand corner of the statistics table so that you'll have a key handy for reading the results.

The left-hand side of the **Statistics By Classification** dialog has a series of checkboxes for selecting the statistics you'd like to see. The **Output Layout** field, on the right-hand side, provides some control over the

Descriptive Statistics for GPA
Categorized by values of WASH and LSAT>160
Date: 03/27/05   Time: 15:34
Sample: 8651 10367 IF GPA>1 AND GPA<5
Included observations: 1639

Mean Std. Dev. Obs.		LSAT>160		
		0	1	All
	0	3.325984	3.463884	3.386349
		0.381066	0.317865	0.361168
		578	450	1028
WASH	1	3.268015	3.445917	3.331489
		0.382462	0.309717	0.367968
		393	218	611
	All	3.302522	3.458021	3.365898
		0.382495	0.315109	0.364573
		971	668	1639

appearance of the table and whether you want "margin" statistics— the "All" row and the "All" column.

Looking at statistics by classification makes sense when the classifying variable has a small set of distinct values. When the classifying variable takes on a large number of values, it's sometimes better to clump together values into a small number of groups or "bins." The **Group into bins if** field in the lower center of the dialog lets you instruct EViews to group different values of the classifying variable into a single bin. (See *Binning Control*, later in this chapter.)

Describing Series—Picturing the Distribution

Sometimes a picture is better than a number. Open a series (or group of series) and choose the **Graph...** view (see Chapter 5, "Picture This!"). While all graphs look at data, the **Distribution**, **Quantile-Quantile**, and **Boxplot** options bear directly on understanding how a set of data is distributed. The **Distribution** option offers a whole set of options, the most familiar one being the **Histogram**.

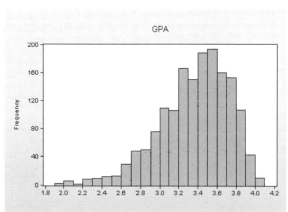

Histograms

A histogram is a graphical representation of the distribution of a sample of data. For the GPAs we see lots of applications around 3.4 or 3.5, and very few around 2.0. EViews sets up bins between the lowest and highest observation and then counts the number of observations falling into each bin. The number of bins is chosen in order to make an attractive picture. Clicking the Options button leads to the **Distribution Plot Customize** dialog, where several customization options are provided. (See the *User's Guide*.)

All the features described in Chapter 5, "Picture This!" and in Chapter 6, "Intimacy With Graphic Objects" can be used for playing with histograms. For example, we can make a categorical graph to compare GPAs of Washington State residents to those of non-residents.

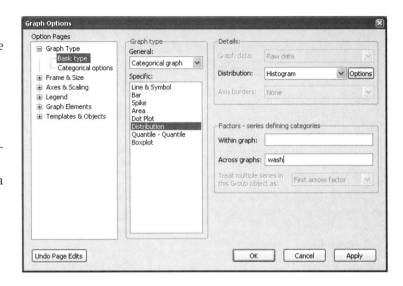

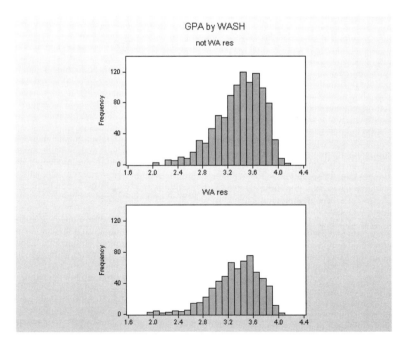

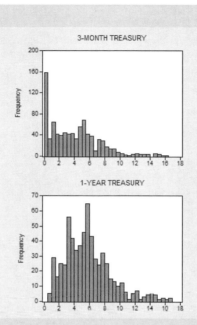

Cautionary hint for graphing multiple series: Individual series in a Group window may have NAs for different observations. As a result distribution graphs may be drawn for different samples. For example, the graph to the right makes it appear that 3-month Treasury rates are much more likely than are 1-year rates to be nearly zero. In fact what's going on is that our sample includes 3-month, but not 1-year, rates from the Great Depression. Looking at a line graph, with the same histograms on the axis border, it becomes evident that the 1-year rates enter our sample at a later date.

Kernel Density Graphs

A kernel density graph is, in essence, a smoothed histogram. Often, a histogram looks choppy because the number of observations in a given bin is subject to random variation. This is particularly true when there are relatively few observations. The kernel density graph smooths the variation between nearby bins. The *User's Guide* describes the various options for controlling the smoothing.

Using the default choices gives a nice picture for our GPA data.

There's no law about the best way to accomplish this smoothing, but the default frequently works well. We see again that applicant grades are concentrated around 3.4 or 3.5, and that there is a long lower tail.

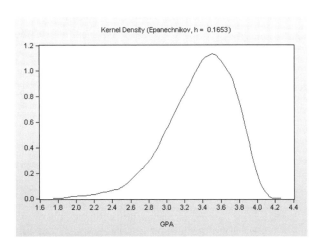

Theoretical Distribution

EViews will fit any of a number of theoretical probability distributions to a series, and then plot the probability density. (You can supply the parameters of the distribution if you prefer.) As an example, we've superimposed a normal distribution on top of the GPA histogram.

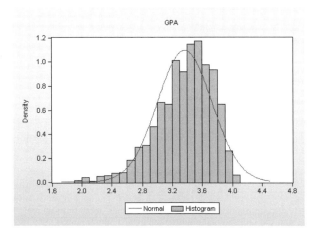

Empirical CDF, Survivor, and Quantile Graphs

Just as a histogram or kernel density plot gives an estimate of the probability density function (PDF), a **Cumulative Distribution** plot presents an estimate of the cumulative distribution function (CDF).

You may find it useful to think of the histogram and kernel density plots as graphical analogs to the Percent column in the one-way tabulation, shown above in *One-Way*, and the cumulative distribution plot as the graphical analog to the Cumulative Percent column. Here's the CDF for GPA.

Survivor and **Quantile** plots provide alternative ways of looking at cumulative distributions.

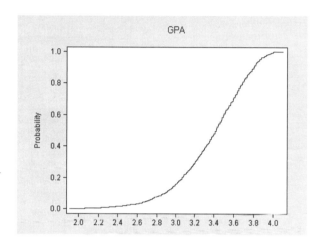

The **Distribution** menu also provides links to a variety of **Quantile-Quantile** graphs and to a set of **Empirical Distribution** tests. **Quantile-Quantile** plots graph the empirical distribution of a series against a variety of theoretical probability distributions (*e.g.*, normal, uniform). **Empirical distribution tests** provide corresponding formal tests of whether a series is drawn from a particular theoretical probability distribution. For more on these topics, see the *User's Guide*—or heck, just click on the relevant menu and see what you get!

Boxplots

Sometimes a picture is better than a table. Boxplots, also called box and whisker diagrams, pack a lot of information about the distribution of a series into a small space. The variety of options are controlled in the **Graph Elements/Boxplots** page of the

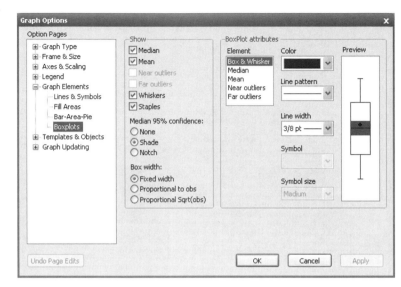

Graph Options dialog. A boxplot of GPA using EViews' defaults is shown here.

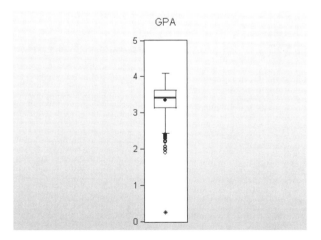

Opening the boxplot

The top and bottom of the box mark 75th and 25th percentile of the distribution. The distance between the two is called the *interquartile range* or *IQR*, because the 75th percentile marks the top quartile (the upper fourth of the data) and the 25th percentile marks the bottom quartile (the bottom fourth of the data).

The width of the box can be set to mean nothing at all (the default) or to be proportional to the number of observations or the square root of the number of observations. (Use the **Box width** radio buttons in the dialog.)

The mean of the data is marked with a solid, round dot. The median of the data is marked with a solid horizontal line. Shading around the horizontal line is used to compare differences between medians; overlapping shades indicate that the medians do not differ significantly. You can change the shading to a notch, if you prefer, as shown in the example below.

The short horizontal lines are called *staples*. The upper staple is drawn through the highest data point that is no higher than the top of the box plus $1.5 \times IQR$ and, analogously, the lower staple is drawn through the lowest data point that is no lower than the bottom of the box minus $1.5 \times IQR$. The vertical lines connecting the staples to the box are called whiskers. Data points outside the staples are called *outliers*. *Near outliers*, those no more than $1.5 \times IQR$ outside the staple, are plotted with open circles, and *far outliers*, those further than $1.5 \times IQR$ outside the staple, are plotted with filled circles.

There Can Be Less Than Meets the Eye Hint: Boxplots tell you a lot about the data, but don't jump to the conclusion that because a point is labeled an "outlier" that it's necessarily got some kind of problem. Even when data is drawn from a perfect normal distribution, just over half a percent of the data will be identified as an outlier in a boxplot.

Boxplots By Categories

Boxplots give quick visual comparisons of different subpopulations. In this plot we're again classifying GPA by Washington residence using the categorical graph tools. We also clicked the notched and proportional to observations radio buttons in the dialog. The distribution of grades is higher for non-

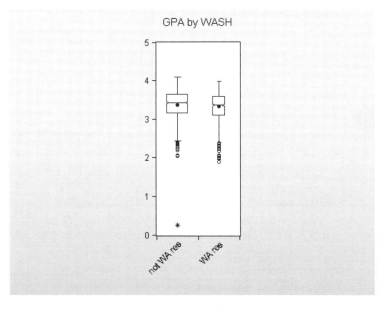

Washington residents, but the ranges for residents and non-residents mostly overlap.

Statistics don't lie, but they can mislead. In this plot, the upper staple for non-residents is higher than the staple for residents. A little investigation shows that, while GPA is measured on a four point scale, one observation for a non-residents was recorded 4.1. Because some schools use something other than a four point scale, we don't know if this GPA is an error or not. But we probably shouldn't conclude anything about the difference between in- and out-of-state applicants based on this one data point.

Tests On Series

Up to this point, we've been looking at ways to summarize the data in a series. Now we move on to formal hypothesis tests. The tests corresponding to the descriptive statistics we've looked at are found under the **Descriptive Statistics & Tests** menu. As an example, having found the mean LSAT in our applicant pool, we might want to test whether it differs from the national average.

| Histogram and Stats |
| Stats Table |
| Stats by Classification... |
| Simple Hypothesis Tests |
| Equality Tests by Classification... |
| Empirical Distribution Tests... |

Simple Hypothesis Tests

Nationally, the average LSAT score is about 152. Looking at the data for University of Washington applicants, we see their average was higher, just over 158. It would be interesting to know whether the difference is meaningful, or whether it's a random statistical fluke.

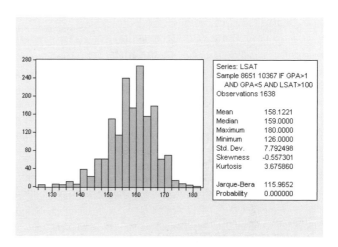

Formally, we want to test the hypothesis that the mean University of Washington score equals 152 and ask whether there is sufficient evidence to reject this hypothesis. We will perform this test after setting the sample to include observations where the GPA is within normal bounds and the LSAT score exceeds 100. Choose **Descriptive Statistics & Tests** and **Simple Hypothesis Tests** and then enter the hypothesized mean in the **Series Distribution Tests** dialog.

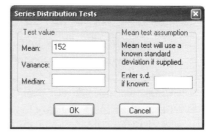

Hint: If you're only testing a mean, you don't need to fill out any other fields. The **Variance** and **Median** fields are for hypothesis tests on the variance or median. In particular, don't enter a previously estimated standard deviation in the **Enter s.d. if known** field. That's only for the (unusual) case in which a standard deviation is known, rather than having been estimated.

EViews conducts a standard *t*-test for this hypothesis, providing both the *t*-statistic and its associated *p*-value. In this case, the *p*-value tells us that *if* the true average LSAT in the applicant pool was 152, the probability of observing the mean LSAT found in our data, 158, is zero to four decimal places. Clearly, applicants to the University of Washington's (very good) law school are better than the average LSAT taker.

Hypothesis Testing for LSAT
Date: 12/20/06 Time: 17:30
Sample: 8651 10367 IF GPA>1 AND GPA<5 AND LSAT>100
Included observations: 1638
Test of Hypothesis: Mean = 152.0000

Sample Mean = 158.1221
Sample Std. Dev. = 7.792498

Method	Value	Probability
t-statistic	31.79660	0.0000

Buzzword hint: We'd say that the average UW applicant LSAT is **statistically significantly different** from the average of all test takers.

Tests By Classification

We know from our work earlier in the chapter that out-of-state applicants have a slightly higher average GPA than do in-state applicants. Is the difference statistically significant? Open the GPA series and use the menu **Equality Tests by Classification…** to get to the **Tests By Classification** dialog. We've filled out the **Series/Group for classify** field with the series WASH, since that's the classifying variable of interest.

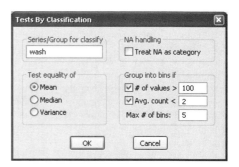

Since there are only two categories in this problem, in-state and out-, we need only look at the reported t-statistic and its associated p-value. If there were more than two categories, we would have to rely on the F-statistic; with exactly two categories, the F- is redundant with the t-.

While the difference between in-state and out-of-state GPAs is very small, statistically it's highly significant.

Test for Equality of Means of GPA
Categorized by values of WASH
Date: 12/06/06 Time: 14:08
Sample: 8651 10367 IF (GPA>1 AND GPA<5 AND LSAT>100)
Included observations: 1638

Method	df	Value	Probability
t-test	1636	2.966237	0.0031
Satterthwaite-Welch t-test*	1259.470	2.951673	0.0032
Anova F-test	(1, 1636)	8.798564	0.0031
Welch F-test*	(1, 1259.47)	8.712371	0.0032

*Test allows for unequal cell variances

Analysis of Variance

Source of Variation	df	Sum of Sq.	Mean Sq.
Between	1	1.164500	1.164500
Within	1636	216.5265	0.132351
Total	1637	217.6909	0.132982

Category Statistics

WASH	Count	Mean	Std. Dev.	Std. Err. of Mean
not WA res	1028	3.386349	0.361168	0.011265
WA res	610	3.331197	0.368199	0.014908
All	1638	3.365810	0.364666	0.009010

Hint: Finding a difference that is statistically significant but very small demonstrates the maxim that with enough data you can accurately identify differences too small for anyone to care about.

Statistical hint: The basic Anova F-test for differences of means assumes that the subpopulations have equal variances. Most introductory statistics classes also teach the Satterthwaite and Welch tests that allow for different variances for different subpopulations.

Time series tests

Five tests of the time-series properties of a series appear in the **View** menu. Exploring these tests would take us too far afield for now, but Correlograms and Unit Root Tests will be discussed in Chapter 13, "Serial Correlation—Friend or Foe?"

Correlogram...
Long-run Variance...
Unit Root Test...
Variance Ratio Test...
BDS Independence Test...

Describing Groups—Just the Facts—Putting It Together

Many of the descriptive features for groups are the same as those for series—except done for each of the series in the group. For example, the descriptive statistics menu for a group offers two choices: **Common Sample**, **Individual Samples**. The choices produce basic descriptive statistics for each series, with two different arrangements for choosing the sample.

<u>C</u>ommon Sample

<u>I</u>ndividual Samples

If you want the same set of observations to go into computing the statistics for each series in the group, be sure to specify **Common Sample**. Using **Individual Samples**, we can see that there were quite a few applicants with valid LSAT scores but not valid GPAs (1707 versus 1638 observations). As a guess, this could reflect applications from undergraduate schools that don't compute grade point averages.

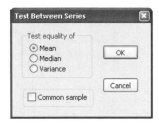

	GPA	LSAT
Mean	3.365810	157.9912
Median	3.420000	159.0000
Maximum	4.100000	180.0000
Minimum	1.910000	126.0000
Std. Dev.	0.364666	7.886239
Skewness	-0.765923	-0.561533
Kurtosis	3.588749	3.596309
Jarque-Bera	183.8092	114.9994
Probability	0.000000	0.000000
Sum	5513.197	269691.0
Sum Sq. Dev.	217.6909	106100.9
Observations	1638	1707

The **Tests of Equality...** view for groups checks whether the mean (or median, or variance) is the same for all the series in the group. (The tests assume that the series are statistically independent.) Here too, you can be sure the same observations are used from each series by picking **Common sample**.

Test Between Series

Test equality of
- Mean
- Median
- Variance

Common sample

OK

Cancel

> Hint: Use **Tests For Descriptive Statistics/Simple Hypothesis Tests** for each individual series to test for a specific value, say that the mean equals 3.14159. Use **Tests For Descriptive Statistics/Equality Tests By Classification...** to test that different subpopulations have the same mean for a series. Use **Tests of Equality...** for groups to see if the mean is equal for different series.

Correlations

It's easy to find the covariances or correlations of all the series in a group by choosing the **Covariance Analysis...** view. By default, EViews will display the covariance matrix for the common samples in the group, but you may instead compute correlations, use individual samples, or compute various other measures of the associations and related test statistics. For example, to compute using individual samples, you

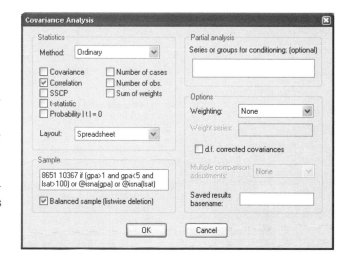

should uncheck the Balanced sample (listwise deletion) box. This setting instructs EViews to compute the covariance or correlation for the first two series using the observations available for both series, then the correlation between series one and series three using the observations available for those two series (in other words, not worrying whether observations are missing for series two), *etc.*

Here, we see the correlation for the two series in the group. Surprisingly, LSAT and GPA are not all that highly correlated. A correlation of only 0.307 means that the information in LSAT is not redundant with the information in GPA, which is why law schools look at both test scores and grades.

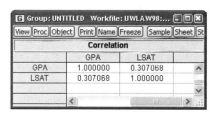

People use correlations a lot more because correlations are unit-free, while the units of covariances depend on the units of the underlying series.

> Hint: Should one use a common sample or not? EViews requires a choice in several of the procedures we're looking at in this chapter.
>
> The most common practice is to find a common sample to use for the entire analysis. That way you know that different answers from different parts of the analysis reflect real differences rather than different inputs. On the other hand, restricting the analysis to a common sample can mean ignoring a lot of data. So there's no absolute right or wrong answer. It's a judgment call.

Cross-Tabs

Cross-tabulation is a traditional method of looking at the relationship between categorical variables. In the simplest version, we build a table in which rows represent one variable and columns another, and then we count how many observations fall into each box. For fun, we've created categorical variables describing grades (4.0 or better, above average but not 4.0, below average) and test scores (above average, below average) with the following commands:

```
series gradecat = (gpa>=4)*1 + (gpa>3.365 and gpa<4)*2 +
    (gpa<=3.365)*3
series testcat = (lsat>158)*1 + (lsat<=158)*2
```

Since GRADECAT is arbitrarily coded as 1, 2, or 3 and TESTCAT is similarly, arbitrarily coded as 1 or 2, we added a value map to each series to make the tables easier to read. See *What Are Your Values?* in Chapter 4, "Data—The Transformational Experience."

Choosing the **N-Way Tabulation...** view and accepting the defaults in the **Crosstabulation** dialog produces the output shown to the right. Let's begin with the table appearing at the bottom.

Table Facts

The first column of the table gives counts for high test-scoring applicants: 5 had top grades, 552 had high—but not "top"—grades, and 306 had low grades—for a total of 863 applicants with "high" (*i.e.*, above average) test scores. Reading across the first row, 5 of the students with top grades had high LSATs, 5 were below average—so there was a total of 10 students with top grades.

```
Tabulation of GRADECAT and TESTCAT
Date: 12/20/06  Time: 17:45
Sample: 8651 10367 IF (GPA>1 AND GPA<5 AND LSAT>100)
Included observations: 1638
Tabulation Summary
```

Variable	Categories
GRADECAT	3
TESTCAT	2
Product of Categories	6

Measures of Association	Value
Phi Coefficient	0.189111
Cramer's V	0.189111
Contingency Coefficient	0.185817

Test Statistics	df	Value	Prob
Pearson X2	2	58.57944	0.0000
Likelihood Ratio G2	2	58.86830	0.0000

Note: Expected value is less than 5 in 16.67% of cells (1 of 6).

Count		TESTCAT		
		High	Low	Total
	Top	5	5	10
GRADECAT	High	552	350	902
	Low	306	420	726
	Total	863	775	1638

Hint: The intersection of a row and column is called a *cell*. For example, there are 350 applicants in the High grade/Low test score cell.

The bottom row reports the totals for each column and the right-most column reports the totals for each row. The Total-Total, bottom right, is the number of observations used in the table.

Table Interpretation

In this applicant pool, there were 5 students with perfect grades and below average LSATs. That's a true fact—but so what? We might be interested in getting counts, but usually what we're trying to do is find out if one variable is related to another. For the data in hand, the obvious question is "Do high test scores and high grades go together?" To begin to answer this question, we return to the **N-Way Tabulation...** menu, this time checking **Table %**, **Row %**, and **Column %** in the **Crosstabulation** dialog.

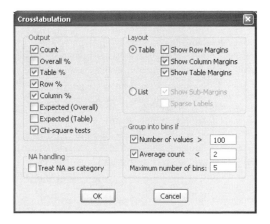

Take a look at the Top grade/Low test score cell again. The first number in the cell tells us, as before, that five applicants had this combination of grade and LSAT. But now we have three additional numbers. The first new number, marked ①, is the Table %, 0.31% (= 5/1638), which tells us the fraction of observations falling in this cell out of all the observations in the table. The Row %, ②, tells us what fraction of top grades (the row) also have low test scores (5/10.) Analogously, the last element in the cell, ③, is the Column % (5/775).

In the same way, table, row, and column percentage are given in the Total column at the right and Total row at the bottom. Looking at the right, we see that perfect grades came from 0.61% of all applicants; that 100% of applicants with perfect grades had perfect grades (telling us that everything in the row is in the row, which isn't very surprising); and that 0.61% of this column had perfect grades (which we already knew from the table % in this cell.)

Tabulation of GRADECAT and TESTCAT
Date: 12/20/06 Time: 17:49
Sample: 8651 10367 IF (GPA>1 AND GPA<5 AND LSAT>100)
Included observations: 1638
Tabulation Summary

Variable	Categories
GRADECAT	3
TESTCAT	2
Product of Categories	6

Measures of Association	Value
Phi Coefficient	0.189111
Cramer's V	0.189111
Contingency Coefficient	0.185817

Test Statistics	df	Value	Prob
Pearson X2	2	58.57944	0.0000
Likelihood Ratio G2	2	58.86830	0.0000

Note: Expected value is less than 5 in 16.67% of cells (1 of 6).

Count % Table % Row % Col		TESTCAT		
		High	Low	Total
	Top	5 0.31 50.00 0.58	5 0.31 ① 50.00 ② 0.65 ③	10 0.61 100.00 0.61
GRADECAT	High	552 33.70 61.20 63.96	350 21.37 38.80 45.16	902 55.07 100.00 55.07
	Low	306 18.68 42.15 35.46	420 25.64 57.85 54.19	726 44.32 100.00 44.32
	Total	863 52.69 52.69 100.00	775 47.31 47.31 100.00	1638 100.00 100.00 100.00

Hint: The row and column percentages given in the Total column and row are sometimes called *marginals* because they give the univariate empirical distribution for grade and test score respectively. So the row and column percentages correspond to the marginal probability distributions of the *joint* probability distribution described by the table as a whole.

Suppose that doing well on the LSAT and having good grades were independent. We'd expect that the percentage of students having both top grades and low test scores would be roughly the overall percentage having top grades times the overall percentage having low test scores. For our data we'd expect $0.61\% \times 47.31\% = 0.2886\%$ to fall into this cell. In fact 0.31 % do fall into this cell—the difference might easily be due to random variation. We could do the same calculation for all the cells and use this as a basis for a formal test of the hypothesis that grades and test scores are independent. That's exactly what's done in the lines marked "Test Statistics" which appear above the table. Formally, if the two series were independent, then the reported test statistics would be approximately χ^2 with the indicated degrees of freedom. The column marked "Prob" gives p-values. So despite what we found in the Top grade/Low test cell, the typical cell percentage is sufficiently different from the product of the marginal percentages that the hypothesis of independence is strongly rejected.

Statistics hint: It's not uncommon to find many cells containing very few observations. As a rule of thumb, when cells are expected to have fewer than five observations, the use of χ^2 test statistics gets a little dicey. In such cases EViews prints a warning message, as it's done here.

N-Way Tabulation with N>2

With two series in a group, the cells are laid out in a two-dimensional rectangle, with the categories for the first series going down and categories for the second series going across. With three series, EViews displays a three-dimensional hyper-rectangle. With four series, the display is a four-dimensional hyper-rectangle, *etc.*

Fortunately, EViews is very clever at detecting older equipment. If you are still using a display limited to two dimensions, rather than one of the newer Romulan units, EViews splits the hyper-rectangle into a series of two-dimensional slices.

As an example, open a group with GRADECAT, TESTCAT, and WASH to add the effect of in-state residency into the mix. Then choose **N-Way Tabulation...** (Reporting of test statistics is turned off simply because the output became very long.)

The first table shows counts for grades and test scores for non-residents. For example, there were four out-of-state residents with top grades and low test scores. The second table gives the same information for Washington residents. Together, these tables describe the *joint* distribution of grades and test scores *conditional* on residency.

The third table gives the joint distribution of grades and test scores, *unconditionally* with respect to residency. In other words, it's the same two-way table we saw before.

You can see that with lots of categories, an N-Way tabulation can be really, really long. If our last series had been 50 states instead of just yes/no for Washington, we'd have gotten 50 conditional tables and one unconditional table. You can imagine how much output there would be with a fourth or fifth variable in the cross-tabulation.

```
Tabulation of GRADECAT and TESTCAT and WASH
Date: 12/20/06  Time: 17:53
Sample: 8651 10367 IF (GPA>1 AND GPA<5 AND LSAT>100)
Included observations: 1638
Tabulation Summary
```

Variable	Categories
GRADECAT	3
TESTCAT	2
WASH	2
Product of Categories	12

Table 1: Conditional table for WASH=0:

Count			TESTCAT High	Low	Total
	Top		5	4	9
GRADECAT	High		372	217	589
	Low		204	226	430
	Total		581	447	1028

Table 2: Conditional table for WASH=1:

Count			TESTCAT High	Low	Total
	Top		0	1	1
GRADECAT	High		180	133	313
	Low		102	194	296
	Total		282	328	610

Table 3: Unconditional table:

Count			TESTCAT High	Low	Total
	Top		5	5	10
GRADECAT	High		552	350	902
	Low		306	420	726
	Total		863	775	1638

Does the order in which the series appear in the group matter? The answer is "no and yes." Whatever order you specify, you get all the possible conditional cell counts. Since you get the same information regardless of the order specified, there's a sense in which the order is irrelevant. (However, which unconditional tables are shown does depend on the order.) However, the series order does affect readability. It generally makes sense to put first the variables you're most interested in comparing. These will be the ones that show up together on each table.

Another approach to improved readability is to arrange series for the easiest screen display. The two rules are:

- The second series should have sufficiently few categories such that the categories can go across the top of the table without forcing you to scroll horizontally. (If you're going to print, think about the width of your paper instead of the width of the screen.)

- The first series should have as many categories as possible. It's easier to look at one long table rather than many short tables. This rule is sometimes limited by the desire to get a complete table to fit vertically on a screen or printed page.

Hint: Sometimes you can get a more useful table by printing in landscape rather than portrait mode.

Hint: Sometimes, when there are too many tables to manage visually, you should stop and think about whether there are also too many tables to help you learn anything.

True Story to End the Chapter

When the author was a college student, he worked as a research assistant for a professor from whom he learned a great deal about many things. One incident was particularly memorable. We had turned in a report, including relevant cross-tabulations, to the government agency which had paid for the research project. Shortly thereafter, a somewhat snippy letter came back pointing out that our analysis had covered a dozen (or so) variables and that the contract required cross-tabulations of *all* the variables, not just those that the research team thought mattered. And that we'd *better* comply. The letter was turned over to me.

I found my mentor the next day and pointed out that the sponsoring agency was asking for about one million pages of printout. He laughed. Told me to mail them the first thousand pages without comment, and said we'd never hear back. I did, and we didn't.

Chapter 8. Forecasting

Prediction is very difficult, especially about the future.
-Niels Bohr

Think what an easier time Bohr would have had if he'd had EViews, instead of just a Nobel prize in physics!

Truth-be-told, the design of a good model on which to base a forecast can be "very difficult," indeed. EViews' role is to handle the *mechanics* of producing a forecast—it's up to the researcher to choose the model on which the forecasts are based. We'll start off with an example of just how remarkably easy the mechanics are, and then go over some of the more subtle issues more slowly.

Just Push the Forecast Button

Our goal is to forecast the growth rate of currency in the hands of the public, G. (You can find "currency.wf1" at the EViews website.) A line graph of the data in the series G appears to the right.

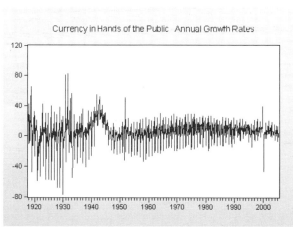

For this example, we're going to model currency growth as a linear function of a time trend, lagged currency growth, and a different constant for each month of the year. We need to estimate an equation for this model before we can make a forecast. Here's the relevant command:

```
ls g @trend g(-1) @expand(@month)
```

The estimation results look fine.

Now, to produce a forecast, *push the* Forecast *button*.

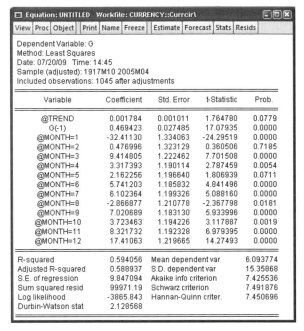

When the **Forecast** dialog opens, uncheck **Forecast graph** and **Forecast evaluation**. (We'll talk about these later.) Set the **Forecast sample** at the lower right to 2000 through the end of the sample. Hit OK .

You're done. The forecasts for G are stored in the series GF.

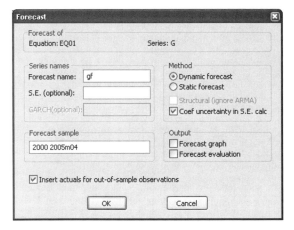

To see how well we did, let's plot actual and forecast currency growth together. Pretty good forecasting, no? Perhaps leaning a little too heavily on seasonal fluctuations, but basically pretty satisfactory.

You now know almost everything you need to forecast in EViews. (We told you the mechanics were easy!)

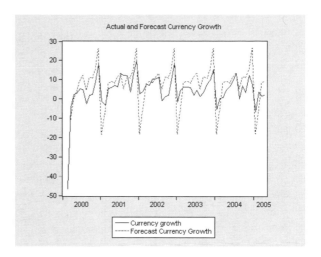

Theory of Forecasting

Let's review a little forecasting theory and then see where EViews fits in.

There are three steps to making an accurate forecast:

1. Formulate a sound model for the variable of interest.

2. Estimate the parameters attached to the explanatory variables.

3. Apply the estimated parameters to the values of the explanatory variables for the forecast period.

Let's call the variable we're trying to forecast y. Suppose that a good way to explain y is with the variable x and that we've decided on the model:

$$y_t = \alpha + \beta x_t + u_t,$$

where in our opening example, x would represent the time trend, lagged currency growth, *etc.*

Choosing a form for the model was Step 1. Now gather data on y_t and x_t for periods $t = 1 \ldots T$ and use one of EViews' myriad estimation techniques—perhaps least squares, but perhaps another method—to assign numerical estimates, $\hat{\alpha}$ and $\hat{\beta}$, to the parameters in the model. You can see the estimated parameters in the equation EQ01 above. That was Step 2.

Finally, let's say that we want to forecast y_τ at all the dates τ starting at T_F and continuing through T_L. This is the *forecast sample*, which is to say the entry marked **Forecast sample** in the lower left part of the **Forecast** dialog. Our forecast will be:

Forecast sample
2000m01 2005m04

$$\hat{y}_\tau = \hat{\alpha} + \hat{\beta} x_\tau$$

In other words, Step 3 consists of multiplying each estimated coefficient from Step 2 by the relevant x value in the forecast period, and then adding up the products. The formalism will turn out to be convenient for our discussion below. For now, let's use the example we've been working with to forecast for November 2004.

The "x" variables in our equation are a time trend, growth the previous month, and a set of dummy (0/1) variables for the month. To forecast, we need the values of each x variable and the estimated coefficient attached to that variable. The required data appear in the following table.

Table 3

x	Estimated Parameters	Value of x	Product
@TREND	0.001784	1047	1.87
$G_{2004m10}$	0.469423	3.4105	1.60
@MONTH = 11	8.321732	1.0	8.32
$\hat{G}_{2004m11}$			11.79
$G_{2004m11}$			12.42
forecast error			0.63

When you click the [Forecast] *button EViews does the same calculation—just faster and with some extra doo-dads available in the output.*

In-Sample and Out-Of-Sample Forecasts

In carrying out Step 3, there's an implicit issue that deserves explicit attention. Before we could start multiplying parameters times x variables in the table above we needed to know the values of x in *the forecast period*.

In our table, the value of @TREND is 1047, the month number in our data for November 2004. (We cheated and looked the number up by giving the command `show @trend`, which opens a spreadsheet view of @TREND.) The November value of lagged currency growth is the October currency growth number, 3.4105. And @MONTH = 11 always equals 1.0 in November.

Suppose we had estimated a better model that used the inflation rate as an explanatory variable? To carry out the forecast, we would need to know the November 2004 inflation rate. But suppose we were forecasting for November 2104? There's no way we're going to be able to plug in the right value of inflation 100 years from now. No inflation rate, no forecast.

The *cardinal rule of practical forecasting* is:

- Know the values of the explanatory variables during the forecast period—or know a way to forecast the required explanatory variables.

We'll return to "know a way to forecast the required explanatory variables" in the next section.

Knowing that you will have to deal with the cardinal rule in Step 3 sometimes influences what you do in Step 1. The corollary to the practical rule of forecasting is:

- *There's not much point in developing a great model for forecasting if you won't be able to carry out the forecast because you don't know the required future values of all of the explanatory variables.*

This aspect of model development is important, but doesn't really have anything to do with using EViews—so we'll leave it at that.

In our example above, we didn't have to face this issue because we were making an *in-sample forecast*; a forecast where $T_L \leq T$. We knew the values of all the explanatory variables for the forecast period because the forecast period was a subset of the estimation period. In-sample forecasting has two advantages: you always have the required data, and you can check the accuracy of your forecast by comparing it to what actually happened. We forecast 11.79 percent currency growth for November 2004. Currency growth was actually 12.42 percent, so the forecast error was a bit above a half a percent. Not too bad.

The alternative to in-sample forecasting is *out-of-sample forecasting*, where $T_F > T$. You have to obey the cardinal rule when forecasting out-of-sample. And sometimes, that's a problem because you lack out-of-sample values of some of the x variables. What's more, the history of forecasting is replete with examples that work well in-sample but fall apart out-of-sample. A common compromise is to *reserve* part of the data by not including it in the estimation sample, effectively pretending that the reserve sample is in the future. Then conduct an out-of-sample forecast over the reserved sample, taking advantage of the known values of the explanatory variables and observed outcomes. We'll walk through this sort of exercise in *Sample Forecast Samples*.

One other disadvantage of in-sample forecasting: It's really hard to get someone to pay you to forecast something that's already happened.

Practical hint: If you're like the author, you usually set up the range of your EViews workfile to coincide with your data sample. Then, when I forecast out-of-sample, I get an error message saying the forecast sample is out of range. When this happens to you, just double-click **Range** in the upper panel of the workfile window to extend the range to the end of your forecasting period.

Dynamic Versus Static Forecasting

Our currency data ends in April 2005. To forecast past that date we need to know the value for @TREND (no problem), which month we're forecasting for (no problem), and the value of currency growth in the month previous to the forecast month (maybe a problem). It's this lagged dependent variable that presents a problem/opportunity. If we're forecasting for May 2005, we're okay because we know the April value. But for June or later we don't have the lagged value of currency growth.

A *static forecast* uses the actual values of the explanatory variables in making the forecast. In our example, we can make static forecasts through May 2005, but no later.

A *dynamic forecast* uses the forecast value of lagged dependent variables in place of the actual value of the lagged dependent variables. If we start a forecast in May 2005, the dynamic forecast $\hat{g}_{2005\,m5}$ is identical to the static forecast. Both use $g_{2005\,m4}$ as an explanatory variable. The dynamic forecast for June uses $\hat{g}_{2005\,m5}$. The static forecast can't be computed because $g_{2005\,q5}$ isn't known.

> Hint: The "^" makes all the difference here. We always have $\hat{g}_{t-1}$ because that's the number we forecast in period $t-1$. We're just "rolling the forecasts forward." In contrast, once we're more than one period past the end of our data sample g_{t-1} is unknown.

The Role of the Forecast Sample

In practice, the difference between static and dynamic forecasting depends on both data availability and the specification of the forecast sample.

> Hint: The data used for the explanatory variables in either static or dynamic forecasting is not in any way affected by the sample period used for equation estimation.

Static forecasting uses values of explanatory variables from the forecast sample. If any of them are missing for a particular date, then nothing gets forecast for that date.

Dynamic forecasting pretends that you don't have any information about the dependent variable during the period covered by the sample forecast—even when you do have the relevant data. In the first period of the forecast sample, EViews uses the actual lagged dependent variables since these actual values are known. In the second period, EViews pretends it doesn't know the value of the lagged dependent variable and uses the value that it had just forecast for the first period. In the third period, EViews uses the value forecast for the second period. And so on. One of the nice things about dynamic forecasting is that the forecasts roll as far forward as you want—assuming, of course, that the future values of the other right-hand side series are also known.

> Mea-very-slightly-culpa: If you've been reading really, really closely you may have noticed that the forecast for November 2004 in the graph shown in *Just Push the Forecast Button* doesn't match the forecast in the table in *Theory of Forecasting*. The former was a dynamic forecast (because that's the EViews default) and the latter was a static forecast (because that's easier to explain).

Static Versus Dynamic in Practice

Static versus dynamic forecasting are used to simulate answers to two different questions.

Suppose in the future you are going to be tasked with forecasting next month's currency growth. When the date arrives you'll have all the necessary data to do a static forecast even though you don't have the data now. Doing a static forecast now simulates the process you'll be carrying out later.

In contrast, suppose you are going to be tasked with forecasting currency growth over the next 12 months. When the date arrives you'll have to do a dynamic forecast. Doing a dynamic forecast now simulates the process you'll be carrying out later.

One last practical detail. You instruct EViews to do a static or dynamic forecast by picking the appropriate radio button in the **Method** field of the **Forecast** dialog. Alternatively, the command `fit` produces a static forecast and the command `forecast` produces as dynamic forecast, as in:

```
forecast gf
```

> Hint: The **Structural (ignore ARMA)** option isn't relevant, in fact is grayed out, unless your equation has ARMA errors. See *Forecasting* in Chapter 13, "Serial Correlation—Friend or Foe?"

Sample Forecast Samples

To check how well your forecasting model works, you want to compare forecasts with what actually happens. One option is to wait until the future arrives and see how things turned out. But the standard procedure is to simulate data arrival by dividing your data sample into an artificial "history" and an artificial "future." Our monthly currency data runs from 1917 through 2005. We'll call the complete sample WHOLERANGE; treat most of the period as "history," HERODOTUS; and reserve the last few years for a "future history," HEINLEIN. If an equation estimated over HERODOTUS does a good job of forecasting HEINLEIN, then we can have some confidence that we can re-estimate over WHOLERANGE and then forecast out into the yet-unseen real future:

```
sample wholeRange @all

sample Herodotus @first 2000

sample Heinlein 2001 @last
```

'int not intended for Americans: Unless you were born in earshot of Bow bells, in which case it's 'oleRange, 'erodotus, and 'einlein—not that h'EViews will h'understand.

Using the command line, we create our forecasts with:

```
smpl herodotus

ls g @trend g(-1) @expand(@month)

smpl heinlein

fit ghein_stat

forecast ghein_dyn

plot g ghein_stat ghein_dyn
```

After a little touch up, our graph looks like this. The static and dynamic forecasts look similar and track actual currency growth well. So using this model to forecast the real future seems promising.

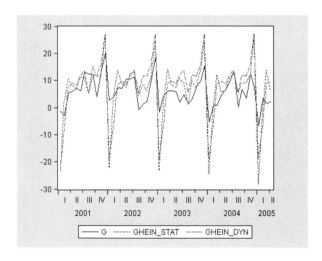

Setting the Sample in the Forecast Dialog

The forecast dialog can be used if you prefer it to typing commands. Enter the forecast sample, HEINLEIN, in the **Forecast sample** field. By default, **Insert actuals for out-of-sample observations** is checked. Under the default, EViews inserts observed G into GHEIN_DYN for data points that aren't included in the HEINLEIN sample. Uncheck this box to have NAs inserted instead. The advantage of inserting actuals is that it sometimes makes for a prettier plot of the forecast values. The

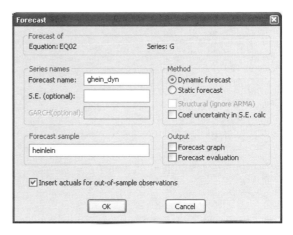

advantage of inserting NAs is that you won't accidentally think you forecasted the values outside HEINLEIN.

Facing the Unknown

So far, we've forecast a number for a particular date—a *point forecast*. There is always some degree of uncertainty around this point forecast. Assuming our model is correctly specified, such uncertainty derives from two sources: coefficient uncertainty and error uncertainty. Our forecast for date τ is $\hat{y}_\tau = \hat{\alpha} + \hat{\beta} x_\tau$ while the actual value of the series we're forecasting will be $y_\tau = \alpha + \beta x_\tau + u_\tau$. The forecast error will be $y_\tau - \hat{y}_\tau = [(\alpha - \hat{\alpha}) + (\beta - \hat{\beta}) x_\tau] + u_\tau$. The term in square brackets is the source of coefficient uncertainty. The error term at the forecast date, u_τ, causes error uncertainty. If you enter a name next to **S.E. (optional)** in the **Forecast** dialog, EViews will save the standard error of the forecast distribution in a series.

It's not unusual to ignore coefficient uncertainty in evaluating a forecast. If you want to exclude the effect of coefficient uncertainty, uncheck **Coef uncertainty in S.E. calc** in the dialog.

We've stored the standard error for our dynamic forecast including coefficient uncertainty as GHEIN_DYN_SE_ALL and analogously, without coefficient uncertainty, under GHEIN_DYN_SE_NOCOEF. Here's a plot of the forecast value and confidence bands, measured as the forecast minus 1.96 standard errors through the forecast plus 1.96 standard errors. You can see that the difference between the confidence intervals with and without coefficient uncertainty is all but invisible to the eye. That's one reason people often don't bother including coefficient uncertainty.

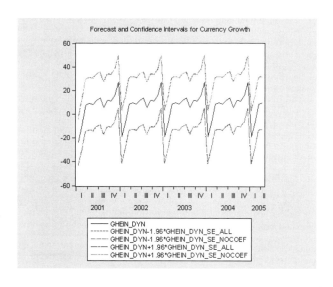

For the record, here's the command that produced the plot (before we added the title and tidied it up):

```
plot ghein_dyn ghein_dyn-1.96*ghein_dyn_se_all ghein_dyn-
    1.96*ghein_dyn_se_nocoef ghein_dyn+1.96*ghein_dyn_se_all
    ghein_dyn+1.96*ghein_dyn_se_nocoef
```

Hint: This plot shows *two* forecasts and *two* associated sets of confidence intervals. Usually, you want to see a single forecast and its confidence intervals. EViews can do that graph automatically, as we'll see next.

Forecast Evaluation

EViews provides two built-in tools to help with forecast evaluation: the **Output** field checkboxes **Forecast graph** and **Forecast evaluation**.

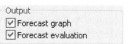

The **Forecast graph** option automates the 95% confidence interval plot.

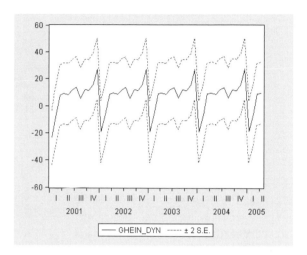

The **Forecast evaluation** option generates a small table with a variety of statistics for comparing forecast and actual values. The **Root Mean Squared Error** (or *RMSE*) is the standard deviation of the forecast errors. (See the *User's Guide* for explanations of the other statistics.)

Forecast: GHEIN_DYN
Actual: G
Forecast sample: 2001M01 2005M04
Included observations: 52

Root Mean Squared Error	8.544296
Mean Absolute Error	6.812486
Mean Absolute Percentage Error	417.2360
Theil Inequality Coefficient	0.391672
Bias Proportion	0.027178
Variance Proportion	0.498255
Covariance Proportion	0.474567

Our forecasts aren't bad, but the confidence intervals shown in the graph above are fairly wide given the observed movement of G. Similarly, the RMSE is not small compared to the standard deviation of G. Looking back at our plot of out-of-sample forecasts versus actuals, one is struck with the fact that the forecasts take wider swings than the data. In the data plot that opened the chapter, you can see that the volatility of currency growth was much greater in the pre-War period than it was post-War. The HERODOTUS sample includes both periods. To get an accurate estimate, and thus an accurate forecast, we like to use as much data as possible. On the other hand, we don't want to include old data if the parameters have changed.

We can rely on a visual inspection of the plots we've made, or we can use a more formal Chow test, which confirms that a change has occurred. (Once again, see the *User's Guide*).

Chow Breakpoint Test: 1950M01
Null Hypothesis: No breaks at specified breakpoints
Varying regressors: All equation variables
Equation Sample: 1917M10 2000M12

F-statistic	21.43691	Prob. F(14,965)	0.0000
Log likelihood ratio	268.8960	Prob. Chi-Square(14)	0.0000
Wald Statistic	300.1167	Prob. Chi-Square(14)	0.0000

If we define an "alternate history" with:

```
sample turtledove 1950 2000

smpl turtledove
```

and re-estimate, we find much smaller seasonal effects and a much higher R^2 in the TURTLEDOVE world than there was according to HEROTODUS.

Glance back at the data plot which opened the chapter. It shows an enormous increase in currency holdings right before the turn of the millennium and a huge drop immediately thereafter. This means that a dynamic forecast starting in the beginning of 2000 uses an anomalous value for lagged G, a problem which is carried forward. In contrast, a static forecast should only have difficulty at the beginning of the forecast period, since thereafter actual lagged G picks up non-anomalous data.

Using this new estimate, shown above to the right, as a basis for a static forecast through the HEINLEIN period, we can set the **Forecast** dialog to save a new forecast, to plot the forecast and confidence intervals, and to show us a new forecast evaluation.

Dependent Variable: G
Method: Least Squares
Date: 12/21/06   Time: 10:20
Sample: 1950M01 2000M12
Included observations: 609

	Coefficient	Std. Error	t-Statistic	Prob.
@TREND	0.009030	0.001215	7.434780	0.0000
G(-1)	0.197162	0.038897	5.068770	0.0000
@MONTH=1	-25.18144	1.216892	-20.69324	0.0000
@MONTH=2	-14.56611	1.347144	-10.81259	0.0000
@MONTH=3	2.035356	1.289985	1.577814	0.1151
@MONTH=4	2.033843	1.055585	1.926744	0.0545
@MONTH=5	-0.393807	1.058826	-0.371928	0.7101
@MONTH=6	4.175762	1.056299	3.953199	0.0001
@MONTH=7	3.546868	1.072860	3.305992	0.0010
@MONTH=8	-7.270580	1.075108	-6.762652	0.0000
@MONTH=9	-2.267576	1.082829	-2.094121	0.0367
@MONTH=10	-1.229835	1.065826	-1.153881	0.2490
@MONTH=11	8.220668	1.061750	7.742565	0.0000
@MONTH=12	13.73250	1.105398	12.42313	0.0000

R-squared	0.812980	Mean dependent var	6.020335
Adjusted R-squared	0.808894	S.D. dependent var	11.36449
S.E. of regression	4.968062	Akaike info criterion	6.066657
Sum squared resid	14685.57	Schwarz criterion	6.168078
Log likelihood	-1833.297	Hannan-Quinn criter.	6.106112
Durbin-Watson stat	2.070689		

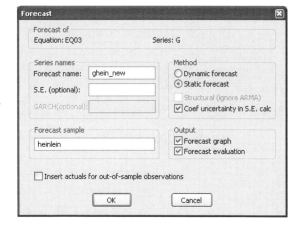

When the **Forecast graph** and the **Forecast evaluation** options are both checked, EViews puts the confidence interval graph and statistics together in one window. We've definitely gotten a bit of improvement from changing the sample.

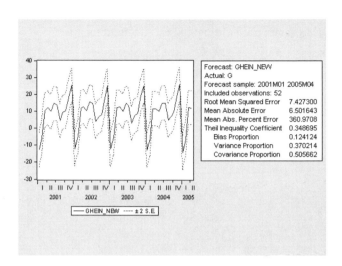

One last plot. The seasonal forecast swings are still somewhat larger than the actual seasonal effects, but the forecast is really pretty good for such a simple model.

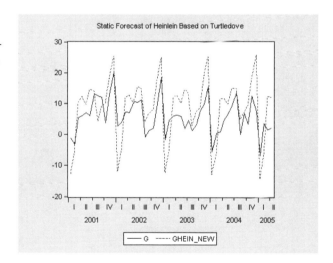

Forecasting Beneath the Surface

Sometimes the variable you want to forecast isn't quite the variable on the left of your estimating equation. There are often statistical or economic modeling reasons for estimating a transformed version of the variable you really care about. Two common examples are using logs (rather than levels) of the variable of interest, and using first differences of the variable of interest.

In the example we've been using, we've taken our task to be forecasting currency growth. If you look at the label for our series G (see *Label View* in Chapter 2, "EViews—Meet Data"), you'll see it was derived from an underlying series for the level of currency, CURR, using the command "series g = 1200*dlog(curr)". Since the function dlog takes first differences of logarithms, we actually made both of the transformations just mentioned.

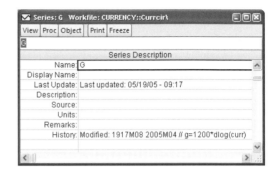

Instead of forecasting growth rates, we could have been asked to forecast the level of currency. In principle, if you know today's currency level and have a forecast growth rate, you can forecast next period's level by adding projected growth to today's level. In practice, doing this can be a little hairy because for more complicated functions it's not so easy to work backward from the estimated function to the original variable, and because forecast confidence intervals (see below) are nonlinear. Fortunately, EViews will handle all the hard work if you'll cooperate in one small way:

- Estimate the forecasting equation using an auto-series on the left in place of a regular series.

As a regular series, the information that G was created from "g = 1200*dlog(curr)" is a historical note, but there isn't any live connection. If we use an auto-series, then EViews understands—and can work with—the connection between CURR and the auto-series. We could use the following commands to define an auto-series and then estimate our forecasting equation:

```
frml currgrowth=1200*dlog(curr)
ls currgrowth @trend currgrowth(-1) @expand(@month)
```

When we hit ⟨Forecast⟩ in the equation window, we get a **Forecast** dialog that looks just a little different. The default choice in the dropdown menu is **Ignore formulae within series**, which means to forecast the auto-series, currency growth in this case.

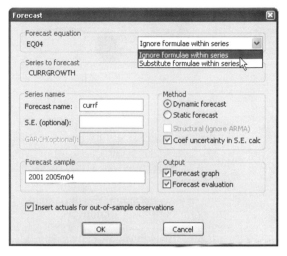

The alternative choice is **Substitute formulae within series**. Choose this option and you're offered the choice of forecasting either the underlying series or the auto-series. We've chosen to forecast the level of currency (and set the forecast sample to match the forecast sample in the previous example).

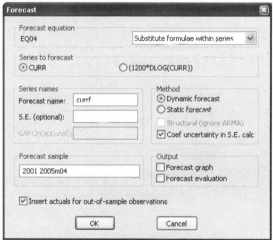

Hint: If you use an expression, for example "1200*dlog(curr)", rather than a named auto-series as the dependent variable, you get pretty much the same choices, although the dialogs look a little different.

Our currency forecast is shown to the right. Note that the forecast turns out to be a little too high.

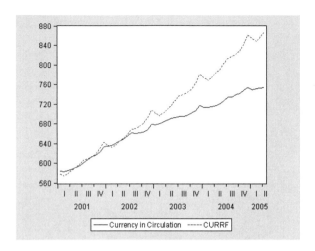

Quick Review—Forecasting

EViews is in charge of the mechanics of forecasting; you're in charge of figuring out a good model. You need to think a little about in-sample versus out-of-sample forecasts and dynamic versus static forecasts. Past that, you need to know how to push the Forecast button.

Chapter 9. Page After Page After Page

An EViews workfile is made up of *pages*. Pages extend our ability to organize and analyze data in powerful ways. Some of these extensions are available with nothing more than a single mouse click, while others require quite a bit of thought. This chapter starts with a look at the easy extensions and gradually works its way through some of the more sophisticated applications.

As a practical matter, most workfiles have only a single page, and you'll never even notice that the page is there. We think of a workfile as a collection of data series and other objects all stuffed together for easy access. In some technical sense, the default workfile contains a single page and all the series, *etc.*, are inside that page. Because almost all EViews operations work on the active page, and because when there is only one page that's the page that's active, the page is effectively transparent in a single-page workfile. In other words, you don't *have* to know about this stuff.

On the other hand, flipping pages can be habit forming. Pages let you do a variety of neat stuff like:

- Pull together unrelated data for easy accessibility. (Easiest)

- Hold multiple frequency data (*e.g.*, both annual and quarterly) in a single workfile. (Easy)

- Link data with differing identifier series into a single analysis. (Moderate)

- Data reduction. (Moderate to hard)

Pages Are Easy To Reach

Every EViews workfile has at least one page. Page names appear as a series of tabs at the bottom of the workfile window. When a workfile is created it contains a single page usually titled "Untitled." You can tell that **Untitled** is the active page—not only because it's the only page there is, but also because the tab for the active page is displayed with a white background and slightly in front of the other tabs.

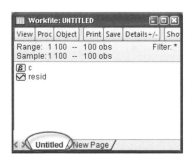

Clicking on a page tab makes that page active. What we see in the workfile window is actually the contents of the active page. For example, choosing the **CPS** tab in the workfile "CPSMar2004 With Pages.wf1" displays data on 136,879 individuals.

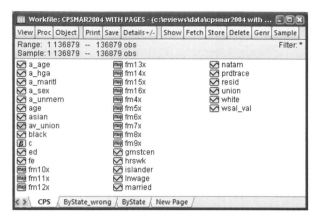

Click instead on the **ByState** tab and we see data on states instead. Both sets of data are stored in the same workfile. Typically we work with one data set at a time, but one of the things we do in this chapter is show how to link data from one workfile page to another.

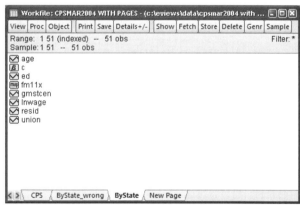

Creating New Pages

To add a second page to a workfile, click on the **New Page** tab to bring up a menu with a number of options. Three of the menu options represent standard methods that are similar to creating a workfile, except that what you actually get is a page within a workfile instead of a new, separate workfile. (We'll get to the other two options later in the chapter.)

Specify by Frequency/Range …
Specify by Identifier Series …
Copy/Extract from Current Page ▸
Load Workfile Page…
Paste from Clipboard as Page

Cancel

Creating A New Page From Scratch

Choosing **Specify by Frequency/Range...**
brings up the familiar **Workfile Create** dialog. You'll see that the field for the workfile
name is greyed out, since you're creating a
page rather than a workfile.

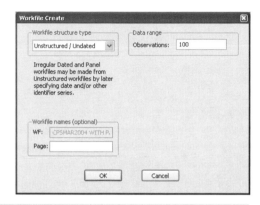

Hint: The **Workfile Create** dialog always gives you the opportunity to name the page
being created, even if you're setting up a separate workfile rather than a page as in this
example. If you leave the **Page** field blank, EViews assigns "Untitled" or "Untitled1,"
etc., for the page name.

Creating A New Page From Existing Data

Paste from Clipboard as Page creates an untitled page by reading the data on the clipboard.
Paste from Clipboard as Page is analogous to right-clicking in an empty area of the EViews
window and choosing **Paste as new Workfile**, except that you get a page within the existing workfile rather than a new, separate workfile.

You can achieve the same effect without using the clipboard by dragging a source file and
dropping it on the **New Page** tab. A plus (" + ") sign will appear when your cursor is over an
appropriate area.

Load Workfile Page... reads an existing workfile from the disk and copies each page in the
disk workfile into a separate page in the active workfile.

Hint: The name **Load Workfile Page...** notwithstanding, this command is perfectly
happy to load data from Excel, text files, or any of the many other formats that EViews
can read. It's not limited to workfiles.

Creating A New Page Based On An Existing Page

Copy/Extract from Current Page brings up a cascading
menu with the two choices shown to the right. The two
options do essentially the same thing. We'll defer a discus-

By Link to New Page...
By Value to New Page or Workfile...

sion of "links" until the section *Wholesale Link Creation* later in this chapter, looking first at **By Value to New Page or Workfile...**.

Copy/Extract from Current Page copies data from the active workfile page into a new page (or a standalone workfile, if you prefer). The command is straightforward once you get over the name. This menu is accessed by clicking on the **New Page** tab, but "Current Page" doesn't mean the new page attached to the tab you just clicked on—it means the currently active page. Just pretend that the command is named **Copy/Extract from *Active* Page**.

Choosing **By Value to New Page or Workfile...** opens the **Workfile Copy By Value** dialog, which has two tabs. The first tab you see, **Extract Spec**, controls what's going to be copied from the active page. By default, everything is copied. If you like, you can change the sample, change which objects are copied, or tell EViews to copy only a random subsample.

The tab **Page Destination** lets you give the about-to-be-created page a name of your choice. This is also the spot for telling EViews whether you want a new workfile or a page in the existing workfile.

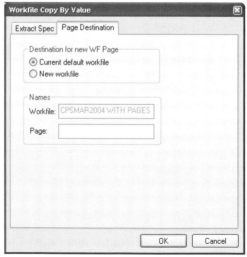

If all you want to do is copy the contents of the existing page into a new page, simply dragging the page tab and dropping it on the **New Page** tab of any workfile. A plus (" + ") sign will appear when your cursor is over an appropriate area.

Messing up hint: EViews doesn't have an Undo function. When you're about to make a bunch of changes to your data and you'd like to leave yourself a way to back out, consider using **Copy/Extract from Current Page** to make a copy of the active page. Then make the trial changes on the copy. If things don't work out, you still have the original data unharmed on the source page.

Renaming, Deleting, and Saving Pages

To rename, delete, or save a page, right-click on the page tab to bring up a context menu with choices to let you—no surprises here—rename, delete, or save the page. The only mild subtlety is that saving a page actually saves an entire workfile containing that page as its only contents. You can also save a page as a workfile on the disk by using the **Proc/Save Current Page...** menu.

Rename Workfile Page...
Delete Workfile Page
Save Workfile Page ...

Cancel

Hint: **Save Workfile Page...** will write Excel files, text files, *etc.*, as well as EViews workfiles.

Backwards compatibility hint: The page feature was first introduced in EViews 5. There are three options if you want a friend with an earlier version to be able to read the data:

- Tell them to upgrade to the current release. There are lots of nifty new features.

- Early versions of EViews will read the first page of a multi-page workfile just fine, but ignore all other pages. So if the workfile has only a single page or if the page of interest is the first one created (the left-most page on the row of page tabs), then there's no problem. If not, you can reorder the pages by dragging the page tabs and dropping them in the desired position. Keep in mind that when reading a file, earlier versions ignore object types that hadn't yet been invented when the earlier version was released.

- Use **Save Workfile Page...** to save the page of interest in a standalone workfile.

Multi-Page Workfiles—The Most Basic Motivation

We'll get to some fancy uses of pages shortly. But don't overlook the simplest reason for using multi-page workfiles: If you have sets of data that you want to keep in one collection, just make each one a page in a workfile. As in the example appearing to the right, it's perfectly okay if the sets of data are unrelated.

To use a particular page, click on the appropriate tab at the bottom of the workfile window, and you're in business.

Multiple Frequencies—Multiple Pages

In Chapter 2, "EViews—Meet Data," we wrote

> Hint: Every variable in an EViews workfile shares a common identifier series. You can't have one variable that's measured in January, February, and March and a different variable that's measured in the chocolate mixing bowl, the vanilla mixing bowl, and the mocha mixing bowl.
>
> Subhint: Well, yes actually, you can. EViews has quite sophisticated capabilities for handling both mixed frequency data and panel data. These are covered later in the book.

It is now "later in the book."

All the data in a *page within a workfile* share a common identifier. For example, one page might hold quarterly data and another might hold annual data. So if you want to keep both quarterly and annual data in one workfile, set up two pages. Even better, you can easily copy data from one page to another, *converting frequencies as needed*.

> Hint: EViews will convert between frequencies automatically, or you can specify your preferred conversion method. More on this below.

The workfile "US Output.wf1" (available on the EViews website) holds data on the U.S. Index of Industrial Production (IP) and on real Gross Domestic Product (RGDP). In contrast to GDP numbers, which are computed quarterly, industrial production numbers are available monthly. For this reason, industrial production is the output measure of choice for comparison with monthly series such as unemployment or inflation. Since the industrial production numbers are available more often and sooner, they're also used to predict GDP. Our task is to use industrial production to forecast GDP.

> Hint: http://research.stlouisfed.org/fred2/ is an excellent source for U.S. macroeconomic data. Among other virtues, FRED can make you an Excel file that EViews will read in about two seconds flat.

> 'nother hint: You can use EViews to search and read data directly from FRED. Select **File/Open/Database...** from the main EViews menu and select **FRED database**. EViews will open a window for examining the FRED database – click on the **Easy Query** button to search the database for series using names, descriptions, or other characteristics. Once you find the desired series, highlight the series names and right-mouse click or drag-and-drop to send the data into a new or existing workfile. See the *User's Guide* for more detail.

Initially, our workfile has two pages. **Indpro** has monthly industrial production data and **Gdpc96** has quarterly GDP data.

To analyze the relation between RGDP and IP, we have to get them into the same page for two reasons:

- Mechanically, only one page is active at a time, so everything we want to use jointly had better be on that page.

- To relate one series to another, at least if we want to use a regression, observations have to match up. This implies that *all the series in a regression need to have the same identifier and therefore the same frequency.*

EViews provides a whole toolkit of ways to move series between pages and to convert frequencies, which we'll take a look at now.

Copy-and-Paste and Drag-and-Drop

Let's decide to work at a monthly frequency. One approach is to click on the **Gdpc96** page tab to make it the active page, then select RGDP and use the right-click context menu to copy.

Next, click to activate on the **Indpro** page and paste.

Equivalently, you can copy RGDP by drag-and-drop the RGDP icon onto the **Indpro** tab. The icon will display a small plus sign when it is ready to be dropped.

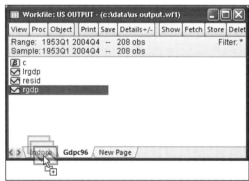

However you copy the data, RGDP appears in the **Indpro** page (not shown). A dual-scale graph gives a quick look at how the two series relate.

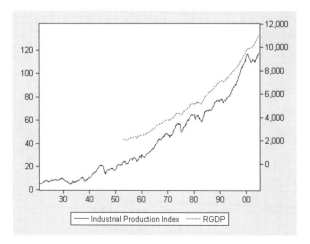

SIP and RGDP are measured in completely different units. IP is simply an index set to 100 in 1997. RGDP is annualized and measured in billions of 1996 dollars. To find a conversion formula, we regress the latter on the former. So when the industrial production number is announced each month, we can get a sneak preview of real GDP with the conversion:

$$RGDP = -338 + 92 \times IP.$$

Equation: UNTITLED   Workfile: US OUTPUT WITH CONVERSIONS::In...

View | Proc | Object | | Print | Name | Freeze | | Estimate | Forecast | Stats | Resids

Dependent Variable: RGDP
Method: Least Squares
Date: 07/20/09   Time: 14:03
Sample (adjusted): 1953M01 2004M12
Included observations: 624 after adjustments

Variable	Coefficient	Std. Error	t-Statistic	Prob.
C	-337.8523	28.48955	-11.85881	0.0000
IP	92.19392	0.417743	220.6954	0.0000

R-squared	0.987391	Mean dependent var	5420.800
Adjusted R-squared	0.987370	S.D. dependent var	2542.141
S.E. of regression	285.6898	Akaike info criterion	14.15089
Sum squared resid	50766806	Schwarz criterion	14.16511
Log likelihood	-4413.078	Hannan-Quinn criter.	14.15642
F-statistic	48706.48	Durbin-Watson stat	0.026340
Prob(F-statistic)	0.000000		

Up-Frequency Conversions

Hold on one second. If GDP is only measured quarterly, how did we manage to use GDP data in a monthly regression? After all, monthly GDP data doesn't exist!

If you were hoping the good data fairy waived her monthly data wand—and will do the same for you—well, sorry that's not what happened. Instead, EViews applied a *low-to-high frequency data conversion rule*. In this case, EViews used a default rule. Let's go over what rules are available, discuss how you can make your own choice rather than accept the default, and then look at how the defaults get set.

> Hint: *Low-to-high frequency* conversion means from annual-to quarterly, quarterly-to-monthly, annual-to-daily, *etc.*

As background, let's take a look at quarterly GDP values for the year 2004 and the monthly values manufactured by EViews.

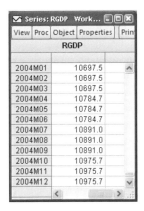

We can see that EViews copied the value of GDP in a given quarter into each month of that quarter. That's a reasonable thing to do. If all we know was that GDP in the first quarter was running at a rate of a trillion dollars a year, then saying that GDP was running at a trillion a year in January, a trillion a year in February, and a trillion a year in March seems like a good start.

What else could we have done? The full set of options is shown at the right. The first choice, **Specified in series**, isn't an actual conversion method: It signals to use whichever method is set as the default in the series being copied.

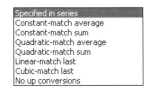

Constant-match average

In the case we're looking at, the conversion method applied (by default) was **Constant-match average**. This instruction parses into two parts: "constant" and "match average." "Constant" means uses the same number in each month in a quarter. "Match average" instructs EViews that the average monthly value chosen has to match the quarterly value for the corresponding quarter.

At this point you may be muttering under your breath, "What do these guys mean, 'the average monthly value?' There only is one monthly value." You have a good point! When converting from low-to-high frequency, saying "constant - match average" is just a convoluted way of saying "copy the value." As we've seen, that's exactly what happened above. Later, we'll see conversion situations where **constant-match average** is much more complex.

Constant-match sum

Suppose that instead of GDP measured at an annual rate, our low frequency variable happened to be total quarterly sales. In a conversion to monthly sales, we'd like the converted January, February, and March to add up to the total of first quarter sales. **Constant-match**

sum takes the low frequency number and divides it equally among the high frequency observations. If first quarter sales were 600 widgets, **Constant-match sum** would set January, February, and March sales to 200 widgets each.

Quadratic-match sum and Quadratic-match average

In 2004, GDP rose every quarter. It's a little strange to assume that GDP is constant across months within a quarter and then jumps at quarter's end. Quadratic conversion estimates a smooth, quadratic, curve using the data from the current quarter and the previous and succeeding quarters. This curve is then used to interpolate the data within the quarter. "Match average" forces the average of the interpolated numbers to match the original quarterly figure, while "match sum" matches on the sum of the generated high frequency numbers.

Linear-match last and Cubic-match last

Both **Linear-match last** and **Cubic-match last** begin by copying the quarterly (more generally, the low frequency source value) into the last monthly observation in the corresponding quarter (more generally, the last corresponding high frequency date). Values for the remaining months are set by linear interpolation between final-months-in-the-quarter for **Linear-match last** and by interpolating along natural cubic splines (see the *User's Guide* for a definition) for **Cubic-match last**.

Down-Frequency Conversions

There's something slightly unsatisfying about low-to-high frequency conversion, in that we're necessarily faking the data a little. There *isn't* any monthly GDP data. All we're doing is taking a reasonable guess. In contrast, high-to-low frequency conversion doesn't involve making up data at all.

If we copy IP from the monthly **Indpro** page and paste it into the quarterly **Gdpc96** page we see the following:

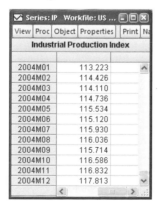
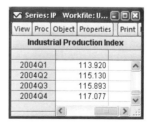

EViews has applied the default high-to-low frequency conversion procedure, which is to average the monthly observations within each quarter. The meanings of the high-to-low frequency conversion options are pretty straightforward. **Sum observations** adds up the monthly observations within a quarter. If we had sales for January, February, and March we would use a **Sum observations** conversion to get total first quarter sales. **First**, **Last**, **Max**, and **Min Observation** all pick out one month within the quarter and use the value for the quarterly value.

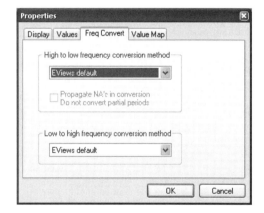

Hint: **First observation** and **Last observation** are especially useful in the analysis of financial price data, where point-in-time data are often preferred over time aggregated data.

Default Frequency Conversions

Every series has built-in default frequency conversions, one for high-to-low and one for low-to-high. These defaults are used when you copy-and-paste from one page or workfile to another. To change the default choices, open the series and click the [Properties] button. Choose the **Freq Convert** tab to access available choices.

The overall **EViews default** is changed using the menu **Options/General Options/Series and Alphas/Frequency Conversion...**.

Paste Special

Sometimes the default frequency conversion method isn't suitable. Instead of using **Paste** to paste a series, use **Paste Special** to bring up all the available conversion options. Drag-and-dropping after right-click selecting will also bring up the **Paste Special** menu.

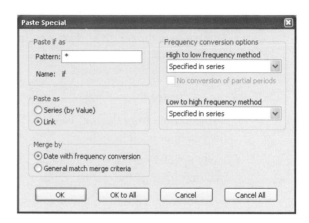

You can choose the conversion method from the fields on the right. In addition, you can enter a new name for the pasted series in the field marked **Pattern**.

Nothing limits copy-and-paste or copy-and-paste-special to a single series. The **Pattern** field lets you specify a general pattern for changing the name of the pasted series. For example, the pattern "*_quarterly" would paste the series X, Y, and Z as X_quarterly, Y_quarterly, and Z_quarterly. For further discussion, see the *User's Guide*.

Links—The Live Connection

Copies of data and the original source are related conceptually, but mechanically they're completely unlinked. Humans understand that a quarterly series for industrial production represents a view of an underlying monthly IP series. But as a mechanical matter, once the copying is done EViews no longer sees any connection between the quarterly data and the original monthly data. A practical consequence of this is that if you change the monthly source data—perhaps because of data revisions, perhaps because you discovered a typo— the derived quarterly data are unaffected. In contrast, EViews uses the concept of a "link" to create a live connection between series in two pages.

A *link* is a live connection. If you define a quarterly IP series as a link to the monthly IP series, EViews builds up an internal connection instead of making a copy of the data. Every time you use the quarterly series EViews retrieves the information from the monthly original, making any needed frequency conversions on the fly. Any change you make to the original will appear in the quarterly link as well.

Aesthetic hint: The icon for a series link, ☑, looks just like a regular series icon, except it's pink. If the link inside the series link is undefined or broken, you'll see a pink icon with a question mark, ?.

> Inconsequential hint: Links save computer memory because only one copy of the data is needed. They use extra computer time because the linked data has to be regenerated each time it's used. Modern computers have so much memory and are so fast that these issues are rarely of any consequence.

Links can be created in three ways:

- **Copy/Extract from Current Page/By Link to New Page…** creates a new page from the active page, linking the new series to the originals on a wholesale basis.

- **Paste Special** provides an option to paste in from the clipboard by linking instead of making copies of the original EViews series.

- Type the command `link` to link in just one series.

Wholesale Link Creation

We looked at the copy part of **Copy/Extract from Current Page** in the section *Creating New Pages*. We turn now to the **By Link to New Page…** option.

By Link to New Page… works just like **Value to New Page or Workfile…** except that links are made for each series instead of copying the values into disconnected series in the destination page. That's it.

> Hint: You can link between pages inside a workfile but not across different workfiles.

One-Or-More-At-A-Time Link Creation

The most common way of creating a link is by copying series on one page and then pasting special on the destination page. Inside the **Paste Special** dialog, choose **Link** in the **Paste as** field. Links for the series, with frequency conversions as specified, will be placed in the destination page.

Note that **Copy/Extract from Current Page** always uses the default frequency conversion for each series. **Paste Special** has the same default behavior, but provides an opportunity in the **Frequency conversion options** field to make an idiosyncratic choice.

Hint: If you've copied multiple series onto the clipboard, you can use the [OK] , [OK to All] , [Cancel] , and [Cancel All] buttons in the **Paste Special** dialog to paste the series in one at a time or to paste them in all at once.

Retail Link Creation

The methods above begin with an existing series, or a whole handful of existing series, and create links from them. You can also create a link in the active page by choosing the **Object** menu or the [Object] button and selecting **New Object.../Series Link.** Or you can type link in the command pane, optionally followed by a name for the link. If you specify a name, a new link appears in the workfile window, although the link isn't yet actually linked to anything. (If you don't specify a name, EViews pops open a view window for the new link and displays an annoying error message "*** Unable to Perform Link ***." Ignore the message and switch to the **Properties...** view.)

Click on the [Properties] button, switch to the **Link Spec** tab, and enter the source series and source workfile page in the **Link to** field. You can also specify the frequency method conversion to be used in the **Frequency conversion options** field.

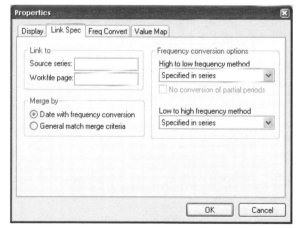

Unlinking

Suppose that the data in your source page is regularly updated, but you want to analyze a snapshot taken at a point in time in the destination page. To freeze the values being linked in, open the link and choose Proc or Object and **Unlink…**. Alternatively, with the workfile window active choose **Object/Manage Links & Formulae…**. The dialog lets you manage links and formulae in your workfile. The

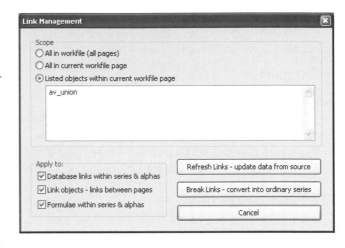

Break Links - convert into ordinary series button, detaches the specified links from their source data and converts them into regular numeric or alpha series using the current values. in all links or just those you list.

> Hint: Of course, you can use the `series` command:
>
>   series frozen_copy_of_series = linked_series
>
> to make a copy of a linked series as an alternative to breaking the link.

Have A Match?

One key to thinking about which data should be collected in a single EViews page is that all the series in a page share a common identifier. One page might hold quarterly series, where the identifier is the date. Another page might hold information about U.S. states, where the identifier might be the state name or just the numbers 1 through 50. What you can't have is one page where some series are identified by date and others are identified by state.

> Reminder: The identifier is the information that appears on the left in a spreadsheet view.

So far, the examples in this chapter have all used dates for identifiers. Because EViews has a deep "understanding" of the calendar, it knows how to make frequency conversions; for example, translating monthly data to quarterly data. So, while data of different frequencies needs to be held in different pages, linking between pages is straightforward.

What do you do when your data series don't all have an identifier in common? EViews provides a two-step procedure:

- Bring all the data which *does* share a common identifier into a page, creating as many different pages as there are identifiers.

- Use "match-merge" to connect data across pages.

The workfile "Infant Mortality Rate.wf1" holds two pages with data by state. The page **Mortality** contains infant mortality rates and the page **Revenue** contains per capita revenue. Is there a connection between the two? Excerpts of the data look like:

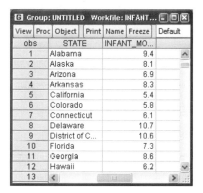

There are days when computers are incredibly annoying. The connection between pages is obvious to us, but not to the computer, because the observations aren't quite parallel in the two pages. The infant mortality data includes an observation for the District of Columbia; the revenue data doesn't. The identifier for the former is a list of observation numbers 1 through 51. For the latter, the identifier is observation numbers 1 through 50. Starting with Florida, there's no identifier in common between the two series because Florida is observation 10 in one page and observation 9 in the other page. Just matching observations by identifier won't work here. Something more sophisticated is needed.

Matching through Links

You can think of the match process as what computer scientists call a "table look-up." Each time we need a value for REV, we want EViews to go to the **Revenue** page and look up the value with the same state name in the **Mortality** page.

We understand that "state" is the meaningful link between the data in the two different pages. We'll tell EViews to bring the data from the **Revenue** page into the **Mortality** page by creating a *link*, and then filling in the **Properties** of the link with the information needed to make a match.

Click on the **Mortality** tab to activate the **Mortality** page. Then create a new link named REV using the menu **Object/New Object/Series Link**. The object ? rev appears in the workfile window with a pink background to indicate a link and a question mark showing that the link hasn't been specified. Double-clicking ? rev opens a view with an error message indicating that the properties of the link haven't been specified yet.

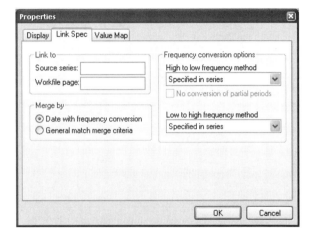

Click the Properties button and then the **Link Spec** tab. The default dialog asks about frequency conversions, which isn't what we need. Click the **General match merge criteria** radio button in the **Merge by** field.

Notice that we now have a new set of fields on the right side of the dialog. Fill out the dialog with the **Source series** and **Workfile page** in the **Link to** field. Since we want to match observations that have the same state names, enter STATE in both the **Source index** and **Destination index** fields. When you close the dialog you'll see that the link icon has switched to ☑ rev , indicating that the link is now complete.

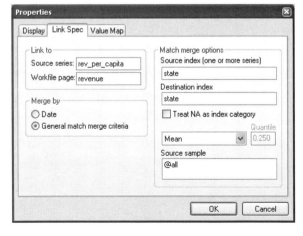

Hint: You may find it more intuitive to think of the **Link to** field as the "Link from" field. Remember that you're specifying the data source here. The destination is always the active page.

A quick glance at the data shows that EViews has made the correct, obvious (to us) connection.

obs	STATE	INFANT_MO...	REV
1	Alabama	9.4	3569.110
2	Alaska	8.1	8459.540
3	Arizona	6.9	2914.980
4	Arkansas	8.3	3892.530
5	California	5.4	4042.070
6	Colorado	5.8	3082.590
7	Connecticut	6.1	4446.900
8	Delaware	10.7	5748.480
9	District of C...	10.6	NA
10	Florida	7.3	2815.430
11	Georgia	8.6	3056.420
12	Hawaii	6.2	4868.910
13	Idaho	6.2	3357.740

We can now use REV just like any other series. EViews will bring data in from the **Revenue** page each time it's needed. For example, a scatter diagram of infant mortality against per capita revenue shows a slight, and surprising, positive association. (The positive association is attributable to the one outlier. Drop Alaska and the picture shifts to a slight negative relation.)

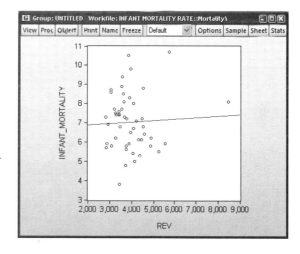

In this example we've used links to match in a case where there really was a common identifier, the computer just didn't know it. Next we turn to matching up series with fundamentally different identifiers.

Matching When The Identifiers Are Really Different

In this next example, our main data set holds observations on individuals. We're going to hook up these individual observations with data specific to each person's state of residence. In order to show off more EViews features, we'll generate the state-by-state data by taking averages from the individual level data.

For a real problem to work on, we're going to try to answer whether higher unionization rates raise wages for everyone, or whether it's just for union members. We begin with a collection of data, "CPSMar2004Extract.wf1", taken from the March 2004 Current Population Survey. We have data for about 100,000 individuals on wage rates (measured in logs, LNWAGE), education (ED), age (AGE), and whether or not the individual is a union member (UNION, 1 if union member, 0 if not). The identifier of this data set is the observation number for a particular individual.

Our goal is to regress log wage on education, age, union membership, and the fraction of the population that's unionized in the state. The difficulty is that the unionized fraction of the state's population is naturally identified by state. We need to find a mechanism to *match* individual-identified data with the state-identified data. We'll do this in several steps.

Let's first make sure that unionization matters at least for the person in the union. The regression results here show a very strong union effect. Controlling for education and age, being a union member raises your wage by about 25 percent!

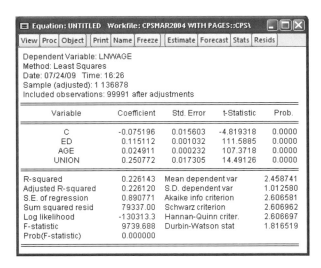

Dependent Variable: LNWAGE
Method: Least Squares
Date: 07/24/09   Time: 16:26
Sample (adjusted): 1 136878
Included observations: 99991 after adjustments

Variable	Coefficient	Std. Error	t-Statistic	Prob.
C	-0.075196	0.015603	-4.819318	0.0000
ED	0.115112	0.001032	111.5885	0.0000
AGE	0.024911	0.000232	107.3718	0.0000
UNION	0.250772	0.017305	14.49126	0.0000

R-squared	0.226143	Mean dependent var	2.458741
Adjusted R-squared	0.226120	S.D. dependent var	1.012580
S.E. of regression	0.890771	Akaike info criterion	2.606581
Sum squared resid	79337.00	Schwarz criterion	2.606962
Log likelihood	-130313.3	Hannan-Quinn criter.	2.606697
F-statistic	9739.688	Durbin-Watson stat	1.816519
Prob(F-statistic)	0.000000		

Specifying A Page By Identifier Series

Our next step is to create a page holding data aggregated to the state level. We want our new page to contain one observation for each of the states observed in the individual data. Clicking on the **New Page** tab brings up a menu including the choice **Specify by Identifier Series…**, which (not surprisingly) is just what we need to specify an identifier series for a new page. In our original page the state identifier is in the series GMSTCEN, so that's what we'll use as the identifier for the new page.

Specify by Frequency/Range …
Specify by Identifier Series …
Copy/Extract from Current Page ▶
Load Workfile Page…
Paste from Clipboard as Page

Cancel

Choosing **Specify by Identifier Series**... brings up the **Workfile Page Create by ID** dialog. Enter GMSTCEN in the **Cross ID series:** field. It's optional, but we've also entered a name for the new page in the **Page** field at the lower right.

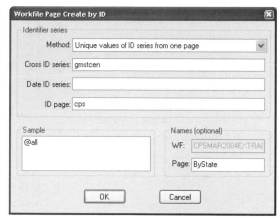

The new page opens containing just the series GMSTCEN. Okay, the new page also contains FM11X—but that's only because FM11X is a value map holding the names of each state.

If we double-click on GMSTCEN, we see that GMSTCEN has also supplied the identifier series for this page, which appears in the left-most, shaded, column of the spreadsheet. Now that we have a page identified by state, we need to fill it up with state-by-state data. One easy method is copy-and-paste. Go back to the individual data page (**Cps**). Ctrl-click on LNWAGE, ED, AGE, and UNION to select the relevant series. Copy, and then click back on the **ByState** tab.

Choose **Paste** from the context menu. Because **Paste** and **Paste Special** are the same here, this brings up the **Paste Special** dialog. We'll discuss the **Match merge options** further in a bit, but EViews has done it's usual good job of guessing what we want done. For now, just note that the field **Contraction method** is set to **Mean** and hit the OK to All button.

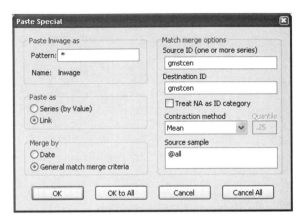

EViews has pasted data into the **ByState** page using what's called a "match-merge." In this case, we've gotten the obvious and desired result. The ED series in the **ByState** page gives the average number of years of education in each state; the UNION series gives the percent unionized, *etc.* Let's back up and talk separately about the "match" step and the "merge" step.

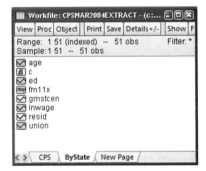

Fib Warning: In fact, we haven't gotten the desired result for a subtle reason involving the sample. Finding the error lets us explore some more features in the next section, *Contracted Data*. For the moment, we'll pretend everything is okay.

Ex-post obvious hint: When you average a 0/1 variable like UNION, you get the fraction coded as a "1." That's because adding up 0/1 observations is the same as counting the number of 1's. So taking the average counts the number of 1's and then divides by the number of observations.

The *match* step connects the identifiers across pages. In this case, we want to connect observations for individuals and observations for states according to whether they have the same state (GMSTCEN) value.

The *merge* step maps the large number of observations for individuals into a single value for each state in the **ByState** page. The default contraction method, Mean, is to average the values for individuals within a state.

Contracted Data

What we've done is called a *contraction*, because we've mapped many data points into one. We can see that the unionization rate in Arkansas—home of the world's largest private employer—is about a half percent and the average education level is three-quarters of a year of college. In Washington—where the state bird is the geoduck—the unionization rate is over three percent and average education is about a year and a half of college.

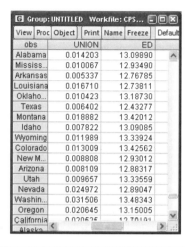

Something's wrong. Unionization rates aren't *that* low. To help investigate, let's copy the data in using a *count merge* instead of a mean merge. We click on the tab to return to the **Cps** page, re-copy the four series, and paste into the **ByState** page as before, except with two differences. In the **Pattern** field in the **Paste Special** dialog we add the suffix "count" to the variable names, so that we don't write over the state means that we computed previously. In the **Contraction method** field, switch to **Number of obs** to get a count of how many observations are being used for each series.

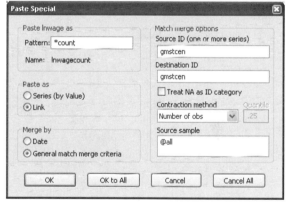

We can see that education and unionization always have the same underlying counts within a state. But the count for LNWAGE is different—and lower—than the count for ED and UNION.

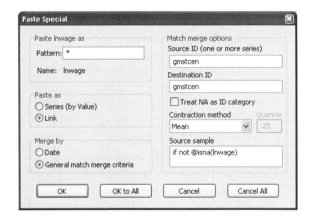

Here's what happened in the mean merge. The contraction computed the mean for each series separately. The Current Population Survey isn't limited to workers, so the state-by-state means have been computed as a fraction of the population. We probably wanted only those who are working. What's more, the variable LNWAGE is coded as NA for anyone who doesn't report a positive salary, including all non-workers. As a result, the state-by-state means for LNWAGE were computed using roughly 25 percent fewer observations than the other variables.

We want a common sample to be used for computing the series means for each state. This can be accomplished by specifying an appropriate sample in the **Source Sample** field in the **Paste Special** dialog. It happens that in this data set the only difference in the sample for the different series is that LNWAGE has a lot of NAs. Toss out the ByState page we made and make a new one, this time entering "if not @isna(lnwage)" in the **Source Sample** field.

Hint: We could have edited the link specifications, but since we had several series, it was faster to just toss the links and start over.

We now have a valid state-by-state dataset. Let's repeat our earlier regression using state-level data. The results are basically the same. The estimated effects of both education and age are a little larger than for the individual data. While the coefficients are highly significant, the standard errors are larger than before. That's what we would expect from the much smaller—99,991 versus 51 observations—sample.

Dependent Variable: LNWAGE
Method: Least Squares
Date: 07/20/09   Time: 14:40
Sample: 1 51
Included observations: 51

Variable	Coefficient	Std. Error	t-Statistic	Prob.
C	-1.538078	0.850213	-1.809051	0.0768
ED	0.153690	0.054388	2.825785	0.0069
AGE	0.046992	0.019479	2.412455	0.0198
UNION	2.553961	1.253813	2.036955	0.0473

R-squared	0.452570	Mean dependent var	2.438082
Adjusted R-squared	0.417628	S.D. dependent var	0.127302
S.E. of regression	0.097149	Akaike info criterion	-1.749965
Sum squared resid	0.443579	Schwarz criterion	-1.598450
Log likelihood	48.62412	Hannan-Quinn criter.	-1.692067
F-statistic	12.95190	Durbin-Watson stat	2.266743
Prob(F-statistic)	0.000003		

In the state-by-state regression, the interpretation of the union coefficient has changed. Because UNION is measured as a fraction, the regression now tells us that for each one percentage point increase in the unionization rate, the average wage rises two and a half percent.

Econometric caution: We're assuming that unionization drives wage rates. Maybe. Or maybe it's been easier for unions to survive in high income states. The latter interpretation would mean that our regression results aren't causal.

Expanded Data

In order to separate out the effect of the average unionization rate from the effect of individual union membership, we need to include both variables in our individual level regression. To accomplish this, we need to *expand* the 51 state-by-state observations on unionization back into the individual page, linking each individual to the average unionization rate in her state of residence.

To expand the data, we make a link going in the other direction. Copy UNION from the **ByState** page and **Paste Special** into the **Cps** page. We'll change the name of the pasted variable to AV_UNION in order to avoid any confusion with the individual union variable.

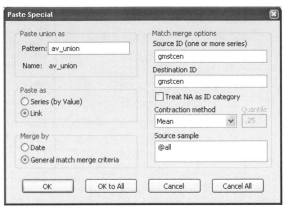

The first few observations in the **Cps** page are shown to the right. Notice that the fourth and fifth person are both from Connecticut. Even though the fourth person is a union member and the fifth person isn't, they have the same value of AV_UNION. We've succeeded in attaching the state-wide average unionization rate to each individual observation.

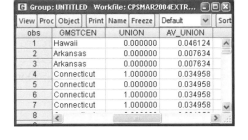

And the answer is? Our regression results show that being a union member raises an individual's wages 23.5 percent. Every additional percentage point of unionization in a state raises everyone's wages 2.65 percent.

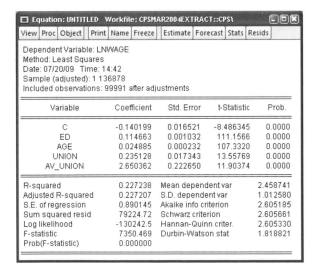

Dependent Variable: LNWAGE
Method: Least Squares
Date: 07/20/09   Time: 14:42
Sample (adjusted): 1 136878
Included observations: 99991 after adjustments

Variable	Coefficient	Std. Error	t-Statistic	Prob.
C	-0.140199	0.016521	-8.486345	0.0000
ED	0.114663	0.001032	111.1566	0.0000
AGE	0.024885	0.000232	107.3320	0.0000
UNION	0.235128	0.017343	13.55769	0.0000
AV_UNION	2.650362	0.222650	11.90374	0.0000

R-squared	0.227238	Mean dependent var		2.458741
Adjusted R-squared	0.227207	S.D. dependent var		1.012580
S.E. of regression	0.890145	Akaike info criterion		2.605185
Sum squared resid	79224.72	Schwarz criterion		2.605661
Log likelihood	-130242.5	Hannan-Quinn criter.		2.605330
F-statistic	7350.469	Durbin-Watson stat		1.818821
Prob(F-statistic)	0.000000			

Hint: As usual, EViews knows more than one way to skin a cat. If we hadn't had any interest in seeing the state-by-state averages, we could have used the @MEANSBY function discussed briefly in Chapter 4, "Data—The Transformational Experience." The following command would produce the same results as we've just seen:

```
ls lnwage c ed age union @meansby(union,gmstcen,"if not
    @isna(lnwage)")
```

Having Contractions

"Contracting" data means mapping many data points into one. Above, when EViews contracted our data from individual to state-level, it used the default contraction method "Mean." EViews provides a variety of methods, shown at the right, in the **Contraction method** field.

| Mean |
| Median |
| Maximum |
| Minimum |
| Sum |
| Sum of Squares |
| Variance (population) |
| Std. Deviation (sample) |
| Skewness |
| Kurtosis |
| Quantile |
| Number of obs |
| Number of NAs |
| First |
| Last |
| Unique values |
| No contractions allowed |

Most of the contraction methods operate just as their names imply, but **No contractions allowed** and **Unique values** are worth a bit of extra comment. These last two options are primarily for error checking. Suppose, as above, that we want to link from state-by-state data to individual data. There should only be one value from each state, so the default contraction **Mean** just copies the state value. However, what if we had somehow messed-up the state-by-state page so that there were two California entries? EViews would average the two entries without any warning. We could instead specify **No contractions allowed**, which instructs EViews to copy the relevant value, but to display an error message if it finds more than one entry for a state. **Unique values** is almost the same as **No contractions allowed**, except that if all the values for a category are identical the link proceeds. In other words, if we had entered California twice with a unionization value of 0.0303, **Unique values** would proceed while **No contractions allowed** would fail.

Q: Can I specify my own function in place of one of the built-in contraction methods?

A: No.

A': Mostly no.

You can't provide your own contraction method, but you may be able to construct a workaround. EViews doesn't provide for contraction by geometric average, for example, but you can roll your own. A geometric average is defined as

$$\hat{x} = \sqrt[n]{\prod_{i=1}^{n} x_i}$$

To do this by hand, define a series `lnx=log(x)` in the source page. Do a contraction using the regular mean method. Finally, exponentiate the resulting series in the destination page, as in `geo_av=exp(lnx)`.

Sometimes, as in this example, this sort of work around is easy—sometimes it isn't.

Two Hints and A GotchYa

In our examples, the **Source ID** and **Destination ID** each specified a single series with the same name. It's perfectly okay to have different names in these fields. EViews matches according to the values found in the respective series. What's more, you can put multiple series in both fields. If we entered "AA BB CC" for the source and "One Two Three" for the destination, EViews would match observations where the value of AA matched the value of ONE and the value of BB matched the value of TWO and the value of CC matched the value of THREE.

Normally, observations with NA in any of the **Source ID** or **Destination ID** series are tossed out of matches. Check the checkbox **Treat NAs as ID Category** to tell EViews to treat NA as a valid value for matching.

And then the "gotchya" risk. When you paste by value, the matching and merging is done right away. When you use a link, the matching and merging is re-executed each time a value of the link is called for. Remember that the link specification has a sample built into it and that this sample is re-evaluated each time the link is recomputed. If the observations included in this sample are changing, be sure that the change is as you intended. Sometimes its better to break links to avoid such unintended changes.

Quick Review

A page is fundamentally a workfile within a workfile. You can use multiple pages simply as a convenient way to store different sets of data together in one workfile.

The real power of pages lies in the fact that each page can have a different identifier. Series can be brought from one page to another either by copying the values in the source page into the destination page, or by creating a live link. If you create a link, EViews will fetch a fresh copy of the data every time the link series is referenced.

Not only will EViews copy data, it will also translate data from one identifier to another. Because EViews is big on calendars, it has a bag of tricks for converting one frequency to another.

Even where the identifier is something other than time, you can contract data by supplying a rule for selecting sets of observations and then summarizing them in a single number. For example, you might contract data on individuals by taking state-wide averages. Inversely, you can also expand data by instructing EViews to look up the desired values in a table.

Chapter 10. Prelude to Panel and Pool

So far, our data has come in a simple, peaceful arrangement. Each series in a workfile begins at the first date in the workfile and ends at the last date in the workfile. What's more, the existence of one series isn't related to the existence of some other series. That is, the series may be related by economics and statistics, but EViews sees them as objects that just happen to be collected together in one place. To pick a prospicient example, we might have one annual data series on U.S. population and another on Canadian population. EViews doesn't "understand" that the two series contain related observations on a single variable—population.

But it might be convenient if EViews did "understand," no?

Not only does EViews have a way to tie together these sort of related series, EViews has two ways: panels and pools. Panels are discussed in depth in Chapter 11, "Panel—What's My Line?" and we cover pools in Chapter 12, "Everyone Into the Pool." Here we do a quick compare and contrast.

A panel can be thought of as a set of cross-sections (countries, people, *etc.*) where each place or person can be followed over time. Panels are widely used in econometrics.

A pool is a set of time-series on a single variable, observed for a number of places or people. Pools are very simple to use in EViews because all you need to do is be sure that series names follow a consistent pattern that tells EViews how to connect them with one another.

In other words, there's a great deal of overlap between panels and pools. We look at an example and then discuss some of the nuances that help choose which is the better setup for a particular application.

Pooled or Paneled Population

We just happen to have annual data on U.S. and Canadian population. The workfile "Pop_Pool_Panel.wf1" contains a page named **Pool** with the pooled population and a page named **Panel** with the paneled population.

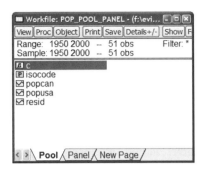 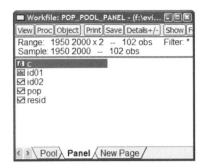

The picture on the left shows the pool approach, which is pretty straightforward. The data run for 51 years, stretching from 1950 through 2000. The two series, POPCAN and POPUSA, hold values for the Canadian and U.S. population, respectively. The object ISOCODE is called a *pool*. ISOCODE holds the words "CAN" and "USA," to tell EViews that POPCAN and POPUSA are series measuring "POP" for the respective countries. In Chapter 12, "Everyone Into the Pool" we meet a variety of features accessed through the pool object that let you process POPCAN and POPUSA either jointly or separately. But if you didn't care about the pool aspect you could treat the data as an ordinary EViews workfile. So one advantage of pools is that the learning curve is very low.

The picture on the right shows the panel approach, which introduces a kind of structure in the workfile that we haven't seen before. The **Range** field now reads "1950 2000 x 2." The data are still annual from 1950 through 2000, but the workfile is structured to contain two cross sections (Canada and the U.S.). All the population measurements are in the single series POP.

Here's a quick peek at the data.

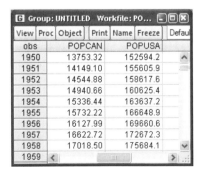

For the pooled data on the left, we see the first few observations for population for Canada and the U.S., each in its own series. The two series have (intentionally and usefully) similar names, but nothing is fundamentally different from what we've seen before.

The panel on the right shows the single series, POP. But look at the row labels—they show both the country name and the year! The rows shown—we've scrolled to roughly the middle of the series—are the Canadian data for the end of the sample followed by the U.S. data for the early years. In a panel, the data for different countries are combined in a single series. We get the all the observations for the first country first, followed by all the observations for the second country. Unlike pools, the panels do introduce a fundamentally new data structure.

You can think of a pool as a sort of *über*-group. A pool isn't a group of series, but it is a set of identifiers that can be used to bring any set of series together for processing. If our workfile had also included the series GDPCAN and GDPUSA, the same ISOCODE pool that connects POPCAN and POPUSA would also connect GDPCAN and GDPUSA. In a panel in contrast, the structure of the data applies to all series in the workfile.

One way to think about the difference between the two structures is seen in the steps needed to include a particular cross section in an analysis. For a panel, all cross sections are included—except for ones you exclude through a smpl statement. In a pool, only those cross sections identified in the pool are included and a smpl statement is used only for the time dimension. The flip side of this is that a panel has one fundamental structure built into the workfile, while in the pool setup you can define as many different pool objects as you like.

> Historical hint: Pools have been part of EViews for a long time, panels are a relatively new feature.

Nuances

If you're thinking that pools are easier to learn about, you're absolutely right. But panels provide more powerful tools.

> Hint: Pools are designed for handling a modest number of time series bundled together, while panels are better for repeated observations on large cross sections. One rule of thumb is that data in which an individual time series has an "interesting" identity (Canada, for example) is likely to be a candidate to be treated as a pool, while large, anonymous (*e.g.*, survey respondent #17529) cross sections may be better analyzed as a panel.

Here's another rule of thumb:

- If you think of yourself as a "time-series person" you'll probably find pools the more natural concept, but if you're a "cross section type" then try out a panel first.

Here's a practical rule:

- If the number of cross sections is really large, you pretty much have to use a panel. What's "really large?" Remember that in a pool each cross-section element has a series for every variable. If the cross section is large enough that typing the names of all the countries (people, *etc.*) is painful, you should probably use a panel.

Hint: The similarities between pools and panels are greater than the differences, and in any event, it's not hard to move back-and-forth between the two forms of organization.

So What *Are* the Benefits of Using Pools and Panels?

We'll spend the next two chapters answering this question. The big answer is that you can control for common elements across observations—or not—as you choose. The smaller answer is that all sorts of data manipulation are made easier because EViews understands how different observations are tied together.

As a quick example from the poolside, here's a set of descriptive statistics done for each country for the whole time series. What's more, it would have been no more trouble to produce these statistics for 20 countries than it was for two.

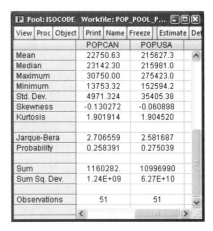

With one click of a different button, we can get descriptive statistics done for each year for all (two) countries grouped together.

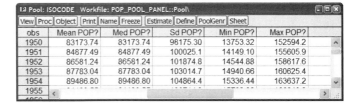

Quick (P)review

If you have a cross-section of time series, put them into a pool. If you have repeated observations on cross-section elements, set up a panel.

Now that you've had a quick taste, proceed to Chapter 11, "Panel—What's My Line?" and Chapter 12, "Everyone Into the Pool" to get the full flavor.

Chapter 11. Panel—What's My Line?

Time series data typically provide one observation in each time period; annual observations of GDP for the United States would be a classic example. In the same way, cross section data provide one observation for each place or person. We might, for example, have data on 2004 GDP for the United States, Canada, Grand Fenwick, *etc. Panel data* combines two dimensions, such as both time and place; for example, 30 years of GDP data on the United States *and* on Canada *and* on Grand Fenwick.

Broadly speaking, we want to talk about three things in this chapter. First, we'll talk about why panel data are so nifty. Next comes a discussion of how to organize panel data in EViews. Finally, we'll look at a few of EViews' special statistical procedures for panel data.

What's So Nifty About Panel Data?

Panel data presents two big advantages over ordinary time series or cross section data. The obvious advantage is that panel data frequently has lots and lots of observations. The not always obvious advantage is that in certain circumstances panel data allows you to control for unobservables that would otherwise mess up your regression estimation.

Panels can be big

It's helpful to think of the observations in a time series as being numbered from 1 to T, even though EViews typically uses dates like "2004q4" rather than $1, 2, 3\ldots$ as identifiers. Cross section data are numbered from 1 to N, it being something of a convention to use T for time series and N for cross sections. Using i to subscript the cross section and t to subscript the time period, we can write the equation for a regression line as:

$$y_{it} = \alpha + \beta x_{it} + u_{it}$$

With a panel, we are able to estimate the regression line using $N \times T$ observations, which can be a whole lot of data, leading to highly precise estimates of the regression line. For example, the *Penn World Table* (Alan Heston, Robert Summers and Bettina Aten, Penn World Table Version 6.1, Center for International Comparisons at the University of Pennsylvania (CICUP), October 2002) has data on 208 countries for 51 years, for a total of more than 10,000 observations. We'll use data from the Penn World Table for our first examples.

Using panels to control for unobservables

A key assumption in most applications of least squares regression is that there aren't any omitted variables which are correlated with the included explanatory variables. (Omitted variables cause least squares estimates to be biased.) The usual problem is that if you don't observe a variable, you don't have much choice but to omit it from the regression. When the unobserved variable varies across one dimension of the panel but not across the other, we can use a trick called *fixed effects* to make up for the omitted variable. As an example, suppose y depends on both x and z and that z is unobserved but constant for a given country. The regression equation can be written as:

$$y_{it} = \alpha + \beta x_{it} + [\gamma z_i + u_{it}]$$

where the variable z is stuffed inside the square brackets as a reminder that, just like the error term u, z is unobservable.

> Hint: The subscript on z is just i, not it, as a reminder that z varies across countries but not time.

The trick of fixed effects is to think of there being a unique constant for each country. If we call this constant α_i and use the definition $\alpha_i = \alpha + \gamma z_i$, we can re-write the equation with the unobservable z replaced by a separate intercept for each country:

$$y_{it} = \alpha_i + \beta x_{it} + u_{it}$$

EViews calls α_i a *cross section fixed effect*.

The advantage of including the fixed effect is that by eliminating the unobservable from the equation we can now safely use least squares. The presence of multiple observations for each country makes estimation of the fixed effect possible.

We could have just as easily told the story above for a variable that was constant over time while varying across countries. This would lead to a *period fixed effect*. EViews panel features allow for cross section fixed effects, period fixed effects, or both.

Setting Up Panel Data

The easiest way to set up a panel workfile is to start with a nonpanel workfile in which one series identifies the period and one series identifies the cross section. The file "PWT61Extract.wf1" has information on both real GDP relative to the United States and on population for a large number of countries for half a century. It also contains a series, ISO-CODE, that holds an abbreviation for each country and a series, YR, for the year.

> Hint: If two dimensions can be used rather than one, why not three dimensions rather than two? Why not four dimensions? EViews only provides built-in statistical support for two-dimensional panels. In the section *Fixed Effects With and Without the Social Contrivance of Panel Structure*, below, you'll learn a technique for handling fixed effects without creating a panel structure. The same technique can be used for estimating fixed effects in third and higher dimensions.

The figure to the right shows observations 1597 through 1610, which happen to be the last few observations for the Central African Republic and the first few observations for Canada. To us humans, it's clear that these are observations for $i = $ CAF,CAN and for $t = 1994\ldots 2000$ and then starting over with $t = 1950\ldots$. In order to set up a panel structure, we need to share this kind of understanding with EViews.

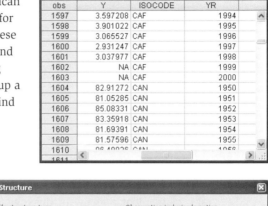

Structuring a panel workfile

To change from a regular to a panel structure, use the **Workfile structure** dialog. Double click on **Range** in the upper pane of the workfile window, or use the menu **Proc/Structure/Resize Current Page**. Choose **Dated Panel** for the **Workfile structure type** and then specify the series containing the cross section (i) and date (t) identifiers. EViews re-organizes the workfile to have a panel

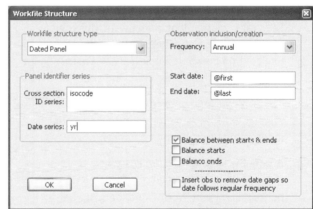

structure (the re-organized workfile is available in the EViews web site as "PWT61PanelExtract.wf1").

EViews announces the panel aspect of the workfile structure by changing the **Range** field in the top panel of the workfile window. We now have 208 cross sections for data from 1950 through 2000.

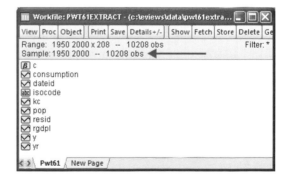

More information about the structure of the workfile is available by pushing the View button and choosing **Statistics** from the menu.

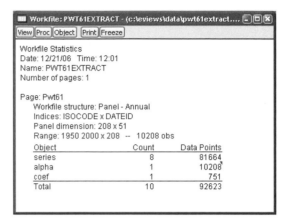

Let's take another look at our data, this time as displayed in the panel workfile. Now the obs column correctly identifies each data point with both country code and year.

That's about all you need to know to set up a panel workfile. One more option is worth mentioning. Should you "balance?"

A panel is said to be *balanced* when every cross section is observed for the same time period. The Penn World Table data are balanced, since there are observations for 1950 through 2000 for every country—although quite a few observations are simply marked NA (not available). If you look at the workfile, you'll see that all the data for the Central African Republic is missing until 1960. (The Central African Republic became independent on August 13, 1960.) The creators of the Penn World Table might have simply omitted these years for the Central African Republic, giving us an *unbalanced* panel. EViews default (if you leave the check box **Balance between starts & ends** in the **Workfile structure** dialog checked) is to make a balanced workfile by inserting empty rows of data where needed. Use **Balance between starts & ends** unless you have a reason not to do so. (See the *User's Guide* for further discussion.)

Panel Estimation

Not that it was much trouble, but we didn't restructure the workfile just to get a prettier display for spreadsheet views. Let's work through an estimation example.

There's a general notion from classical Solow growth theory that high population growth leads to lower per capita output, conditional on available technologies. We can test this theory by regressing gross domestic product per capita relative to the United States on the rate of population growth, measured as the change in the log of population. Results from a simple regression seem to support such a theory. At least, we can say that the coefficient is statistically significant. In fact, looking at the p-value, the coefficient is off-the-scale significant.

Equation: UNTITLED   Workfile: PWT61EXTRACT::Pwt61

View | Proc | Object | | Print | Name | Freeze | | Estimate | Forecast | Stats | Resids

Dependent Variable: Y
Method: Panel Least Squares
Date: 07/20/09   Time: 11:58
Sample: 1950 2000 IF ISOCODE <> "USA"
Periods included: 50
Cross-sections included: 153
Total panel (unbalanced) observations: 5622

Variable	Coefficient	Std. Error	t-Statistic	Prob.
C	44.93176	0.546861	82.16302	0.0000
D(LOG(POP))	-901.0468	23.83234	-37.80773	0.0000

R-squared	0.202772	Mean dependent var	27.76428
Adjusted R-squared	0.202630	S.D. dependent var	25.58963
S.E. of regression	22.85041	Akaike info criterion	9.096170
Sum squared resid	2934433.	Schwarz criterion	9.098531
Log likelihood	-25567.34	Hannan-Quinn criter.	9.096993
F-statistic	1429.424	Durbin-Watson stat	0.102652
Prob(F-statistic)	0.000000		

But is the effect of population growth important? We can try to get a better handle on this by comparing a couple of countries; let's use the Central African Republic and Canada, since they're at opposite ends of the development spectrum. Set the sample using:

```
smpl if isocode="CAF" or ISOCODE="CAN"
```

Reminder: Variable names aren't case sensitive in EViews ("isocode" and "ISOCODE" mean the same thing), but string comparisons using " = " are. In this particular data set country identifiers have been coded in all caps. "CAN" works. "can" doesn't.

Now open a window on population growth with the command:

```
show d(log(pop))
```

Hint in two parts: The function d() takes the first difference of a series, and the first difference of a log is approximately the percentage change. Hence "d(log(pop))" gives the percentage growth of population.

Hint: Lags in panel workfiles work correctly—in other words, EViews knows that a lag means the previous observation for the same country. Notice in the window to the right that the 1950 value of D(LOG(POP)) is—correctly—NA. Even though the observation for the year 2000 for Canada appears immediately before 1950 Switzerland in the spreadsheet, EViews understands that the observations are not sequential.

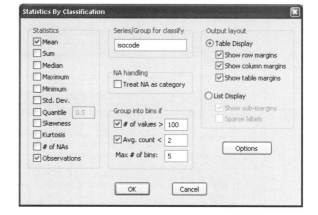

Use the [View] button to choose **Descriptive Statistics & Tests/Stats by Classification**.... Use ISOCODE as the classifying variable.

The average value of population growth was 2.2 percent per year in the Central African Republic and 1.6 percent in Canada. If we multiply the difference in population growth rates, 0.008, by the estimated regression coefficient, -901, we predict that relative GDP in the Central African Republic should be 7 percentage points lower than in Canada. Population growth appears to have a very large effect.

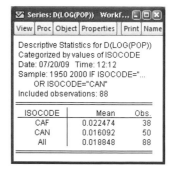

Convenience hint: It wasn't necessary to restrict the sample to the two countries of interest. Limiting the sample just made the output window shorter and easier to look at.

Is the apparent effect of population growth on output real, or is it a spurious result? It's easy to imagine that population growth is picking up the effect of omitted variables that we can't measure. To the extent that the omitted variables are constant for each country, fixed effects estimation will control for the omissions.

> Econometric digression: The regression output includes a hint that something funky is going on. The Durbin-Watson statistic (see Chapter 13, "Serial Correlation—Friend or Foe?") indicates very, very high serial correlation. This suggests that if the error for a country in one year is positive then it's positive in all years, and if it's negative once then it's always negative. High serial correlation in this context provides a hint that we've left out country specific information.

Setting the sample back to everything except the United States, click the [Estimate] button and then choose the Panel Options tab. Set **Effects specification** to Cross-section **Fixed**. This instructs EViews to include a separate intercept, α_i, for each country.

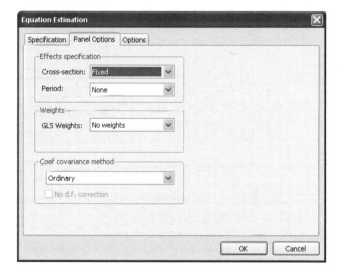

In our new regression results, the effect of population growth is reduced to about one 1/100th of the previous estimate. This confirms our suspicion that the previous estimate had omitted variables—and apparently ones that mattered a lot.

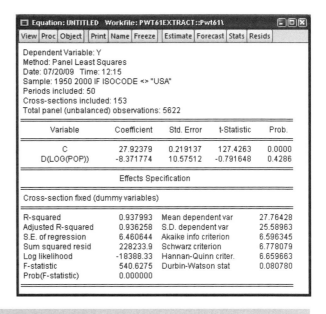

Equation: UNTITLED   Workfile: PWT61EXTRACT::Pwt61\

View | Proc | Object | Print | Name | Freeze | Estimate | Forecast | Stats | Resids

Dependent Variable: Y
Method: Panel Least Squares
Date: 07/20/09   Time: 12:15
Sample: 1950 2000 IF ISOCODE <> "USA"
Periods included: 50
Cross-sections included: 153
Total panel (unbalanced) observations: 5622

Variable	Coefficient	Std. Error	t-Statistic	Prob.
C	27.92379	0.219137	127.4263	0.0000
D(LOG(POP))	-8.371774	10.57512	-0.791648	0.4286

Effects Specification

Cross-section fixed (dummy variables)

R-squared	0.937993	Mean dependent var	27.76428
Adjusted R-squared	0.936258	S.D. dependent var	25.58963
S.E. of regression	6.460644	Akaike info criterion	6.596345
Sum squared resid	228233.9	Schwarz criterion	6.778079
Log likelihood	-18388.33	Hannan-Quinn criter.	6.659663
F-statistic	540.6275	Durbin-Watson stat	0.080780
Prob(F-statistic)	0.000000		

> Hint: **Fixed/Random Effects Testing** offers a formal test for the presence of fixed effects. Look for it on the **View** menu.

We can take a look at the estimated values of the fixed effects for each country by looking at the **Fixed/Random Effects/Cross-section Effects** view. The reported values of the cross-section fixed effects are the intercept for country i, α_i, less the average intercept. So it's not very surprising that the effect for Canada is positive and the effect for the Central African Republic is negative.

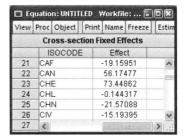

Equation: UNTITLED   Workfile: ...

View | Proc | Object | Print | Name | Freeze | Estim

Cross-section Fixed Effects

	ISOCODE	Effect
21	CAF	-19.15951
22	CAN	56.17477
23	CHE	73.44862
24	CHL	-0.144317
25	CHN	-21.57088
26	CIV	-15.19395
27		

> Hint: When using fixed effects, the constant term reported in regression output is the average value of α_i.

Since the results differ dramatically, it would be nice to have some assurance that the fixed effects are really there. Panel estimates include extra coefficient testing views. **Choose Fixed/Random Effects Testing/Redundant Fixed Effects - Likelihood Ratio**. In this case, the statistical evidence, as shown by the p-value, is overwhelmingly in favor of keeping fixed effects in the model.

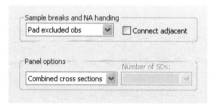

Pretty Panel Pictures

EViews offers extra ways of looking at the panel structured data—especially in graphs. When you select the **Graph...** view for data in a panel structured workfile, the dialog offers additional panel options in the bottom right corner.

Choosing **Combined cross sections** gives the figure to the right. Mean anything to you? Me neither. There are just too many darn lines in this picture.

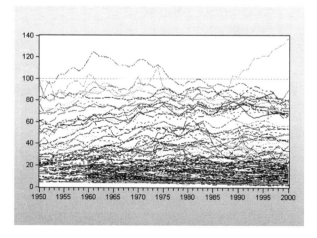

Looking at all possible cross sections isn't always very informative. This is one case where too much data means too little information. **Combined cross sections** works much better when there are only a small number of countries. If we limit the sample to the Central African Republic and Canada, as we did above, the plot is much more informative.

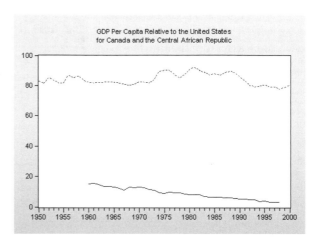

Hint: EViews doesn't produce a legend for this sort of graph by default. You can double-click on the graph, go to the legend portion of the dialog, and tell it do so.

Going through the same process, we can choose **Individual cross sections** to get a different picture of the same data. Where the previous graph visually emphasized the difference in income levels between the Central African Republic and Canada, this graph is better at showing the relative trends over time.

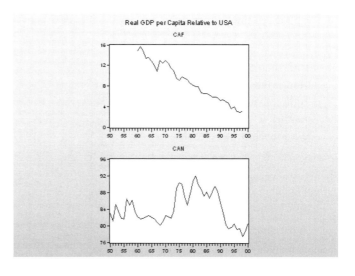

More Panel Estimation Techniques

We've merely brushed the surface of the panel estimation techniques that EViews provides, discussing fixed effects models and a couple of panel-special graphing techniques. The EViews *User's Guide* devotes an entire chapter to panel estimation. Here are a few items you may want to check out:

- Fixed effects in the time dimension, or in time and cross section simultaneously.

- Random effect models.

- A variety of procedures for estimating coefficient covariances.

- A variety of panel-oriented GLS (generalized least squares) techniques.

- Dynamic panel data estimation.

- Panel unit root tests.

One Dimensional Two-Dimensional Panels

Panels are designed for data that's inherently two dimensional. Effectively, data are grouped by both cross section and time period. Grouping data is sometimes useful even when there is only one dimension to group along. In other words, sometimes it's useful to pretend that data comes in a panel even when it doesn't. In particular, this can be a useful trick for estimating separate intercepts for each group.

Information on wages (in logs), education (in years), age, race, and state was collected as part of the Current Population Survey (CPS) in March 2004. The workfile "CPSMAR2004extract.wf1" contains an extract with usable data for about 100,000 individuals. We can use this data to test the theory that Asians earn more than others after accounting for observable differences such as education and age. A standard method for looking at this kind of question is to regress wages on education, age and a dummy variable for being Asian. We then ask whether the "Asian effect" is positive. Using the CPS data we get the results shown here.

Equation: UNTITLED	Workfile: CPSMAR2004EXTRACT::CPS\

View | Proc | Object | Print | Name | Freeze | Estimate | Forecast | Stats | Resids

Dependent Variable: LNWAGE
Method: Least Squares
Date: 07/20/09   Time: 13:13
Sample (adjusted): 1 136878
Included observations: 99991 after adjustments

Variable	Coefficient	Std. Error	t-Statistic	Prob.
C	-0.080370	0.015618	-5.146007	0.0000
ED	0.115398	0.001035	111.5470	0.0000
AGE	0.025093	0.000232	108.2062	0.0000
ASIAN	0.025921	0.014093	1.839287	0.0659

R-squared	0.224544	Mean dependent var	2.458741
Adjusted R-squared	0.224521	S.D. dependent var	1.012580
S.E. of regression	0.891691	Akaike info criterion	2.608646
Sum squared resid	79500.93	Schwarz criterion	2.609026
Log likelihood	-130416.5	Hannan-Quinn criter.	2.608761
F-statistic	9650.877	Durbin-Watson stat	1.817140
Prob(F-statistic)	0.000000		

Junk science alert: Asian-Americans are an especially diverse socio-economic group. Other than the American tendency to use race to classify everything, it's not clear why fourth and fifth generation Japanese-Americans should be lumped together with recent Hmong refugees. For a serious scientific investigation, we'd have to turn to a data source other than the CPS in order to get a more meaningful socio-economic breakdown.

Our regression results suggest that Asians earn two-and-a-half percent more than the rest of the population, after accounting for age and education (although the significance level is a smidgen short of the 5 percent gold standard). However, the Asian population isn't distributed randomly across the United States. If Asians are relatively more likely to live in high wage areas, our regression might be unintentionally picking up a location effect rather than a race effect.

We can look at this issue by including dummy variables for the 51 states (DC too, eh?). This can be done directly (and we'll do it directly in the next section) but it can be very convenient to pretend that each state identifies a cross section in a panel so that we can use EViews panel estimation tools. In other words, let's fake a panel.

Double-click on **Range** to bring up the **Workfile structure** dialog. Set the dialog to **Undated Panel**—since there aren't any dates—and uncheck **Balance between starts and ends**—since there isn't anything to balance.

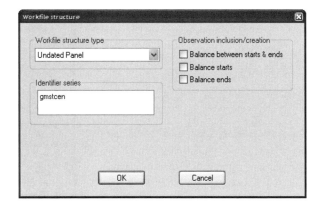

Now that we have a (pretend) panel, we can re-run the estimation and then use the estimation options to include cross section fixed effects.

Our new results estimate that the Asian effect is negative (although not significantly so) rather than positive. Our speculation that the positive Asian effect was picking up location effects appears to be correct.

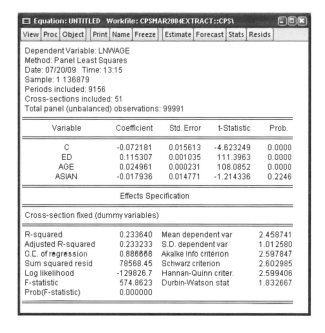

Fixed Effects With and Without the Social Contrivance of Panel Structure

EViews provides a large set of features designed for panel data, but fixed effects estimation is the most important. In terms of econometrics, specifying fixed effects in a linear regression is a fancy way of including a dummy variable for each group (country or state in the examples in this chapter). You're free to include these dummy variables manually, if you wish.

There is a special circumstance under which including dummies manually is required. Once in a while, you may have three (or more) dimensional panel data. Since EViews panels are limited to two dimensions, the only way to handle a third dimension of fixed effects is by adding dummy variables in that third dimension by hand.

Hint: All else equal, choose the dimension with the fewest categories as the one to be handled manually.

There is a fairly common circumstance under which including dummies manually may be preferred. If *all* you're after is fixed effects, why bother setting up a panel structure? Adding dummies into the regression is easier than restructuring a workfile.

There is one circumstance under which you should almost certainly use panel features rather than including dummies manually. If you have lots and lots of categories, panel estimation of fixed effects is *much* faster. Internally, panel estimation uses a technique called *"sweeping out the dummies"* to factor out the dummies before running the regression, drastically reducing computational issues. (The time required to compute a linear regression is quadratic in the number of variables.) Additionally, when the number of dummy variables reaches into the hundreds, EViews will sometimes produce regression results using panel estimation for equations in cases in which computation using manually entered dummies breaks down.

Manual dummies—How To

The easy way to include a large number of dummies is through use of the @expand function. @expand was discussed in Chapter 4, "Data—The Transformational Experience," so here's a quick review. Add to the least squares command:

```
@expand(cross_section_identifier, @droplast)
```

where the option @droplast drops one dummy to avoid the *dummy variable trap.*

> Econometric reminder: The dummy variable trap is what catches you if you attempt to have an intercept and a complete set of dummies in a regression.

For example,

```
ls lnwage c ed age asian @expand(gmstcen, @droplast)
```

gives the results to the right.

The regression is identical to our earlier fixed effect results. You do have to remember that the constant term has a different interpretation. In the fixed effect panel estimation, the reported constant is the average α_i and the reported fixed effects are the deviations from that average for each category. When using

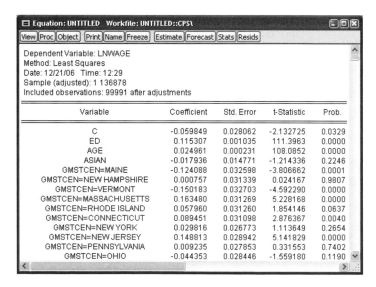

Equation: UNTITLED Workfile: UNTITLED::CPS\				
View Proc Object Print Name Freeze Estimate Forecast Stats Resids				
Dependent Variable: LNWAGE				
Method: Least Squares				
Date: 12/21/06 Time: 12:29				
Sample (adjusted): 1 136878				
Included observations: 99991 after adjustments				
Variable	Coefficient	Std. Error	t-Statistic	Prob.
C	-0.059849	0.028062	-2.132725	0.0329
ED	0.115307	0.001035	111.3963	0.0000
AGE	0.024961	0.000231	108.0852	0.0000
ASIAN	-0.017936	0.014771	-1.214336	0.2246
GMSTCEN=MAINE	-0.124088	0.032598	-3.806662	0.0001
GMSTCEN=NEW HAMPSHIRE	0.000757	0.031339	0.024167	0.9807
GMSTCEN=VERMONT	-0.150183	0.032703	-4.592290	0.0000
GMSTCEN=MASSACHUSETTS	0.163480	0.031269	5.228168	0.0000
GMSTCEN=RHODE ISLAND	0.057960	0.031260	1.854146	0.0637
GMSTCEN=CONNECTICUT	0.089451	0.031098	2.876367	0.0040
GMSTCEN=NEW YORK	0.029816	0.026773	1.113649	0.2654
GMSTCEN=NEW JERSEY	0.148813	0.028942	5.141829	0.0000
GMSTCEN=PENNSYLVANIA	0.009235	0.027853	0.331553	0.7402
GMSTCEN=OHIO	-0.044353	0.028446	-1.559180	0.1190

@expand, the reported constant is the intercept for the dropped category and the reported dummy coefficients are the difference between the category intercept and the intercept for the dropped category.

Quick Review—Panel

The panel feature lets you analyze two dimensional data. Convenient features include prettier identification of your data in spreadsheet views and some extra graphic capabilities. The use of fixed effects in regression is straightforward, and often critical to getting meaningful estimates from regression by washing out unobservables. The examples in this chapter used cross-section fixed effects, but you can use period fixed effects—or both cross section and period fixed effects—just as easily. See Chapter 12, "Everyone Into the Pool" for a different approach to two dimensional data. The *User's Guide* describes several advanced statistical tools which can be used with panels.

Chapter 12. Everyone Into the Pool

Suppose we want to know the effect of population growth on output. We might take Canadian output and regress it on Canadian population growth. Or we might take output in Grand Fenwick and regress it on Fenwickian population growth. Better yet, we can *pool* the data for Canada and Grand Fenwick in one combined regression. More data—better estimates. Of course, we'll want to check that the relationship between output and population growth is the same in the two countries before we accept combined results.

Pooling data in this way is so useful that EViews has a special facility—the "pool" object—to make it easy to work with pooled data. We begin this chapter with an illustration of using EViews' pools. Then we'll look at some slightly fancy arrangements for handling pooled data.

Getting Your Feet Wet

The file "PWT61PoolExtract.wf1" (available from the EViews website) contains annual data on population and output (relative to the United States) extracted from the Penn World Tables for the G7 countries (Canada, France, Germany, Great Britain, Italy, Japan, and the United States). The first thing you'll notice is that there are lots of population and output series, one for each country. We use pools to study behavior common to all the countries. The second thing you'll notice is that series names have two parts: a series component identifying the series, and a cross-section component identifying the cross-section element—the country in this example. So POPCAN is population for Canada and POPFRA is population for France. YCAN is Canadian output and YFRA is French output. There's just one rule you have to remember about series set up in a pool:

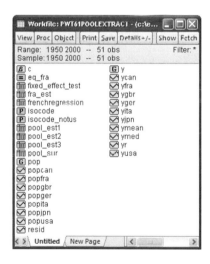

- Pooled series aren't any different from any other series; they're simply ordinary series conveniently named with common components.

In other words, pool series have neither any special features nor any special restrictions. The only thing going on is that their names are set up conveniently to identify the country (or other cross-sectional element) with which they're associated. For example, the command:

```
ls yfra c d(log(popfra))
```

gives us the regression of output on population growth for France. The reported effect of population growth is statistically significant and rather large. (Given historical magnitudes in French rates of population growth, the effect accounts for a decrease in output of about 10 percent relative to US output.)

Dependent Variable: YFRA
Method: Least Squares
Date: 07/17/09   Time: 14:29
Sample (adjusted): 1951 2000
Included observations: 50 after adjustments

Variable	Coefficient	Std. Error	t-Statistic	Prob.
C	75.47372	2.342993	32.21252	0.0000
D(LOG(POPFRA))	-920.3221	306.2157	-3.005470	0.0042

R-squared	0.158380	Mean dependent var	69.08886
Adjusted R-squared	0.140846	S.D. dependent var	7.538449
S.E. of regression	6.987430	Akaike info criterion	6.765281
Sum squared resid	2343.561	Schwarz criterion	6.841762
Log likelihood	-167.1320	Hannan-Quinn criter.	6.794405
F-statistic	9.032851	Durbin-Watson stat	0.156600
Prob(F-statistic)	0.004208		

Reverse causation alert: There's good reason to believe that countries becoming richer leads to lower population growth. Thus there's a real issue of whether we're picking up the effect of output on population growth rather than population growth on output. The issue is real, but it hasn't got anything to do with illustrating the use of pools, so we won't worry about it further.

Into the Pool

- Pooled series aren't any different from any other series, but Pool objects let us do some nifty tricks with them.

The first step in pooled analysis is to give EViews a list of the suffixes, CAN, FRA, *etc.*, that identify the countries. Click on the Object button, select **New Object...** and choose **Pool**.

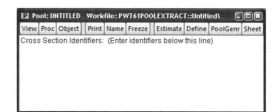

Hint: The cross-section identifier needn't be placed as a suffix. You can stick it anywhere in the series name so long as you're consistent.

Simply type the country identifiers—one per line—into the blank area and then name the pool by clicking on the Name button. In our example the window ends up looking as shown to the right.

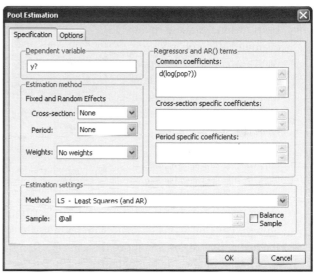

Click on the Estimate button in the Pool window. For this first example, enter "Y?" in the **Dependent variable** field and "C D(LOG(POP?))" in the **Common coefficients** field.

- In a pooled analysis, the "?" in the variable names gets replaced with the ids listed in the pool object.

Clicking OK gives us a regression that's just like the regression on French data reported above— except that this time we've combined the data for all six countries. Let's see what's changed. First, we have 280 observations instead of 50. Second, the reported effect of population has switched sign. The French-only result was negative as theory predicts. The pooled result is positive.

Dependent Variable: Y?
Method: Pooled Least Squares
Date: 07/17/09 Time: 14:40
Sample (adjusted): 1951 2000
Included observations: 50 after adjustments
Cross-sections included: 6
Total pool (unbalanced) observations: 280

Variable	Coefficient	Std. Error	t-Statistic	Prob.
C	68.42578	1.139282	60.06045	0.0000
D(LOG(POP?))	244.6215	119.9112	2.040022	0.0423

R-squared	0.014749	Mean dependent var		70.18130
Adjusted R-squared	0.011205	S.D. dependent var		12.56390
S.E. of regression	12.49331	Akaike info criterion		7.895380
Sum squared resid	43390.99	Schwarz criterion		7.921343
Log likelihood	-1103.353	Hannan-Quinn criter.		7.905794
F-statistic	4.161690	Durbin-Watson stat		0.027688
Prob(F-statistic)	0.042293			

Everyone Into the Pool May Not Be Fun

The advantage of pooling data is that a great deal of data is brought to bear on the problem. The potential disadvantage is that a simple pool forces the coefficients to be identical across countries. Does this make sense in our example? We probably do want the coefficient on population growth to be the same for each country, because the theory isn't of much use if population growth doesn't have a predictable effect. In contrast, there's no reason for the intercept to be the same for each country. We know that countries have different levels of GDP for reasons unrelated to population growth. Let's retry this estimate with an individual intercept for each country. Go back to the estimation dialog and move the constant from the **Common coefficients** field into **Cross-section specific coefficients**.

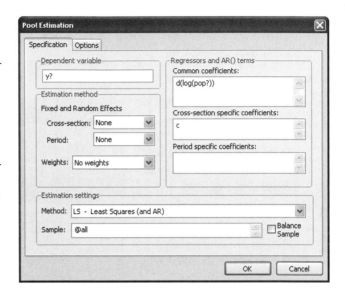

Now we're asking for a separate intercept for each country. The estimated effect of population growth is negative as we had expected. And the increased sample size has raised the *t*-statistic on population growth from 3 to 5.

Dependent Variable: Y?
Method: Pooled Least Squares
Date: 07/17/09 Time: 14:41
Sample (adjusted): 1951 2000
Included observations: 50 after adjustments
Cross-sections included: 6
Total pool (unbalanced) observations: 280

Variable	Coefficient	Std. Error	t-Statistic	Prob.
D(LOG(POP?))	-754.0516	141.7995	-5.317729	0.0000
CAN--C	96.09819	2.670078	35.99079	0.0000
FRA--C	74.32020	1.700051	43.71644	0.0000
GBR--C	72.90192	1.466834	49.70018	0.0000
GER--C	74.37765	1.809296	41.10860	0.0000
ITA--C	66.22264	1.508854	43.88937	0.0000
JPN--C	69.14969	1.834263	37.69889	0.0000

R-squared	0.404168	Mean dependent var	70.18130
Adjusted R-squared	0.391072	S.D. dependent var	12.56390
S.E. of regression	9.804086	Akaike info criterion	7.428158
Sum squared resid	26240.79	Schwarz criterion	7.519028
Log likelihood	-1032.942	Hannan-Quinn criter.	7.464606
F-statistic	30.86376	Durbin-Watson stat	0.085267
Prob(F-statistic)	0.000000		

Observation about life as a statistician: Running estimates until you get results that accord with prior beliefs is not exactly sound practice. The risk isn't that the other guy is going to do this intentionally to fool you. The risk is that it's awfully easy to fool yourself unintentionally.

There's nothing special about moving the constant term into the **Cross-section specific coefficients** field. You can do the same for any variable you think appropriate.

Fixed Effects

Okay—that first sentence was a fib. There *is* something special about the constant. The cross-section specific constant picks up all the things that make one country different from another that aren't included in our model. Such differences occur so frequently that EViews has a built-in facility for allowing for such country-specific constants. Country-specific constants are called *fixed effects*. Push [Estimate] again, take the constant term out of the specification entirely and set **Estimation method** to **Cross-section: Fixed**.

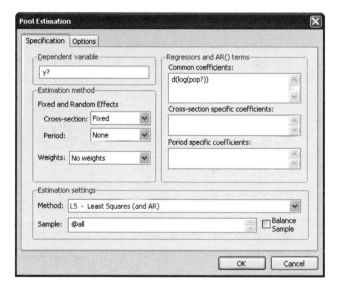

Hint: The econometric issues surrounding fixed effects in pools are the same as for panels. See Chapter 11, "Panel—What's My Line?"

Fixed effect estimation puts in an intercept for every country, and changes slightly how the results are reported. The intercept is now reported in two parts. (Nothing else in the report changes.) The line marked "C" reports the average value of the intercept for all the countries in the sample. The lines marked for the individual countries give the country's intercept as a deviation from that overall average. In this example the overall average intercept is 76 and the intercept for Canada is 96 (20 above 76).

Dependent Variable: Y?
Method: Pooled Least Squares
Date: 07/17/09   Time: 14:42
Sample (adjusted): 1951 2000
Included observations: 50 after adjustments
Cross-sections included: 6
Total pool (unbalanced) observations: 280

Variable	Coefficient	Std. Error	t-Statistic	Prob.
C	75.59272	1.174237	64.37601	0.0000
D(LOG(POP?))	-754.0516	141.7995	-5.317729	0.0000
Fixed Effects (Cross)				
CAN--C	20.50547			
FRA--C	-1.272522			
GBR--C	-2.690795			
GER--C	-1.215073			
ITA--C	-9.370082			
JPN--C	-6.443027			

Effects Specification

Cross-section fixed (dummy variables)

R-squared	0.404168	Mean dependent var	70.18130
Adjusted R-squared	0.391072	S.D. dependent var	12.56390
S.E. of regression	9.804086	Akaike info criterion	7.428158
Sum squared resid	26240.79	Schwarz criterion	7.519028
Log likelihood	-1032.942	Hannan-Quinn criter.	7.464606
F-statistic	30.86376	Durbin-Watson stat	0.085267
Prob(F-statistic)	0.000000		

Testing Fixed Effects

Fixed effects specifications are common enough that EViews builds in a test for country specific intercepts against a single, common, intercept. After a pooled estimate specifying fixed effects, choose [View] and then the menu **Fixed/Random Effects Testing/Redundant Fixed Effects - Likelihood Ratio**. Both F- and χ^2-tests appear at the top of the view. Since the hypothesis of a common intercept is wildly rejected, there's more to the fixed effect specification than just that it gives results that we like.

Redundant Fixed Effects Tests
Pool: ISOCODE_NOTUS
Test cross-section fixed effects

Effects Test	Statistic	d.f.	Prob.
Cross-section F	35.684935	(5,273)	0.0000
Cross-section Chi-square	140.822284	5	0.0000

Cross-section fixed effects test equation:
Dependent Variable: Y?
Method: Panel Least Squares
Date: 07/17/09   Time: 14:44
Sample (adjusted): 1951 2000
Included observations: 50 after adjustments
Cross-sections included: 6
Total pool (unbalanced) observations: 280

Variable	Coefficient	Std. Error	t-Statistic	Prob.
C	68.42578	1.139282	60.06045	0.0000
D(LOG(POP?))	244.6215	119.9112	2.040022	0.0423

R-squared	0.014749	Mean dependent var	70.18130
Adjusted R-squared	0.011205	S.D. dependent var	12.56390
S.E. of regression	12.49331	Akaike info criterion	7.895380
Sum squared resid	43390.99	Schwarz criterion	7.921343
Log likelihood	-1103.353	Hannan-Quinn criter.	7.905794
F-statistic	4.161690	Durbin-Watson stat	0.027688
Prob(F-statistic)	0.042293		

Playing in the Pool—Data

Pooled series are just plain-old series that share a naming convention. All the usual operations on series work as expected. But there are some extra features so that you can examine or manipulate all the series in a pool in one operation.

> Hint: It's fine to have multiple pool objects in the workfile. They're just different lists of identifiers, after all.

Spreadsheet Views

Pools have two special spreadsheet views, stacked and unstacked, chosen by pushing the [Sheet] button or choosing the **View/Spreadsheet (stacked data)...** menu. For either view, the first step is to specify the desired series when the **Series List** dialog opens. Enter the names of the series you'd like to see, using the conventions that a series *with* a question mark means replace that question mark with each of the country ids in turn. A series with no question mark means use the series as usual, repeated for each country. The way we've filled in the dialog here asks EViews to display D(LOG(POPCAN)), D(LOG(POPFRA)), *etc.*, for YCAN, YFRA, *etc.*, and for D(LOG(POPUSA)) separately.

Stacked View

The spreadsheet opens with all the data for Canada followed by all the data for France, *etc.* The data for POPUSA gets repeated next to each country. Notice how the identifier FRA-1950 in the **obs** column gives the cross-section identifier followed by the date—in other words, country and year.

This is called the *stacked view.* You can imagine putting together all the data for Canada, then stacking on all the data for France, *etc.* We'll return to the idea of a stacked view when we talk about loading in pooled data below.

Unstacked View

Re-arranging the spreadsheet into the "usual order," that is by date, is called the *unstacked view*. Clicking the Order+/- button flicks back-and-forth between stacked and unstacked views.

obs	D(LOG(POP?))	Y?	D(LOG(POP...
CAN-1951	0.028371	81.05285	0.019545
FRA-1951	0.009569	50.17182	0.019545
GBR-1951	0.001978	67.22717	0.019545
GER-1951	NA	NA	0.019545
ITA-1951	0.006390	39.37976	0.019545
JPN-1951	0.014235	-23.11203	0.019545
CAN-1952	0.027588	85.08331	0.019170
FRA-1952	0.007117	51.59016	0.019170
GBR-1952	0.001974	66.42880	0.019170
GER-1952	NA	NA	0.019170
ITA-1952	0.006349	39.99177	0.019170
JPN-1952	0.015196	24.39119	0.019170
CAN-1953	0.026847	83.35918	0.012579
FRA-1953	0.007067	51.23390	0.012579
GBR-1953	0.001970	68.43254	0.012579
GER-1953	NA	NA	0.012579
ITA-1953	0.006309	41.91782	0.012579
JPN-1953	0.013825	24.66796	0.012579
CAN-1954	0.026145	81.69391	0.018576
FRA-1954	0.009346	54.41555	0.018576
GBR-1954	0.001967	73.22035	0.018576
GER-1954			

Pooled Statistics

The **Descriptive Statistics...** view offers a number of ways to slice and dice the data in the pool. We've put two pooled series (with the "?" marks) and one non-pooled series in the dialog so you can see what happens as we try out each option.

First, look at the **Sample** radio buttons on the right. The presence of missing data, NAs, means that the samples available for one series may differ from the sample available for another. You can see above, for example, that Canada, France, and Great Britain have data starting in 1950, but that German data begins later. **Common** sample instructs EViews to use only those observations available for all countries for a *particular* series, while **Balanced** sample requires observations for all countries for *all* series entered in the dialog. **Individual** sample means to use all the observations available.

Stacked Data Statistics

The default **Data Organization** is **Stacked data**, which stacks the series for all countries together for the purpose of producing descriptive statistics. For example, we see that GDP per capita in our six pooled countries averaged just over 70 percent of U.S. GDP per capita. (Y is measured relative to U.S. GDP.)

Date: 05/16/05 Time: 08:59
Sample: 1950 2000
Common sample

	D(LOG(POP?))	Y?	D(LOG(POPUSA))
Mean	0.007176	70.18130	0.011598
Median	0.005901	71.78911	0.010431
Maximum	0.030214	91.97449	0.019545
Minimum	-0.004612	23.11203	0.008761
Std. Dev.	0.006238	12.56390	0.003142
Skewness	1.343328	-1.449204	1.297714
Kurtosis	5.253966	5.841244	3.316759
Jarque-Bera	143.4823	192.1901	79.76011
Probability	0.000000	0.000000	0.000000
Sum	2.009408	19650.76	3.247495
Sum Sq. Dev.	0.010855	44040.56	0.002754
Observations	280	280	280
Cross sections	6	6	6

Stacked - Means Removed

Specifying **Stacked - means removed** in **Descriptive Statistics** produces some pretty funny looking output, but it turns out that this method is just what we want for answering certain questions. EViews subtracts the means for each country before generating the descriptive statistics. As a consequence, the means are always zero, which looks pretty funny.

The raison d'être for **Stacked - means removed** is to see statistics other than the means and medians. (The medians aren't zero, but they're pretty close.)

Date: 05/16/05 Time: 09:05
Sample: 1950 2000
Common sample
Cross section specific means subtracted

	D(LOG(POP?))	Y?	D(LOG(POPUSA))
Mean	0.000000	0.000000	0.000000
Median	-0.000203	0.594645	-0.001082
Maximum	0.014619	26.52773	0.007734
Minimum	-0.008025	-39.65170	-0.003050
Std. Dev.	0.004139	10.18800	0.003081
Skewness	0.894852	-1.246273	1.206397
Kurtosis	4.252254	6.372645	3.202128
Jarque-Bera	55.66381	205.1877	68.39503
Probability	0.000000	0.000000	0.000000
Sum	0.000000	0.000000	0.000000
Sum Sq. Dev.	0.004780	28958.90	0.002648
Observations	280	280	280
Cross sections	6	6	6

According to the **Stacked data** statistics, the standard deviation of annual U.S. population growth was $3/10^{ths}$ of one percent, while the standard deviation for the pooled countries was $6/10^{ths}$ of one percent. This looks like population growth was much more variable for the countries in the pooled sample. Whether this is the correct conclusion depends on a subtle point. Some of the countries have relatively high population growth and some have lower growth. The standard deviation for **Stacked data** includes the effect of variability across countries and across time, while the standard deviation reported for the United States is looking only at variability across time. The **Stacked - means removed** report takes out cross-country variability, reporting the time series variation within a country, averaged across the pooled sample. This standard deviation is just over $4/10^{ths}$ of one percent. So the typical country in our pooled sample has only slightly higher variability in population growth than the United States.

The choice to remove means or not before computing descriptive statistics isn't a right-or-wrong issue. It's a way of answering different questions.

Cross Section Specific Statistics

Choosing the **Cross section specific** radio button generates descriptive statistics for each country separately, one column for each country for each series. In our example we have six reports from D(LOG(POP?)), six from Y?, and one from D(LOG(POPUSA)), an excerpt of which is shown below.

Date: 05/16/05 Time: 09:37
Sample: 1950 2000

	D(LOG(POPCAN))	D(LOG(POPFRA))	D(LOG(P...	D(LOG(P...	D(LOG(P...	D(LOG(P...	YCAN	YFRA
Mean	0.012202	0.004983	0.002384	0.001860	0.002336	0.006728	84.90463	73.48369
Median	0.011689	0.004712	0.002979	0.001227	0.001688	0.006087	86.01774	74.47637
Maximum	0.029485	0.009391	0.005307	0.008694	0.006783	0.023088	91.97449	78.21751
Minimum	0.008067	0.003332	-0.000604	-0.004612	5.48E-05	0.001580	77.39386	66.29604
Std. Dev.	0.003909	0.001495	0.001685	0.003827	0.002067	0.004699	4.427662	3.229485
Skewness	3.011855	1.537113	-0.456707	0.264405	0.834429	1.541362	-0.176956	-0.707828
Kurtosis	13.97230	5.048113	2.003455	2.103459	2.449095	5.940986	1.589700	2.578399
Jarque-Bera	195.8455	17.05705	2.284284	1.354282	3.860733	22.69072	2.642747	2.727286
Probability	0.000000	0.000198	0.319135	0.508067	0.145095	0.000012	0.266769	0.255727
Sum	0.366057	0.149478	0.071511	0.055795	0.070067	0.201854	2547.139	2204.511
Sum Sq. Dev.	0.000443	6.48E-05	8.24E-05	0.000425	0.000124	0.000640	568.5215	302.4577
Observations	30	30	30	30	30	30	30	30

Empirical aside: If you're following along on the computer, you can scroll the output to see that three of the countries in the pooled sample have population growth standard deviations much lower than the U.S. and three have standard deviations a little above that of the U.S.

Time Period Specific Statistics

Time period specific is the flip side of **Cross section specific**. **Time period specific** pools the whole sample together and then computes mean, median, *etc.*, for each date.

obs	Mean D(LOG(POP?))	Med D(LOG(POP?))	Sd D(LOG(POP?))	Min D(LOG(PO
1950	NA	NA	NA	N,
1951	0.012109	0.009569	0.010134	0.00197
1952	0.011645	0.007117	0.010110	0.00197
1953	0.011204	0.007067	0.009720	0.00197
1954	0.011056	0.009346	0.009580	0.00196
1955	0.011433	0.006953	0.008811	0.00392
1956	0.011471	0.008859	0.007956	0.00390
1957	0.012641	0.009091	0.009940	0.00583
1958	0.012101	0.010152	0.006714	0.00579
1959	0.011614	0.008611	0.009744	0.00384
1960	0.010942	0.009600	0.006772	0.00574
1961	0.010870	0.008982	0.005287	0.00667
1962	0.012354	0.009320	0.005491	0.00678
1963	0.011914	0.010174	0.005709	0.00622
1964	0.010915	0.010278	0.004688	0.00680
1965	0.010626	0.009231	0.004436	0.00662
1966	0.009841	0.008292	0.005106	0.00537
1967	0.009623	0.007780	0.004849	0.00576
1968	0.007557	0.006313	0.005039	0.00333
1969	0.010487	0.008041	0.006690	0.00446

You can save the time period specific statistics into series. Click the [Proc] button and choose **Make Periods Stats series**....

Check boxes for the desired descriptive statistics and EViews will (1) create the requested series, YMEAN, YMED, *etc.*, and (2) open an untitled group displaying the new series.

Getting Out of the Pool

Pooled series are plain old series, so the pool object provides a number of tools for manipulating pooled plain old EViews objects in convenient ways. A number of useful procedures involving pools appear under the **Proc** menu.

Hint: If you don't see the procedures for pools listed under the Proc menu, be sure that the pool window is active. Clicking the Proc button in a pool window gets you to the same menu.

Pool Series Generation

Much of our analysis on the pool has used percentage population growth, measured as D(LOG(POP?)). We might want to generate this as a new series for each country. Manually, we could give six commands of the form:

```
series dlpcan = d(log(popcan))
series dlpfra = d(log(popfra))
```

…

To automate the task, hit the PoolGenr button and enter the equation using a "?" everywhere you want the country identifier to go. The entry "DLP? = D(LOG(POP?))" generates all six series.

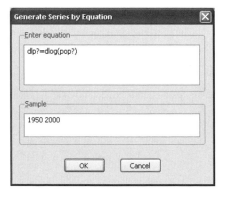

Hint: `genr` is a synonym for the command `series` in generating data. Hence the name on the button, "PoolGenr."

Pool Series Degeneration

To delete a pile of series, choose **Delete Pool series…**. from the **Proc** menu. This deletes the series. It doesn't affect the pool definition in any way.

Making Groups

As you've seen, there are lots of ways to manipulate a group of pooled series from the pool window. But sometimes it's easier to include all the series in a standard EViews group and then use group procedures. Plotting pooled series is one such example. Choose **Make Group…** from the **Proc** menu and enter the series you want in the **Series List** dialog. An untitled group will open.

If we like, we could make a quick plot of Y for the pooled series by switching the group to a graph view. (See Chapter 5, "Picture This!")

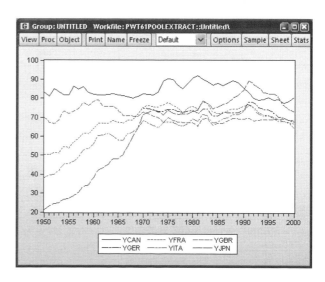

More Pool Estimation

You won't be surprised that estimates with pools come with lots of interesting options. We touch on a few of them here. For complete information, see the *User's Guide*.

Residuals

Return to the first pooled estimate in the chapter, the one with a common intercept for all series. Pick the menu **View/Residuals/Graphs**. The first thing you'll notice is that squeezing six graphs into one window makes for some pretty tiny graphs.

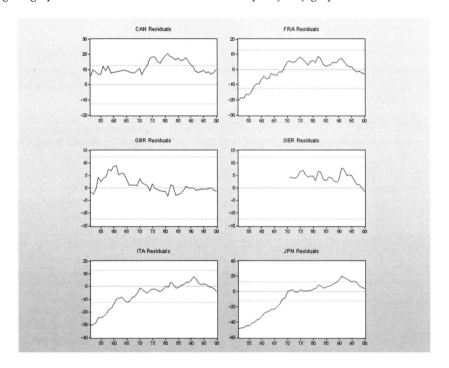

Residuals are supposed to be centered on zero. The second thing you'll notice is that the residuals for Canada are all strongly positive, those for Germany are mostly positive and Italy's residuals are nearly all negative, so the residuals are *not* centered on zero. That's a hint that the country equations should have different intercepts.

We can get different intercepts by specifying fixed effects. Let's look at the residual plots from the fixed effects equation we estimated. This time, each country's residual is centered around zero.

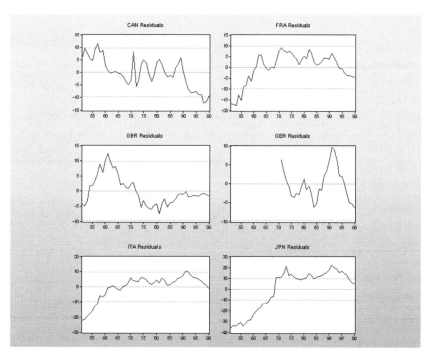

Grabbing the Residual Series

If six graphs in one window is looking a little hard to read, think what sixty-six graphs would look like! **Proc/Make Residuals** generates series for the residuals from each country, RESIDCAN, RESIDFRA, *etc.*, and puts them into a group window. From there, it's easy to make any kind of group plot we'd like. Here's one to which we've added a title and zero line. It's pretty clear from this picture that the fit for Japan is problematic.

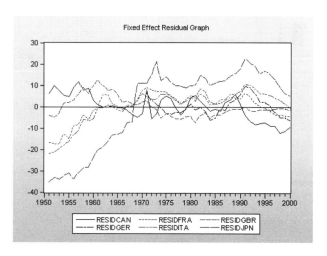

Our model doesn't take into account the post-War Japanese recovery - and it shows! (If this were a real research project we'd have to stop and deal with the misspecification issue. Employing the literary device *suspension of disbelief*, we'll just proceed onward.)

Residual Correlations

Clicking on **View/Residuals/Correlation Matrix** gives us a table showing the correlation of the residuals. The correlations involving Japan and Italy are particularly high.

Pool: ISOCODE_NOTUS   Workfile: PWT61POOLEXTRACT::Untitled\
View Proc Object Print Name Freeze Estimate Define PoolGenr Sheet

Residual Correlation Matrix

	CAN	FRA	GBR	GER	ITA	JPN
CAN	1.000000	-0.276989	0.154012	0.061364	-0.558845	-0.584563
FRA	-0.276989	1.000000	-0.079641	0.149119	0.889344	0.755364
GBR	0.154012	-0.079641	1.000000	0.134813	-0.198263	-0.539393
GER	0.061364	0.149119	0.134813	1.000000	0.159259	0.102686
ITA	-0.558845	0.889344	-0.198263	0.159259	1.000000	0.903301
JPN	-0.584563	0.755364	-0.539393	0.102686	0.903301	1.000000

The menu **View/Residuals/Covariance Matrix** gives variances and covariances instead of correlations. Note that the variance of

Pool: ISOCODE_NOTUS   Workfile: PWT61POOLEXTRACT::Untitled\
View Proc Object Print Name Freeze Estimate Define PoolGenr Sheet

Residual Covariance Matrix

	CAN	FRA	GBR	GER	ITA	JPN
CAN	34.14641	-11.11523	4.180378	1.524866	-25.97868	-63.70409
FRA	-11.11523	47.15911	-2.540432	4.354747	48.58535	96.73923
GBR	4.180378	-2.540432	21.57637	2.662975	-7.326277	-46.72594
GER	1.524866	4.354747	2.662975	18.08399	5.387706	8.143726
ITA	-25.97868	48.58535	-7.326277	5.387706	63.28573	134.0135
JPN	-63.70409	96.73923	-46.72594	8.143726	134.0135	347.7978

the residuals for Japan, 347.8, is ten times the variance for Canada.

Generalized Least Squares and Heteroskedasticity Correction

Relaxation hint: This is a book about EViews, not an econometrics tome. If the title of this section just pushed past your comfort zone, skip ahead to the next topic.

One of the assumptions underlying ordinary least squares estimation is that all observations have the same error variance and that errors are uncorrelated with one another. When this assumption isn't true reported standard errors from ordinary least squares tend to be off and you forego information that can lead to improved estimation efficiency. The tables above suggest that our pooled sample has both problems: correlation across observations and differing variances. EViews offers a number of options in the **Weights** menu in the **Pool Estimation** dialog, shown to the right, for dealing with heteroskedasticity. We'll touch on a couple of them.

No weights
Cross-section weights
Cross-section SUR
Period weights
Period SUR

Country Specific Weights

To allow for a different variance for each country, choose **Cross-section weights**. Compare these estimates to those we saw in *Everyone Into the Pool May Not Be Fun*, on page 292. The estimated effect of growth is much smaller. The standard error is also smaller, but it shrunk by less than the coefficient did. It would have been nicer if the *t*-statistic had become larger rather than smaller, at least if "nicer" is interpreted as providing support to our preconceived notions.

As you might guess, the menu choice **Period weights** is analogous to **Cross-section weights**, allowing for different variances for each time period instead of each country.

Dependent Variable: Y?
Method: Pooled EGLS (Cross-section weights)
Date: 07/17/09 Time: 16:22
Sample (adjusted): 1951 2000
Included observations: 50 after adjustments
Cross-sections included: 6
Total pool (unbalanced) observations: 280
Linear estimation after one-step weighting matrix

Variable	Coefficient	Std. Error	t-Statistic	Prob.
C	71.24291	0.709014	100.4817	0.0000
D(LOG(POP?))	-147.9298	86.54592	-1.709264	0.0885
Fixed Effects (Cross)				
CAN--C	15.10145			
FRA--C	-1.127769			
GBR--C	-0.387397			
GER--C	2.007452			
ITA--C	-7.564365			
JPN--C	-7.226390			

Effects Specification

Cross-section fixed (dummy variables)

Weighted Statistics

R-squared	0.560258	Mean dependent var	105.7350
Adjusted R-squared	0.550593	S.D. dependent var	45.76257
S.E. of regression	9.026674	Sum squared resid	22244.27
F-statistic	57.96979	Durbin-Watson stat	0.105388
Prob(F-statistic)	0.000000		

Unweighted Statistics

R-squared	0.364290	Mean dependent var	70.18130
Sum squared resid	27997.03	Durbin-Watson stat	0.040912

Cross-country Correlations

To account for correlation of errors across countries as well as different variances, choose **Cross-section SUR**. This option requires *balanced* samples —ones that all have the same start and end dates. So if your pool isn't balanced—ours isn't—you'll also need to check the **Balance Sample** checkbox at the lower right of the dialog. The estimated effect of population growth is now quite small, but statistically very significant.

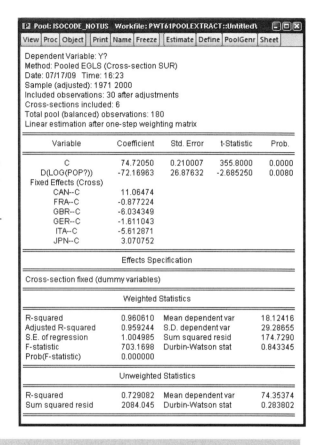

```
Dependent Variable: Y?
Method: Pooled EGLS (Cross-section SUR)
Date: 07/17/09   Time: 16:23
Sample (adjusted): 1971 2000
Included observations: 30 after adjustments
Cross-sections included: 6
Total pool (balanced) observations: 180
Linear estimation after one-step weighting matrix
```

Variable	Coefficient	Std. Error	t-Statistic	Prob.
C	74.72050	0.210007	355.8000	0.0000
D(LOG(POP?))	-72.16963	26.87632	-2.685250	0.0080
Fixed Effects (Cross)				
CAN--C	11.06474			
FRA--C	-0.877224			
GBR--C	-6.034349			
GER--C	-1.611043			
ITA--C	-5.612871			
JPN--C	3.070752			

Effects Specification

Cross-section fixed (dummy variables)

Weighted Statistics

R-squared	0.960610	Mean dependent var	18.12416
Adjusted R-squared	0.959244	S.D. dependent var	29.28655
S.E. of regression	1.004985	Sum squared resid	174.7290
F-statistic	703.1698	Durbin-Watson stat	0.843345
Prob(F-statistic)	0.000000		

Unweighted Statistics

R-squared	0.729082	Mean dependent var	74.35374
Sum squared resid	2084.045	Durbin-Watson stat	0.283802

Nomenclature hint: *SUR* stands for Seemingly Unrelated Regression.

Period SUR provides the analogous model where errors are correlated across periods within each country's observations.

More Options to Mention

If you're in an exploring mood, note that EViews will do random effects as well as fixed effects (in the **Estimation method** field of the **Specification** tab of the **Pool Estimation** dialog) and **Period specific coefficients** just as it does **Cross-section specific coefficients** (**Regressors and AR() terms**). The **Options** tab provides a variety of methods for robust estimation of standard errors, and also options for controlling exactly how the estimation is done. These are, of course, discussed at length in the *User's Guide*.

Getting Data In and Out of the Pool

Since pooled series are just ordinary series, you're free to load them into EViews any way that you find convenient. But there are two data arrangements that are common: *unstacked* and *stacked*. These data arrangements correspond to the spreadsheet arrangements we saw in *Spreadsheet Views* earlier in the chapter. Unstacked data are read through a standard **File/Open**. (See Chapter 2, "EViews—Meet Data.") EViews provides some special help for stacked data.

Importing Unstacked Data

Here's an excerpt of an Excel spreadsheet with unstacked data.

	A	B	C	D	E	F	G	H	
1	yr	ycan	yfra	ygbr	yger	yita	yjpn	yusa	
2	1950	82.912723	50.5084213	69.8522627	#N/A	38.2405647	21.3147443	100	
3	1951	81.052846	50.1718216	67.2271715	#N/A	39.3797631	23.1120264	100	
4	1952	85.0833059	51.5901598	66.4287985	#N/A	39.9917745	24.3911922	100	
5	1953	83.3591796	51.2338972	68.4325399	#N/A	41.9178248	24.6679595	100	
6	1954	81.6939082	54.4155543	73.2203468	#N/A	45.0865893	26.7221542	100	
7	1955	81.5759565	53.6333057	71.8266032	#N/A	45.4169103	27.176685	100	
8	1956	86.4803641	56.6182518	73.249934	#N/A	46.8931849	28.7378419	100	
9	1957	84.8500982	59.0927652	74.4278311	#N/A	48.96212	30.5277451	100	
10	1958	86.1393285	61.7984348	77.3896696	#N/A	52.5932701	33.267279	100	

I◄ ◄ ► ►I \ pwt61poolunstacked /

Since we have ordinary series with conveniently chosen names, load in the spreadsheet in the usual way, create a pool object with suffixes CAN, FRA, *etc.*, and bob's your uncle.

Importing Stacked Data—The Direct Method

Here's an excerpt of an Excel spreadsheet with stacked data—stacked by cross-section. We've hidden some of the rows so you can see the whole pattern. All the data for the first country appears first, stacked on top of the data for the second country, *etc.* While Y and POP appear in the first row, the country specific series names, such as YCAN, don't appear.

	A	B	C	D	
1	ID	YEAR	Y	POP	
2	CAN	1950	82.91272	13753.32	
3	CAN	1951	81.05285	14149.1	
4	CAN	1952	85.08331	14544.88	
5	CAN	1953	83.35918	14940.66	
6	CAN	1954	81.69391	15336.44	
52	CAN	2000	80.6619	30750	
53	FRA	1950	50.50842	42718.14	
54	FRA	1951	50.17182	43128.89	
55	FRA	1952	51.59016	43436.95	
56	FRA	1953	51.2339	43745.02	
57	FRA	1954	54.41555	44155.77	
103	FRA	2000	66.29604	60431.2	
104	GBR	1950	69.85226	50473.98	
105	GBR	1951	67.22717	50573.93	
106	GBR	1952	66.4288	50673.88	
107	GBR	1953	68.43254	50773.82	
108	GBR	1954	73.22035	50873.77	
109	GBR	1955	71.8266	51073.67	
110	GBR	1956	73.24993	51273.57	
111	GBR	1957	74.42783	51573.41	
112	GBR	1958	77.38967	51873.26	
113	GBR	1959	76.07212	52073.15	

I◄ ◄ ► ►I \ pool stacked cross

We want EViews to help out by attaching the identifiers in the first column to the series names beginning with Y and POP. With the pool window active, choose the menu **Proc/Import Pool data (ASCII,XLS,WK?)**.... Fill out the dialog with the names of the series to import, as in the example to the right. Hit OK and EViews will get everything properly attached.

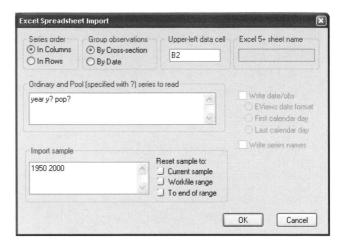

Not surprisingly, stacked by date is the flipped-on-the-side version of stacked by cross-section. Here's an excerpt. The same **Proc/Import Pool data (ASCII,XLS,WK?)...** command works fine—just choose the **By Date** radio button instead of **By Cross-section**.

	A	B	C	D
1	ID	YEAR	Y	POP
2	CAN	1950	82.91272	13753.32
3	FRA	1950	50.50842	42718.14
4	GBR	1950	69.85226	50473.98
5	GER	1950		
6	ITA	1950	38.24056	46799.91
7	JPN	1950	21.31474	83105.04
8	CAN	1951	81.05285	14149.1
9	FRA	1951	50.17182	43128.89
10	GBR	1951	67.22717	50573.93
11	GER	1951		
12	ITA	1951	39.37976	47099.91
13	JPN	1951	23.11203	84296.51
14	CAN	1952	85.08331	14544.88

pool stacked date

Importing Stacked Data—The Indirect Method

Sometimes, a little indirection makes life go more smoothly. In the case at hand, it's often easier to simply read your data into EViews by the methods you're already familiar with (for example, we might read in our data by drag-and-dropping the file onto the EViews desktop and clicking on 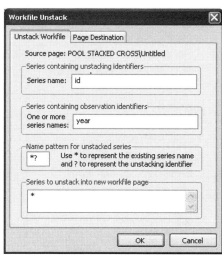 OK to accept the defaults) and then work with it in panel form (see Chapter 11, "Panel—What's My Line?"), or transform it into pooled form using **Proc/Reshape Current Page/Unstack in New Page**.... and filling out the **Workfile Unstack** dialog as shown.

Click OK and you have a new page set up in pooled form. In fact, to help out EViews has even set up a pool object for you.

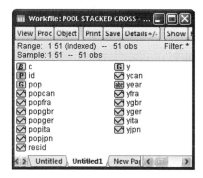

Exporting Stacked Data

Typically, unstacked data are easier to operate on, but sometimes stacked data are easier for humans to read. The inverse of **Proc/Import Pool data (ASCII,XLS,WK?)…** is **Proc/Export Pool data (ASCII,XLS,WK?)…**. Choose **By Date** or **By Cross-section** and away you go.

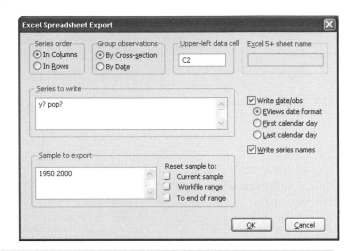

Hint: EViews includes the "?" in the series name in the output file. You might choose to manually delete the "?" in the exported file to improve the appearance of the output.

Exporting Stacked Data—A Little Indirection Here Too

Not surprisingly, there's an indirect method for exporting, too. To stack data in a new page in preparation for using any of the usual export tools, choose **Proc/Reshape Current Page/Stack in New Page…**. In the **Workfile Stack** dialog, enter the name of the pool object. Click OK for a nicely stacked page.

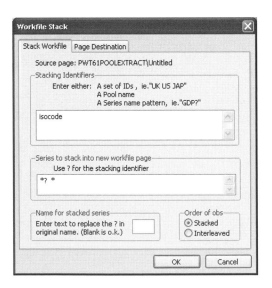

Quick Review—Pools

The pool feature lets you analyze multiple series observed for the same variable, such as GDP series for a number of countries. You can pool the data in a regression with common coefficients for all countries. You can also allow for individual coefficients by cross-section or by period for any variable. Fixed and random effect estimators are built-in. And because pooled series are just plain old series with a clever naming convention, all of the EViews features are directly available. See Chapter 11, "Panel—What's My Line?" for a different approach to two dimensional data.

Chapter 13. Serial Correlation—Friend or Foe?

In a first introduction to regression, it's usually assumed that the error terms in the regression equation are uncorrelated with one another. But when data are ordered— for example, when sequential observations represent Monday, Tuesday, and Wednesday—then we won't be very surprised if neighboring error terms turn out to be correlated. This phenomenon is called *serial correlation*. The simplest model of serial correlation, called first-order serial correlation, can be written as:

$$y_t = \beta x_t + u_t$$
$$u_t = \rho u_{t-1} + \epsilon_t, \quad 0 \le |\rho| < 1$$

The error term for observation t, u_t, carries over part of the error from the previous period, ρu_{t-1}, and adds in a new *innovation*, ϵ_t. By convention, the innovations are themselves uncorrelated over time. The correlation comes through the ρu_{t-1} term. If $\rho = 0.9$, then 90 percent of the error from the previous period persists into the current period. In contrast, if $\rho = 0$, nothing persists and there isn't any serial correlation.

If left untreated, serial correlation can do two bad things:

- Reported standard errors and t-statistics can be quite far off.

- Under certain circumstances, the estimated regression coefficients can be quite badly biased.

When treated, three good things are possible:

- Standard errors and t-statistics can be fixed.

- The statistical efficiency of least squares can be improved upon.

- Much better forecasting is possible.

We begin this chapter by looking at residuals as a way of spotting visual patterns in the regression errors. Then we'll look at some formal testing procedures. Having discussed detection of serial correlation, we'll turn to methods for correcting regressions to account for serial correlation. Lastly, we talk about forecasting.

Fitted Values and Residuals

A regression equation expresses the dependent variable, y_t as the sum of a modeled part, βx_t, and an error, u_t. Once we've computed the estimated regression coefficient, $\hat{\beta}$, we can make an analogous split of the dependent variable into the part explained by the regression, $\hat{y}_t \equiv \hat{\beta} x_t$ and the part that remains unexplained, $e_t \equiv y_t - \hat{\beta} x_t$. The explained part, $\hat{y}_t$, is called the *fitted* value. The unexplained part, e_t, is called the *residual*. The residuals are estimates of the errors, so we look for serial correlation in the errors (u_t) by looking for serial correlation in the residuals.

EViews has a variety of features for looking at residuals directly and for checking for serial correlation. Exploration of these features occupies the first half of this chapter. Additionally, you can capture both fitted values and residuals as series that can then be investigated just like any other data. The command `fit` *seriesname* stores the fitted values from the most recent estimation and the special series RESID automatically contains the residuals from the most recent estimation.

> Hint: Since RESID changes after the estimation of every equation, you may want to use **Proc/Make Residual Series...** to store residuals in a series which won't be accidentally overwritten.

As an example, the first command here runs a regression using data from the workfile "NYSEVOLUME.wf1":

```
ls logvol c @trend @trend^2 d(log(close(-1)))
```

Equation: UNTITLED   Workfile: NYSEVOLUME::Quarterly

View | Proc | Object | | Print | Name | Freeze | | Estimate | Forecast | Stats | Resids

Dependent Variable: LOGVOL
Method: Least Squares
Date: 07/17/09   Time: 10:42
Sample (adjusted): 1896Q4 2004Q1
Included observations: 430 after adjustments

Variable	Coefficient	Std. Error	t-Statistic	Prob.
C	-0.126809	0.104280	-1.216036	0.2246
@TREND	-0.011342	0.000949	-11.95094	0.0000
@TREND^2	5.89E-05	1.86E-06	31.72172	0.0000
D(LOG(CLOSE(-1)))	0.821073	0.310635	2.643206	0.0085

R-squared	0.953438	Mean dependent var		1.628945
Adjusted R-squared	0.953110	S.D. dependent var		2.449342
S.E. of regression	0.530381	Akaike info criterion		1.578816
Sum squared resid	119.8355	Schwarz criterion		1.616619
Log likelihood	-335.4455	Hannan-Quinn criter.		1.593744
F-statistic	2907.712	Durbin-Watson stat		0.349207
Prob(F-statistic)	0.000000			

The next commands save the fitted values and the residuals, and then open a group—which we changed to a line graph and then prettied up a little.

```
fit logvol_fitted
series logvol_resid = logvol - logvol_fitted
show logvol logvol_fitted logvol_resid
```

You'll note that the model does a good job of explaining volume after 1940, where the residuals fluctuate around zero, and not such a good job before 1940, where the residuals look a lot like the dependent variable.

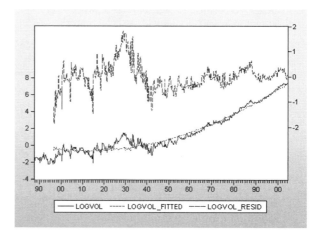

Econometric hint: We're treating serial correlation as a statistical issue. Sometimes serial correlation is a hint of misspecification. Although it's not something we'll investigate further, that's probably the case here.

Visual Checks

Every regression estimate comes with views to make looking at residuals easy. If the errors are serially correlated, then a large residual should generally be followed by another large residual; a small residual is likely to be followed by another small residual; and positive followed by positive and negative by negative. Clicking the [View] button brings up the **Actual, Fitted, Residual** menu.

> Actual,Fitted,Residual Table
> Actual,Fitted,Residual Graph
> Residual Graph
> Standardized Residual Graph

Choosing **Actual, Fitted, Residual Graph** switches to the view shown to the right. The actual dependent variable (LOGVOL in this case) together with the fitted value appear in the upper part of the graph and are linked to the scale on the right-hand axis. The residuals are plotted in the lower area, linked to the axis on the left.

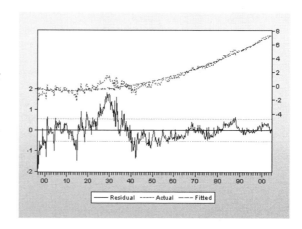

The residual plot includes a solid line at zero to make it easy to visually pick out runs of positive and negative residuals. Lightly dashed lines mark out ± 1 standard error bands around zero to give a sense of the scaling of the residuals.

It's useful to see the actual, fitted, and residual values plotted together, but it's sometime also useful to concentrate on the residuals alone. Pick **Residual Graph** from the **Actual, Fitted, Residual** menu for this view. In this example there are long runs of positive residuals and long runs of negative residuals, providing strong visual evidence of serial correlation.

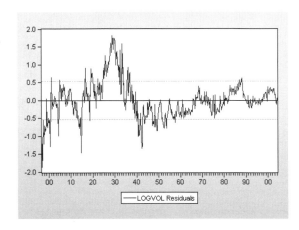

Another way to get a visual check is with a scatterplot of residuals against lagged residuals. In the plot to the right we see that the lagged residual is quite a good predictor of the current residual, another very strong indicator of serial correlation.

The Correlogram

Another visual approach to checking for serial correlation is to look directly at the empirical pattern of correlations between residuals and their own past values. We can compute the correlation between e_t and

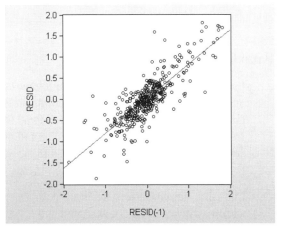

e_{t-1}, the correlation between e_t and e_{t-2}, and so on. Since the correlations are of the residual series with its (lagged) self, these are called *autocorrelations*. If there is no serial correlation, then all the correlations should be approximately zero—although the reported values will differ from zero due to estimation error.

Hint: For the first-order serial correlation model that opens the chapter, $u_t = \rho u_{t-1} + \epsilon_t$, the autocorrelations equal $\rho, \rho^2, \rho^3 \ldots$.

To plot the autocorrelations of the residuals, click the [View] button and choose the menu **Residual Diagnostics/Correlogram - Q-Statistics....** Choose the number of autocorrelations you want to see—the default, 36, is fine—and EViews pops up with a combined graphical and numeric look at the autocorrelations. The unlabeled

Date: 12/22/06 Time: 05:35
Sample: 1896Q4 2004Q1
Included observations: 430

Autocorrelation	Partial Correlation		AC	PAC	Q-Stat	Prob
		1	0.819	0.819	290.53	0.000
		2	0.748	0.235	533.59	0.000
		3	0.725	0.204	762.10	0.000
		4	0.707	0.135	979.99	0.000
		5	0.659	-0.008	1170.0	0.000
		6	0.630	0.035	1344.0	0.000
		7	0.593	-0.023	1498.6	0.000
		8	0.579	0.053	1646.0	0.000
		9	0.574	0.079	1791.5	0.000

column in the middle of the display, gives the lag number (1, 2, 3, and so on). The column marked AC gives estimated autocorrelations at the corresponding lag. This correlogram shows substantial and persistent autocorrelation.

The left-most column gives the autocorrelations as a bar graph. The graph is a little easier to read if you rotate your head 90 degrees to put the autocorrelations on the vertical axis and the lags on the horizontal, giving a picture something like the one to the right showing slowing declining autocorrelations.

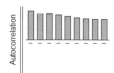

Testing for Serial Correlation

Visual checks provide a great deal of information, but you'll probably want to follow up with one or more formal statistical tests for serial correlation. EViews provides three test statistics: the Durbin-Watson, the Breusch-Godfrey, and the Ljung-Box Q-statistic.

Durbin-Watson Statistic

The Durbin-Watson, or DW, statistic is the traditional test for serial correlation. For reasons discussed below, the DW is no longer the test statistic preferred by most econometricians. Nonetheless, it is widely used in practice and performs excellently in most situations. The Durbin-Watson tradition is so strong that EViews routinely reports it in the lower panel of regression output.

The Durbin-Watson statistic is unusual in that under the null hypothesis (no serial correlation)

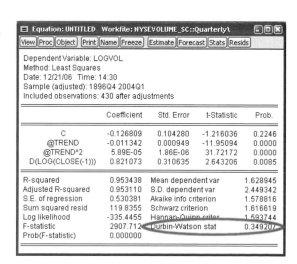

the Durbin-Watson centers around 2.0 rather than 0. You can roughly translate between the Durbin-Watson and the serial correlation coefficient using the formulas:

$$DW = 2 - 2\rho$$

$$\rho = 1 - (DW/2)$$

If the serial correlation coefficient is zero, the Durbin-Watson is about 2. As the serial correlation coefficient heads toward 1.0, the Durbin-Watson heads toward 0.

To test the hypothesis of no serial correlation, compare the reported Durbin-Watson to a table of critical values. In this example, the Durbin-Watson of 0.349 clearly rejects the absence of serial correlation.

> Hint: EViews doesn't compute p-values for the Durbin-Watson.

The Durbin-Watson has a number of shortcomings, one of which is that the standard tables include intervals for which the test statistic is inconclusive. *Econometric Theory and Methods*, by Davidson and MacKinnon, says:

> *...the Durbin-Watson statistic, despite its popularity, is not very satisfactory.... the DW statistic is not valid when the regressors include lagged dependent variables, and it cannot be easily generalized to test for higher-order processes.*

While we recommend the more modern Breusch-Godfrey in place of the Durbin-Watson, the truth is that the tests usually agree.

> Econometric warning: But never use the Durbin-Watson when there's a lagged dependent variable on the right-hand side of the equation.

Breusch-Godfrey Statistic

The preferred test statistic for checking for serial correlation is the Breusch-Godfrey. From the [View] menu choose **Residual Diagnostics/Serial Correlation LM Test...** to pop open a small dialog where you enter the degree of serial correlation you're interested in testing. In other words, if you're interested in first-order serial correlation change **Lags to include** to 1.

The view to the right shows the results of testing for first-order serial correlation. The top part of the output gives the test results in two versions: an F-statistic and a χ^2 statistic. (There's no great reason to prefer one over the other.) Associated p-values are shown next to each statistic. For our stock market volume data, the hypothesis of no serial correlation is easily rejected.

The bottom part of the view provides extra information showing the auxiliary regression used to create the test statistics reported at the top. This extra regression is sometimes interesting, but you don't need it for conducting the test.

Breusch-Godfrey Serial Correlation LM Test:

F-statistic	918.0997	Prob. F(1,425)	0.0000
Obs*R-squared	293.9342	Prob. Chi-Square(1)	0.0000

Test Equation:
Dependent Variable: RESID
Method: Least Squares
Date: 07/23/09   Time: 10:29
Sample: 1896Q4 2004Q1
Included observations: 430
Presample missing value lagged residuals set to zero.

Variable	Coefficient	Std. Error	t-Statistic	Prob.
C	0.011076	0.058730	0.188584	0.8505
@TREND	-6.29E-05	0.000534	-0.117595	0.9064
@TREND^2	1.81E-07	1.05E-06	0.173053	0.8627
D(LOG(CLOSE(-1)))	-0.725945	0.176578	-4.111188	0.0000
RESID(-1)	0.834519	0.027542	30.30016	0.0000

R-squared	0.683568	Mean dependent var	-2.78E-16
Adjusted R-squared	0.680590	S.D. dependent var	0.528523
S.E. of regression	0.298702	Akaike info criterion	0.432821
Sum squared resid	37.91981	Schwarz criterion	0.480075
Log likelihood	-88.05659	Hannan-Quinn criter.	0.451480
F-statistic	229.5249	Durbin-Watson stat	2.185386
Prob(F-statistic)	0.000000		

Ljung-Box Q-statistic

A different approach to checking for serial correlation is to plot the correlation of the residual with the residual lagged once, the residual with the residual lagged twice, and so on. As we saw above in *The Correlogram*, this plot is called the *correlogram* of the residuals. If there is no serial correlation then correlations should all be zero, except for random fluctuation. To see the correlogram, choose **Residual Diagnostics/Correlogram - Q-statistics…** from the [View] menu. A small dialog pops open allowing you to specify the number of correlations to show.

The correlogram for the residuals from our volume equation is repeated to the right. The column headed "Q-Stat" gives the Ljung-Box Q-statistic, which tests for a particular row the hypothesis that all the correlations up to and including that row equal zero. The column marked "Prob" gives the corresponding p-value. Continuing

Date: 12/22/06   Time: 05:35
Sample: 1896Q4 2004Q1
Included observations: 430

Autocorrelation	Partial Correlation		AC	PAC	Q-Stat	Prob
		1	0.819	0.819	290.53	0.000
		2	0.748	0.235	533.59	0.000
		3	0.725	0.204	762.10	0.000
		4	0.707	0.135	979.99	0.000
		5	0.659	-0.008	1170.0	0.000
		6	0.630	0.035	1344.0	0.000
		7	0.593	-0.023	1498.6	0.000
		8	0.579	0.053	1646.0	0.000
		9	0.574	0.079	1791.5	0.000

along with the example, the Q-statistic against the hypothesis that both the first and second correlation equal zero is 553.59. The probability of getting this statistic by chance is zero to three decimal places. So for this equation, the Ljung-Box Q-statistic agrees with the evidence in favor of serial correlation that we got from the Durbin-Watson and the Breusch-Godfrey.

> Hint: The number of correlations used in the Q-statistic does *not* correspond to the order of serial correlation. If there is first-order serial correlation, then the residual correlations at all lags differ from zero, although the correlation diminishes as the lag increases.

More General Patterns of Serial Correlation

The idea of first-order serial correlation can be extended to allow for more than one lag. The correlogram for first-order serial correlation always follows geometric decay, while higher order serial correlation can produce more complex patterns in the correlogram, which also decay gradually. In contrast, moving average processes, below, produce a correlogram which falls abruptly to zero after a finite number of periods.

Higher-Order Serial Correlation

First-order serial correlation is the simplest pattern by which errors in a regression equation may be correlated over time. This pattern is also called an *autoregression* of order one, or AR(1), because we can think of the equation for the error terms as being a regression on one lagged value of itself. Analogously, second-order serial correlation, or AR(2), is written $u_t = \rho_1 u_{t-1} + \rho_2 u_{t-2} + \epsilon_t$. More generally, serial correlation of order p, AR(p), is written $u_t = \rho_1 u_{t-1} + \rho_2 u_{t-2} + \ldots + \rho_p u_{t-p} + \epsilon_t$.

When you specify the number of lags for the Breusch-Godfrey test, you're really specifying the order of the autoregression to be tested.

Moving Average Errors

A different specification of the pattern of serial correlation in the error term is the *moving average*, or *MA*, error. For example, a moving average of order one, or MA(1), would be written $u_t = \epsilon_t + \theta \epsilon_{t-1}$ and a moving average of order q, or MA(q), looks like $u_t = \epsilon_t + \theta_1 \epsilon_{t-1} + \ldots + \theta_q \epsilon_{t-q}$. Note that the moving average error is a weighted average of the current innovation and past innovations, where the autoregressive error is a weighted average of the current innovation and past errors.

> Convention Hint: There are two sign conventions for writing out moving average errors. EViews uses the convention that lagged innovations are added to the current innovation. This is the usual convention in regression analysis. Some texts, mostly in time series analysis, use the convention that lagged innovations are subtracted instead. There's no consequence to the choice of one convention over the other.

Conveniently, the Breusch-Godfrey test with q lags specified serves as a test against an MA(q) process as well as against an AR(q) process.

Autoregressive Regressive Moving Average (ARMA) Errors

Autoregressive and moving average errors can be combined into an *autoregressive-moving average*, or *ARMA*, process. For example, putting an AR(2) together with an MA(1) gives you an ARMA(2,1) process which can be written as $u_t = \rho_1 u_{t-1} + \rho_2 u_{t-2} + \epsilon_t + \theta \epsilon_{t-1}$.

Correcting for Serial Correlation

Now that we know that our stock volume equation has serial correlation, how do we fix the problem? EViews has built-in features to correct for either autoregressive or moving average errors (or both!) of any specified order. (The corrected estimate is a member of the class called *Generalized Least Squares*, or *GLS*.) For example, to correct for first-order serial correlation, include "AR(1)" in the regression command just as if it were another variable. The command:

```
ls logvol c @trend @trend^2 d(log(close(-1))) ar(1)
```

gives the results shown. The first thing to note is the additional line reported in the middle panel of the output. The serial correlation coefficient, what we've called ρ in writing out the equations, is labeled "AR(1)" and is estimated to equal about 0.84. The associated standard error, t-statistic, and p-value have the usual interpretations. In our equation, there is very strong evidence that the serial correlation coefficient doesn't equal zero— confirming all our earlier statistical tests.

Dependent Variable: LOGVOL
Method: Least Squares
Date: 07/17/09   Time: 11:13
Sample (adjusted): 1897Q1 2004Q1
Included observations: 429 after adjustments
Convergence achieved after 5 iterations

Variable	Coefficient	Std. Error	t-Statistic	Prob.
C	0.151610	0.365446	0.414863	0.6785
@TREND	-0.013476	0.003235	-4.165858	0.0000
@TREND^2	6.26E-05	6.19E-06	10.12327	0.0000
D(LOG(CLOSE(-1)))	-0.123767	0.150632	-0.821654	0.4117
AR(1)	0.836549	0.025884	32.31920	0.0000

R-squared	0.986452	Mean dependent var		1.637021
Adjusted R-squared	0.986325	S.D. dependent var		2.446463
S.E. of regression	0.286095	Akaike info criterion		0.346600
Sum squared resid	34.70453	Schwarz criterion		0.393937
Log likelihood	-69.34577	Hannan-Quinn criter.		0.365294
F-statistic	7718.214	Durbin-Watson stat		2.269181
Prob(F-statistic)	0.000000			

| Inverted AR Roots | .84 | | | |

Now let's look at the top panel, where we see that the number of observations has fallen from 430 to 429. EViews uses observations from before the start of the sample period to estimate AR and MA models. If the current sample is already at the earliest available observation, EViews will adjust the sample used for the equation in order to free up the pre-sample observations it needs.

There's an important change in the bottom panel too, but it's a change that isn't explicitly labeled. The summary statistics at the bottom are now based on the innovations (ϵ) rather than the error (u). For example, the R^2 gives the explained fraction of the variance of the dependent variable, including "credit" for the part explained by the autoregressive term.

Similarly, the Durbin-Watson is now a test for remaining serial correlation after first-order serial correlation has been corrected for.

Serial Correlation and Misspecification

Econometric theory tells us that if the original equation was otherwise well-specified, then correcting for serial correlation should change the standard errors. However, the estimated coefficients shouldn't change by very much. (Technically, both the original and corrected results are "unbiased.") In our example, the coefficient on D(LOG(CLOSE(-1))) went from positive and significant to negative and insignificant. This is an informal signal that the dynamics in this equation weren't well-specified in the original estimate.

Higher-Order Corrections

Correcting for higher-order autoregressive errors and for moving errors is just about as easy as correcting for an AR(1)—once you understand one very clever notational oddity. EViews requires that if you want to estimate a higher order process, you need to include all the lower-order terms in the equation as well. To estimate an AR(2), include AR(1) and AR(2). To estimate an AR(3), include AR(1), AR(2), and AR(3). If you want an MA(1), include MA(1) in the regression specification. And as you might expect, you'll need MA(1) and MA(2) to estimate a second-order moving average error.

> Hint: Unlike nearly all other EViews estimation procedures, MA requires a continuous sample. If your sample includes a break or NA data, EViews will give an error message.

Why not just type "AR(2)" for an AR(2)? Remember that a second-order autoregression has two coefficients, ρ_1 and ρ_2. If you type "AR(1) AR(2)," both coefficients get estimated. Omitting "AR(1)" forces the estimate of ρ_1 to zero, which is something you might want to do on rare occasion, probably when modeling a seasonal component.

Autoregressive and moving average errors can be combined. For example, to estimate both an AR(2) and an MA(1) use the command:

```
ls logvol c @trend @trend^2 d(log(close(-1))) ar(1) ar(2) ma(1)
```

The results, shown to the right, give both autoregressive coefficients and the single moving average coefficient. All three ARMA coefficients are significant.

Dependent Variable: LOGVOL
Method: Least Squares
Date: 07/17/09   Time: 11:14
Sample (adjusted): 1897Q2 2004Q1
Included observations: 428 after adjustments
Convergence achieved after 13 iterations
MA Backcast: 1897Q1

Variable	Coefficient	Std. Error	t-Statistic	Prob.
C	1.093273	0.911345	1.199626	0.2310
@TREND	-0.020058	0.006892	-2.910531	0.0038
@TREND^2	7.30E-05	1.18E-05	6.172038	0.0000
D(LOG(CLOSE(-1)))	0.278013	0.180387	1.541204	0.1240
AR(1)	1.305267	0.111769	11.67826	0.0000
AR(2)	-0.330825	0.103548	-3.194887	0.0015
MA(1)	-0.726684	0.081767	-8.887205	0.0000

R-squared	0.987528	Mean dependent var		1.645901
Adjusted R-squared	0.987351	S.D. dependent var		2.442394
S.E. of regression	0.274693	Akaike info criterion		0.269897
Sum squared resid	31.76716	Schwarz criterion		0.336285
Log likelihood	-50.75799	Hannan-Quinn criter.		0.296117
F-statistic	5555.989	Durbin-Watson stat		1.986655
Prob(F-statistic)	0.000000			

Inverted AR Roots	.96	.34	
Inverted MA Roots	.73		

Another Way to Look at the ARMA Coefficients

Equations that include ARMA parameters have an **ARMA Structure...** view which brings up a dialog offering four diagnostics. We'll take a look at the **Correlogram** view here and the **Impulse Response** view in the next section.

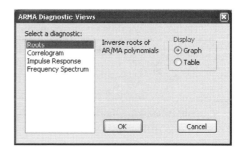

Here's the correlogram for the volume equation estimated above with an AR(1) specification. The correlogram, shown in the top part of the figure, uses a solid line to draw the theoretical correlogram corresponding to the estimated ARMA parameters. The spikes show the empirical correlogram of the residuals - the same values as we saw in the residual correlogram earlier in the chapter.

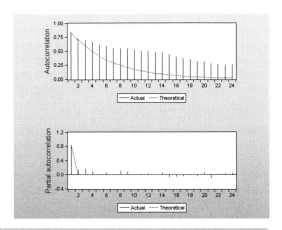

Nomenclature Hint: The theoretical correlogram corresponding to the estimated ARMA parameters is sometimes called the *Autocorrelation Function* or *ACF.*

The solid line (theoretical) and the top of the spikes (empirical) don't match up very well, do they? The pattern suggests that an AR(1) isn't a good enough specification, which we already suspected from other evidence.

Here's the analogous correlogram from the ARMA(2,1) model we estimated earlier. In this more general model the theoretical correlogram and the empirical correlogram are much closer. The richer specification is probably warranted.

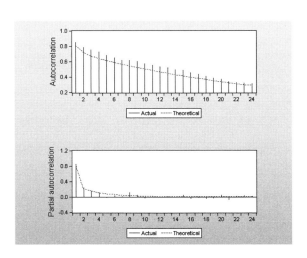

The Impulse Response Function

Including ARMA errors in forecasts sometimes makes big improvements in forecast accuracy a few periods out. The further out you forecast, the less ARMA errors contribute to forecast accuracy. For example, in an AR(1) model, if the autoregressive coefficient is estimated as 0.9 and the last residual is e_T, then including the ARMA error in the forecast adds

$0.9\,e_T$, $0.81\,e_T$, $0.729\,e_T\ldots$ in the first three forecasting periods. As you can see, the ARMA effect gradually declines to zero.

You can see that two elements determine the contribution of ARMA errors to the forecast: the value of the last residual and how quickly the weights decline. The value of the last residual depends on the starting date for the forecast, but the weights can be plotted using **ARMA Structure…/Impulse Response**.

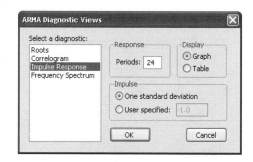

The weights are multiplied either by the standard error of the regression, if you choose **One standard deviation**, or by a value of your own choosing. Here's the plot for our AR(1) model set to **User specified:** 1.0. Even after two years, 28 percent of the final residual will remain in the forecast.

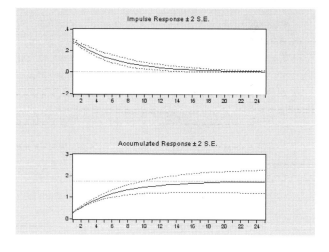

Forecasting

When we discussed forecasting in Chapter 8, "Forecasting," we put off the discussion of forecasting with ARMA errors—because we hadn't yet discussed ARMA errors. Now we have! The intuition about forecasting with ARMA errors is straightforward. Since errors persist in part from one period to the next, forecasts of the left-hand side variable can be improved by including a forecast of the error term.

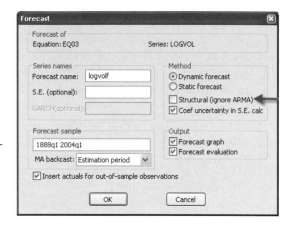

EViews makes it very easy to include the contribution of ARMA errors in forecasts. Once you push the [Forecast] button all you have to do is not do anything—in other words, the default procedure is to include ARMA errors in the forecast. Just don't check the **Structural (ignore ARMA)** checkbox.

Static Versus Dynamic Forecasting With ARMA errors

When you include ARMA errors in your forecast, you still need to decide between "static" and "dynamic" forecasting. The difference is best illustrated with an example. We have data on NYSE volume through the first quarter of 2004. Let's forecast volume for the last eight quarters of our sample, based on the model including an AR(1) error. Since we know what actually happened in that period, we can compare our forecast with reality to see how well we've done.

> Nomenclature hint: This is sometimes called *in-sample* forecasting, see Chapter 8, "Forecasting."

The first quarter of our forecast period is 2002q2. First, EViews will multiply the right hand side variables for 2002q2 by their respective estimated coefficients. Then EViews adds in the contribution of the AR(1) term: 0.8365 times the residual from 2002q1 (the final period before the forecast began).

The second period of our forecast is 2002q3. Now EViews will multiply the right hand side variables for 2002q3 by their respective estimated coefficients. Then there's a choice: should we add in 0.8365 times the residual from 2002q2, or should we use 0.8365^2 times the residual from 2002q1? The former is called a *static* forecast and the latter a *dynamic* forecast. The static forecast uses all information in our data set, while the dynamic forecast uses only information through the start of the estimation sample. The static forecast uses the best available information, so it's likely to be more accurate. On the other hand, if we were truly forecasting into an unknown future, dynamic forecasting would be the only option. Static forecasting requires calculation of residuals during the forecast period. If you don't know the true values of the left-hand side variable, you can't do that. Therefore dynamic forecasting is generally a better test of how well multi-period forecasts would work when forecasting for real.

Using our AR(1) model, we've constructed three forecasts: dynamic, static, and structural (ignore ARMA), this last forecast leaving out the contribution of the ARMA terms entirely. The static and dynamic forecasts are identical for the first period; they're supposed to be, of course. In general, the static forecast tracks the actual data best, followed by the dynamic forecast, with the structural forecast coming in last.

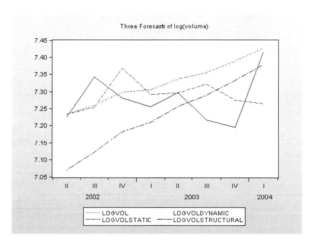

Three Forecasts of log(volume)

ARMA and ARIMA Models

The basic approach of regression analysis is to model the dependent variable as a function of the independent variables. The addition of ARMA errors augments the regression model with additional information about the persistence of errors over time. A widely used alternative—variously called Time Series Analysis or Box-Jenkins analysis, or ARMA or ARIMA modeling—directly models the persistence of the dependent variable. Estimation of ARMA or ARIMA models in EViews is very easy. We begin with a short digression into the "unit root problem" and then work through a pure time series model of NYSE volume.

Who Put the I in ARIMA?

Series that explode over time can be statistically problematic. Most of statistical theory requires that time series be *stationary* (non-explosive), as opposed to *nonstationary* (explosive). This is an over-simplification of some fairly complex issues. But looking at a graph of LOGVOL, it's clear that volume has exploded over time. This suggests—but doesn't prove—that a time series model of the level of LOGVOL might be dicey. A

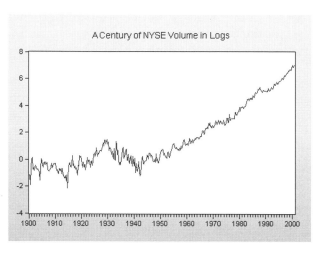

A Century of NYSE Volume in Logs

standard solution to this problem is to build a model of the first difference of the variable instead of modeling the level directly. Given such a differenced model, we then need to "integrate" the first differences to recover the levels. So an ARMA model of the first difference is an AR-Integrated-MA, or *ARIMA*, model of the level.

> Hint: If you know $dy_1 \equiv y_1 - y_0$, $dy_2 \equiv y_2 - y_1$, *etc.*, then you can find y_1 by adding dy_1 to y_0. You can find y_2 by adding dy_2 and dy_1 to y_0, and so forth. Adding up the first differences is the source of the term "integrated."

Unit Root Tests

A series that's stationary in first differences is said to possess a *unit root*. EViews provides a battery of unit root tests from the **View/Unit Root Test...** menu. For our purposes, the default test suffices. (The *User's Guide* has an extended discussion of both EViews options and of the different tests available.)

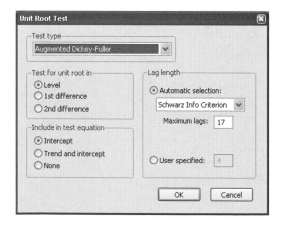

For this test, the null hypothesis is that there *is* a unit root. An excerpt of our test results are shown to the right. Because the hypothesis of a unit root is *not* rejected, we'll build a model of first differences.

Null Hypothesis: LOGVOL has a unit root
Exogenous: Constant
Lag Length: 3 (Automatic based on SIC, MAXLAG=17)

		t-Statistic	Prob.*
Augmented Dickey-Fuller test statistic		0.829999	0.9945
Test critical values:	1% level	-3.444311	
	5% level	-2.867590	
	10% level	-2.570055	

*MacKinnon (1996) one-sided p-values.

> Hint: The first difference of LOGVOL can be written in two ways: D(LOGVOL) or LOGVOL-LOGVOL(-1). The two are equivalent.

> Hint: Once in a great while, it's necessary to difference the first difference in order to get a stationary time series. If it's necessary to difference the data d times to achieve stationarity, then the original series is said to be "integrated of order d," or to be an $I(d)$ series. The complete specification of the order of an ARIMA model is ARIMA(p, d, q), where a plain old ARMA model is the special case ARIMA(p, 0, q).
>
> By the way, the d() function generalizes in EViews so that d(y, d) is the dth difference of Y.

ARIMA Estimation

Here's a plot of D(LOGVOL). No more exploding.

Building an ARIMA model of LOGVOL boils down to building an ARMA model of D(LOGVOL). It's traditional to treat the dependent variable in an ARMA model as having mean zero. One way to do this is to use the expression "D(LOGVOL)-@MEAN(D(LOGVOL))" as the dependent variable, but it's just as easy to include a constant in the estimate.

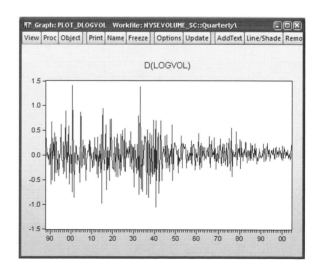

So with that build up, here's how to estimate an ARIMA(1,1,1) model in EViews:

```
ls d(logvol) c ar(1) ma(1)
```

That wasn't very hard. The results are shown to the right. Both ARMA coefficients are off-the-scale significant. The R^2 isn't very high, but remember that we're explaining changes—not levels—of volume.

To estimate higher order ARIMA models, just include more AR and MA terms in the command line.

Dependent Variable: D(LOGVOL)
Method: Least Squares
Date: 07/17/09 Time: 14:16
Sample (adjusted): 1888Q3 2004Q1
Included observations: 463 after adjustments
Convergence achieved after 6 iterations
MA Backcast: 1888Q2

Variable	Coefficient	Std. Error	t-Statistic	Prob.
C	0.019347	0.005532	3.497459	0.0005
AR(1)	0.398073	0.086300	4.612635	0.0000
MA(1)	-0.746012	0.062466	-11.94272	0.0000

R-squared	0.125147	Mean dependent var		0.019253
Adjusted R-squared	0.121343	S.D. dependent var		0.298833
S.E. of regression	0.280116	Akaike info criterion		0.299234
Sum squared resid	36.09395	Schwarz criterion		0.326044
Log likelihood	-66.27271	Hannan-Quinn criter.		0.309789
F-statistic	32.90134	Durbin-Watson stat		1.991050
Prob(F-statistic)	0.000000			

Inverted AR Roots	.40
Inverted MA Roots	.75

ARIMA Forecasting

Forecasting from an ARIMA model pretty much consists of pushing the Forecast button and then setting the options in the **Forecast** dialog as you would for any other equation. You'll notice one new twist: The dependent variable is D(LOGVOL), but EViews defaults to forecasting the level variable, LOGVOL.

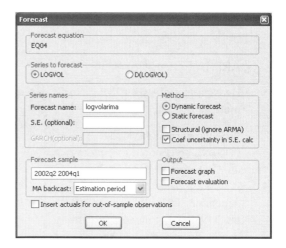

Here's our ARIMA-based forecast, together with the regres-
sion-based forecast generated
earlier. In the example at hand,
the ARIMA based forecast gets
a bit closer to the true data.

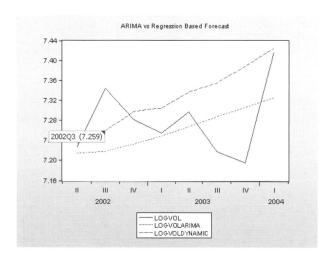

Quick Review

You can check for persistence in regression errors with a variety of visual aids as well as with formal statistical tests. Regressions are easily corrected for the presence of ARMA errors by the addition of AR(1), AR(2), *etc.*, terms in the `ls` command.

ARMA and ARIMA models are easily estimated by using the `ls` command without including any exogenous variables on the right. Forecasting requires nothing more than pushing the `Forecast` button.

Chapter 14. A Taste of Advanced Estimation

Estimation is econometric software's raison d'être. This chapter presents a quick taste of some of the many techniques built into EViews. We're not going to explore all the nuanced variations. If you find an interesting flavor, visit the *User's Guide* for in-depth discussion.

Weighted Least Squares

Ordinary least squares attaches equal weight to each observation. Sometimes you want certain observations to count more than others. One reason for weighting is to make sub-population proportions in your sample mimic sub-population proportions in the overall population. Another reason for weighting is to downweight high error variance observations. The version of least squares that attaches weights to each observation is conveniently named *weighted least squares*, or WLS.

In Chapter 8, "Forecasting" we looked at the growth of currency in the hands of the public, estimating the equation shown here. We used ordinary least squares for an estimation technique, but you may remember that the residuals were much noisier early in the sample than they were later on. We might get a better estimate by giving less weight to the early observations.

Dependent Variable: G
Method: Least Squares
Date: 12/21/06   Time: 15:06
Sample (adjusted): 1917M10 2005M04
Included observations: 1045 after adjustments

	Coefficient	Std. Error	t-Statistic	Prob.
@TREND	0.001784	0.001011	1.764780	0.0779
G(-1)	0.469423	0.027485	17.07935	0.0000
@MONTH=1	-32.41130	1.334063	-24.29519	0.0000
@MONTH=2	0.476996	1.323129	0.360506	0.7185
@MONTH=3	9.414805	1.222462	7.701508	0.0000
@MONTH=4	3.317393	1.190114	2.787459	0.0054
@MONTH=5	2.162256	1.196640	1.806939	0.0711
@MONTH=6	5.741203	1.185832	4.841496	0.0000
@MONTH=7	6.102364	1.199326	5.088160	0.0000
@MONTH=8	-2.866877	1.210778	-2.367798	0.0181
@MONTH=9	7.020689	1.183130	5.933996	0.0000
@MONTH=10	3.723463	1.194226	3.117887	0.0019
@MONTH=11	8.321732	1.192328	6.979395	0.0000
@MONTH=12	17.41063	1.219665	14.27493	0.0000

R-squared	0.594056	Mean dependent var	6.093774
Adjusted R-squared	0.588937	S.D. dependent var	15.35868
S.E. of regression	9.847094	Akaike info criterion	7.425536
Sum squared resid	99971.19	Schwarz criterion	7.491876
Log likelihood	-3865.843	Hannan-Quinn criter.	7.450696
Durbin-Watson stat	2.128568		

As a rough and ready adjustment after looking at the residual plot, we'll choose to give more weight to observations from 1952 on and less to those earlier.

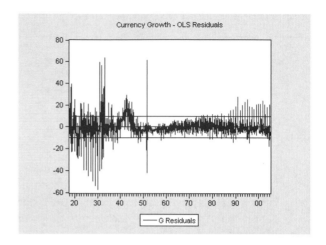

We used a **Stats By Classification...** view of RESID to find error standard deviations for each subperiod.

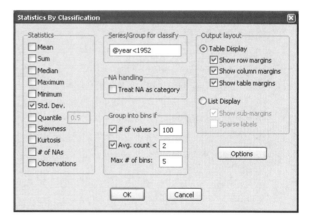

You can see that the residual standard deviation falls in half from 1952. We'll use this information to create a series, ROUGH_W, for weighting observations:

```
series rough_w = 14*(@year<1952) +
    6*(@year>=1952)
```

Descriptive Statistics for RESID
Categorized by values of @YEAR<1952
Date: 12/21/06 Time: 15:09
Sample (adjusted): 1917M10 2005M04
Included observations: 1045 after
    adjustments

@YEAR<1...	Std. Dev.
0	5.592399
1	14.00910
All	9.785594

That's the heart of the trick in instructing EViews to do weighted least squares—you need to create a series which holds the weight for every observation. When performing weighted least squares using the default settings, EViews then multiplies each observation by the weight you supply. Essentially, this is equivalent to replicating each observation in proportion to its weight.

Hint: In fact, if the weight is w_i, the EViews default scaling multiplies the data by $w_i/\overline{w}$—the observation weight divided by the mean weight. In theory this makes no difference, but sometimes the denominator helps with numerical computation issues.

The Weighted Option

Open the least squares equation EQ01 in the workfile, click the [Estimate] button, and switch to the **Options** tab. In the **Weights** group-box, select **Inverse std.dev.** from the **Type** dropdown and enter the weight series in the **Weight series** field. Notice that we've entered 1/ROUGH_W. That's because 1/ROUGH_W is roughly proportional to the inverse of the error standard deviation. As is generally true in EViews, you can enter an expression wherever a series is called for.

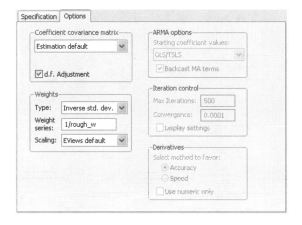

The weighted least squares estimates include two summary statistics panels. The first panel is calculated from the residuals from the weighted regression, while the second is based on unweighted residuals. Notice that the unweighted R^2 from weighted least squares is a little lower than the R^2 reported in the original ordinary least squares estimate, *just as it should be.*

Dependent Variable: G
Method: Least Squares
Date: 07/15/09   Time: 17:15
Sample (adjusted): 1917M10 2005M04
Included observations: 1045 after adjustments
Weighting series: 1/ROUGH_W
Weight type: Inverse standard deviation (EViews default scaling)

Variable	Coefficient	Std. Error	t-Statistic	Prob.
@TREND	0.003049	0.000852	3.580363	0.0004
G(-1)	0.432967	0.027779	15.58629	0.0000
@MONTH=1	-26.96734	1.051277	-25.65197	0.0000
@MONTH=2	-5.124309	1.033504	-4.958192	0.0000
@MONTH=3	8.382050	0.977922	8.571291	0.0000
@MONTH=4	4.123760	0.902597	4.568772	0.0000
@MONTH=5	1.619529	0.914298	1.771336	0.0768
@MONTH=6	5.952679	0.907029	6.562829	0.0000
@MONTH=7	5.087558	0.926393	5.491792	0.0000
@MONTH=8	-5.141760	0.932315	-5.515047	0.0000
@MONTH=9	3.303105	0.902891	3.658366	0.0003
@MONTH=10	1.338879	0.904249	1.480654	0.1390
@MONTH=11	10.36768	0.904327	11.46452	0.0000
@MONTH=12	14.68181	0.955980	15.35787	0.0000

Weighted Statistics

R-squared	0.716645	Mean dependent var	6.114959
Adjusted R-squared	0.713072	S.D. dependent var	13.13395
S.E. of regression	6.932504	Akaike info criterion	6.723626
Sum squared resid	49549.46	Schwarz criterion	6.789965
Log likelihood	-3499.095	Hannan-Quinn criter.	6.748786
Durbin-Watson stat	2.065267	Weighted mean dep.	6.128286

Unweighted Statistics

R-squared	0.565252	Mean dependent var	6.093774
Adjusted R-squared	0.559770	S.D. dependent var	15.35868
S.E. of regression	10.19046	Sum squared resid	107064.7
Durbin-Watson stat	2.088948		

Heteroskedasticity

One of the statistical assumptions underneath ordinary least squares is that the error terms for all observations have a common variance; that they are *homoskedastic*. Varying variance errors are said, in contrast, to be *heteroskedastic*. EViews offers both tests for heteroskedasticity and methods for producing correct standard errors in the presence of heteroskedasticity.

Tests for Heteroskedastic Residuals

The **Residual Diagnostics/Heteroskedasticity Tests...** view of an equation offers variance heteroskedasticity tests, including two variants of the White heteroskedasticity test. The White test is essentially a test of whether values of the right-hand side variables—and/or their cross terms, x_1^2, $x_1 \times x_2$, x_2^2, *etc.*—help explain the squared residuals. To perform a White test with only the squared terms (no cross terms), you should uncheck the **Include White cross terms** box.

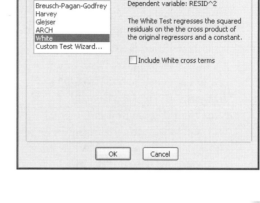

Here are the results of the White test (without cross terms) on our currency growth equation. The *F*- and χ^2- statistics reported in the top panel decisively reject the null hypothesis of homoskedasticity. The bottom panel— only part of which is shown—shows the auxiliary regression used to compute the test statistics.

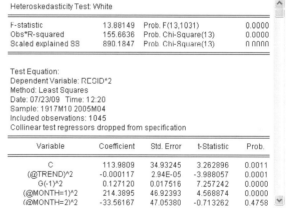

Heteroskedasticity Test: White

F-statistic	13.88149	Prob. F(13,1031)	0.0000
Obs*R-squared	155.6636	Prob. Chi-Square(13)	0.0000
Scaled explained SS	890.1847	Prob. Chi-Square(13)	0.0000

Test Equation:
Dependent Variable: RESID^2
Method: Least Squares
Date: 07/23/09   Time: 12:20
Sample: 1917M10 2005M04
Included observations: 1045
Collinear test regressors dropped from specification

Variable	Coefficient	Std. Error	t-Statistic	Prob.
C	113.9809	34.93245	3.262896	0.0011
(@TREND)^2	-0.000117	2.94E-05	-3.988057	0.0001
G(-1)^2	0.127120	0.017516	7.257242	0.0000
(@MONTH=1)^2	214.3895	46.92393	4.568874	0.0000
(@MONTH=2)^2	-33.56167	47.05380	-0.713262	0.4758

Heteroskedasticity Robust Standard Errors

One approach to dealing with heteroskedasticity is to weight observations such that the weighted data are homoskedastic. That's essentially what we did in the previous section. A different approach is to stick with least squares estimation, but to correct standard errors to account for heteroskedasticity. Click the Estimate button in the equation window and switch to the **Options** tab. Select either **White** or **HAC (Newey-West)** in the drop-down in the **Coefficient covariance matrix** group. As an example, we'll trumpet the White results.

Compare the results here to the least squares results shown on page 333. The coefficients, as well as the summary panel at the bottom, are identical. This reinforces the point that we're still doing a least squares estimation, but adjusting the standard errors.

The reported t-statistics and p-values reflect the adjusted standard errors. Some are smaller than before and some are larger. Hypothesis tests computed using **Coefficient Diagnostics/Wald-Coefficient Restrictions...** correctly account for the adjusted standard errors. The **Omitted Variables** and **Redundant Variables** tests do not use the adjusted standard errors.

Dependent Variable: G
Method: Least Squares
Date: 07/23/09   Time: 12:22
Sample (adjusted): 1917M10 2005M04
Included observations: 1045 after adjustments
White heteroskedasticity-consistent standard errors & covariance

Variable	Coefficient	Std. Error	t-Statistic	Prob.
@TREND	0.001784	0.001279	1.395297	0.1632
G(-1)	0.469423	0.054169	8.665832	0.0000
@MONTH=1	-32.41130	2.400069	-13.50432	0.0000
@MONTH=2	0.476996	2.038404	0.234005	0.8150
@MONTH=3	9.414805	1.235400	7.620856	0.0000
@MONTH=4	3.317393	0.991803	3.344809	0.0009
@MONTH=5	2.162256	0.893950	2.418766	0.0157
@MONTH=6	5.741203	1.014540	5.658922	0.0000
@MONTH=7	6.102364	0.939989	6.491950	0.0000
@MONTH=8	-2.866877	1.120103	-2.559476	0.0106
@MONTH=9	7.020689	1.282562	5.473958	0.0000
@MONTH=10	3.723463	1.418071	2.625724	0.0088
@MONTH=11	8.321732	1.114829	7.464582	0.0000
@MONTH=12	17.41063	1.432653	12.15272	0.0000

R-squared	0.594056	Mean dependent var	6.093774
Adjusted R-squared	0.588937	S.D. dependent var	15.35868
S.E. of regression	9.847094	Akaike info criterion	7.425536
Sum squared resid	99971.19	Schwarz criterion	7.491876
Log likelihood	-3865.843	Hannan-Quinn criter.	7.450696
Durbin-Watson stat	2.128568		

Nonlinear Least Squares

Much as Molière's bourgeois gentil-homme was pleased to discover he had been speaking prose all his life, you may be happy to know that in using the `ls` command you've been doing nonlinear estimation all along! Here's a very simple estimate of trend NYSE volume growth from the data set "NYSEVolume.wf1":

```
ls volume c @trend
```

Dependent Variable: VOLUME
Method: Least Squares
Date: 12/21/06 Time: 15:35
Sample: 1888Q1 2004Q1
Included observations: 465

	Coefficient	Std. Error	t-Statistic	Prob.
C	-153.1447	21.24266	-7.209300	0.0000
@TREND	1.062245	0.079253	13.40316	0.0000

R-squared	0.279540	Mean dependent var	93.29618
Adjusted R-squared	0.277984	S.D. dependent var	269.9802
S.E. of regression	229.4063	Akaike info criterion	13.71316
Sum squared resid	24366427	Schwarz criterion	13.73097
Log likelihood	-3186.309	Hannan-Quinn criter.	13.72017
F-statistic	179.6446	Durbin-Watson stat	0.014841
Prob(F-statistic)	0.000000		

Switch to the **Representations** view and look at the section titled "Estimation Equation." The least squares command orders estimation of the equation $volume = \alpha + \beta \times$ @trend , except that since EViews doesn't display Greek letters, C(1) is used for α and C(2) is used for β .

Estimation Command:
========================
LS VOLUME C @TREND

Estimation Equation:
========================
VOLUME = C(1) + C(2)*@TREND

Substituted Coefficients:
========================
VOLUME = -153.144694905 + 1.06224514869*@TREND

If you double-click on ⓑ c you'll see that the first two elements of C equal the just-estimated coefficients. In fact, every time EViews estimates an equation it stores the results in the vector C.

Hint: It may look curious that C(1), C(2), *etc.* seem to be labeled R1, R2, and so on. R1 and R2 are generic labels for row 1 and row 2 in a coefficient vector. The same setup is used generally for displaying vectors and matrices.

The key to nonlinear estimation is:

- Feed the `ls` command a formula in place of a list of series.

If you enter the command:

```
ls volume = c(1) + c(2)*@trend
```

you get precisely the same results as above. The only difference is that the formula in the command is reported in the top panel and that C(1) and C(2) appear in place of series names.

Dependent Variable: VOLUME
Method: Least Squares
Date: 12/21/06 Time: 15:39
Sample: 1888Q1 2004Q1
Included observations: 465
VOLUME = C(1) + C(2)*@TREND

Variable	Coefficient	Std. Error	t-Statistic	Prob.
C(1)	-153.1447	21.24266	-7.209300	0.0000
C(2)	1.062245	0.079253	13.40316	0.0000

R-squared	0.279540	Mean dependent var	93.29618
Adjusted R-squared	0.277984	S.D. dependent var	269.9802
S.E. of regression	229.4063	Akaike info criterion	13.71316
Sum squared resid	24366427	Schwarz criterion	13.73097
Log likelihood	-3186.309	Hannan-Quinn criter.	13.72017
F-statistic	179.6446	Durbin-Watson stat	0.014841
Prob(F-statistic)	0.000000		

Hint: Unlike series where a number in parentheses indicates a lead or lag, the number following a coefficient is the coefficient number. C(1) is the first element of C, C(2) is the second element of C, and so on.

Naming Your Coefficients

Least squares with a series list always stores the estimated coefficients in C, but you're free to create other coefficient vectors and use those coefficients when you specify a formula. To create a coefficient vector, give the command coef(n) *newname*, replacing *n* with the desired length of the coefficient vector and *newname* with the vector's name. Here's an example:

```
coef(1) alpha

coef(2) beta

ls volume = alpha(1) + beta(1)*@trend
```

The results haven't changed, but the names given to the estimated coefficients have. As a side effect, the results are stored in ALPHA and BETA, not in C.

Dependent Variable: VOLUME
Method: Least Squares
Date: 12/21/06   Time: 15:41
Sample: 1888Q1 2004Q1
Included observations: 465
VOLUME = ALPHA(1) + BETA(1)*@TREND

Variable	Coefficient	Std. Error	t-Statistic	Prob.
ALPHA(1)	-153.1447	21.24266	-7.209300	0.0000
BETA(1)	1.062245	0.079253	13.40316	0.0000

R-squared	0.279540	Mean dependent var		93.29618
Adjusted R-squared	0.277984	S.D. dependent var		269.9802
S.E. of regression	229.4063	Akaike info criterion		13.71316
Sum squared resid	24366427	Schwarz criterion		13.73097
Log likelihood	-3186.309	Hannan-Quinn criter.		13.72017
F-statistic	179.6446	Durbin-Watson stat		0.014841
Prob(F-statistic)	0.000000			

Notice that the slope coefficient has been stored in BETA(1), and that since we didn't reference BETA(2) nothing has been stored in it.

Hint: Since every new estimate specified with a series list replaces the values in C, it makes sense to use a different coefficient vector for values you'd like to keep around.

Coefficient vectors aren't just for storing results. They can also be used in computations. For example, to compute squared residuals one could type:

```
series squared_residuals=(volume-alpha(1)-beta(1)*@trend)^2
```

Hint: It would, of course, been easier in this example to enter:

```
series squared_residuals=resid^2
```

But then we wouldn't have had the opportunity to demonstrate how to use coefficients in a computation.

Making It Really Nonlinear

To estimate a nonlinear regression, enter a nonlinear formula in the `ls` command. For example, to estimate the equation $volume = \alpha t^{\beta}$ use the command:

```
ls volume =
    c(1)*(1+@trend)^c(2)
```

Notice the big improvement in R^2 over the linear model.

You can place most any nonlinear formula you like on the right hand side of the equation.

Dependent Variable: VOLUME
Method: Least Squares
Date: 12/21/06   Time: 15:42
Sample: 1888Q1 2004Q1
Included observations: 465
Convergence achieved after 108 iterations
VOLUME = C(1)*(1+@TREND)^C(2)

Variable	Coefficient	Std. Error	t-Statistic	Prob.
C(1)	5.73E-08	1.17E-07	0.488334	0.6255
C(2)	3.769148	0.317653	11.86563	0.0000

R-squared	0.561730	Mean dependent var	93.29618
Adjusted R-squared	0.560784	S.D. dependent var	269.9802
S.E. of regression	178.9250	Akaike info criterion	13.21610
Sum squared resid	14822559	Schwarz criterion	13.23392
Log likelihood	-3070.744	Hannan-Quinn criter.	13.22311
Durbin-Watson stat	0.023714		

If you're lucky, getting a nonlinear estimate is no harder than getting a linear estimate. Sometimes, though, you're not lucky. While EViews uses the standard closed-form expression for finding coefficients for linear models, nonlinear models require a search procedure. The line in the top panel "Convergence achieved after 108 iterations" indicates that EViews tried 108 sets of coefficients before settling on the ones it reported. Sometimes no satisfactory estimate can be found. Here are some tricks that may help.

Re-write the formula

Notice we actually estimated $volume = \alpha(1 + t)^{\beta}$ instead of $volume = \alpha t^{\beta}$. Why? The first value of @TREND is zero, and in this particular case EViews had difficulty raising 0 to a power. This very small re-write got around the problem without changing anything substantive. Sometimes one expression of a particular functional form works when a different expression of the same function doesn't.

Fiddle with starting values

EViews begins its search with whatever values happen to be sitting in C. Sometimes a search starting at one set of values succeeds when a search at different values fails. If you have good guesses as to the true values, use those guesses for a starting point. One way to change starting values is to double-click on 🅱 c and edit in the usual way. You can also use the `param` statement to change several coefficient values at once, as in:

```
param c(1) 3.14159 c(2) 2.718281828
```

Change iteration limits

If the estimate runs but doesn't converge, give the same command again. Since EViews stores the last estimated coefficients in C, the second estimation run picks up exactly where the first one left off.

Alternatively, click the [Estimate] button and switch to the Options tab. Try increasing **Max iterations**. You can also put a larger number in the **Convergence** field, if you're willing to accept potentially less accurate answers.

2SLS

For consistent parameter estimation, the *sine non qua* assumption of least squares is that the error terms are uncorrelated with the right hand side variables. When this assumption fails, econometricians turn to *two-stage least squares*, or *2SLS*, a member of the *instrumental variable*, or *IV*, family. 2SLS augments the information in the equation specification with a list of instruments—series that the econometrician believes to be correlated with the right-hand side variables and uncorrelated with the error term.

As an example, consider estimation of the "new Keynesian Phillips curve," in which inflation depends on expected future inflation and unemployment—possibly lagged. In the following oversimplified specification,

$$\pi_t = \alpha + \beta \pi^e_{t+1} + \gamma un_{t-1}$$

we expect $\beta \approx 1$ and $\gamma < 0$. Using monthly U.S. data in "CPI_AND_UNEMPLOYMENT.wf1", we could try to estimate this equation by least squares with the command:

```
ls inf c inf(1)
    unrate(-1)
```

Dependent Variable: INF
Method: Least Squares
Date: 12/21/06   Time: 15:44
Sample (adjusted): 1948M02 2005M02
Included observations: 685 after adjustments

	Coefficient	Std. Error	t-Statistic	Prob.
C	1.086076	0.554900	1.957248	0.0507
INF(1)	0.495433	0.033356	14.85304	0.0000
UNRATE(-1)	0.136110	0.094558	1.439444	0.1505

R-squared	0.250938	Mean dependent var	3.691521
Adjusted R-squared	0.248741	S.D. dependent var	4.340267
S.E. of regression	3.761935	Akaike info criterion	5.492114
Sum squared resid	9651.769	Schwarz criterion	5.511951
Log likelihood	-1878.049	Hannan-Quinn criter.	5.499790
F-statistic	114.2358	Durbin-Watson stat	2.244407
Prob(F-statistic)	0.000000		

Notice that the estimated coefficients are very different from the coefficients predicted by theory. The coefficient on future inflation is approximately 0.5, rather than 1.0, and the coefficient on unemployment is positive. The econometric difficulty is that by using actual future inflation as a proxy for expected future inflation, we introduce an "errors-in-variables" problem. We'll try a 2SLS estimate, using lagged information as instruments.

> Econometric digression: If a right-hand side variable in a regression is measured with random error, the equation is said to suffer from *errors-in-variables*. Errors-in-variables leads to biased coefficients in ordinary least squares. Sometimes this can be fixed with 2SLS.

The 2SLS command uses the same equation specification as does least squares. The equation specification is followed by an "@" and the list of instruments. The command name is tsls.

> Hint: It's tsls rather than 2sls because the convention is that computer commands start with a letter rather than a number.

Thus, to get 2SLS results we can give the command:

```
tsls inf c inf(1)
    unrate(-1) @ c
    unrate(-1) inf(-1)
    inf(-2)
```

The coefficient on future inflation is now close to 1.0, as theory predicts. The coefficient on unemployment is negative, albeit small and not significant.

Dependent Variable: INF
Method: Two-Stage Least Squares
Date: 07/16/09 Time: 10:33
Sample (adjusted): 1948M02 2005M02
Included observations: 685 after adjustments
Instrument specification: C UNRATE(-1) INF(-1) INF(-2)

Variable	Coefficient	Std. Error	t-Statistic	Prob.
C	-0.348687	0.707908	-0.492560	0.6225
INF(1)	1.131316	0.086191	13.12567	0.0000
UNRATE(-1)	-0.028002	0.118688	-0.235932	0.8136

R-squared	-0.148225	Mean dependent var	3.691521
Adjusted R-squared	-0.151592	S.D. dependent var	4.340267
S.E. of regression	4.657638	Sum squared resid	14795.03
F-statistic	88.70490	Durbin-Watson stat	2.819037
Prob(F-statistic)	0.000000	Second-Stage SSR	9036.479
Instrument rank	4	J-statistic	0.059248
Prob(J-statistic)	0.807688		

> Hint: By default, if you don't include the constant, C, in the instrument list, EViews puts one in for you. You can tell EViews not to add the constant by unchecking the **Include a constant** box in the estimation dialog.

Did you notice the R^2 in the 2SLS output? It's *negative*. This means that the equation fits the data really poorly. That's okay. Our interest here is in accurate parameter estimation.

Generalized Method of Moments

What happens if you put together nonlinear estimation and two-stage least squares? While EViews will happily estimate a nonlinear equation using the tsls command, nowadays econometricians are more likely to use the *Generalized Method of Moments,* or *GMM.*

Two-stage least squares can be thought of as a special case of GMM. GMM extends 2SLS in two dimensions:

- GMM estimation typically accounts for heteroskedasticity and/or serial correlation.

- GMM specification is based on an orthogonality condition between a (possibly nonlinear) function and instruments.

As an example, suppose instead of the tsls command above we gave the gmm command:

```
gmm inf c inf(1) unrate(-1) @ c unrate(-1) inf(-1) inf(-2)
```

The resulting estimate is close to the 2SLS estimate, but it's not identical. By default, EViews applies one of the many available options for estimation that is robust to heteroskedasticity and serial correlation.

Dependent Variable: INF
Method: Generalized Method of Moments
Date: 07/16/09   Time: 10:35
Sample (adjusted): 1948M02 2005M02
Included observations: 685 after adjustments
Linear estimation with 1 weight update
Estimation weighting matrix: HAC (Bartlett kernel, Newey-West fixed
    bandwidth = 7.0000)
Standard errors & covariance computed using estimation weighting matrix
Instrument specification: C UNRATE(-1) INF(-1) INF(-2)

Variable	Coefficient	Std. Error	t-Statistic	Prob.
C	-0.330258	0.392670	-0.841057	0.4006
INF(1)	1.130012	0.080548	14.02913	0.0000
UNRATE(-1)	-0.030009	0.068855	-0.435828	0.6631

R-squared	-0.146591	Mean dependent var	3.691521
Adjusted R-squared	-0.149953	S.D. dependent var	4.340267
S.E. of regression	4.654323	Sum squared resid	14773.98
Durbin-Watson stat	2.819580	Instrument rank	4
J-statistic	0.018783	Prob(J-statistic)	0.890990

Clicking the Estimate button reveals the GMM **Specification** tab. The entire right side of this tab is devoted to the choice of robust estimation methods. See the *User's Guide* for more information.

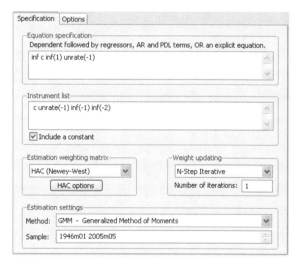

Orthogonality Conditions

The basic notion behind GMM is that each of the instruments is orthogonal to a specified function. You can specify the function in any of three ways:

- If you give the usual—dependent variable followed by independent variables—series list, the function is the residual.

- If you give an explicit equation, linear or nonlinear, the function is the value to the left of the equal sign minus the value to the right of the equal sign.

- If you give a formula with no equal sign, the formula is the function.

See *System Estimation*, below, for a brief discussion of GMM estimation for systems of equations.

Limited Dependent Variables

Suppose we're interested in studying the determinants of union membership and that, coincidentally, we have data on a cross-section of workers in Washington State in the workfile "CPSMAR2004WA.wf1". The series UNION is coded as one for union members and zero for non-members. Between four and five percent of workers in our sample are members of a union.

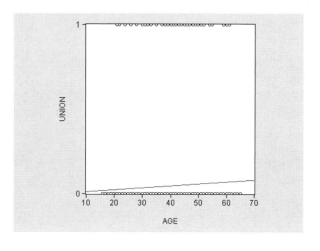

Union Member (yes/no) in Washington State, March 2004	
Series: UNION	
Sample 1 1759	
Observations 1759	
Mean	0.043775
Median	0.000000
Maximum	1.000000
Minimum	0.000000
Std. Dev.	0.204652
Skewness	4.459813
Kurtosis	20.88993
Jarque-Bera	29288.05
Probability	0.000000

Is age an important determinant of union membership? We might run a regression to see. According to the least squares results, age is highly significant statistically (the t-statistic is 2.8), but doesn't explain much of the variation in the dependent variable (the R^2 is low).

Dependent Variable: UNION
Method: Least Squares
Date: 12/21/06   Time: 15:50
Sample: 1 1759
Included observations: 1759

	Coefficient	Std. Error	t-Statistic	Prob.
C	-0.001568	0.016883	-0.092896	0.9260
AGE	0.001156	0.000412	2.804930	0.0051

R-squared	0.004458	Mean dependent var	0.043775
Adjusted R-squared	0.003891	S.D. dependent var	0.204652
S.E. of regression	0.204253	Akaike info criterion	-0.337774
Sum squared resid	73.30110	Schwarz criterion	-0.331552
Log likelihood	299.0723	Hannan-Quinn criter.	-0.335474
F-statistic	7.867676	Durbin-Watson stat	1.761318
Prob(F-statistic)	0.005088		

We can also look at the regression on a scatter plot. The dependent variable is all zeros and ones. The predicted values from the regression lie on a continuous line. While the regression results aren't necessarily "wrong," what does it mean to say that predicted union membership is 0.045? Either you are a member of a union, or you are not a member of a union!

This example is a member of a class called *limited dependent* variable problems. EViews provides estimation methods for binary dependent variables, as in our union membership example, ordered choice models, censored and truncated models (*tobit* being an example), and count models. The *User's Guide* provides its usual clear explanation of how to use these models in EViews, as well as a guide to the underlying theory. We'll illustrate with the simplest model: logit.

Logit

Instead of fitting zeros and ones, the logit model uses the right-hand side variables to predict the *probability* of being a union member, *i.e.*, of observing a 1.0. One can think of the model as having two parts. First, an *index s* is created, which is a weighted combination of the explanatory variables. Then the probability of observing the outcome depends on the cumulative distribution function (cdf) of the index. Logit uses the cdf of the logistic distribution; probit uses the normal distribution instead.

The `logit` command is straightforward:

```
logit union c age
```

The coefficients shown in the output are the coefficients for constructing the index. In this case, our estimated model says:

$$s = -4.23 + 0.028 \times age$$

$$prob(union = 1) = 1 - F(-s)$$

$$F(s) = e^s / (1 + e^s)$$

Dependent Variable: UNION
Method: ML - Binary Logit (Quadratic hill climbing)
Date: 07/23/09   Time: 16:00
Sample: 1 1759
Included observations: 1759
Convergence achieved after 6 iterations
Covariance matrix computed using second derivatives

Variable	Coefficient	Std. Error	z-Statistic	Prob.
C	-4.234841	0.447392	-9.465608	0.0000
AGE	0.028066	0.010102	2.778213	0.0055

McFadden R-squared	0.012502	Mean dependent var	0.043775
S.D. dependent var	0.204652	S.E. of regression	0.204371
Akaike info criterion	0.357301	Sum squared resid	73.38559
Schwarz criterion	0.363523	Log likelihood	-312.2459
Hannan-Quinn criter.	0.359600	Deviance	624.4917
Restr. deviance	632.3981	Restr. log likelihood	-316.1991
LR statistic	7.906377	Avg. log likelihood	-0.177513
Prob(LR statistic)	0.004926		

Obs with Dep=0	1682	Total obs	1759
Obs with Dep=1	77		

Textbook hint: Textbooks usually describe the relation between probability and index in a logit with $prob(union = 1) = F(s)$ rather than $prob(union = 1) = 1 - F(-s)$. The two are equivalent for a logit (or a probit), but differ for some other models.

Logit's **Forecast** dialog offers a choice of predicting the *index s*, or the probability. Here we predict the probability.

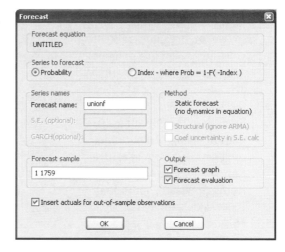

The graph shown to the right plots the probability of union membership as a function of age. For comparison purposes, we've added a horizontal line marking the unconditional probability of union membership. A 60 year old is about three times as likely to be in a union as is a 20 year old.

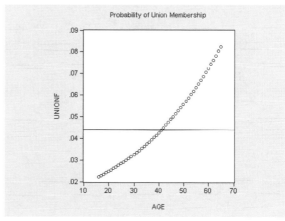

ARCH, etc.

Have you tried **About EViews** on the **Help** menu and then clicked the ⌗Credits⌗ button? Only one Nobel prize winner (*so far!*) appears in the credits list. Which brings us to the topic of *autoregressive conditional heteroskedasticity*, or *ARCH*. ARCH, and members of the extended ARCH family, model time-varying variances of the error term. The simplest ARCH model is:

$$y_t = \hat{\alpha} + \hat{\beta} x_t + e_t$$

$$\sigma_t^2 = \gamma_0 + \gamma_1 e_{t-1}^2$$

In this ARCH(1) model, the variance of this period's error term depends on the squared residual from the previous period.

The residuals from the currency data used earlier showed noticeably persistent volatility, a sign of a potential ARCH effect. In EViews, all the action in specifying ARCH takes place in the **Specification** tab of the **Equation Estimation** dialog. To get to the right version of the **Specification** tab, choose **ARCH - Autoregressive Conditional Heteroskedasticity** in the **Method** dropdown of the **Estimation settings** field.

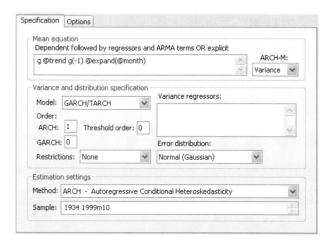

Hint: Unlike nearly all other EViews estimation procedures, ARCH requires a continuous sample. Define an appropriate sample in the **Specification** tab. If your sample includes a break, EViews will give an error message. In this example, we had to use a subset of our data to accommodate the continuous sample requirement.

ARCH coefficients appear below the structural coefficients. The ARCH coefficient—our estimated γ_1 —is both large, 0.75, and statistically significant, $t = 8.4$.

Dependent Variable: G
Method: ML - ARCH (Marquardt) - Normal distribution
Date: 12/21/06 Time: 16:05
Sample: 1934M01 1999M10
Included observations: 790
Convergence achieved after 116 iterations
Variance backcast used with parameter = 0.7
GARCH = C(15) + C(16)*RESID(-1)^2

	Coefficient	Std. Error	z-Statistic	Prob.
@TREND	0.005261	0.000617	8.524239	0.0000
G(-1)	0.549819	0.023067	23.83544	0.0000
(@MONTH)=1	-32.39236	0.833258	-38.87435	0.0000
(@MONTH)=2	-4.982209	0.822267	-6.059112	0.0000
(@MONTH)=3	8.084118	0.858691	9.414470	0.0000
(@MONTH)=4	1.682949	0.757272	2.222383	0.0263
(@MONTH)=5	0.140919	0.814614	0.172989	0.8627
(@MONTH)=6	4.073757	0.691534	5.890903	0.0000
(@MONTH)=7	2.043162	0.766317	2.666209	0.0077
(@MONTH)=8	-9.185011	0.554304	-16.57034	0.0000
(@MONTH)=9	0.832339	0.873454	0.952928	0.3406
(@MONTH)=10	-1.063576	0.982500	-1.082520	0.2790
(@MONTH)=11	8.088314	0.641873	12.60111	0.0000
(@MONTH)=12	13.17102	0.667944	19.71874	0.0000

Variance Equation				
C	18.25251	1.039234	17.56343	0.0000
RESID(-1)^2	0.753232	0.089309	8.434040	0.0000

R-squared	0.705928	Mean dependent var	6.991178
Adjusted R-squared	0.700229	S.D. dependent var	12.79553
S.E. of regression	7.005730	Akaike info criterion	6.369390
Sum squared resid	37988.11	Schwarz criterion	6.464013
Log likelihood	-2499.909	Hannan-Quinn criter.	6.405761
Durbin-Watson stat	2.114299		

In addition to the usual results, the **View** menu offers **Garch Graph**. **Garch Graph** provides a plot of the predicted conditional variance or the conditional standard deviation. Selecting **Garch Graph/Conditional Variance**, we see that higher variances occur early and late in the sample, plus an enormous spike in 1952.

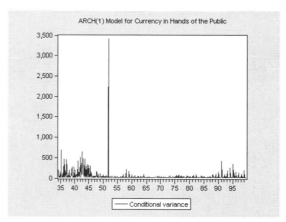

Perhaps the variance spike is really there, or perhaps ARCH(1) isn't the best model. EViews offers a wide choice from the extended ARCH family. The **Model** dropdown offers four broad choices. Each broad choice is further refined with various options. Most simply, you can specify the order of the ARCH or GARCH (Generalized ARCH) model in the dialog fields just below **Model**.

You can also choose from a variety of error distributions using the **Error distribution** dropdown.

| Normal (Gaussian) |
| Student's t |
| Generalized Error (GED) |
| Student's t with fixed df. |
| GED with fixed parameter |

One of the most interesting applications of ARCH is to put the time-varying variance back into the structural equation. This is called *ARCH-in-mean*, or *ARCH-M*, and is added to the specification using the **ARCH-M** drop-down menu in the upper right of the **Specification** tab.

| None |
| Std. Dev. |
| Variance |
| Log(Var) |

Here we've changed the model to GARCH(1,1) and entered the variance in the structural equation. EViews labels the structural coefficient of the ARCH-M effect GARCH. Notice that the structural effect of ARCH-M is almost significant at the five percent level.

Dependent Variable: G
Method: ML - ARCH (Marquardt) - Normal distribution
Date: 12/21/06   Time: 16:08
Sample: 1934M01 1999M10
Included observations: 790
Convergence achieved after 57 iterations
Variance backcast used with parameter = 0.7
GARCH = C(16) + C(17)*RESID(-1)^2 + C(18)*GARCH(-1)

	Coefficient	Std. Error	z-Statistic	Prob.
GARCH	0.013651	0.007426	1.838330	0.0660
@TREND	0.009112	0.000877	10.39123	0.0000
G(-1)	0.382047	0.039720	9.618625	0.0000
(@MONTH)=1	-31.20559	1.124634	-27.74732	0.0000
(@MONTH)=2	-12.22195	1.168382	-10.46058	0.0000
(@MONTH)=3	5.179291	1.054092	4.913510	0.0000
(@MONTH)=4	2.093547	0.720438	2.905936	0.0037
(@MONTH)=5	-1.979770	0.947610	-2.089224	0.0367
(@MONTH)=6	4.141952	0.872925	4.744912	0.0000
(@MONTH)=7	2.067415	0.993113	2.081752	0.0374
(@MONTH)=8	-9.814432	1.147446	-8.553285	0.0000
(@MONTH)=9	-2.229448	0.850166	-2.622366	0.0087
(@MONTH)=10	-2.462779	0.862287	-2.856102	0.0043
(@MONTH)=11	8.490929	0.831617	10.21015	0.0000
(@MONTH)=12	11.90415	0.969121	12.28345	0.0000

Variance Equation				
C	0.224294	0.113214	1.981149	0.0476
RESID(-1)^2	0.109608	0.012830	8.542772	0.0000
GARCH(-1)	0.892461	0.011893	75.03785	0.0000

R-squared	0.689416	Mean dependent var	6.991178
Adjusted R-squared	0.682576	S.D. dependent var	12.79553
S.E. of regression	7.209049	Akaike info criterion	6.211605
Sum squared resid	40121.14	Schwarz criterion	6.318056
Log likelihood	-2435.584	Hannan-Quinn criter.	6.252523
Durbin-Watson stat	1.777332		

Is the 0.014 estimated GARCH-M coefficient large? Again, we look at the conditional variance using the **Garch Graph** menu item. In a few periods, the conditional variance reaches 400 to 500, so the structural effect is on the order of 6 or 7 (the estimated coefficient multiplied by the estimated conditional variance.) That's larger than several of the monthly dummies. But for most of the sample, the GARCH-M effect is relatively small.

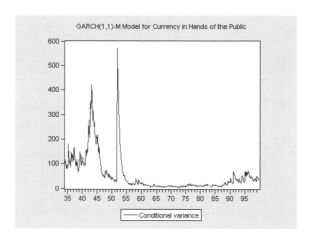

Maximum Likelihood—Rolling Your Own

Despite EViews' extensive selection of estimation techniques, sometimes you want to custom craft your own. EViews provides a framework for customized maximum likelihood estimation (mle). The division of labor is that you provide a formula defining the contribution an observation makes to the likelihood function, and EViews will produce estimates and the expected set of associated statistics. For an example, we'll return to the weighted least squares problem which opened the chapter. This time, we'll estimate the variances and coefficients jointly.

Our first step is to create a new LogL object, using either the **Object/New Object...** menu or a command like:

```
logl weighted_example
```

Opening ⊠ weighted_example brings up a text area for entering definitions. Think of the commands here as a series of `series` commands—only without the command name `series` being given—that EViews will execute in sequential order. These commands build up the definition of the contribution to the likelihood function. The file also includes one line with the keyword `@logl`, which identifies which series holds the contribution to the likelihood function.

Let's take apart our example specification shown to the right. We broke the definition of the error term into two parts simply because it was easier to type. The first equation defines the seasonal component. The second equation is the difference between observed currency growth and predicted currency growth. The third equation defines

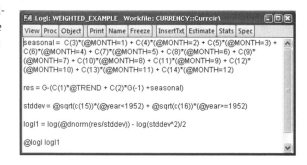

the error term standard deviation as coming from either the early-period variance, C(15), or the late-period variance, C(16). Note that all these definitions depend on the values in the coefficient vector C, and will change as EViews tries out new coefficient values.

The fourth line defines LOGL1, which gives the contribution to the log likelihood function, assuming that the errors are distributed independent Normal. The last line announces to EViews that the contributions are, in fact, in LOGL1.

> Hint: We didn't really type in that long seasonal component. We copied it from the representations view of the earlier least squares results, pasted, and did a little judicious editing.

The maximum likelihood coefficients are close to the coefficients estimated previously. We've gained formal estimates of the variances, along with standard errors of the variance estimates.

The *User's Guide* devotes an entire chapter to the ins and outs of maximum likelihood estimation. Additionally, EViews ships with over a dozen files illustrating definitions of likelihood functions across a wide range of examples.

LogL: WEIGHTED_EXAMPLE
Method: Maximum Likelihood (Marquardt)
Date: 12/21/06   Time: 16:28
Sample: 1917M08 2005M04 IF G AND G(-1)
Included observations: 1043
Evaluation order: By observation
Convergence achieved after 118 iterations

	Coefficient	Std. Error	z-Statistic	Prob.
C(3)	-26.25158	0.794494	-33.04186	0.0000
C(4)	-6.780918	0.894377	-7.581725	0.0000
C(5)	7.610450	0.895578	8.497812	0.0000
C(6)	3.815713	0.805500	4.737074	0.0000
C(7)	1.078785	1.310473	0.823203	0.4104
C(8)	5.554133	0.928298	5.983135	0.0000
C(9)	4.461885	1.201398	3.713910	0.0002
C(10)	-6.031965	1.180381	-5.110184	0.0000
C(11)	2.049911	1.059985	1.933906	0.0531
C(12)	0.351983	1.069359	0.329153	0.7420
C(13)	10.29977	0.866584	11.88548	0.0000
C(14)	13.71585	1.006266	13.63045	0.0000
C(1)	0.003943	0.000774	5.091304	0.0000
C(2)	0.420402	0.023339	18.01322	0.0000
C(15)	242.7087	10.32781	23.50050	0.0000
C(16)	18.87754	0.780028	24.20111	0.0000

Log likelihood	-3530.549	Akaike info criterion	6.800670
Avg. log likelihood	-3.384994	Schwarz criterion	6.876602
Number of Coefs.	16	Hannan-Quinn criter.	6.829470

Hint: Unlike nearly all other EViews estimation procedures, maximum likelihood won't deal with missing data. The series defined by @logl must be available for every observation in the sample. Define an appropriate sample in the **Estimation** dialog. If you accidentally include missing data, EViews will give an error message identifying the offending observation.

System Estimation

So far, all of our estimation has been of the one-equation-at-a-time variety. System estimation, in contrast, estimates jointly the parameters of two or more equations. System estimation offers three econometric advantages, at the cost of one disadvantage. The first plus is that a parameter can appear in more than one equation. The second plus is that you can take advantage of correlation between error terms in different equations. The third advantage is that cross-equation hypotheses are easily tested. The disadvantage is that if one equation is misspecified, that misspecification will pollute the estimation of all the other equations in the system.

Worthy of repetition hint: If you want an estimated coefficient to have the same value in more than one equation, system estimation is the only way to go. Use the same coefficient name and number, *e.g.*, C(3), in each equation you specify. The jargon for this is "constraining the coefficients." Note that you can constrain some coefficients across equations and not constrain others.

To create a system object either give the system command or use the menu **Object/New Object....** Enter one or more equation specifications in the text area. We've added data on the growth in bank vault cash, GV, to our data set on growth in currency in the hands of the public, G. The specification shown is identical for both cash components.

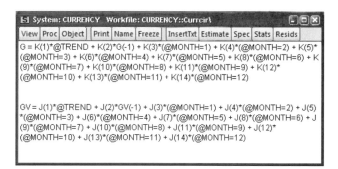

Hint: It helped to copy-and-paste from the representations view of the earlier least squares results, and then to use **Edit/Replace** to change the coefficients from "C" to "K" and "J."

Before we can estimate the system shown, we need to create the coefficient vectors K and J. That can be done with the following two commands given in the command pane, not in the system window:

```
coef(14) j
coef(14) k
```

EViews provides a long list of estimation methods which can be applied to a system. Click the Estimate button to bring up the **System Estimation** dialog and then choose an estimation method from the **Method** dropdown.

| Ordinary Least Squares |
| Weighted L.S. (equation weights) |
| Seemingly Unrelated Regression |
| Two-Stage Least Squares |
| Weighted Two-Stage Least Squares |
| Three-Stage Least Squares |
| Full Information Maximum Likelihood |
| GMM - Cross Section (White cov.) |
| GMM - Time series (HAC) |
| ARCH - Conditional Heteroskedasticity |

Choosing **Ordinary Least Squares** produces estimates for both equations. (The output is long; only part is shown here.) Note that the results for currency in the hands of the public are precisely the same as those we saw previously. We asked for equation-by-equation ordinary least squares, and that's what we got—the equivalent of a bunch of `ls` commands.

System: CURRENCY
Estimation Method: Least Squares
Date: 12/21/06   Time: 16:26
Sample: 1917M10 2005M04
Included observations: 1048
Total system (unbalanced) observations 1589

	Coefficient	Std. Error	t-Statistic	Prob.
K(1)	0.001784	0.001011	1.764780	0.0778
K(2)	0.469423	0.027485	17.07935	0.0000
K(3)	-32.41130	1.334063	-24.29519	0.0000
K(4)	0.476996	1.323129	0.360506	0.7185
K(5)	9.414805	1.222462	7.701508	0.0000
K(6)	3.317393	1.190114	2.787459	0.0054
K(7)	2.162256	1.196640	1.806939	0.0710
K(8)	5.741203	1.185832	4.841496	0.0000
K(9)	6.102364	1.199326	5.088160	0.0000
K(10)	-2.866877	1.210778	-2.367798	0.0180
K(11)	7.020689	1.183130	5.933996	0.0000
K(12)	3.723463	1.194226	3.117887	0.0019
K(13)	8.321732	1.192328	6.979395	0.0000
K(14)	17.41063	1.219665	14.27493	0.0000
J(1)	-0.061689	0.016994	-3.630060	0.0003
J(2)	0.025066	0.014397	1.741005	0.0819
J(3)	94.54043	16.45760	5.744485	0.0000
J(4)	-16.31821	16.17205	-1.009038	0.3131
J(5)	4.977493	16.02635	0.310582	0.7562
J(6)	54.45108	16.05498	3.391538	0.0007
J(7)	60.28574	16.10434	3.743446	0.0002
J(8)	61.47900	16.12961	3.811563	0.0001
J(9)	70.42382	16.14572	4.361763	0.0000
J(10)	54.86403	16.17497	3.391909	0.0007
J(11)	85.04242	16.16317	5.261494	0.0000
J(12)	49.94944	16.22960	3.077675	0.0021
J(13)	63.92924	16.18388	3.950181	0.0001
J(14)	116.2615	16.21876	7.168331	0.0000

Determinant residual covariance	355371.4

Equation: G = K(1)*@TREND + K(2)*G(-1) + K(3)*(@MONTH=1) + K(4)
  (@MONTH=2) + K(5)(@MONTH=3) + K(6)*(@MONTH=4) + K(7)
  (@MONTH=5) + K(8)(@MONTH=6) + K(9)*(@MONTH=7) + K(10)
  (@MONTH=8) + K(11)(@MONTH=9) + K(12)*(@MONTH=10) + K(13)
  (@MONTH=11) + K(14)(@MONTH=12)
Observations: 1045

R-squared	0.594056	Mean dependent var	6.093774
Adjusted R-squared	0.588937	S.D. dependent var	15.35868
S.E. of regression	9.847094	Sum squared resid	99971.19
Prob(F-statistic)	2.128568		

Equation: GV = J(1)*@TREND + J(2)*GV(-1) + J(3)*(@MONTH=1) + J(4)
  (@MONTH=2) + J(5)(@MONTH=3) + J(6)*(@MONTH=4) + J(7)
  (@MONTH=5) + J(8)(@MONTH=6) + J(9)*(@MONTH=7) + J(10)
  (@MONTH=8) + J(11)(@MONTH=9) + J(12)*(@MONTH=10) + J(13)

Instead of equation-by-equation least squares, we might try a true systems estimator, such as seemingly unrelated regressions (SUR). The upper portion of the SUR results is shown to the right.

System: CURRENCY
Estimation Method: Seemingly Unrelated Regression
Date: 12/21/06   Time: 16:28
Sample: 1917M10 2005M04
Included observations: 1048
Total system (unbalanced) observations 1589
Linear estimation after one-step weighting matrix

	Coefficient	Std. Error	t-Statistic	Prob.
K(1)	0.001785	0.001004	1.777117	0.0757
K(2)	0.469372	0.027300	17.19319	0.0000
K(3)	-32.40994	1.325089	-24.45870	0.0000
K(4)	0.475915	1.314230	0.362124	0.7173
K(5)	9.414121	1.214239	7.753101	0.0000
K(6)	3.317469	1.182109	2.806400	0.0051
K(7)	2.162418	1.188591	1.819312	0.0691
K(8)	5.741283	1.177856	4.874351	0.0000
K(9)	6.102642	1.191259	5.122852	0.0000
K(10)	-2.866474	1.202633	-2.383497	0.0173
K(11)	7.020700	1.175172	5.974189	0.0000
K(12)	3.723774	1.186194	3.139263	0.0017
K(13)	8.321959	1.184308	7.026851	0.0000
K(14)	17.41115	1.211460	14.37203	0.0000
J(1)	-0.061681	0.016774	-3.677238	0.0002
J(2)	0.025187	0.014210	1.772505	0.0765
J(3)	94.26694	16.24433	5.803067	0.0000

The estimated coefficients haven't changed much in this example. The difference between the two estimates is that the latter accounts for correlation between the two equations, while the former doesn't. The **Residuals/Correlation Matrix** view shows the estimated cross-equation correlation. In this case, there is very little correlation—that's why the SUR estimates came out about the same the estimates from equation-by-equation least squares.

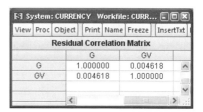

Because coefficient estimates from all the equations are made jointly, cross-equation hypotheses are easily tested. For example, to check the hypothesis that the coefficients on trend are equal for cash in the hands of the public and vault cash, choose **View/Coefficient Diagnostics/Wald Coefficient Tests…** and fill out the **Wald Test** dialog in the usual way.

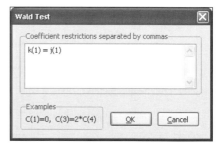

The answer, which is unsurprising given the reported coefficients and standard errors, is "No, the coefficients are not equal."

Wald Test:
System: CURRENCY

Test Statistic	Value	df	Probability
Chi-square	14.26742	1	0.0002

Null Hypothesis Summary:

Normalized Restriction (= 0)	Value	Std. Err.
-J(1) + K(1)	0.063466	0.016802

Restrictions are linear in coefficients.

Vector Autoregressions—VAR

In Chapter 8, "Forecasting," we discussed predictions based on ARMA and ARIMA models. This kind of forecasting generalizes, at least in the case of autoregressive models, to multiple dependent variables through the use of *vector autoregressions* or *VARs*. While VARs can be quite sophisticated (see the *User's Guide*), at its heart a VAR simply takes a list of series and regresses each on its own past values as well as lags of all the other series in the list.

Create a VAR object either through the **Object** menu or the var command. The [Estimate] button opens the VAR Specification dialog. Enter the variables to be explained in the **Endogenous Variables** field.

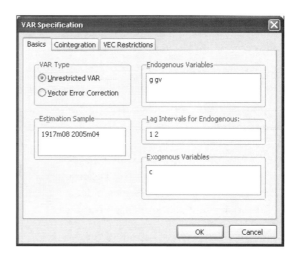

EViews estimates least squares equations for both series.

Impulse response

To answer the question "How do the series evolve following a shock to the error term?" click the `Impulse` button. The phrase "following a shock" is less straightforward than it sounds. In general, the error terms will be correlated across equations, so one wants to be careful about shocking one equation but not the other. And how big a shock? One unit? One standard deviation?

Vector Autoregression Estimates
Date: 12/21/06   Time: 16:34
Sample (adjusted): 1960M02 2005M04
Included observations: 539 after adjustments
Standard errors in ( ) & t-statistics in [ ]

	G	GV
G(-1)	0.325270	2.538929
	(0.03920)	(0.28462)
	[8.29740]	[8.92044]
G(-2)	-0.378807	-1.206638
	(0.03955)	(0.28718)
	[-9.57702]	[-4.20172]
GV(-1)	-0.026723	0.261115
	(0.00581)	(0.04216)
	[-4.60150]	[6.19288]
GV(-2)	-0.001473	-0.006644
	(0.00205)	(0.01487)
	[-0.71892]	[-0.44672]
C	7.696707	-1.377166
	(0.50323)	(3.65366)
	[15.2946]	[-0.37693]

R-squared	0.282985	0.209469
Adj. R-squared	0.277614	0.203547
Sum sq. resids	40682.97	2144550.
S.E. equation	8.728421	63.37201
F-statistic	52.68859	35.37380
Log likelihood	-1930.085	-2998.619
Akaike AIC	7.180279	11.14515
Schwarz SC	7.220072	11.18495
Mean dependent	7.054272	10.52969
S.D. dependent	10.26954	71.00966

Determinant resid covariance (dof adj.)	300498.3
Determinant resid covariance	294949.1
Log likelihood	-4923.849
Akaike information criterion	18.30742
Schwarz criterion	18.38700

You control how you deal with these questions on the **Impulse Definition** tab. For illustration purposes, let's consider a unit shock to each error term.

Once we choose a specification, we get a set of *impulse response functions*. We get a plot of the response over time of each endogenous variable to a shock in each equation. In other words, we see how G responds to shocks to both the G equation and the GV equation, and similarly, how GV responds to shocks to the GV equation and the G equation.

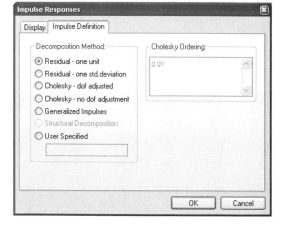

By default (there *are* other options) we get one figure containing all four impulse response graphs. The line graph in the upper left-hand corner shows that following a shock to the G equation, G wiggles around for a quarter or so, but by the fifth quarter the response has effectively dissipated. In contrast, the upper right-hand corner graph shows that G is effectively unresponsive to shocks in the GV equation.

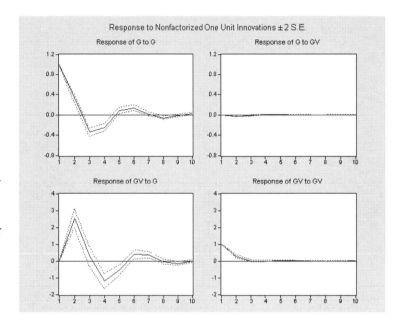

Hint: The dashed lines enclose intervals of plus or minus two standard errors.

Variance decomposition

How much of the variance in G is explained by shocks in the G equation and how much is explained by shocks in the GV equation? The answer depends on, among other things, the estimated coefficients, the estimated standard error of each equation, and the order in which you evaluate the shocks. **View/Variance Decomposition...** leads to the **VAR Variance Decompositions** dialog where you can set various options.

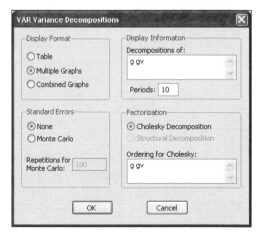

The variance decomposition shows one graph for the variance of each equation from each source. The horizontal axis tells the number of periods following a shock to which the decomposition applies and the vertical axis gives the fraction of variance explained by the shock source. In this example, most of the variance comes from

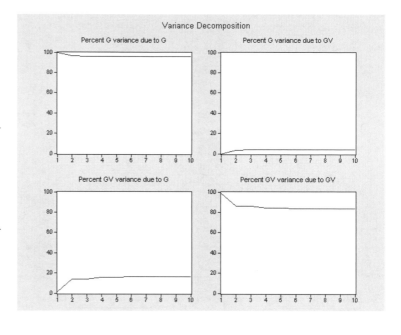

the "own-shock" (*i.e.*, G-shocks effect on G), rather than from the shock to the other equation.

Forecasting from VARs

In order to forecast from a VAR, you need to use the model object. An example is given in *Simulating VARs* in Chapter 15, "Super Models."

Vector error correction, cointegration tests, structural VARs

VARs have become an important tool of modern econometrics, especially in macroeconomics. Since the *User's Guide* devotes an entire chapter to the subject, we'll just say that the VAR object provides tools that handle everything listed in the topic heading above this paragraph.

Quick Review?

A quick review of EViews' advanced estimation features suggests that a year or two of Ph.D.-level econometrics would help in learning to use all the available tools. This chapter has tried to touch the surface of many of EViews advanced techniques. Even this extended introduction hasn't covered everything that's available. For example, EViews offers a sophisticated state-space (Kalman filter) module. As usual, we'll refer you to the *User's Guide* for more advanced discussion.

Chapter 15. Super Models

Most of EViews centers on using data to estimate something we'd like to know, often the parameters of an equation. The model object turns the process around, taking a model made up of linear or nonlinear, (possibly) simultaneous equations and finding their solution. We begin the chapter with the solution of a simple, familiar model. Next, we discuss some of the ways that models can be used to explore different scenarios. Of course, we'll link the models to the equations you've already learned to estimate.

Your First Homework—Bam, Taken Up A Notch!

Odds are that your very first homework assignment in your very first introductory macroeconomics class presented a model something like this:

$$Y \equiv C + I + G$$

$$C = \overline{C} + mpc \times Y$$

Your assignment was to solve for the variables Y (GDP), and C (consumption), given information about I (investment) and G (government spending).

Cultural Imperialism Apologia: If you took the course outside the United States, the national income identity probably included net exports as well.

But that consumption function is econometrically pretty unsophisticated. (We'll carefully avoid any questions about the sophistication of a model consisting solely of a national income identity and a consumption function.) A more modern consumption function might look like this:

$$\ln C_t = \alpha + \lambda \ln C_{t-1} + \beta \ln Y_t$$

The page **Real** in the workfile "Keynes.wfl" contains annual national income accounting data for the U.S. from 1959 through 2000. It also includes an estimated equation, 🖩 consumption , for this more modern consumption function.

```
┌─────────────────────────────────────────────────────────────────────┐
│ ▣ Equation: CONSUMPTION  Workfile: KEYNES::Real\          ▣▣▣        │
├─────────────────────────────────────────────────────────────────────┤
│ View│Proc│Object│ │Print│Name│Freeze│ │Estimate│Forecast│Stats│Resids│
├─────────────────────────────────────────────────────────────────────┤
│ Dependent Variable: LOG(CONS)                                         │
│ Method: Two-Stage Least Squares                                       │
│ Date: 07/16/09  Time: 11:39                                           │
│ Sample (adjusted): 1961 2000                                          │
│ Included observations: 40 after adjustments                           │
│ Instrument specification: C LOG(CONS(-1)) LOG(CONS(-2))               │
├──────────────┬────────────┬───────────┬────────────┬─────────────────┤
│  Variable    │ Coefficient│ Std. Error│ t-Statistic│     Prob.       │
├──────────────┼────────────┼───────────┼────────────┼─────────────────┤
│       C      │  -0.564032 │  0.186948 │  -3.017052 │    0.0046       │
│ LOG(CONS(-1))│   0.391655 │  0.168305 │   2.327051 │    0.0255       │
│    LOG(Y)    │   0.646231 │  0.180833 │   3.573644 │    0.0010       │
├──────────────┴────────────┴───────────┴────────────┴─────────────────┤
│ R-squared          0.999361   Mean dependent var        8.140632     │
│ Adjusted R-squared 0.999326   S.D. dependent var        0.397565     │
│ S.E. of regression 0.010321   Sum squared resid         0.003941     │
│ F-statistic        28889.16   Durbin-Watson stat        1.063241     │
│ Prob(F-statistic)  0.000000   Second-Stage SSR          0.009581     │
│ Instrument rank           3   J-statistic               1.44E-28     │
└─────────────────────────────────────────────────────────────────────┘
```

Creating A Model

This model isn't so easy to solve as is the Keynesian cross. The consumption function introduces both nonlinear $(\ln Y_t)$ and dynamic (C_{t-1}) elements. Fortunately, this sort of number-crunching is a breeze with EViews' modeling facility.

To get started with making an EViews model, use **Object/New Object…** to generate a model named KEYNESCROSS.

The new model object opens to an empty window, as shown. We're going to type the first equation in manually, so hit the ⬚Text button.

Type in the national income accounting identity. When you're done, the window should look something like the picture shown to the right.

Hint: Since C is a reserved name in EViews, we've substituted CONS for *C*.

Hint: In this example, we typed in one equation and copied another from an estimated equation in the workfile. You're free to mix and match, although in real work most equations are estimated. In addition to linking in an equation object, you can also link in SYS and VAR objects.

Let's find out whether we and EViews have had a meeting of the minds on how to interpret the model. Click Equations to switch to the equations view, which tells us what EViews is thinking. (You may get a warning message about recompiling the model. It can be ignored.) One line appears for each equation. (So far, there *is* only one equation.)

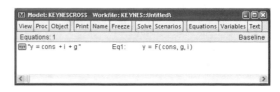

Double-click on an equation for more information; for example, the **Properties** of the first equation are shown to the right. Since this is the national income accounting identity, it should really be marked as an identity. Click the **Identity** radio button on the lower right of the dialog, and then OK to return to the equations view.

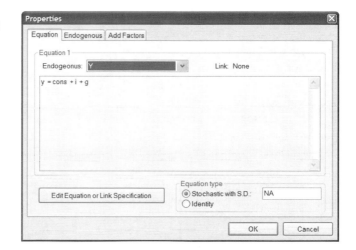

To complete the model, we need to bring in the consumption function. The estimated consumption function is stored in the workfile as ▣ consumption . Select this equation in the workfile window, and then copy-and-paste or drag-and-drop it into the model window. EViews checks to be sure that you really want to link the estimated consumption function into the model. Since you do, choose Yes .

The model is now complete.

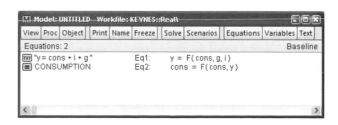

Solving the Model

So what's the homework
answer? Click ⌊Solve⌋. The **Model
Solution** dialog appears with
lots and lots of options. We're
not doing anything fancy, so
just hit ⌊ OK ⌋. EViews will
find a numerical solution for the
simultaneous equation model
we've specified.

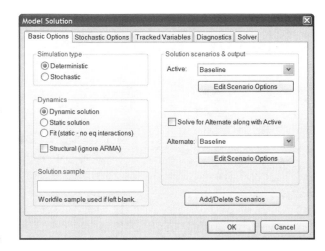

Two windows display new
information. The model solution messages window (below
right) provides information
about the solution. The workfile
window (below left) has
acquired two series ending with the suffix "__0."

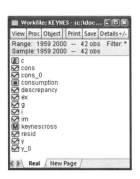

The model window gives details of the solution technique used. Complicated models can be
hard for even a computer to solve, but this model is not complex, so the details aren't very
interesting. Note at the bottom of the window that EViews solved the model essentially
instantly.

Wow hint: The model is nonlinear. There is no closed form solution. This doesn't
bother EViews in the slightest! (Admittedly, some models are harder for a computer to
solve.)

The model solver created new series containing the solution values. To distinguish these
series from our original data, EViews adds "_0" to the end of the name for each solved

series. That's the source of the series CONS_0 and Y_0 that now appears in the workfile window.

> Hint: EViews calls a series with the added suffix an *alias*.

Open a group in the usual way to look at the solutions. The solution for GDP is close to the real data, although it isn't perfect.

obs	Y	Y_0
1959	2441.300	NA
1960	2501.800	2487.488
1961	2560.000	2549.774
1962	2715.200	2700.850
1963	2834.000	2835.239
1964	2998.600	2992.443
1965	3191.100	3185.228
1966	3399.100	3427.493
1967	3484.600	3569.726
1968	3652.700	3726.350
1969	3765.400	3852.002
1970	3771.900	3836.083
1871		

Making A Better Model

If we'd like the solution to be closer to the real data, we need a better model. In the example at hand, we know that we've left exports and imports out of the model. Switch to the text view and edit the identity so it looks as shown here.

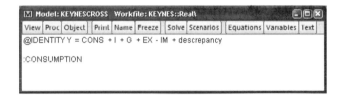

@IDENTITY Y = CONS + I + G + EX - IM + descrepancy

:CONSUMPTION

> Hint: *Discrepancy?* What discrepancy? Well for our data, consumption, investment, government spending, and net exports don't quite add up to GDP.
>
> Welcome to the real world.

Click Solve again.

Looking At Model Solutions

Since EViews placed
the results CONS_0
and Y_0 in the work-
file, we can examine
our solution using any
of the usual tools for
looking at series. In
addition, the model
object has tools con-
venient for this task in
the **Proc** menu.
Choose **Proc/Make
Graph...** to bring up
the **Make Graph** dia-
log and click OK .

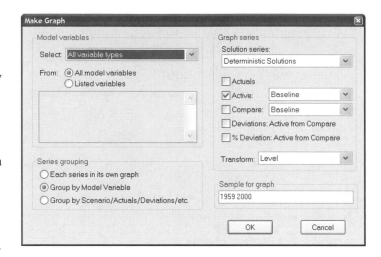

The graph window that opens shows the time path for all the variables in our homework
model.

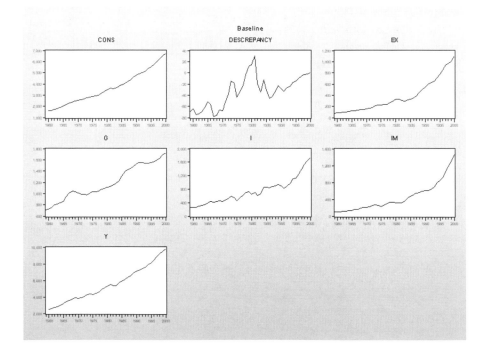

If you prefer to see all the series on a single graph, choose the radio button **Group by Scenario/Actuals/Deviations/etc.** in the **Make Graph** dialog. To make the graph prettier, we've reassigned Y and CONS to the right axis. (See *Left and Right Axes in Group Line Graphs* in Chapter 5, "Picture This!")

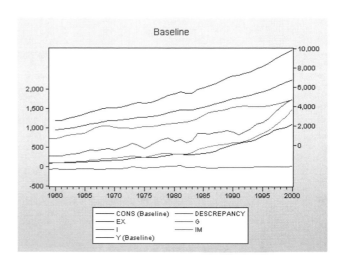

Comparing Actual Data to the Model Solution

Return again to the **Make Graph** dialog. This time choose **Listed variables**, enter Y in the text field, and check the checkbox **Compare** and choose **Actuals** on the dropdown menu. Click **Group by Model Variable** so that all the GDP data will appear on the same graph. If you'd like, also check **% Deviation: Active from Compare.**

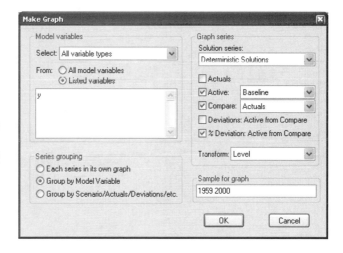

You can see that we now do a
much better job of matching the
real data.

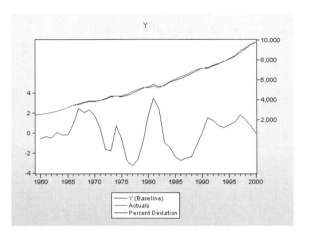

More Model Information

Before we see what else we can do
with a model, let's explore a bit to
see what else is stored inside.

Model Variables

Click the [Variables] button to switch the
model to the variables view. We see
that CONS and Y are marked with an
[En] icon, while the remaining variables are marked with an [X] icon to
distinguish the former as endogenous
from the latter, which are exogenous.

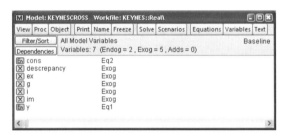

Teminology hint: *Exogenous* variables are determined outside the model and their values are not affected by the model's solution. *Endogenous* variables are determined by
the solution of the model. Think of exogenous variables as model inputs and endogenous variables as model outputs.

Model Equations

Equations View

Return to the equations view.
The left column shows the
beginning of the equation. The
column on the right shows how
EViews is planning on solving
the model: income is a function
of consumption, investment,

and government spending; consumption is a function of income and consumption (well, lagged consumption actually).

> Hint: How come the equation shows only CONS + I + G? What happened to exports and imports—not to mention that discrepancy thing? In the equation view, EViews displays only enough of each equation so that you can remember which equation's which. To see the full equation, switch to the text view or look at the equation's **Properties**.

Equation Properties

Double-click in the view on ▣ consumption to bring up the **Properties** dialog. As you can see, the model has pulled in the estimated coefficients as well as the estimated standard error of the regression. We're looking at a live link. If we re-estimated the consumption equation, the new estimates would automatically replace the current estimates in the model.

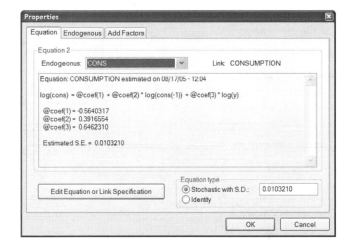

> Hint: The estimated standard error is used when you ask EViews to execute a stochastic simulation, a feature we won't explore, referring you instead to the *User's Guide*.

Numerical accuracy

Computers aren't nearly so bright as your average junior high school student, so they use numerical methods which come up with approximate solutions. If you'd like a "more accurate" answer, you need to tell EViews to be more fussy. Click Solve and choose the **Solver** tab. Change **Convergence** to "1e-09", to get that one extra digit of accuracy.

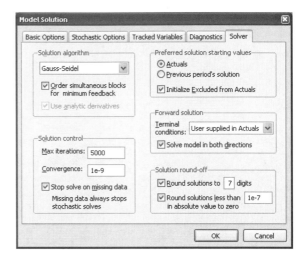

Vanity hint: In the problem at hand, all we're doing is making the answer look pretty.

In more complicated problems a smaller convergence limit has the advantage that it helps assure that the computer reaches the right answer. The disadvantages are that the solution takes longer, and that sometimes if you ask for extreme accuracy no satisfactory answer can be found.

Accurately understanding accuracy: Don't confuse numerical accuracy with model accuracy. The solver options control numerical accuracy. These options have nothing to do with the accuracy of your model or your data. The latter two are far more important. Unfortunately, you can't improve model or data accuracy by clicking on a button.

Your Second Homework

Odds are that your second homework assignment in your first introductory macroeconomics class asked what would happen to GDP if G were to rise. In other words, how do the results of this new scenario differ from the baseline results?

Making Scenarios

EViews puts a single set of assumptions about the inputs to a model together with the resulting solution in a *scenario*. The solutions based on the original data are called the *Baseline*. So the solutions to our first homework problem are stored in the baseline scenario. Choosing **Scenarios...** from the **View** menu brings up the **Scenario Specification** dialog with the **Select Scenario** tab showing. The Baseline scenario that's showing was automatically created when we solved the model.

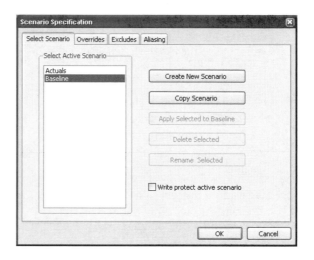

A look at the aliasing tab shows that the suffix for Baseline results is "_0." The fields are greyed out because EViews assigns the suffix for the Baseline.

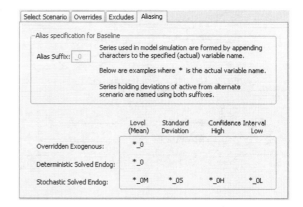

We want to ask what would happen in a world in which government spending were 10 (billion dollars) higher than it was in the real world. This is a new scenario, so click [Create New Scenario] on the **Select Scenario** tab. Scenario 1 is associated with the alias "_1". If you like, you can rename the new scenario to something more meaningful or change the suffix, but we'll just click [OK] for now.

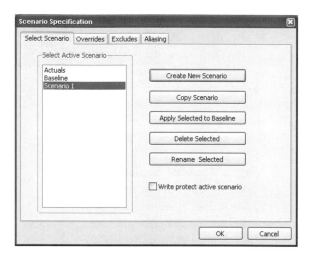

We want to instruct EViews to use different values of G in this scenario. We'll create the series G_1 with the command:

```
series g_1 = g + 10
```

Hint: We chose the name "G_1" because the suffix has to match the scenario alias.

Overriding Baseline Data

Back in the model window click [Variables] and then right-click on G and choose **Properties...**.

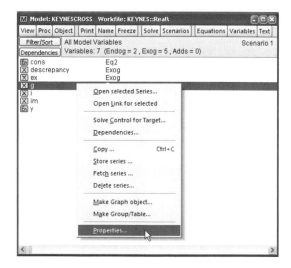

On the **Properties** dialog, check **Use override in series in scenario** to instruct EViews to substitute G_1 for G.

Now Solve .

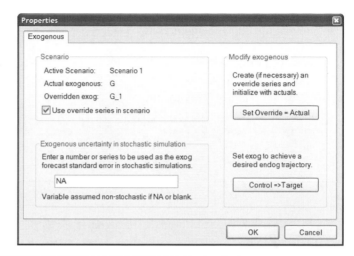

Hint: You can override an exogenous variable but you cannot override an endogenous variable because the latter would require a change to the structure of the model.

New series Y_1 and CONS_1 appear in the workfile. Return to **Proc/Make Graph...** in the model window, choose **Listed Variables**, list Y, and check **Compare**. As you can see in the dialog, many options are available. We're asking for a comparison of the baseline solution to the new scenario. We can show the difference between the two—by checking one of the **Deviations** boxes—in either units or as a percentage.

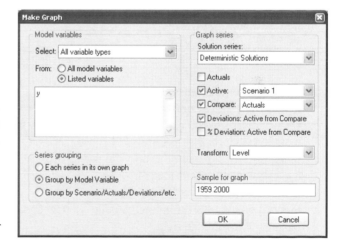

Our new graph (which we have prettied-up) shows both baseline and scenario 1 results. Putting the deviation on a separate scale makes it easier to see the effect of this fiscal policy experiment. With a little luck, these results will get us a very good grade.

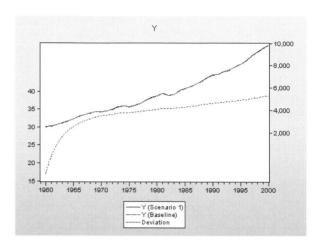

Simulating VARs

Models can be used for solving complicated systems of equations under different scenarios, as we've done above. Models can also be used for forecasting dynamic systems of equations. This is especially useful in forecasting from vector autoregressions.

> Hint: The [Forecast] feature in equations handles dynamic forecasting from a single equation quite handily. Here we're talking about forecasting from multiple equation models.

Open the workfile "currency-model.wf1" which contains the vector autoregression esti-mated in Chapter 14, "A Taste of Advanced Estimation." Cre-ate a new model object named CURRENCY_FORECAST. Copy

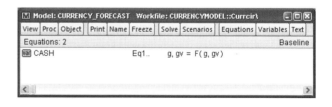

the VAR object CASH from the workfile window and paste it into the model, which now looks as shown to the right.

Double-click on the equation. The equation for G (growth in currency in the hands of the public) has been copied in together with the estimated coefficients and the estimated standard error of the error terms in the equation. Remember, this is a live *link,* so:

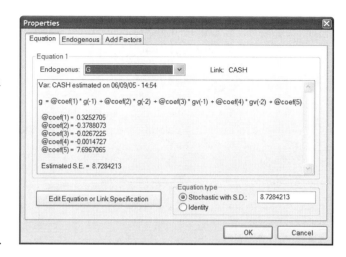

- If you re-estimate the VAR, the model will know to use the re-estimated coefficients.

We can now use the model to forecast from the VAR. Click Solve, set the Solution sample to 2001 2005, and hit OK . Then do **Proc/Make Graph.**... Check both **Actuals** and **Active** and set the **Sample for Graph** to 2000M1 2005M4.

In this particular example, the vector autoregres-

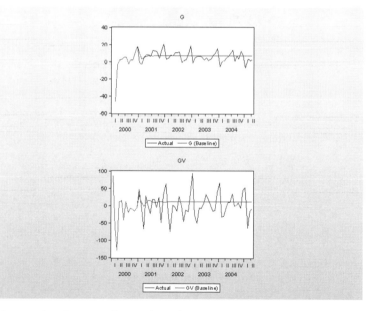

sion did a good job of forecasting for several periods and essentially flatlined by a year out.

> Hint: If you prefer, instead of creating a model and then copying in a VAR you can use **Proc/Make Model** from inside the VAR to do both at once.

The model taught in our introductory economics course was linear because it's hard for people to solve nonlinear models. Computers are generally fine with nonlinear models, although there are some nonlinear models that are too hard for even a computer to solve. For the most part though, the steps we just walked through would have worked just as well for a set of nonlinear equations.

Rich Super Models

The model object provides a rich set of facilities for everything from solving intro homework problems to solving large scale macroeconometric models. We've only been able to touch the surface. To help you explore further on your own, we list a few of the most prominent features:

- Models can be nonlinear. Various controls over the numerical procedures used are provided for hard problems. Diagnostics to track the solution process are also available when needed.

- Add factors can be used to adjust the value of a specified variable. You can even use add factors to adjust the solution for a particular variable to match a desired target.

- Equations can be implicit. Given an equation such as $\log y = x^2$, EViews can solve for y. Add factors can be used for implicit equations as well.

- Stochastic simulations in which you specify the nature of the random error term for each equation are a built-in feature. This allows you to produce a statistical distribution of solutions in place of a point estimate.

- Equations can contain future values of variables. This means that EViews can solve dynamic *perfect foresight* models.

- Single-variable control problems of the following sort can be solved automatically. You can specify a target path for one endogenous variable and then instruct EViews to change the value of one exogenous variable that you specify in order to make the solved-for values of the endogenous variable match the target path.

Quick Review

A model is a collection of equations, either typed in directly or linked from objects in the workfile. The central feature of the model object is the ability to find the simultaneous solution of the equations it contains. Models also include a rich set of facilities for exploring various assumptions about the exogenous driving variables of the model and the effect of shocks to equations.

Chapter 16. Get With the Program

EViews comes with a built-in programming language which allows for very powerful and sophisticated programs. Because the language is very high level, it's ideal for automating tasks in EViews.

> Hint: Because EViews' programming language is very high-level, it's not very efficient for the kind of tasks which might be coded in C or Java.

> Hint: To become a proficient author, you read great literature. In the same vein, to become a skilled EViews programmer you should read EViews programs. EViews ships with a variety of sample programs. You can find them under **Help/Quick Help Reference/Sample Programs & Data**. *Appendix: Sample Programs* at the end of these chapters includes several of the sample programs with annotations.

I Want To Do It Over and Over Again

If you have repetitive tasks, create an EViews program and run it as needed. EViews programs are *not* objects stored in the workfile. You don't make them with **Object/New Object…**. An EViews program is held either in a program window created with **File/New/Program** or in a text file on disk ending with the extension ".prg".

> Hint: Clicking the Save button in a program window saves the file to disk with the extension ".prg". But you're free to create EViews programs in your favorite text editor or any word processor able to save standard ASCII files.

The program window at the right holds three standard commands. Every time you click Run these three commands are executed.

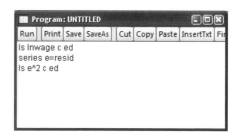

Hint: If you choose the **Quiet** radio button in the **Run Program** dialog (not shown here; see below), programs execute faster and more peacefully. But **Verbose** is sometimes helpful in debugging.

As a practical matter, you probably don't want to run the same regression on the same series over and over and over. On the other hand, you might very well want to apply the same data transformation to a number of different data sets. For example, the Current Population Survey (CPS) records various measures of educational attainment, but doesn't provide a "years of education" variable. The program "transformcps_ed.prg" translates the series A_HGA that appears in the data supplied in the CPS into years of education, ED. When new CPS data are released each March, we can run transformcps_ed again to re-create ED.

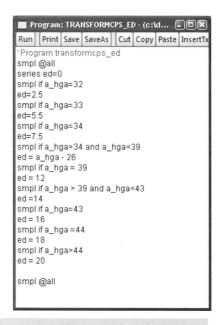

Documentary Hint: It's sometimes important to keep a record of your analysis. While you can print lines typed in the command pane, or save them to disk as "COMMAND.log", point-and-click operations aren't recorded for posterity. Entering commands in a program and then running the program is the best way to create an audit trail in EViews.

Documentation Hint: Anything to the right of an apostrophe in a program line is treated as a comment. Writing lots of comments will make you happy later in life.

You Want To Have An Argument

You might want to run the same regression over and over again on different series. Our first program regressed LNWAGE on ED and then looked to see if there is a relation between the squared residuals and ED. Suppose we want to execute the same procedure with AGE and then again with UNION as the right-hand side variable.

Instead of writing three separate programs, we write one little program in which the right-hand side variable is replaced by an *evaluated string variable argument*. In an EViews program:

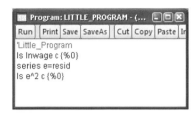

- A *string variable* begins with a "%" sign, holds text, and only exists during program execution. You may declare a string variable by entering the name, an equal sign, and then a quote delimited string, as in:

      %y = "abc"

- EViews automatically defines a set of string variables using *arguments* passed to the program in the **Program arguments (%0 %1...)** field of the **Run Program** dialog. The string variable %0 picks up the first string entered in the field. The string variable %1 picks up the second string. *Etc.*

- You may refer to a string variable in a program using its name, as in "%Y". EViews will replace the string value with its string contents, "ABC". In some settings, we may be interested, not in the actual string variable *value*, but rather in an *object named* "ABC". An *evaluated* string is a string variable name placed between squiggly braces, as in "{%0}", which tells EViews to use the name, names, or name fragment given by the string value.

For example, if we enter "age" in the **Run Program** dialog, EViews will replace "{%0}" in the program lines,

    ls lnwage c {%0}
    series e = resid
    ls e^2 c {%0}

and then execute the following commands:

    ls lnwage c age
    series e = resid
    ls e^2 c age

If we had entered UNION in the dialog, the regressions would have been run on UNION instead of AGE.

Program Variables

String variables live only while a program is being executed. They aren't stored in the workfile. While they live, you can use all the same string operations on string variables as you can on an alpha series.

Hint: A string variable in a program is a single string—not one string per observation, as in an alpha series.

Hint: If you want to keep your string after the program is executed and save it in the workfile, you should use put it into a string object.

In addition to string variables, programs also allow *control variables*. A control variable holds a number instead of a string, and similarly lives only while the program is alive. Control variables begin with an "!" as in "!I".

Hint: And if you want to keep your number after the program is executed and save it in the workfile, you should use put it into a scalar object.

String and control variables and string and scalar objects can be defined directly in a program.

Hint: When read aloud, the exclamation point is pronounced "bang," as in "bang eye."

We've written a slightly silly program which runs four regressions, although the real purpose is to illustrate the use of control variables. Running this program is equivalent to entering the commands:

```
smpl if fe=0
ls lnwage c ed
smpl if fe=1
ls lnwage c ed
smpl if fe=0
ls lnwage c age
smpl if fe=1
ls lnwage c age
```

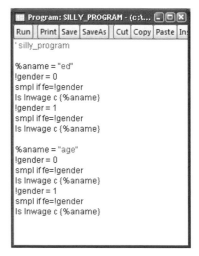

Loopy

Program loops are a powerful method of telling EViews to repeatedly execute commands without you having to repeatedly type the commands. Loops can use either control variables or string variables.

A loop begins with a `for` command, with the rest of the line defining the successive values to be taken during the loop. A loop ends with a `next` command. The lines between `for` and `next` are executed for each specified loop value. Most commonly, loops with control variables are used to execute a set of commands for a sequence of numbers, 0, 1, 2,…. In contrast, loops with string variables commonly run the commands for a series of names that you supply.

Number loops

The general form of the `for` command with a control variable is:

```
for !control_variable=!first_value to !last_value step !stepvalue
    'some commands go here
next
```

If the step value is omitted, EViews steps the control variable by 1.

The program "count.prg" counts to 100, displaying the count on the status line. Most econometricians can count to 100 on their own, so this program is rarely seen in the wild. We captured this unusual specimen because it provides a particularly pristine example of a numerical loop.

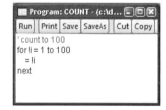

For something a bit more likely to be of practical use, we've simplified "silly_program.prg" by putting the values 0 and 1 in a loop instead of writing out each statement twice. In "less_silly_program.prg", !GENDER is the control variable, !FIRST_VALUE is 0 and !LAST_VALUE is 1.

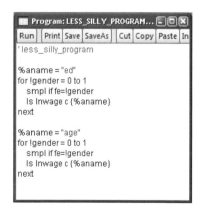

String Loops

A `for` command with a string variable has a string variable followed by a list of strings (no equal sign).

Each string is placed in turn in the string variable and the lines between `for` and `next` are executed.

```
for %string string1 string2 string3
    'some commands go here
next
```

The commands between for and next are executed first with the string "string1" replacing "%string", then with "string2", *etc.*

To further simplify "less_silly_program.prg" so that we don't have to write our code separately for ED and for AGE, we can add a `for` command with a string variable.

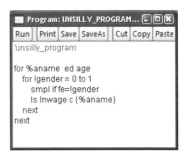

Program: UNSILLY_PROGRAM...

Run | Print | Save | SaveAs | Cut | Copy | Paste

```
'unsilly_program

for %aname ed age
  for !gender = 0 to 1
    smpl if fe=!gender
    ls lnwage c {%aname}
  next
next
```

Hint: Loops are much easier to read if you indent.

Other Program Controls

In addition to the command form used throughout *EViews Illustrated*, commands can also be written in "object form." In a program, use of the object form is often the easiest way to set options that would normally be set by making choices in dialog boxes.

Sometimes you don't want the output from each command in a program. For example, in a Monte Carlo study you might run 10,000 regressions, saving one coefficient from each regression for later analysis, but not otherwise using the regression output. (A Monte Carlo study is used to explore statistical distributions through simulation techniques.) Creating 10,000 equation objects is inefficient, and can be avoided by using the object form. For example, the program:

```
for !i = 1 to 10000
    ls y c x
next
```

runs the same regression 10,000 times, creating 10,000 objects and opening 10,000 windows. (Actually, you aren't allowed to open 10,000 windows, so the program won't run.) The program:

```
equation eq
for !i = 1 to 10000
```

```
        eq.ls y c x
    next
```

uses the object form and creates a single object with a single, re-used window.

> Hint: Prefacing a line in a program with the word do also suppresses windows being opened. do doesn't affect object creation.

EViews offers other programming controls such as if-else-endif, while loops, and sub-routines. We refer you to the *Command and Programming Reference*.

A Rolling Example

Here's a very practical problem that's easily handled with a short program. The workfile "currency rolling.wf1" has monthly data on currency growth in the variable G. The commands:

```
    smpl @all
    ls g c g(-1)
    fit gfoverall
```

estimate a regression and create a forecast. Of course, this example uses current data to estimate an equation, which is then used to forecast for the previous century. We might instead perform a *rolling regression*, in which we estimate the regression over the previous year, use that regression for a one year forecast, and then do the same for the following year.

The program "rolling_currency.prg", shown to the right, does what we want. Note the use of a for loop to control the sample—a common idiom in EViews. Note also that we "re-used" the same equation object for each regression to avoid opening multiple windows.

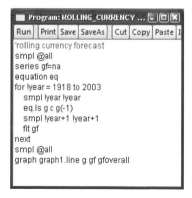

```
'rolling currency forecast
smpl @all
series gf=na
equation eq
for !year = 1918 to 2003
    smpl !year !year
    eq.ls g c g(-1)
    smpl !year+1 !year+1
    fit gf
next
smpl @all
graph graph1.line g gf gfoverall
```

For this particular set of data, the rolling forecasts are much closer to the actual data than was the overall forecast.

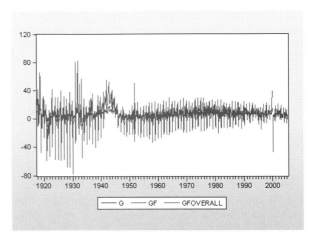

Quick Review

An EViews program is essentially a list of commands available to execute as needed. You can make the commands apply to different objects by providing arguments when you run the program. You can also automate repetitive commands by using numerical and string "for…next" loops. An EViews program is an excellent way to document your operations, and compared to manually typing every command can save a heck of a lot of time!

Nearly all operations can be written as commands suitable for inclusion in a program. Simple loops are quite easy to use. A limited set of matrix operations are available for more complex calculations. However, it's probably best to think of the program facility as providing a very sophisticated command and batch scripting language rather than a full-blown programming environment.

And if you come across a need for something not built in, see the—no, not the *User's Guide* this time—see the 900 + page *Command and Programming Reference*.

> Hint: If you want to learn more about writing EViews programs, start with Chapter 17, "EViews Programming" in the *User's Guide*.

Appendix: Sample Programs

Rolling forecasts

The dynamic forecast procedure for an equation produces multi-period forecasts with the same set of estimated parameters. Suppose instead that you want to produce multi-period forecasts by reestimating the parameters as new data become available. To be more specific, suppose you want to produce forecasts up to 4 periods ahead from each subsample where each subsample is moved 4 periods at a time.

The following program uses a `for` loop to step through the forecast periods. Notice how `smpl` is used first to control the estimation period, and is then reset to the forecast period. Temporary variables are used to get around the problem of the forecast procedure overwriting forecasts from earlier windows.

```
' set window size
!window = 20

' get size of workfile
!length = @obsrange

' declare equation for estimation
equation eq1
' declare series for final results
series yhat     ' point estimates
series yhat_se' forecast std.err.

' set step size
!step = 4

' move sample !step obs at a time
for !i = 1  to  !length-!window+1-!step step !step
    ' set sample to estimation period
    smpl @first+!i-1 @first+!i+!window-2
    ' estimate equation
    eq1.ls y c y(-1) y(-2)
    ' reset sample to forecast period
    smpl @first+!i+!window-1 @first+!i+!window-2+!step
    ' make forecasts in temporary series first
    eq1.forecast(f=na) tmp_yhat tmp_se
    ' copy data in current forecast sample
    yhat = tmp_yhat
    yhat_se = tmp_se
next
```

Monte Carlo

Earlier in the chapter, we briefly touched on the idea of a Monte Carlo study. Here's a more in depth example.

A typical Monte Carlo simulation exercise consists of the following steps:

1. Specify the "true" model (data generating process) underlying the data.

2. Simulate a draw from the data and estimate the model using the simulated data.

3. Repeat step 2 many times, each time storing the results of interest.

4. The end result is a series of estimation results, one for each repetition of step 2. We can then characterize the empirical distribution of these results by tabulating the sample moments or by plotting the histogram or kernel density estimate.

The following program sets up space to hold both the simulated data and the estimation results from the simulated data. Then it runs many regressions and plots a kernel density for the estimated coefficients.

```
' store monte carlo results in a series
' checked 4/1/2004

' set workfile range to number of monte carlo replications
wfcreate mcarlo u 1 100

' create data series for x
' NOTE: x is fixed in repeated samples
' only first 10 observations are used (remaining 90 obs missing)
series x
x.fill 80, 100, 120, 140, 160, 180, 200, 220, 240, 260

' set true parameter values
!beta1 = 2.5
!beta2 = 0.5

' set seed for random number generator
rndseed 123456

' assign number of replications to a control variable
!reps = 100

' begin loop
for !i = 1 to !reps
    ' set sample to estimation sample
    smpl 1 10

    ' simulate y data (only for 10 obs)
    series y = !beta1 + !beta2*x + 3*nrnd

    ' regress y on a constant and x equation
    eq1.ls y c x
    ' set sample to one observation
    smpl !i !i

    ' and store each coefficient estimate in a series
    series b1 = eq1.@coefs(1)
    series b2 = eq1.@coefs(2)
```

```
next
' end of loop

' set sample to full sample
smpl 1 100

' show kernel density estimate for each coef
freeze(gra1) b1.kdensity
' draw vertical dashline at true parameter value
gra1.draw(dashline, bottom, rgb(156,156,156)) !beta1
show gra1

freeze(gra2) b2.kdensity
' draw vertical dashline at true parameter value
gra2.draw(dashline, bottom, rgb(156,156,156)) !beta2
show gra2
```

Descriptive Statistics By Year

Suppose that you wish to compute descriptive statistics (mean, median, *etc.*) for each year of your monthly data in the series IP, URATE, M1, and TB10. One approach would be to link the data into an annual page, see Chapter 9, "Page After Page After Page," and then compute the descriptive statistics in the newly created page.

Here's another approach, which uses the `statsby` view of a series to compute the relevant statistics in two steps: first create a year identifier series, and second compute the statistics for each value of the identifier.

```
' change path to program path
%path = @runpath
cd %path

' get workfile
%evworkfile = "..\data\basics"
load %evworkfile

' set sample
smpl 1990:1 @last

' create a series containing the year identifier
series year = @year

' compute statistics for each year and
' freeze the output from each of the tables
for %var ip urate m1 tb10
    %name = "tab" + %var
```

```
        freeze({%name}) {%var}.statby(min,max,mean,med) year
        show {%name}
    next
```

More Samples

These sample programs were all taken from online help, found under **Help/Quick Help Reference/Sample Programs & Data.** Over 50 programs, together with descriptions and related data, are provided. Reading the programs is an excellent way to pick up advanced techniques.

Chapter 17. Odds and Ends

An odds and ends chapter is a good spot for topics and tips that don't quite fit anywhere else. You've heard of **F**requently **A**sked **Q**uestions. Think of this chapter as **P**ossibly **H**elpful **A**uxiliary **T**opics.

> Daughter hint: Oh daddy, that's *so* 90's.

How Much Data Can EViews Handle?

EViews holds workfiles in internal memory, *i.e.,* in RAM, as opposed to on disk. Eight bytes are used for each number, so storing a million data points (1,000 series with 1,000 observations each, for example) requires 8 megabytes. That's more memory than there is in a voice-only cell phone, but less than in a typical Palm Pilot, and much less than in an MP3 player.

Data capacity isn't an issue unless you have truly massive data needs, perhaps processing public use samples from the U.S. Census or records from credit card transactions. Current versions of EViews do have an out-of-the box limit of 4 million observations per series, but this may be adjusted.

> Hint: Student versions of EViews place limits on the amount of data that may be saved and omit some of EViews' more advanced features.

How Long Does It Take To Compute An Estimate?

Probably not long enough for you to care about.

On the author's somewhat antiquated PC, computing a linear regression with ten right-hand side variables and 100,000 observations takes roughly one eye-blink.

Nonlinear estimation can take longer. First, a single nonlinear estimation step, *i.e.,* one *iteration*, can be the equivalent of computing hundreds of regressions. Second, there's no limit on how many iterations may be required for a nonlinear search. EViews' nonlinear algorithms are both fast and accurate, but hard problems can take a while.

Freeze!

EViews' objects change as you edit data, change samples, reset options, *etc.* When you have table output that you want to make sure *won't* change, click the `Freeze` button to open a new window, disconnected from the object you've been working on—and therefore frozen. You've taken a snapshot. Nothing prevents you from editing the snapshot—that's the standard approach for customizing a table for example—but the frozen object won't change unless you change it.

> Hint: Any untitled EViews object will disappear when you close its window. If you want to keep something you've frozen, use the Name button.

Frozen graphs offer more sophisticated behavior than frozen tables. When you have graphical output and click on the Freeze button, EViews opens a dialog prompting you to choose **Auto Update Options**. Selecting **Off** means that the frozen graph acts exactly like a frozen table; it is a snapshot of the current graph that is disconnected from the original object. If you choose **Manual** or **Automatic** EViews will create a frozen ("chilled") graph snapshot of the current graphical output that can update itself when the data in the original object changes.

Every frozen object is kept either as a table, shown in the workfile window with the 🎛 icon, or a graph, shown with the 🎛 icon. No matter how an object began life, once frozen you can adjust its appearance by using customization tools for tables or graphs.

A Comment On Tables

Every object has a label view providing a place to enter remarks about the object. Tables take this a step further. You can add a comment to any cell in a table. Select a cell and choose **Proc/Insert/Edit Comment…** or right-click on a cell to bring up the context menu.

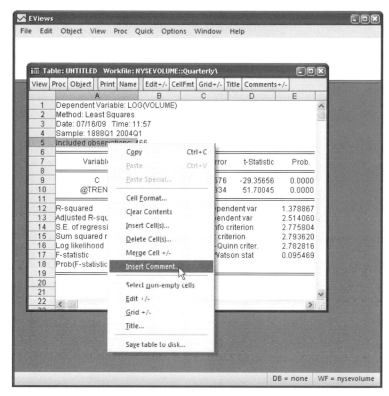

Cells with comments are marked with little red triangles in the upper right-hand corner. When the mouse passes over the cell, the comment is displayed in a note box.

Saving Tables and Almost Tables

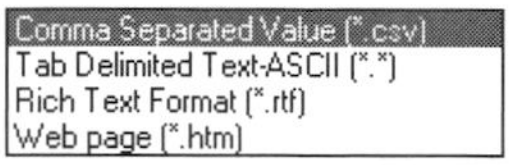

It's nice to look at output on the screen, but eventually you'll probably want to transfer some of your results into a word processor or other program. One fine method is copy-and-paste. You can also save any table as a disk file through **Proc/Save table to disk…** or the **Save table to disk…** context menu item when you right-click in the table. Either way, you get a nice list of choices for the table format on disk.

> Comma Separated Value (*.csv)
> Tab Delimited Text-ASCII (*.*)
> Rich Text Format (*.rtf)
> Web page (*.htm)

If you're planning on reading the table into a spreadsheet or database program, choose **Comma Separated Value** or **Tab Delimited Text-ASCII**. If the table's eventual destination is a word processor, you can use Rich Text Format to preserve the formatting that EViews has built into the table.

> Hint: If you're looking at a view of an object that would become a table if you froze it—regression output or a spreadsheet view of a series are examples—**Save table to disk…** shows up on the right-click menu even though it isn't available from **Proc**.

Saving Graphs and Almost Graphs

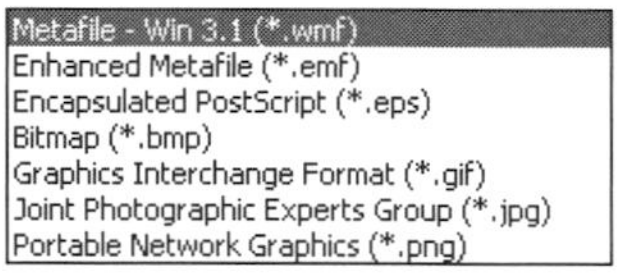

Saving graphs works much like saving tables. In addition to using copy-and-paste to transfer your graph into another program, you can save any graph as a disk file through **Proc/Save graph to disk…** or the **Save graph to disk…** context menu item when you right-click in the graph. Simply select one of the available graph disk formats.

> Metafile - Win 3.1 (*.wmf)
> Enhanced Metafile (*.emf)
> Encapsulated PostScript (*.eps)
> Bitmap (*.bmp)
> Graphics Interchange Format (*.gif)
> Joint Photographic Experts Group (*.jpg)
> Portable Network Graphics (*.png)

> Hint: If you're looking at a view of an object that would become a graph if you froze it—**Save graph to disk…** shows up on the right-click menu.

Unsubtle Redirection

Inside Output

You hit [Print] and output goes out, right? Not necessarily, as EViews provides an option that allows you to *redirect* printer output to an EViews *spool* object. The spool object collects output that would otherwise go to the printer. This gives you an editable record of the work you've done.

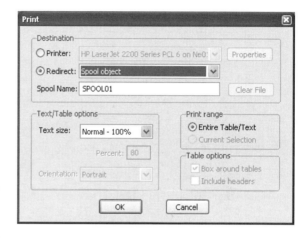

The window below is scrolled so that you can see part of a table and part of a graph, each of which had previously been redirected to this spool. Objects are listed by name in the left pane and object contents are displayed in the right pane.

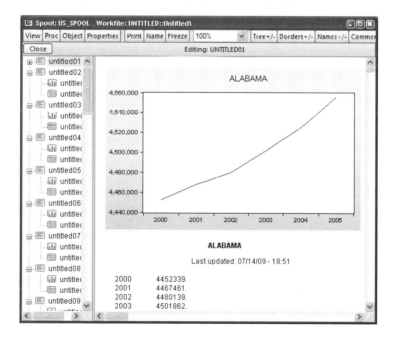

Outside Output

You hit [Print] and output—at least output that doesn't stay inside—goes to the printer, right? Not necessarily, as EViews provides an option that allows you to *redirect* printer output to a disk file instead. Choosing the **Redirect** radio button in the **Print** dialog leads to output destination choices. **RTF file** adds the output to the end of the specified file in a format that is easily read by word processing programs. **Text file** writes text output as a standard (unformatted) text file and sends graphic output to the printer. **Frozen objects** freezes the object that you said to "print" and stores it in the active workfile.

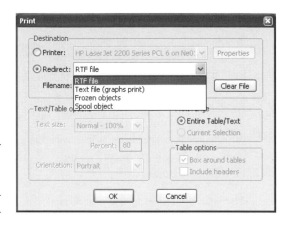

Hint: Use the command pon in a program (see Chapter 16, "Get With the Program") to make every window print (or get redirected) as it opens. Poff undoes pon. Unfortunately, pon and poff don't work from the command line, only in programs.

Objects and Commands

When we type:

```
ls lnwage c ed
```

it looks like we've simply typed a regression command. But behind the scenes, EViews has created an equation object just like those we see stored in the workfile with the ▣ icon. The difference is that the equation object is untitled, and so not stored in the workfile. Internally, all commands are carried out as operations applied to an object. Rather than give the ls command, we could have issued the two commands:

```
equation aneq

aneq.ls lnwage c ed
```

The first line creates a new equation object named ANEQ. The second applies the ls operation to ANEQ. The dot between ANEQ and ls is object-oriented notation connecting the object, aneq, with a particular command, ls.

The two lines could just as easily have been combined into one, as in:

```
equation aneq.ls lnwage c ed
```

So `ls` is actually an operation defined on the equation object. Similarly, `output` is a view of an equation object.

The command:

```
aneq.output
```

opens a view of ANEQ displaying the estimation output.

Do you need to understand the abstract concepts of objects, object commands, and object views? No, everything can be done by combining point-and-click with typing the straightforward commands that we've used throughout *EViews Illustrated*. But if you prefer doing everything via the command line, or if you want an exact record of the commands issued, you may find the fine-grain control offered by objects helpful.

Equation: ANEQ Workfile: CPSMAR2004 WITH PAGES::CPS\					
View Proc Object Print Name Freeze Estimate Forecast Stats Resids					

Dependent Variable: LNWAGE
Method: Least Squares
Date: 07/14/09 Time: 19:08
Sample (adjusted): 1 136878
Included observations: 99991 after adjustments

Variable	Coefficient	Std. Error	t-Statistic	Prob.
C	0.644901	0.014902	43.27598	0.0000
ED	0.133724	0.001076	124.2275	0.0000

R-squared	0.133705	Mean dependent var	2.458741
Adjusted R-squared	0.133697	S.D. dependent var	1.012580
S.E. of regression	0.942463	Akaike info criterion	2.719380
Sum squared resid	88813.86	Schwarz criterion	2.719570
Log likelihood	-135954.7	Hannan-Quinn criter.	2.719437
F-statistic	15432.47	Durbin-Watson stat	0.325892
Prob(F-statistic)	0.000000		

The *Command and Programming Reference* includes extensive tables documenting each object type and the commands and views associated with each.

Workfile Backups

When you save a workfile EViews keeps the previous copy on disk as a backup, changing the extension from ".wf1" to ". ~ f1". For example, the first time you save a workfile named "foo," the file is saved as "foo.wf1". The second time you save foo, the name of the first file is changed to "foo. ~ f1" and the new version becomes "foo.wf1". The third time you save foo, the first file disappears, the second incarnation is changed to "foo. ~ f1", and the third version becomes "foo.wf1".

It's okay to delete backup versions if you're short on disk space. On the other hand, if something goes wrong with your current workfile, you can recover the data in the backup version by changing the backup filename to a name with the extension "wf1". For example, to read in "foo. ~ f1". change the name to "hope_this_saves_my_donkey.wf1" and then open it from EViews.

> Etymological Hint: "Foo" is a generic name that computer-types use to mean "any file" or "any variable." "Foo" is a shortened version of "foobar." "Foobar" derives from the World War II term "fubar," which itself is an acronym for "Fouled Up Beyond All Recognition" (or at least that's the acronymization given in family oriented books such as the one you are reading). The transition from "fubar" to "foobar" is believed to have arisen from the fact that if computer types could spell they wouldn't have had to give up their careers as English majors. (For further information, contact the Professional Organization of English Majors^{TM}.)

Updates—A Small Thing

Objects in workfiles are somewhere between animate and inanimate. If you open a graph view of a series and then change the data in the series, the graph will update before your very eyes. If you open an **Estimation Output** view of an equation and then change the data in one of the series used in the equation, nothing at all will happen.

Some views update automatically and some don't.

Mostly, the update-or-not decision reflects design guesses as to what the typical user would like to have happen. To be sure estimates, *etc.*, reflect the latest changes you made to your data, redo the estimates.

Updates—A Big Thing

Quantitative Micro Software (QMS) posts program updates to www.eviews.com as needed. Bug fixes are posted as soon as they become available. Serious bugs are very rare, and bugs outside the more esoteric areas of the program are very, *very*, rare.

QMS also posts free, minor enhancements from time to time and, once-in-a-while, posts updated documentation. On occasion, QMS releases a minor version upgrade (5.1 from 5.0, for example) free-of-charge to current users. Some of these "minor" upgrades include quite significant new features. It pays to check the EViews website.

If you'd like, you can use the automatic updating feature to can check for new updates every day, and install any available updates. The automatic update feature can be enabled or disabled from the main **Options** menu under the

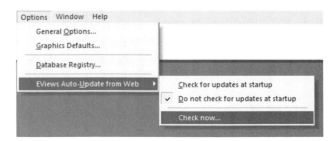

EViews Auto-Update from Web menu item. Or manually check for updates from by selecting **Check now...** or by selecting **EViews Update** from the **Help** menu.

Ready To Take A Break?

If EViews is taking so long to compute something that you'd like it to give up, hit the **Esc** (Escape) key. EViews will quit what it's doing and pay attention to you instead.

Help!

It is conceivable that you've read *EViews Illustrated* and, nonetheless, may someday need more help. The **Help** menu has all sorts of goodies for you. Complete electronic versions of the *User's Guide*, *Command and Programming Reference*, and *Object Reference* are just a **Help** menu click away. **Quick Help Reference** provides quick links to summaries of commands, object properties, *etc.* **EViews Help Topics...** leads to extensive, indexed and searchable help on nearly everything in EViews, plus nice explanations of the underlying econometrics. Most of the material in the help system gives the same information found in the manuals, but sometimes it's easier and faster to find what you're after in the help system.

Odd Ending

We hope *EViews Illustrated* has helped, but reading is rarely quite so enlightening as doing. It's time to click buttons and pull down menus and type stuff in the command pane and generally have fun trying stuff out.

Chapter 18. Optional Ending

EViews devotes an entire menu to setting a myriad of **Options**. A little bit of one-time customization makes EViews a lot more comfortable, and detailed customization can really speed along a big project.

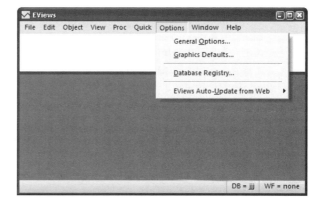

We'll explore options in three levels of detail, starting in this section with what you absolutely have to know. The next section gives you our personal recommendations for changing settings. The final section of the chapter walks through all the other important options.

> Recapitulation note: Parts of the discussion here repeat advice given in earlier chapters.

Required Options

If it's required, then it really isn't an option—is it? That's the message of this little subsection. Many users live fulfilled and truly happy lives without ever messing with the **Options** menu. This is *okay*. EViews' designers have chosen very nice defaults for the options. Feel free to leave them as they are.

Option-al Recommendations

Here's how you should reset your options. Trust me. We'll talk about why later.

These options can be found under the **General Options...** menu item.

Window Behavior

In the **Windows/Window behavior** dialog, under **Warn on close** uncheck **Series-Matrices-Coefficients**, **Groups**, **Tables-Graphs**, and **Equation-Sys-VAR-Pool-Model**. Under **Allow only one untitled** uncheck everything to cut down on unnecessary alert boxes.

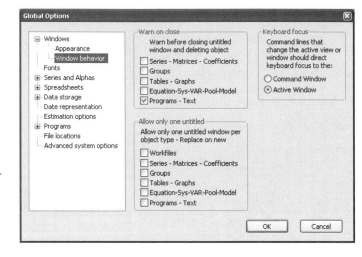

Alpha Truncation

In the **Series and Alphas/Alpha truncation** dialog, enter a large number in the **Maximum number of characters per observation** field. Try 256, or even 1,000

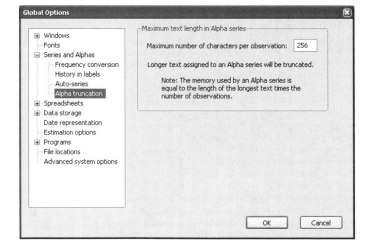

Workfile Storage Defaults

In the **Data storage/Workfile Save** dialog, check **Use compression**. One exception—don't do this if you need to share workfiles with someone using an older (before 5.0) version of EViews. Uncheck **Prompt on each Save**.

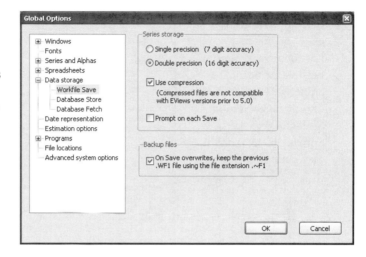

Date Representation

If you're American, which includes Canadian for the very limited purpose of this sentence, skip this paragraph. Americans write dates Month/Day/Year. Most of the world prefers the order Day/Month/Year. If you operate in the latter area, click the **Day/Month/Year** radio button.

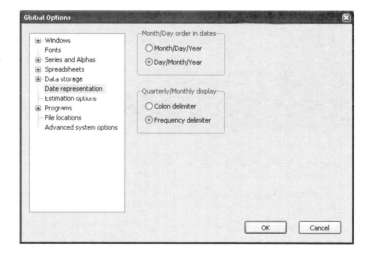

Spreadsheet Defaults

Americans can skip this one too. Americans separate the integer and fractional parts of numbers with a decimal point. If you prefer a comma, check **Comma as decimal** in the **Spreadsheets/Data display** dialog.

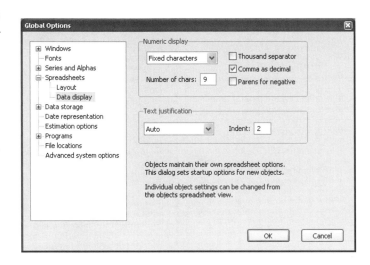

More Detailed Options

My personal recommendation? If you've made the changes above, don't worry about other option settings for now. As you become more of a power user, you will find some personal customization helpful. The remainder of this chapter is devoted to customization hints.

Window Behavior

When EViews opens a new window, the window title is "Untitled"—unless you've explicitly given a name. Named objects are stored in the workfile; untitled objects aren't. Commands like `ls` and `show` create untitled objects. So does freezing an object. If you do a lot of exploring, you'll create many such untitled objects.

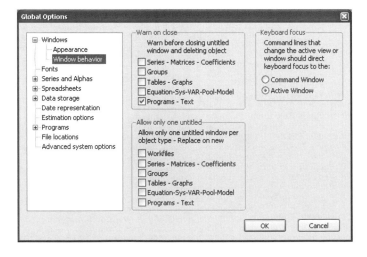

Unchecking **Warn on close** lets you close throw-aways without having to deal with a delete confirmation dialog. On the other hand, once in a while you'll delete something you meant to name and save.

As suggested earlier, you'll probably want to uncheck most of the options in **Allow only one untitled**. Doing so lets you type a sequence of `ls` commands, for example, without having to close windows between commands. The downside is that the screen can get awfully cluttered with accumulated untitled windows.

Keyboard Focus

The radio button **Keyboard focus** directs whether typed characters are "sent" by default to the command pane or to the currently active window. Most people leave this one alone, but if you find that you're persistently typing in the command pane when you meant to be editing another window, try switching this button and see if the results are more in line with what your fingers intended.

Font Options

The **Fonts** dialog controls default fonts in the workfile display, in spreadsheets, and in tables. Font selection is an issue about what looks good to you, so turn on whatever turns you on.

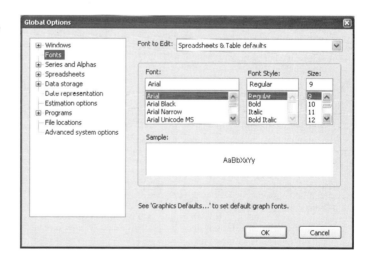

Frequency Conversion

The **Series and Alphas/Frequency conversion** dialog lets you reset the default frequency conversions. Usually there's a way to control the conversion method used for individual conversions. Sometimes—copy-and-paste, for example—there isn't.

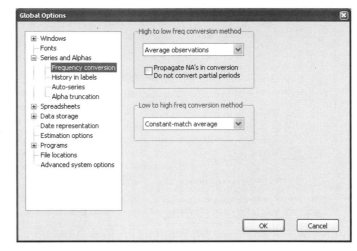

See *Multiple Frequencies—Multiple Pages* in Chapter 9, "Page After Page After Page" for an extended discussion of frequency conversion.

Alpha Truncation

EViews sometimes truncates text in alpha series. You probably don't want this to happen. Unless you're storing large amounts of data in alpha series, increase the maximum number of characters so that nothing ever gets truncated. With modern computers, "large amounts of data" means on the order of 10^5 or 10^6 observations.

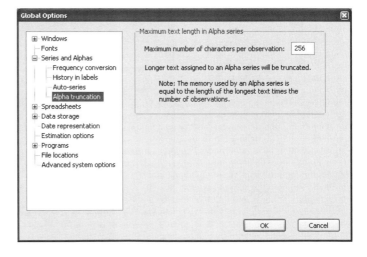

Spreadsheet Defaults

Aside from the comments in *Option-al Recommendations* above, there's really nothing you need to change in the **Spreadsheets** defaults section. Looking at the **Layout** page, you may *want* to check one or more of the **Edit mode on** checkboxes. If you do, then the corresponding spreadsheets open with editing permitted. Leaving edit mode off gives you a lit-

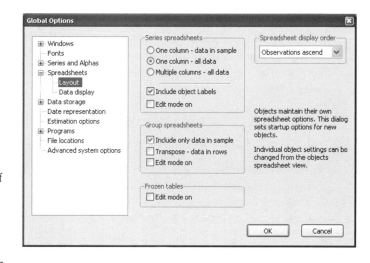

tle protection against making an accidental change and economizes on screen space by suppressing the edit field in the spreadsheet. This is purely a matter of personal taste.

Workfile Storage Defaults

Back in the old days, computer storage was a scarce commodity. Data was often stored in "single precision," offering about seven digits of accuracy in four bytes of storage. Today, data are usually represented in "double precision," giving 16 digits of accuracy in eight bytes of storage. Since raw data aren't likely to be accurate to more than seven digits, single precision seems

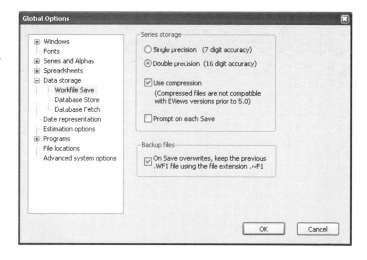

sufficient. However, numerical operations can introduce small errors. EViews holds all internal results in double precision for this reason. Using double precision when storing the workfile on the disk preserves this extra accuracy. Using single precision cuts file size in half, but causes some accuracy to be lost.

Internally, each observation in a series takes up eight bytes of storage. There's no great reason you should care about this as either you have enough memory—in which case it doesn't matter—or you don't have enough memory—in which case your only option is to buy some more. And as a practical matter, unless you're using millions of data points the issue will never arise.

> Hint: **Workfile Save Options** have no effect on the amount of RAM (internal storage) required. They're just for disk storage.

Use compression tells EViews to squish the data before storing to disk. When much of the data takes only the values 0 or 1, which is quite common, disk file size can be reduced by nearly a factor of 64. This level of compression is unusual, but shrinkage of 90 percent happens regularly. Unlike use of single precision, compression does not cause any loss of accuracy.

The truth is that disk storage is so cheap that there's no reason to try to conserve it. While disk storage itself is rarely a limiting factor, moving around large files is sometimes a nuisance. This is especially true if you need to email a workfile.

Earlier releases of EViews (before 5.0) can read single precision, but not compressed files.

> Hint: There's no reason not to use compression, so use it, unless someone using a version of EViews earlier than 5.0 needs to read the file, in which case—don't.

Estimation Defaults

The **Estimation options** dialog lets you set defaults for controlling the iteration process and internal computation of derivatives in nonlinear estimation. There's nothing wrong with the out-of-the-box defaults, although some people do prefer a smaller number for the **Convergence** value. You can also set these controls as needed for a specific estimation problem, but if you do

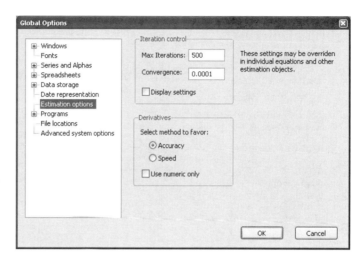

lots of nonlinear estimation, you may find it convenient to reset the defaults here.

File Locations

As a rule, EViews users never mess with the **File locations** settings. But you may be exceptional, since you're reading a chapter on setting options. Power users sometimes keep around several different sets of options, each fine-tuned for a particular purpose. The **EViews Paths** dialog lets you pick a path for each option setting.

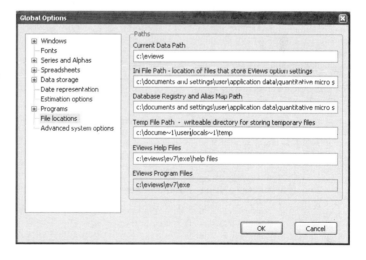

EViews automatically names its options-storing-file "EViews.ini". To store multiple versions of "EViews.ini", fine tune your options to suit a particular purpose, then reset the **Ini File Path** to a unique path for each version you wish to save. There's no browsing for "EViews.ini", and the name

"EViews.ini" is hard-coded into the program, so to use multiple option sets you need to remember the paths in which you've stored each set.

Graphics Defaults

Going back to the **Options** menu and clicking on **Graphics Defaults**, you'll see the **Graph Options** dialog is enormous, with many sections. These options set the defaults used for options when you first create a graph. The same tabs appear on the **Graph Options** dialog for an individual graph, so

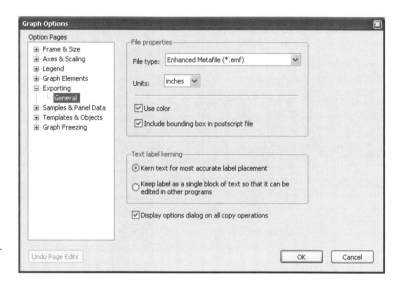

they've effectively already been discussed at length in *Options, Options, Options* in Chapter 6, "Intimacy With Graphic Objects." One of the pages, **Exporting**, doesn't appear as an option for an individual graph, but we discussed this tab in the same chapter in *The Impact of Globalization on Intimate Graphic Activity*.

The default format for saving graphics is **Enhanced Metafile (*.emf)**. EMF is almost always the best choice. However, you may want to switch to **Encapsulated PostScript (*.eps)** if you send output to *very* high resolution devices. If you're a LaTeX user, you may also find eps files easier to deal with. You may also save files to **Graphics Interchange Format (*.gif)**, **Portable Network Graphics (.png)**, **Joint Photographic Experts Group (*.jpg)** and **Bitmap (*.bmp)** files. GIF and PNG files are particularly useful if you wish to include graphs in web pages.

Quick Review

If fine-tuning doesn't ring your chimes, you can safely avoid the **Options** menu entirely. On the other hand, if you're regularly resetting an option for a particular operation, the **Options** menu will let you reset the option once and for all.

Index